INDUSTRIAL WOMEN, 1760–1914

INDUSTRIAL WOMEN, 1760–1914

Edited by
Deborah Simonton

Volume I
Women in Industrial Handwork

Routledge
Taylor & Francis Group
LONDON AND NEW YORK

First published 2026
by Routledge
4 Park Square, Milton Park, Abingdon, Oxon OX14 4RN

and by Routledge
605 Third Avenue, New York, NY 10158

Routledge is an imprint of the Taylor & Francis Group, an informa business

For Product Safety Concerns and Information please contact our EU representative GPSR@taylorandfrancis.com. Taylor & Francis Verlag GmbH, Kaufingerstraße 24, 80331 München, Germany.

British Library Cataloguing-in-Publication Data
A catalogue record for this book is available from the British Library

ISBN: 978-1-032-49910-9 (set)
ISBN: 978-1-032-49913-0 hbk (vol I)
ISBN: 978-1-003-67666-9 ebk (vol I)

DOI: 10.4324/9781003676669

Typeset in Times New Roman
by Apex CoVantage, LLC

CONTENTS

IMAGES

ACKNOWLEDGEMENTS

This volume, and its sisters, owe a great debt to the extensive digitisation projects that have made the study of history far easier. While some in this collection are difficult to find, the growth of the internet and the generosity of these projects are a boon to students and scholars alike. Although slightly insidious to mention only a few, the Hathi Trust, Internet Archive, Gale, the Wellcome Collection, as well as The Metropolitan Museum of Art and the Yale Centre for British Art are important resources. Local and individual resource centres and archives and digital projects like The Wedgwood Archives at the Victoria and Albert Museum, British History Online, the London Lives Project and the Friends Library make studying women in industry a much easier task than twenty years ago.

I am grateful to many people who swiftly and helpfully answered questions about materials and copyright and provided access and occasionally located the originals for me. The V&A were helpful, even trying to define a word that we had to give up on. So, thanks to Silvia Haldane, Lead Textile Conservator and Silvija Banic in the Textile Department. And thanks also to Isabelle Gapomo at the Wellcome Collection. And to Catriona MacDonald and Dauvit Brown, who enabled me to use the British Linen Company Correspondence, edited by Alastair Durie. I am grateful to Anne Montenach for supplying documentary French sources, though the translations are mine. I hope she approves.

At Routledge, Eve Setch is always a support, answering a myriad of questions, providing ideas, reading material and is very good for a few laughs along the way. Simon Alexander has picked up this project with aplomb and has been a good colleague as this project unfolded.

I also appreciate the support and energy I get from my band of historical colleagues, Katie Barclay, Elaine Chalus, Alison Duncan, Marjo Kaartinen and Anne Montenach, who over the years have become my comfort zone. Without them life would be much sadder. My sister is always there, and her (virtual) presence brightens my day. Thanks to David who tolerates, cooks and drinks wine with me, and our two wonderful Irish Setters, known as the girlies, Cally and Clio, who insist on walks and treats.

GENERAL INTRODUCTION

INDUSTRIAL WOMEN

Women and industrial work are at the heart of the Industrial Revolution. They were often the most numerous workers, certainly in early textile factories, and important contributors to the protoindustrial workforce based on domestic industry. Women's contributions underpinned much of the success of early industrial developments, often beginning as children. The character of the workforce, the work they did and the impact on homes were significant aspects of industrial society. So were the laws and customs they worked under, as well as their responses and resistance to restrictive working practices.

And yet, the concept of 'women in industry' raises several questions, not the least of which is, who are women in industry? And indeed, what is industry? To start with the second, industry is often conceived as factory work. Certainly, factory work is industry, but this is a limiting concept. We instinctively think of manufacturing industries tied up with mechanisation and factories. The image of the textile factory is ubiquitous, and women who worked in them were highly visible symbols of industry and of women's work from the later eighteenth century. While this disguises the variety of women's work and women's work in industry, it remains a potent image. But we need to think more carefully about this, because while it has particular reference when we think about gender and women in the industrial workplace, it excludes a large number of industrial women. Expanding our thinking to manufacturing draws in a wider set of ideas and options, so that making things, or at least parts of things, is a more helpful approach, since industrial women embraced a wider range of products and activities, like milliners, silversmiths and printers.

Not surprisingly the OED has multiple definitions of 'industry'. Excluding obsolete ones, these include:

- Exertion, effort, hard work.
- Productive work, trade, or manufacture. In later use *esp.*: manufacturing and production carried out on a commercial basis, typically organised on a large scale and requiring the investment of capital.

- Manufacturing or production, and those involved in it.
- A particular form or sector of productive work, trade, or manufacture. In later use also more generally: any commercial activity or enterprise.
- Any activity portrayed as a flourishing and highly productive commercial enterprise.

Notably then, the OED expands the concept of industry and thus of industrial women to include a much wider range. Indeed, it even accepts 'any commercial activity or enterprise'. Much of the contemporary literature also uses 'industry' as an activity: working people were meant to be industrious and to learn and practice habits of industry.

This collection of documentary sources follows this broader approach in identifying who industrial women were. While it tends to avoid primarily commercial enterprises, it expands our understanding of women in industry to cover a broad group of women workers. Some come to mind readily: artisan and handicraft workers; women in domestic and protoindustries; machine operators and minders; sweated workers and outworkers; enterprising craft and skilled women; and mine workers. These overlapped chronologically as industry did not develop along a continuum of one type of work passing to another. For example, in towns like Sheffield, Aberdeen or Belfast in the middle of the nineteenth century all operated at the same time. In the textile industries, they were milliners, seamstresses, handworkers in luxury manufacturing and homeworkers either in protoindustries or the sweated trades, mill hands, merchants and brokers, amongst others. In metal working, they were workshop and factory workers making a wide range of small metal goods, finishers, burnishers as well as silversmiths with their own marks. In many respects the phrase 'industrial women' disguises a great deal of what women contributed to the workforce and especially to the manufacturing world. So, when we look at the meanings of the word, we recognise that industrial women are far more than factory girls, and that a broader sense of industry brings far more women into play.

But there are also other women in industry who, while not necessarily overlooked, are nevertheless not usually perceived as industrial women. They are the businesswomen and entrepreneurs who worked in, managed and financed industrial concerns from the smallest to the largest. Indeed, it is curious, but not surprising. There is a growing and vigorous historiography on women in business which has captured the significance of women in family firms especially but also as independent women managing their concerns. A characteristic of this research, however, is that it amalgamates all forms of business and entrepreneurship. This is logical since the characteristics of women's business activity are replicated across service, retail and commercial sectors. At the same time, much of the research has concentrated on trades and commerce, reflecting the focus and volume of women's entrepreneurship. Women industrialists comprised a significant number between 1750 and 1914 – there is no doubt that industrial businesswomen can be found across the terrain. Certainly, fewer than men, but where they are found, their role could be significant and longstanding. This is not really about numbers but a foray into changing the narrative that business belongs to men. Firms could be both large and small. Women were active in large firms, like the Darbys of Coalbrookdale, or the women of the Krupp family in Essen. However, if we look at smaller ones, often single-generation ones, women are far more plentiful. The data from Aberdeen represents a shift from 179 business owners in 1824 to 533 in 1890, or from 79 to 197 in manufacturing businesses.[1] Stana Nenadic argued that in nineteenth-century Britain, 'the largest group of women entrepreneurs – comprising almost twenty-two thousand who employed the labour of others in 1891 – were those in the women's garment trades.'[2] They could operate successfully for some time, sometimes in partnership but also on their own account.

Geoffrey Tweedale listed fourteen women cutlery manufacturers in nineteenth-century Sheffield; eleven were probably widows who operated the businesses from eleven to fifteen years, except one who went bankrupt in two years. Some partnered sons for part of the time, but three seemed to retain ownership until their death when sons inherited. One firm was run by the daughters of the founder and another two by single or separated women.[3] Many such firms lasted a substantial period, notably the Darbys of Coalbrookdale, Shropshire, and Jesse Buyers, ships chandler of Aberdeen, and milliners Reeves and Gibbon of Colchester and Bath, Margaret Cameron of Edinburgh and Isabella Alexander of Aberdeen. They can be found across the period 1750 to 1914.[4] The fact they spanned the entire period is significant. Recent research indicates that rather than the nineteenth century being a period of dramatic and oppressive change for women, there was a high degree of continuity as women continued to own and operate business enterprises. This echoes conclusions of Beatrice Craig for Northern France, Hannah Barker for the North of England, Jennifer Aston for Birmingham and mine for Aberdeen.[5]

Industrial work of all sorts also embraced far more females than adult women. Many were girls, aged under twenty-one. They could begin at home, in crafts and protoindustries; they could be apprenticed either by their parents or parishes or charities; they could be industrial servants. 'Servant' was in fact a common term for a single working woman regardless of age. They could be married, single or widowed; they could be mothers – or not. They could be heads of household if their 'man' had left or died. They could be migrants, temporary or permanent. They could be free or slave labour. Industrial women were indeed a widely diversified group. They did not all work in towns either. The putting out system was built on female rural industrial labour and the first factories themselves, like Cromford in Derbyshire, Penicuik or New Lanark in Scotland and Pawtucket, Rhode Island were built to harness waterpower, available where there was a plentiful year-round water source. These factories relied on several related industries including smithing of all sorts, as the textile and other industries expanded.

Before turning to women and their industrial history, a word about industry as an employer of the female labour force is in order. For most of the last three centuries, industry was not the main employer of women. Certainly, large numbers worked in family production units, largely uncounted and unsung, but agricultural activities remained important for women across Europe until the middle of the twentieth century. Britain, however, varied from this pattern and in terms of 'employment' they were under 10 per cent of female labour – an important distinction is that women were not necessarily paid and therefore this work merged with the cottage industries and domestic responsibilities, especially for married women. Farm service was a normal route for unmarried women, while in the nineteenth century to the first world war, domestic service became a significant employer of women and girls as demand grew.

> The increase was linked to a rise in the number of prosperous households in expanding urban areas, population growth, and a marked increase in the number of young in the population. While artisanal and factory industry competed for young single female labour, neither could absorb those unable to find work in the countryside. Numbers grew rapidly from the 1830s, peaking in the last decades of the century [at nearly 50 per cent of the female labour force] . . . Before 1880, employment opportunities changed little, though in industrial areas, factories provided an option which girls sometimes alternated with service or substituted for service altogether . . . then a slow but distinctive decline set in; and by 1900, clearly fewer girls and a smaller proportion of the female labour force turned to domestic service.[6]

A snapshot of women's employment in these three areas illustrates the relative balance between them. British census data, while notoriously under-recording female employment in the nineteenth century, shows how service was a dominant employer, and only approached parity in 1911 (Table 1). Comparable data is not available for the United States, but in 1900, 19.0 per cent of the female labour force remained in agriculture, 28.7 per cent in domestic service and 25.2 per cent in manufacturing.[7]

In this context, then, industrial work of all sorts remained second to domestic service, at around 45 per cent of the female labour force. This result does not undermine the significance of industrial work but helps to place perspective on the female work force.

Table 1 Female Labour in Britain, Selected occupations, 1841 and 1911, based on census data.[8]

	Agriculture	*Manufacturing*	*Service*
1841	3.4%	35.2%	57.4%
1911	2.2%	44.9%	47.3%

WOMEN AND INDUSTRIAL HISTORY

The story of women in industry is shaped by three intertwining histories and historiographies: economic and social histories of industry and industrialisation, the history of work as well as histories of women and gender, and especially women's work. Much of these discussions are embedded in developments in northern Europe and later in North America, and it is this story that this collection comprises. Documenting the industrial history of much of the rest of the world must wait not only for a different volume but also for a more mature global working women's history.[9] The history of industrialisation is dominated by discussions of the industrial revolution, and yet as intimated industry has a much longer and much debated history. Craftwork and domestic industries predated the Industrial Revolution and indeed continued to operate in parallel. For many decades some domestic industries expanded alongside mechanised factory branches of the industry concerned. Often factory manufacturing, homework and sweated industries operated in tandem. As Eric Hobsbawm suggested, the obvious way to expand was to extend domestic industry, not to build large scale units.[10] As there was a largely untapped labour force in the countryside, it was plausible to put work out to take advantage of the skills of women who could also juggle such work with other tasks. Much the same was true of men as farming was rarely a year-round activity.

Industrial development was a vital factor in women's working lives. Much 'new' manufacturing was based on dispersed units of production, from cottages to workshops, located in town and country. They were small-scale and not far removed from the homestead, if at all, and based on the industries and skills of traditional crafts and domestic manufacture. Thus, handicraft work and domestic industry were important aspects of industrial working, engaging large numbers of women, although often this was not waged work, but piecework for which the price paid for the piece went into a family 'pot'.[11] Peasants had always manufactured goods in their own homes to meet their own needs or for sale. They had worked in forges, mines or other rural industries. Traditional rural crafts continued to exist, but from the mid-seventeenth century, the numbers involved in domestic manufacture of goods for market sale swelled, mainly in textile industries like woollens and linen.

Labelled 'protoindustrialisation', Franklin Mendels developed the theory in his 1969 doctoral dissertation on the rural linen industry in eighteenth-century Flanders and popularised it in his 1972 article based on that work. Mendels believed that 'surplus' family labour turned to production for the market, provided income at slack periods and fostered population growth which became a in a self-sustaining process that created the labour, capital and entrepreneurial skill that led to industrialisation.[12] As Pat Hudson explained,

> Proto-industrialisation is considered to be a phase in the development of modern industrial economics which preceded and paved the way for industrialisation proper. Mendels . . . had two basic propositions. First,

> the proto-industrial phase was dominated by the spread of rural domestic manufacturing which linked more and more families to the pulse of national and international markets. Secondly, rural industrialisation was so widespread and so dynamic economically and socially that it became the major force propelling economies in the direction of phase two, or industrial capitalism proper, based in centralised urban production.[13]

Other historians developed these ideas, notably Hans Medick, who in 1976 argued that the family economy of the agrarian peasantry, based firmly on land and inheritance, underwent fundamental change in its motivation and function to become the family economy of the proto-industrial cottage worker. Together with Peter Kriedte and Jürgen Schlumbohm, he expanded the theory into a broad account of the transformation of European society from feudalism to industrial capitalism.[14] The theory has, however, been seen both as exciting and influential in explaining the shifts in industrial development and at the same time the model is too uncritical of the variations in local economies and undervalues the range of variables affecting the economic life of most families of the working orders whose strategies were conducted in the context of wider market forces, an increasing level of waged labour and a higher incidence of day labour and geographic mobility. Its concern with labour supply tended to omit those who did not live in a family economy, nor did it adequately explain and describe many urban workplaces and strategies. In particular, it was unsatisfactory as an explanation of the transition to industrialisation and factory developments. Many protoindustries did not translate directly to factory industry, and often factory industry developed in a location different from that of the protoindustry. A classic example is the extensive woollen trades of Essex, which did not transform into factory working, and the cloth trade went into severe decline in the eighteenth and early nineteenth centuries

Features of the concept which are useful are the concepts of 'strategies', interdependence and the centrality of women and children and their labour to a household's response to economic conditions. Whether in an agricultural or a domestic industry setting, women's labour as wife or daughter was significant. The interdependency of household or family members was an important feature of their economic participation. Co-residence was not essential since one strategy for balancing the requirements of the household involved apprenticing, hiring out or sending out children. Similarly, another strategy involved importing labour, from either kin or non-kin. This labour was also not necessarily co-resident. A woman's work must be seen within this context. The importance and frequently pivotal role of the wife meant that she was neither powerless nor dependent. Not only was she economically active, but as household manager she often determined and manipulated the strategies for survival. The strategies employed by a family were not simply in the context of family and subsistence, though these were important.[15] Other considerations, such as transmission of culture, played a part. Also increasing reliance on wages may well have changed family relationships and affected plebeian responses linked to culture, custom and control.[16]

Women's industrial work was a central part of this thesis, as it is to Neil McKendrick's depiction of 'The Consumer Revolution of the Eighteenth Century' and to Jan de Vries' concept of the 'industrious revolution'. McKendrick saw women as pivotal to stimulating demand by drawing on greater access to family and personal income, dominating consumer choice, especially for household and personal items, and arguing that their desire for small consumer goods like metal pins and buttons expanded the domestic market for such products.[17] He went further, claiming that women had a 'pent up desire' to compete with their betters and laying new consumer demand at the door of the 'the mill girl who wanted to dress like a duchess . . . helped create the industrial revolution'.[18] In 1993, de Vries argued there was an 'industrious revolution' which connected changing household behaviour and new consumer markets. Driven by the prospect of novelties, exotics and luxuries, he argues that people worked harder, more hours and were more fully employed, especially women and children in order to buy into life's little luxuries.[19] As explanations for the emergence of a commercial economy developed, women became closely identified as consumers, and less associated with their long-standing roles as contributors to household production. This discourse undermined women's roles as producers and makers in industry, and played into the image of women as subordinate, as helpers and as unskilled.

Organisational structures were important to how women's industrial work was perceived. Much of women's commercial industrial work appeared supplementary and complementary to male work, e.g. carding and spinning while men wove. The rate paid for the finished product, in this case cloth, represented the whole effort. In the process, their participation was interpreted as subsidiary and subordinate. Because their work was secondary, it was cheap. Although their status may have improved in domestic industry compared to the agrarian world, 'their labour was still far cheaper than . . . in workshops or early factories.'[20] As families turned more and more to waged activities, men continued to draw the equivalent of the 'family wage' while women regularly were paid less. The relative invisibility of their work thus tended to disadvantage women once there was a growing reliance on wages, which made it difficult for women to support themselves, or dependents.

The period to 1840 remained an era of domestic manufacture, while textiles, the largest domestic industry and large-scale manufacture, persisted as significant women's employment. They were so crucial to the economy that a Belgian proverb warned, 'Cut off the thumbs of the linen spinsters and Flanders will starve.' When factory spinning shifted pressure to weaving, the demand for weavers enabled women to establish themselves relatively easily in this 'male' trade because they were cheaper and seen as malleable, whereas men were more likely to resist coming into the factories, and often shifted to other work when it was available. Men were also quicker to combine into unions and to try to enforce minimum wages and apprenticeship regulations to protect their position; using traditional artisan rhetoric and their apprenticeships, they claimed 'their just reward'. But tensions between men who hired family members and journeymen who saw women as competition meant they ultimately failed.

While the late eighteenth century was a period of self-sustained economic growth, especially in Britain, the effect and significance of changes in industrial organisation by the end of the century must not be over-emphasised. The growth in textile mills took place only after 1770, rotary steam power after 1785, and industrial development remained substantially unmechanised relying on large numbers of unskilled workers. The dramatic changes brought by factory working in some regions sometimes obscures the fact that it never was the major occupation and that much industrial organisation continued to centre on the home and small workshop. Throughout Europe and the United States, numerous processes were converted to factory working, primarily during the period of 1820–1870.

Manufactories tended to spring up in rural areas when the need for waterpower determined their location, like at Cromford in Derbyshire or Penicuik, in Scotland, both hilly areas with copious and consistent water supplies. Only when forms of power like steam, coal and electricity became central to production did entrepreneurs build large urban factories. In the United States, too, factory formation, like at Lowell, relied initially on waterpower, but like rural mills in Britain, strategies had to be developed to bring workers to the factory. At Cromford, workers' housing enabled Arkwright to bring whole families to the mill; he established a school and a working community. At Lowell, the Boston Manufacturing Company similarly set out to create a community, drawing primarily on daughters of farmers with few other opportunities to earn, by enticing them with monthly cash wages and room and board in a comfortable boarding-house. As some of the sources in this collection show, while they worked long hours there was also a philanthropic spirit to the enterprise, providing social activities and education.

The story of industrialisation and factory manufacturing is usually told as a story of male entrepreneurs, inventors and investors who shifted manufacturing from home-like settings to increasingly large-scale factories. In these, men were seen as managers, supervisors, overlookers and machinists, while women were simply 'operatives'. In many of the documents in this collection, the term is used as though there was no gender attached. In fact, operatives were clearly gendered. The conventional emphasis in historical writing on late eighteenth-century textile and factory development is misleading in describing women's work. It implies that women were newly brought into the work force largely as millworkers, while in practice, women had been and continued to be employed throughout the economy in all forms of industrial organisation. Accelerated growth generated new opportunities for women, but the loss of work in traditional lines was probably greater than the new creations.[21] Urban industry undermined rural production and women's jobs as faster and cheaper manufacturing processes made the techniques of cottage industry uneconomic. Therefore, the range of women's work declined, and a sharper division of labour emerged, since men and women often worked in distinct sectors of the economy, not only at different tasks. Men were more likely to hang on to artisanal work, while women became more clearly 'operatives'. Women's work tended to remain outwork, and with mechanisation and centralisation, they often switched tasks. At the same time, new female jobs were created as more goods and markets developed, predominantly in textiles, clothing, paper and tobacco. However, women who lost jobs in rural industry were not necessarily the ones who gained new jobs. In the process of the changing shape of industry, women became a more visible and, indeed, essential workforce. As cottage, workshop and factory organisation existed side-by-side throughout the period, with them came different interpersonal relationships between co-workers, managers, masters and owners. Likewise, the work-discipline and the value placed on industrial time varied.[22]

Maxine Berg challenged the 'traditional' interpretations of the industrial revolution indicating that more recent research on 'patterns of economic growth raised important questions for the significance of women's work.' Not only did she question interpretations that saw industrialisation as rapid, but she also argued there was significant 'continuity rather than discontinuity in the growth of output and productivity during the years of England's classic industrial revolution.'[23] She pointed to an increasing acceptance of the more gradual approach using social as well as economic factors, although she also acknowledged that this is contested. Significantly, she suggested that the newer considerations of economic change nevertheless left a 'glaring omission' in that women's labour was rarely factored into the equation. Instead of asking what effect the industrial revolution had on women, she turned this around to ask what impact the gender division of labour had on the understanding of industrialisation, thus concentrating on labour supply rather than indices of industrial production and not limiting the discussion to male labour supply. Indeed, Anthony Wrigley commented, somewhat dismissively, 'In some of the most dynamic industries, such as cotton textiles, a high proportion of the labour force was female. . . . If information were available for the whole labour force, therefore, the numbers and percentages just given would be changed somewhat.[24] Berg's contention is that industry in the eighteenth and early nineteenth centuries relied on a largely female labour force, mainly in textiles: there were important counter examples, such as the metal trades, but textiles were largely a driver of the industrial revolution, whether in cottages or factories relied extensively on female workers. Additionally, those industries 'at the forefront of technological and organisational change were . . . industries employing women's labour.'[25] The same technological and technological changes in early US industrial development mirrored the changes in division of labour and productivity. Berg acknowledged that data on women was less robust than that for men, but she argues that,

> The dominant parts of the manufacturing sector were employers of higher proportions of women than of men, and women rather than men were employed in the new progressive industries to which most of the productivity gain in industry has been attributed.

Furthermore, she pointed out that as women and children were assumed to be the key workforce, 'machines and processes were invented with this workforce in mind.'[26] For example, she has shown how spinning jennies were designed to be operated by young girls, since they were uncomfortable for adults to use for any length of time. Writing at much the same time, Sonja Rose also emphasised that in the nineteenth century,

> Machines designed to be worked by skilled workers were built to be operated by people with the hands, height, and weight of an average male, unless a manufacturer had in mind reducing labor costs by replacing men with women and therefore contracted with a machine maker to build a machine that would be suitable for female bodies.[27]

More work needs to be done to understand the sources of gain in industrial productivity married to the high labour intensity of a largely female workforce. It is unlikely to be only cheaper labour and docility that shaped this development.[28]

The factory became an alternative migratory route for young females in place of farm and domestic service, and it was common for girls to swap between them. In Halstead, Essex, many female weavers left Courtauld's silk factory for short periods of time, because of the 'pull of domestic service', and it was not uncommon for young girls to try both factory work and domestic service.[29] Their income mattered to families. Jeanne Bouvier's mother sent her to a silk factory outside Lyon, and when she did not get a pay rise, she beat Jeanne, accusing her of being lazy.[30]

The image of the mill girl obscures the number of married women in factories. The most common factory employees in Roubaix were childless wives, while single women and married mothers with children under five worked reduced hours. Fewer worked as children grew up; potentially mothers and daughters traded off work. Employers were ambivalent. Cowan's paper mill, Penicuik, Scotland, in 1865 claimed, 'With a view to prevent the neglect of children in their homes, we do not employ the mothers of young children in our works, . . . [except] widows or women deserted by their husbands, or having husbands unable to earn a living.'[31] In Essex, no one expected married women at Courtauld's silk factory to give up millwork, even those with well-paid husbands.[32] Demand for female labour could pose problems for families, though, as a Lancashire woman explained: 'So large is the demand for female labour, that fifty women can find employment where the man fails. . . . Thus, it is quite true that many women do keep their husbands'.[33] Many had no choice and migrated to towns where factory textiles dominated. Sometimes they changed occupations. On balance, if legislation did not restrict girls' work, probably the majority of female workers in centralised units were young and unmarried. However, the number of married women who worked in mills and workshops is sufficient to make it clear that women utilised whatever strategies suited their own particular needs. Since the demand for female labour was so great, and since jobs were scarce for men in textile towns, it placed an even greater premium on married women's work. Many single mothers also worked in textile mills. If women needed income, and work was available in a mill or workshop, they were likely to take it up. We should not be blind to the variety of patterns which existed, and the strategies employed by women who had to earn. From their point of view, it was pragmatic to continue in the work one knew to make ends meet, provided arrangements could be made for the children.

At the turn of the twentieth century, homeworking and sweated workshops were little changed, and these jobs sat at the defining moment between a domestic economy and industrial activity. It expanded with increased demand for popularly priced clothing, toys and luxury goods previously only available to the leisured classes, accompanied by a reduction in prices and sophisticated division of labour in the workshops. Department stores that created 'dream worlds' for mass consumption, and a burgeoning white-collar labour force together with skilled and semi-skilled workers' families generated a vast new internal market for such goods.[34] Many women turned to outwork to meet household needs, including wives and daughters of labourers, tailors, artisans and merchants; some needy 'surplus' bourgeois women relied on sewing as a 'respectable' trade. Often irregular male employment and seasonal or cyclical unemployment, meant women had to work, becoming essential to family income. Parisienne Victorine Brocher sewed boots when her master shoemaker husband was unfit or out of work. Family needs often interrupted her, and she complained about the necessity for married women to work '12 or 14 hours for pitiful wages, forced to leave their children or aged parents untended'.[35] Neither married nor single women fit a single pattern. They took whatever was available, altering domestic strategies as necessary. The range and quality of outwork was vast: dressmakers, shirtmakers, seamers, milliners, staymakers, footwear and glove stitchers. They made umbrellas, walking sticks, artificial flowers, paper, sacks, bags, boxes, tassels, dolls' clothes and feather decorations. Factories or large workshops linked to networks of agents was a common way to put work out to rural communities. In Derry, Ireland, shirt factories encouraged women to take work home, salaried agents put work out and outstations allowed them to work *in situ* or take materials home.[36]

The homework system put women in a particularly vulnerable position, since employers dictated pay, completion dates and fined 'unsatisfactory' work. To achieve subsistence income, women had to work long, hard hours. Homework theoretically resolved the work and childcare conundrum, though intensive work was incongruous with household responsibilities. A London shirtmaker told Mayhew in 1849 that she usually worked from four in the morning until nine or ten at night in summer, 'as long as I can see', while a seamstress stayed up half the night to do housework after her husband had gone to bed.[37] Only better-off workingwomen could afford to set their own pace. Many single women preferred the relative freedom of homework to the constraints of domestic service. An English lace runner said, 'I like it better than the factory, though we can't get so much. We have our liberty at home and get our meals comfortable, such as they are.'[38] Many women chose to work at home precisely because they could attend children, despite the conflicts this involved.

The growth of 'ready-made', or *confection*, expanded needlework, but also destroyed skilled female trades like millinery, mantuamaking and dressmaking. Self-employed, they worked in dispersed locations and usually lacked the strong craft solidarity that tailors used to fight ready-made. Subcontracting created a fundamental gender change in needle trades: men became owners and subcontractors. They had greater access to capital, and closely identified with ownership and management, it was easier for them to take control. Thus, women lost their craft status as the distinction between skilled and unskilled workers died. Workshops introduced machines on a large scale, mechanising and centralising garmentmaking by 1860. Sewing machines facilitated decentralisation but certainly did not cause it. They sped up sewing, raised expectations of productivity and increased hours of work, stress and exhaustion. Women provided their machine and absorbed overheads, becoming an even more attractive workforce. Breaking down the production process meant the skill content deteriorated. Ottilie Baader, included in this collection, described how this exacerbated the boring, repetitious character of work:

> A session lasted from 6 am to 12 am, with one hour pause for lunch. . . . year after year at the sewing machine, always just collars and cuffs in front of me, one dozen after another. Life had no value, I was just a work machine and had no future prospects.[39]

At the same time, one of the most important female occupations, garmentmaking, began to decline so that by 1910 the trend was apparent across Europe. By 1915, Belfast Health Reports reported 'outwork in the city has been reduced as employers prefer it to be done on their premises because of punctuality, combined with sending it to the country districts where it can be embroidered at a cheaper rate.' In Glasgow, homeworkers in garment trades declined by a quarter between 1901 and 1911.[40]

THE INDUSTRIAL HOME

From the mid-eighteenth century to the first world war, a bourgeoisie emerged whose views and values fashioned much of urban society, affecting those who were neither part of this buoyant class nor privy to its wealth and status. From domestic arrangements to industrial capitalism and representative democracy, bourgeois values had a significant impact and were central to understanding gender. Largely coming from the new middle class of industrialists and industrial capitalism, their views shaped perceptions of the working woman and her middle-class counterparts. Married women especially had long had the main responsibility for maintaining the household and caring for family members; single women expected this to be their future and domestic service was seen as a natural workspace for them, preparatory to managing their own homes. An idealised view, it nevertheless shaped the context into which industrial women worked. From cottage industry to homework and piecework, the assumption was that these were 'by-employments' to their real work of housekeeping. Thus, they were seen as casual, part-time workers, supplementary labour, subordinate to men who were 'real' workers and breadwinners.

Needless to say, this conception was partly fact and partly fiction. Most women worked because they needed to, and industrial trades provided this opportunity. Few households could survive on a single income, and a remarkable number of single and widowed women headed households making them the key 'breadwinner'. Domesticity was a powerful construct, and many working-class men and women identified with its attractions especially in the last half of the century as incomes improved. Yet, it was unrealistic for most for whom poverty and poor living conditions made daily life a struggle. Their physical environments meant that separate spaces simply did not exist; men and women worked together in cottages, crowded tenements, workshops and factories. Home was hardly a haven.

Cottages crowded with equipment including looms, spindles and other paraphernalia which meant that households were both workshop and living space. Children were often left to fend for themselves; for example, Sarah Stephenson, born in 1738, commented in her biography, 'When I was about six years of age, I had a narrow escape of being burned to death, by falling on the fire when no one else was in the room.'[41] Certainly, caring for children was not all absorbing and reflected the realities of the economic and labour needs of the household. In the Montpellier region during silkworm season,

> the women are constantly busy with gathering mulberry leaves or with the worms themselves. The children are neglected, suffer, and die. The habit of seeing such a great number perish in this season has given rise to a proverb which says that "in the time you see the silkworm rise, the most kids go to paradise".[42]

Similar problems faced women in urban households and as slums and overcrowding developed during the nineteenth century; domestic space hardly improved. Rapidly expanding manufacturing towns with industrial debris created fresh problems, including urban sewage, smoke and other industrial detritus. These made it harder to clean house and contributed to the move to suburbs for those who could afford to. Workingwomen coped with shared privies, crumbling plaster, bugs, rats and overcrowding. Although increasingly prosperous homes had piped water and sewage, workingwomen still had to fetch it. In 1850, the British General Board of Health estimated that it took two days' work each week to fetch twenty pails (500 lbs) of water necessary for a labouring family's needs. Rural conditions were often little better, and in 1913, 62 per cent of British rural houses lacked piped water. The idea that homework enabled women to work to their own rhythms was contradicted by the hours required and the low pay almost all such industries entailed. Rarely did women have any control over these factors, although flowermakers were sometimes seen as an exception. Jacob Riis' accounts of *How the Other Half Lived*, initially a short article in *Scribner's Magazine* in 1889, are indicative. Photographing and describing the conditions of urban workers in New York in the 1890s, his work is testimony to the unsavoury and virtually impossible conditions in which many industrial families lived. In Britain, Henry Mayhew recorded similar images from London in the 1840s in *London Labour and the London Poor*, originally serialised in the *Morning Chronicle*. In an age of enquiries, Fréderic LePlay similarly recorded the lives of European working people, and in 1855, he published *Les Ouvriers Européens* (*The European Workers*), a series of thirty-six monographs on the budgets of typical families selected from a wide range of industries.[43]

A further issue was provision of housing for single working women. In Europe generally, boarding houses and female-only housing was frowned upon or usually unavailable. Rental flats, flat-sharing, staying with family and sometimes boarding with kin provided accommodation. But in the United States, housing for young women was provided almost from the outset, with the Lowell Mills in Massachusetts being the outstanding example where a virtual community was created around single mill girls. Other mills followed suit, with varying degrees of success and a variety of amenities. With them often came strictures on behaviour and other conditions. Such accommodations were not comprehensive, however, and single American women often had to follow the same route as European girls.

Industrial training was available throughout the period. In the eighteenth and early nineteenth century, this was largely apprenticeships. Girls took up apprenticeship in prominent trades, millinery and mantuamaking the most pronounced, with good premiums and useful training. But most were likely to be parish apprenticeships, often to trades, like metalwork, textiles or pottery. However, the majority were sent to domestic service, and much of the literature continued to focus on girls' anticipated roles as mother and wife. Indeed, much of the training offered was in housewifery skills at schools. The quality and utility of their training was variable but could provide a livelihood and might have served them well on marriage.[44] As the nineteenth century progressed, training became a more significant issue, in parallel with the woman's movement and growing feminism. Thus, tracts increasingly promoted 'industrial training' while college programmes also began to include industrial subjects, especially in North America, where young women were more successful at entering secondary and higher education than in Britain. Yet, in all cases, there were persistent tensions with the ideology of womanhood and a concern with women being able to look after their homes and families. Some were successful well-directed endeavours, providing work-related training for both young men and women, and in the American South, for 'Indians' and 'Coloreds' [their language].

FEMALE AGENCY

Women were not passive in the road to industrialisation, and they certainly took whatever opportunities that lay before them. They also reacted to poor working and living conditions. Although working women were slower to 'combine' into unions and friendly societies than men, they did so from the eighteenth century. Female friendly societies emerged in several industrial areas, with Frederick Morton Eden reporting on large numbers of them across Britain. Many were initiated by middle-class women intending to create a safety net for working women; a few were begun by working women themselves; and in some they shared management with middle-class benefactors. Primarily a sick club, these helped support women in sickness, injury and pregnancy, and usually provided for funeral expenses. Members, both the 'management' and the workers themselves, paid into the fund and therefore benefitted under conditions laid out in the regulations. Women took strike action, with union membership or without, for better pay, for better conditions, against layoffs and short-time working. In Vienna in 1898, Amalie Seidl provoked the first strike of women simply by speaking to promote the importance of May Day and the ways that union organisation could improve their pay and conditions.[45] In Britain, the strike against Bryant and May, the match-making company, was of similar significance.

There was a clear link between feminist groups and individuals and efforts to improve the industrial woman's life, living and working conditions. To cite one example, Florence Kelley became a lifelong social campaigner. Born to abolitionist parents in Philadelphia in 1859, she graduated from Cornell University, studied in Europe, joined the German Social Democratic Workers' Party and translated many of their works. Her translation of a selection from Friedrich Engels, *The Condition of the Working-Class in England in 1844*, is in Volume Three.[46] She worked with Jane Addams at Hull House and became the first woman to become the Chief Factory Inspector for Illinois. Furthermore, she became the head of the National Consumers League (NCL), helped organise the National Advancement of Colored People (NAACP) and in 1911, she founded the National Labor Committee. As a feminist and suffragist, she became the Vice President of the National American Woman Suffrage Association and was a founding member of the Women's International League for Peace and Freedom.[47] She authored or contributed to several documents in this collection, in addition to the translation mentioned earlier, showing some of the breadth of her interests. Other authors could claim a similar diverse pedigree, including American Jane Addams, Englishwomen Beatrice Webb and B. L. Hutchins (Elizabeth Leigh Hutchins), Scotswoman Margaret Irwin, and Austrians Adelheid Popp and Amalie Seidl, all of whom feature in this collection. These authors illustrate the significance of women's voices in the work to understand and reform women's industrial working along with their other interests.

This collection brings together key sources for this industrial transition and women's role in it. It focuses both on the process and on women's contribution, echoing Berg by addressing the issue of what impact the gender division of labour had on the understanding of industrialisation as well as how women operated within industrial work. It also looks to female agency and how both authors and workers articulated their positions in industry. The set comprises four volumes, each taking up a different aspect of women in industry. Volume One concentrates on women's role in industrial work located at home or workshops. It comprises domestic industries, protoindustries and the later developments of workshops, outwork and sweated trades. Notably, this volume uses the thread of home working to tie together kinds of work often seen as separate, e.g. cottage industry and sweated industry, and marks the changes over time. It also brings into focus some of the issues facing married women especially. Volume Two focuses on industrialisation and factory working. In doing so, it marks the different choices single and married women had and the issues which emerged as urban industry impacted rural industries. Both of these volumes consider kinds of work, the types of workers employed and their tasks, and the volumes address the conditions under which women worked. Volume Three takes on the industrial home addressing the social and living conditions of women in industry. While not all documents specify women, this is implicit in talking about the character of homes, the role of women in those homes and the wider social conditions that shaped how industrial women managed domestic responsibilities. An important section of this volume includes essays that expose what authors believed woman's domestic role should have been, together with what they blamed as the reasons for their failure as wives and mothers. Others are less moralistic and depict the realities of slums and poor housing. Further sections explore the kinds of industrial training that authors argued should be provided for girls and women and the kinds of employer housing and residential provision, especially for single women. While lifecycle runs as a question though all four volumes, it is most explicit in Volume Three. Volume Four deals most directly with issues of law, power and resistance. It takes account of pressures to change legislation and women's resistance to their working status and conditions. It also examines some self-help initiatives organised by benefactors and women themselves.

It must be stressed that the individual volumes are not self-standing since most authors had more than one agenda, so an essay frequently addressed several issues at once. The volumes also include several selections from some authors. Thus, documents were allocated to volumes where they best fit the story of that volume, helping to create a more holistic picture. All four volumes illustrate changes over time, both in the issues discussed as well as reflecting changes in the wider concern about industry and especially in the social concerns that came to the forefront. For example, in Volume One we see the shift from a primarily small-scale family working environment in the late eighteenth century to the concerns with sweated industries of the early twentieth century. The documents naturally reflect the interests of the authors, so Daniel Defoe was concerned with productivity and English manufactures, while Arthur Young's remarks were based on his interest in agricultural development, with industry as a side interest. Frederick Morton Eden was concerned with the poor law and poverty. But all three give glimpses into the industrial production of cottages and protoindustries. At the other end of the time period, we see the impact of concerns with social welfare, with groups like the Fabian Society and feminists coming to the fore in explaining and pressing for reforms in working conditions. Volume Two marks the spread of factories which was apparent in both Britain and America, especially Massachusetts. By mid-century, many commentators selected were part of the debate over factory legislation and its pros and cons, and these were followed by more and more reports from factory inspectors in both countries. Again, these commentaries reflect the changing priorities of society over time more broadly. A similar pattern can be seen in Volumes Three and Four, as industrial working became more common and indeed visible, and as women's economic and domestic issues became more central to social concern.

The geographical coverage necessarily is weighted towards Great Britain, with many of the earlier documents focused on the late eighteenth century. Similarly, documents on the British factory reform movement and poor law movements of the middle years of the nineteenth century reflect the importance of these debates and initiatives on the wider history of industrial women. Frequently, American documents cite them in making the case for changes in the United States. The same forms of early industry did not exist in the United States and factory development came later. Waterpower fuelled industry by 1800, and by 1820 Lowell, Massachusetts, was designed as a planned manufacturing centre. Lowell girls became iconic mill girls, and several of their writings are included. The development of Lowell was deliberate, and the documents illustrate significant differences in the experiences of these girls from those in Britain, and indeed in Europe. Europe is least represented in the collection, but a sample of documents shows how industry was not only an Anglo-American story.

The collection is designed to be varied, so as suggested previously, there are essays expressing opinions, others which attempt statistical analysis, while others report on fact-finding missions and inspections. Some documents are government reports and debates in Parliament, while newspapers are included to bring to life the immediacy of some events. Those reporting catastrophes tend also to be dramatic, sometimes lurid and as one author claimed 'thrilling'. The people living through these events probably did not agree with him.[48] Where possible, women's voices are included, the majority of which fall into the later period of the story, as few autobiographical materials from women survive from the earlier period. However, some testimonies and other documents which suggest women's responses to their situation, and perhaps a comment on their agency, do find their way into the volumes from the period before 1820. A strategy used throughout the collection is documents on a single theme. So, for example, milliners and dressmakers figure as a running theme across the volumes, allowing us to follow the trajectory of an industry where women could make a good living and could run their own business across the whole of the period of the collection. This was not always true, of course, as this group also elided with sweated industries. The world of printing also makes up a running thread, from Susan Traill, printer in eighteenth-century Aberdeen, to printers reported by factory inspectors, and finally to the compositors' struggle in early twentieth-century Edinburgh. A feature of women's work, especially in the earlier period, is that the documents tend to be short, sometime cryptic. Thus, a strategy of creating 'clusters' was employed to capture these worlds. So Volume One has a cluster around the putting-out system, another on the letters of the British Linen company and their protoindustrial strategy of training and using female labour, and another on girl apprentices and workers. Volume Two has a similar cluster based on the Factory Commission Reports in 1842, and Volume Four has one on an Atlanta Cotton Mills strike, 1899, where white women rejected working with blacks, and one on the British Match Girl's strike of 1888, using reports by Annie Besant. The intention was to use an array of materials which capture the spirit of industrialisation and the part of industrial women. In doing so, it builds on the initial questions: who are women in industry? And indeed, what is industry? It takes a broad view of industrial women, including not only the women who worked in it but also those who commentated on it, those who found ways to support themselves and their families and those who strove to reform practices.

NB. Biographical details were drawn from a variety of sources, especially the *Oxford Dictionary of National Biography*, *Britannica*, and other similar biographical dictionaries as well as from prefaces and introductions to the documents themselves.

Editing Notes: Generally this collection follows the grammar and spelling of the original authors, thus misspellings are usually different conventions than today, such as "expence" not expense. Sometimes the difference depends on nationality of the author, so that American conventions are followed for Americans and British ones for British authors. However, this is highly inconsistent, as several British authors followed American conventions. Translations from non-English languages are the editor's and use British English. Not all notes have been included, either because they were not useful or went off in tangents that were not strictly relevant to the story of industrial women. A few silent edits were required, but largely these are as the original authors intended.

Notes

1 Deborah Simonton, *Gender in the European Town* (Routledge, 2023), 143.
2 Stana Nenadic, 'The Social Shaping of Business Behaviour in the Nineteenth-Century Women's Garment Trades'. *Journal of Social History*, 31, 3 (1998): 626.
3 Geoffrey Tweedale, 'Backstreet capitalism: An analysis of the family firm in the nineteenth-century Sheffield cutlery industry', *Business History*, 55, 6 (2013): 884.
4 See in Simonton, *Gender in the European Town* (Routledge, 2023).
5 Hannah Barker, *The Business of Women, Female Enterprise and Urban Development in Northern England, 1760–1830.* (Oxford University Press, 2006); Beatrice Craig, *Female Enterprise: Behind the Discursive Veil in Nineteenth-Century Northern France*. (Palgrave Macmillan, 2017); Jennifer Aston, 'Female Business Ownership in Birmingham 1849–1901', *Midland History*, 37, 2 (Autumn 201): 187–206; Simonton, *Gender in the European Town*, especially 142–45, and see bibliography.
6 Deborah Simonton, *A History of European Women's Work* (Routledge, 1998), 97–98.
7 United States. Bureau of the Census Historical Statistics of the United States: Colonial Times to 1957, 1960, Series D 72–122. Major Occupation Group of the Economically Active Population, by Sex: 1900 to 1950; see also, Xuesheng You 'The Missing

Half: Female employment in Victorian England and Wales', Cambridge Group for the History of Population, [2019?] https://www.campop.geog.cam.ac.uk/research/occupations/outputs/onlineatlas/femaleemployment.pdf. Accessed 24 September 2024.

8 B.R. Mitchell, *International Historical Statistics: Europe*, 4th ed. (Macmillan, 1998), 160.

9 Janine Lanza, Amanda Lewis Nang'ea and Deborah Simonton, *The Routledge History of Global Women's Work* (Routledge, forthcoming); see also Teresa A. Meade and Merry E, Wiesner-Hanks, *A Companion to Global Gender History* (Wiley-Blackwell, 2020).

10 Eric J. Hobsbawm, *The Age of Revolution, 1789–1848* (Weidenfeld and Nicolson, 1962), 55.

11 See the discussion of alternative forms of industrial organisation in Berg, *Age of Manufactures* (Routledge, 1994), 84–90.

12 Franklin F. Mendels, 'Proto-industrialization: the first phase of the industrialization process'. *Journal of Economic History*, 32, 1 (1972): 241–261.

13 Pat Hudson, 'Protoindustrialisation', *ReFresh*, Spring 10, 1990, 1.

14 The debate about proto-industry and its relationship to 'preindustrial' and 'industrial' society and the dynamic of economic and social change are outlined in Pat Hudson, 'Protoindustrialisation', *ReFresh*, Spring 10, 1990, 1. and Sheilagh C. Ogilvie and Markus Cerman, 'The Theories of Protoindustrialisation', in *European Proto-Industrialization: An Introductory Handbook* (Cambridge University Press, 1996), 1–11, and L.A. Clarkson, *Proto-Industrialization: The First Phase of Industrialization?* (Macmillan, 1985).

15 See also Clarkson's criticism, *Proto-Industrialization The First Phase of Industrialization?* (Macmillan, 1985), 48.

16 On plebeian culture, custom and control see Berg, *Age of Manufactures, Industry, Innovation and Work in Britain, 1700 –1820.* Fontana Press, 1994, chapter 7; Medick, 'Protoindustrial Family', 303; Hans Medick, 'Plebeian Culture in the transition to capitalism,' in *Culture, Ideology and Politics, essays for Eric Hobsbawm*, Raphael Samuel and Gareth Stedman Jones, eds. (Routledge, 1983*)*, 84–113, E. P. Thompson, 'Patrician Society, Plebeian Culture,' *Journal of Social History*, 7, 4 (Summer 1974): 382–405

17 Neil McKendrick, 'The Consumer Revolution in Eighteenth-Century England,' in *The Birth of a Consumer Society*, Neil McKendrick, John Brewer and J. H. Plumb, eds. (Hutchinson and Co. Ltd, 1983), 23.

18 Neil McKendrick, 'Home Demand and Economic Growth, A New View of the Role of Women and Children in the Industrial Revolution.' In *Historical Perspectives, Studies in English Thought and Society*, 152–210, Neil McKendrick, ed. (Europa Publications, 1974), 200, 209.

19 Jan de Vries, 'Between Purchasing Power and the World of Goods: Understanding the Household Economy in Early Modern Europe,' in *Consumption and World of Goods*, John Brewer and Roy Porter, eds. (Routledge, 1993), 85–132; and *The Industrious Revolution* (Cambridge, Cambridge University Press, 2006).

20 Berg, *Age of Manufactures, Industry, Innovation and Work in Britain, 1700 – 1820.* Fontana Press, 1994, 155.

21 For examples and a detailed discussion see Berg, *Age of Manufactures, Industry, Innovation and Work in Britain, 1700 – 1820.* Fontana Press, 1994, 108–25. See also Eric Richards, 'Women in the British Economy Since about 1700, an Interpretation,' *History*, 59, 197 (June 1974): 344.

22 See E. P. Thompson, 'Time, Work Discipline, and Industrial Capitalism.' In *Essays in Social History*, M. W. Flinn and T. C. Smout, eds (Clarendon Press, 1974), 39–77.

23 Berg, Maxine, 'What Difference did Women's Work Make to the Industrial Revolution?', *History Workshop*, 35 (1993 Spring): 22. See also Maxine Berg, 'Women's Work and the Industrial Revolution', *ReFresh*, 12, Spring 1991.

24 E. Anthony Wrigley, *Continuity, Chance, and Change. The Character of the Industrial Revolution in England* (Cambridge, 1988), 85.

25 Berg, 'What Difference did Women's Work Make to the Industrial Revolution?', *History Workshop*, 35 Spring 1993 30.

26 Berg, 'What Difference did Women's Work Make to the Industrial Revolution?', *History Workshop*, 35 Spring 1993, 34.
27 Sonya O. Rose, *Limited Livelihoods Gender and Class in Nineteenth Century England*, (Taylor & Francis Group: 1992), 29.
28 Berg, 'What Difference did Women's Work Make to the Industrial Revolution?', *History Workshop*, 35 Spring 1993, 41.
29 Judy Lown, *Women and Industrialization: Gender at Work in Nineteenth-century England* (Polity Press: 1990), 60.
30 Jeanne Bouvier, *My Memoirs*, in *The French Worker*, Mark Traugott, ed. (The University of California Press, 1993), 348.
31 Quoted in John Holley, 'The two family economies of Industrialism: Factory Workers in Victorian Scotland', *Journal of Family History*, 6 (1981): 64.
32 Lown, *Women and Industrialization Gender at Work in Nineteenth-century England* (Polity Press: 1990), 36, 81.
33 Ellen Barlee, *A visit to Lancashire in December 1862* (Seely, 1863), 32.
34 Rosalind Williams, *Dream Worlds: Mass Consumption in Late Nineteenth-century France* (University of California Press, 1982).
35 Victorine B[rocher], *Souveniers d'une morte vivante* (Librarie A Lapie, 1976), 61.
36 Brenda Collins, 'Sewing Outwork in Ulster,' in *Markets and Manufacturers in Early Industrial Europe*, Maxine Berg, ed. (Routledge, 1991), 141–42, 148–50.
37 Paul Thompson and Eileen Yeo. *Unknown Mayhew* (Penguin, 1984), 122–23, 251.
38 G.B. *Parliamentary Papers, Factory Commission*, 1833, C2, 17.
39 Ottilie Baader, *Ein steiniger Weg. Lebenserinnerungen einer Sozialistin* (1921) [A Rocky Path: Reminiscences of a Female Socialist], 3rd ed., Marie Juchacz ed. (J.H.W. Dietz Nachf., 1979), 19–20. Author Translation.
40 Collins 'Sewing Outwork,'152, 155–56n36; Alice J. Albert, 'Fit Work for Women: Sweated Home-workers in Glasgow, c. 1875–1914,' in *The World is Ill Divided: Women's Work in Scotland in the Nineteenth and Early Twentieth Centuries*. Eleanor Gordon and Esther Breitenbach, eds, (Edinburgh: Edinburgh University Press 1990), 158–177.
41 Sarah Stephenson, *Memoirs Life and Travels in the Service of the Gospel of Sarah Stephenson* (Friends Library: 1807), 2.
42 Hugh Cunningham, *Children and Childhood in Western Society since 1500* (Longman, 1995), 107–108.
43 Jacob Riis, *How the Other Half Lives: Studies among the Tenements of New York* (Charles Scribner's and Sons, 1890); Henry Mayhew, *London Labour and the London Poor; a cyclopaedia of the condition and earnings of those that will work, those that cannot work, and those that will not work*. 3 vols. (G. Newbold: 1851); Fréderic Le Play, *Les Ouvriers Européens: Travaux, Vie Domestique Et Condition Morale Des Populations,* 2nd ed., (A. Mame et fils, 1877).
44 Deborah Simonton, *The Education and Training of Eighteenth-Century English Girls, with special reference to the working classes*, PhD Thesis, University of Essex, 1988.
45 Amalie Seidl, 'Der erste Arbeiterinnenstreik in Wien [The First Women's Strike in Vienna], in *Gedenkbuch 20 Jahre österreichische Arbeiterinnenbewegung* [Memories, 20 years of the Austrian Women Workers Journey], Adelheid Popp, ed. (Kommissionsverl. der Wr. Volksbuchhandlung "Vorwärts": 1912), 66–69.
46 Friedrich Engels, *The Condition of the Working-Class in England in 1844*. Translated: Florence Kelley (George Allen and Unwin, 1892).
47 Arlisha R. Norwood, 'Florence Kelley', National Women's History Museum, 2017. https://www.womenshistory.org/education-resources/biographies/florence-kelley, accessed 25 September 2024.
48 [Pemberton Mill Disaster], *An Authentic History of the Lawrence Calamity [including] a chapter of Thrilling highlights*, (John Dyer and Co.: 1860).

INTRODUCTION TO VOLUME I

Women in Industrial Handwork

Across the period from 1750 to 1914, women worked at home and in workshops on a range of crafts, trades and tasks. However, these roles have often been divided, with historical thinking splitting them into the eighteenth-century domestic or cottage industries and the nineteenth- and twentieth-century sweated industries. Such a demarcation thus overlooks the similarities in the kinds of work they did, the locations they worked in and the power relations that controlled the work processes. Certainly, there were differences in these categories of work, but the similarities are striking. Focusing on domestic industry, trades and sweated work demonstrates how continuous industrial handwork was throughout the period. Certainly, some handwork was tool-based, with looms, spinning jennies, stocking frames and sewing machines, for example, but largely it was handwork. Workplaces changed, but for the most part the home remained an important locus for women's industrial work. Where there was a sufficient concentration of women, industries might be brought into workshops where women continued to produce a single item, but when the tasks could be divided, they might work on only part of an item, like sewing collars and cuffs, or finishing a pair of trousers, a feature prominent in sewing outwork especially. Merchants and employers controlled the amount of work that was available, fixing prices and rates of pay, controlling the delivery of materials and sales. Rarely did women gain control of their work in these situations. However, women did take advantage of entrepreneurial opportunities and dictated their own work and that of other women.

Women were also foremost in criticising the work practices affecting industrial women. In the late nineteenth century and early twentieth centuries, commentators increasingly addressed the characteristics of women's industrial work, especially in the sweated trades. To do so, they looked back to cottage industries, which provided a template for many of the circumstances which shaped industrial handwork. Often prompted by their activities in the women's and suffrage movements and benefitting from access to university education and to jobs like factory inspection, many commentators were women, like B.L Hutchins in Britain and Edith Abbott in the United States (docs. 1, 2).

DOMESTIC INDUSTRIES

Cottage industries and family workshops were long-standing modes of production where many women worked in a household as a member of a family or a servant in residence. Initially such domestic industries provided items for the home, but surpluses were marketed and became an important income source for families (Image 1).[1] Many but not all these industries were in textiles, and other handicrafts like metalwork, pottery and leatherwork were familiar enterprises, often in workshops nearby or associated with homes. Increasing population growth and agricultural change meant that more people looked for alternatives to support themselves, and as many plots provided only subsistence, women increasingly turned to commercialised forms of work. The protoindustries, commission system in America, the *Verlager* system in German areas and *protoindustrie* in France, capitalised on this labour force, but specifically marketed goods commercially. A familiar pattern involved a merchant supplying raw materials and collecting them for finishing and sale. In Yorkshire, many woollen weavers organised their own raw materials, production and sale, whereas the families of the English West Country were more reliant on clothiers and merchants to supply wool and arrange finishing and sales. As an industrial system, English domestic industries were highly praised by commentators like Daniel Defoe (doc. 3), Arthur Young (docs. 4, 5, 7), Adam Smith (doc. 6) and Frederick Morton Eden (doc. 8). They were interested in promoting British industry and commerce to improve the wealth of the nation, and they uniformly described a family pattern of working, subsuming women's work to the household. They also frequently commented on a woman's primary role as housekeeper alongside her industrial work, remarking on women's industrial role only in passing. While sometimes referencing women's unemployment – suggesting laziness at times – they promoted the image of a well-dressed, contented family resulting from this system.

Women worked in cottage industries on a uniquely large scale and were important in the transition to protoindustries. Entrepreneurs were drawn to the countryside because large numbers of skilled women requiring income made them attractive and affordable employees. Women's motives were primarily financial, to support themselves and to contribute to household support. Though young women left for service or later factory work, married women or mothers were the mainstay of these industries, since work that could be carried out around other household tasks was particularly attractive. Like much of women's work, domestic industries were largely task-orientated and perceived as 'casual' and supplementary, even when it took up most of women's time. However, the need to produce enough to earn enough to support even herself required a strenuous effort and was not 'casual' in any sense of the word. As 'casual, supplementary' work, it never gained recognition as a primary source of income, affecting both the level of wages and the perceptions of women's income as 'pin money'.

Commentators saw women's so-called natural abilities and nimble fingers as suiting them to many of the manipulative tasks associated with cottage industries, a feature that carried over to sweated trades. They were the spinners of Europe, working in every thread and fabric. The female culture associated with spinning was illustrated by the *spinnstuben*, *écreignes* or *veillées*, where women came together to spin and talk, usually on winter evenings when they could share heat and light. Women also wove, sometimes alternating with men who were seen as the skilled master-weavers (doc. 9). Single women and widows might work in a family setting, but they also worked on their own, in other's homes or workshops and in clusters of women who pooled their labour. A distinctive feature of lace-making in Ireland, Normandy, Picardy, Flanders and Belgium was that women controlled all stages of production, whilst in most other domestic industries women were limited to preparatory or minor finishing tasks dependent on male workers. It required little capital investment, and women worked on their own, hired a few co-workers or worked with daughters.

In some instances, competing demands for women's labour precipitated the drive to find cheaper labour. In the second half of the century, work was moved to the Scottish Highlands and Islands to meet the need for cheap yarn, because better paid employment for women in the main weaving areas enticed women away from spinning into muslin embroidery, bleachfields and mills. David Loch's tour of Scotland in 1778 (doc. 10) and the *Statistical Account of Scotland* (doc. 11) described the importance of these industries while the British Linen Company was responsible for much of the employment of women as linen thread spinners (doc. 12). Notably, merchants saw it as necessary to provide training for women in the highlands, having concern for the quality of the final product, with the Linen Company and Aberdeen City Council providing spinning teachers.

Domestic industries clearly overlapped with homework and factory work, which was more appealing to young single women. They often left rural areas for towns to take up domestic service, and factory spinning provided them with a better wage. As a result, women gradually lost home spinning, with a specific impact on married women who had to decide whether to follow the work or stay where work was disappearing (docs. 13, 14, 15).

INDUSTRY AND WORKSHOPS

While domestic industries dominated many women's working lives, others found their way into other trades and workplaces. Increasingly, many domestic and rural industries moved into workshops, and for many of the working classes, their experience of work, even after factories entered the industrial world, was in small workshops, sometimes clustered into yards with separate operators, or single ones in smaller towns. And some, like the metal trades, sometimes worked at a single forge but also in a larger workshop setting. Matthew Bolton and Josiah Wedgwood both began their works in a small workshop setting and expanded as they became more successful and with investment and use of new inventions.

The trades of metalwork, especially nails, and of pottery are suggestive of the situation in workshops. Metalwork was already divided into multiple tasks, and children could be apprenticed to remarkably small parts of it. In Staffordshire in the eighteenth century, over a hundred separate metal trades took apprentices (Image 2, doc. 16).[2] The work was hard, and while girls were generally healthy from the exercise, they were also fatigued. The work did not require literacy, and observers' comments indicate that it positively discouraged schooling.[3] William Hutton's description of the nailmakers in Birmingham in 1783 are largely narrative, while about a century later, they were included in Robert Sherard's 'White Slaves of England' (docs. 17, 18). However, both men focused on the men. Nail-making was little changed, with nailing sheds fixed to the houses and systems of putting-out still operated at the end of the nineteenth century.[4]

Access to skilled industrial work tended to require apprenticeship, and formal apprenticeship applied to girls as well as boys, and authors of guides for parents wishing to place their children in apprenticed trades recognised this (docs. 19, 20, 21). They suggested several trades, and while some echoed women's work in domestic industries, they also included skilled work as auxiliaries in clockmaking, stay and bodice making and in a number of sewing trades and lacemaking, amongst others. These guides and apprenticeships are not representative of the breadth of trades women found their way into, however. They worked as awl-blade makers, bell founders, bellows, edge-tool, lock and hinge makers, iron founders and platers in the Birmingham metal trades. Three-quarters of women in Genevan criminal cases worked in sewing, watchmaking, textiles, laundering and the ever-present domestic service, but also as furriers, silk millers or hatmakers. Female silversmiths ran businesses and worked in production in the London craft as well as in clockmaking.[5] The trade guides tended to reflect trades coded as female, and thus they overlooked numerous others and reserved most industries for men. Edith Abbot put paid to the notion that these trades were restricted to men with a vast list of industries employing women in early America.[6]

Often using a system whereby women – usually girls – worked with a man as an assistant, the traditions of the cottage industries carried on into workshops. Yet, by the late eighteenth century the master might have become more of a manager and businessman than worker. In silversmithing, many hands were involved, so that men were usually hammermen and women were burnishers, and the master who left a mark may have had little to do with the actual piece. Women were frequently associated with retailing and accounts, but they as well as men took responsibility for final pieces, like Newcastle upon Tyne goldsmith Ann Robertson. Louisa Courtauld, member of one of the most famous families of goldsmiths, was one of the leading business owners in England, with a wide exporting and retailing network. Women also made silver goods from buttons, seen by Robert Campbell as 'a pretty ingenious business . . . women work for a mere trifle' to silverplaters in Sheffield who earned 'very good wages'.[7]

Although all trades had high-class as well as jobbing workers, the prestige trades drew the highest premiums for training apprentices, and women could make a name in them. English apprenticeship records demonstrate that girls were a significant proportion of apprentices (c. 9 per cent overall, doc. 22). Similarly, though in fewer numbers, guild and corporation records refer to females as mistresses and apprentices.[8] Also traditionally guilds allowed wives and daughters of members to work in a trade and to continue as full guild members after husbands' or fathers' deaths.[9] Also, many women gained their trading position because contemporaries accepted seven years' experience as equivalent to apprenticeship, although not within the terms of the law. Some girls who worked for their fathers were no doubt as carefully taught as boys. Others were apprenticed on the same conditions as brothers and served a formal term and those with the best chance of a *métier* were girls apprenticed privately by family or friends, about 4 per cent of these children.[10] When they completed their apprenticeship, they could set up as independent mistresses, legally the masters' equivalent, and take apprentices themselves. Some girls were hired rather than apprenticed. Parish indentures showed a strikingly different pattern since almost 30 per cent of pauper apprentices were girls, whose chances of learning a skill were weaker (doc. 24).

For many, these were good jobs and some shops clean and the workers healthy, but use of chemicals and the range of employers indicate these were not uniformly safe and salubrious (doc. 25). Working conditions increasingly became an issue in the nineteenth century, beginning with the first Factory Acts (see Vol. 4), initially focusing on women and children. Workshops and the sweated trades became an important public issue by the 1880s. Most workshops were not covered by the Factory Acts, which only applied to shops employing more than fifty workers. The Lords Select Committee on Sweating took up nailmaking as one of its concerns in 1889 (doc. 26). Education legislation from the 1870s meant that child workers were restricted or prevented from working. This is noticeable in the testimonies of girls, who were above school age for the most part, and who supplied detailed information on their working experiences (doc. 27). *The Englishwoman's Review* commented on the power relations and the complaints of china painter workers who argued that the men discriminated against them, asserting their claim for the property of their skill (doc. 28).

In skilled trades, the line between employer and worker was very fine, but while traces of craft and quality handmade work remained, increasingly it was lost as was the status associated with it. For example, flowermakers exercised more control over their work than many women, remaining 'mistresses of production' (Image 4). They claimed a *métier*, believing that work at home 'in an industry requiring taste, talent, and time for careful work might enhance a woman's self-image, while filling her pocketbook.'[11] Often homeworkers, by the beginning of the twentieth century it was largely outwork or had moved into workshops which could be crowded. In 1912, Caroline Milhaud found that a very good living could still be made, but about a third of workers depended on public relief (doc. 29).[12]

A CASE STUDY: MILLINERS AND SEAMSTRESSES

Sewing was a primary form of industrial work occupying and women of all ages and stations. At the lower end, it eventually became depressed and a sweated trade, while those at the top, commanding good apprenticeship premiums and providing a high-class service, did very well indeed. Milliners, and their sisters the mantuamakers, *modistes* and *marchandes de mode*, were skilled artisans, businesswomen and tradeswomen (Image 5).[13] Milliners especially could make comfortable profits in the second half of the eighteenth century; village women did less well, and workwomen might struggle, even before the days of sweating. To be successful, women needed a good knowledge of fashion and usually capital to set up on their own, so they could 'make vast profits on every article they deal in'. Girls with the right qualities of gentility, literacy and with some 'fancy and imagination' would 'hardly fail of procuring, in this branch of business, a comfortable and genteel support'. Commentators emphasised the importance of fashion, 'taste and fancy' and 'a quickness in discerning, imitating, and improving upon the various fashions'. Yet contemporaries saw a 'dark side' to this trade, criticising milliners and their workers of a tendency to loose morals and subject to the wiles of men who frequented the shops. While Robert Campbell was the most misogynist and outspoken critic, Joseph Collyer was less strident, but both reflect a problematic character of the trade. In the eighteenth century, milliners were frequently lampooned as prostitutes in disguise.[14] Thus, in millinery advertisements, 'women negotiated most carefully between the competing claims to skill, reputation, fashion and price' (docs. 30–33).[15]

Millinery and mantua making were trades where women could establish themselves most easily as entrepreneurs, like high-class milliners in the capitals and provincial cities like Colchester and Bath. These were solidly middling women, drawing on connections from their locations and access to the fashions of London and Bath. They regularly apprenticed young women and charged fees higher than most for male apprentices, ranging from £20 to over £50 for a short three- or four-year term.[16] These were carefully managed respectable firms, and they were well-esteemed in their communities. Mantuamakers and dressmakers often worked for milliners, as well as on their own, and while they earned less they were usually better placed than most who worked as auxiliaries sewing in other workshops. However, an investigation into hat makers in Paris argued that, while they may not be as unhappy as many others in other parts of France, 'they are nevertheless not as happy as the public believes' (doc. 34). Notably, the idea of a milliner mutated as time passed and in 1910, Alice Barrows struggled to define it as a single trade. Instead of a woman who worked with hats, fashion accessories and decoration, and who often hired a mantuamaker to make the basic dress, it was 'not easy to describe the millinery trade clearly because the essence of the description is to show that it cannot be made clear' (doc. 35). This disquiet reflected the vast range of sewing work that women undertook.

Sewing was the foremost female industry, closely identified with their roles as wives and mothers, linked to their feminine identity, and identified as a proficiency that was essential to women of all classes. While it was seen as something to be learned at home, utilising women's 'natural' abilities, schools, from fashionable boarding schools to charity schools, frequently taught sewing as both appropriate and as preparation for work.[17] Mary Wollstonecraft advocated plain sewing, mantuamaking, millinery, etc. as part of the education for those girls intended for domestic employments or mechanical trades. Thus, it *did* have to be learned, but for females it was seen as operating outside the recognised structure of artisanal training. It was non-guild work and was a frequent occupation of women at home. They also worked in workshops, perhaps sewing buttons on for a tailor, or stitching gloves and stockings for a glover or stocking weaver, who might or might not be a husband or son. As workers relying primarily on the fashion trades, they were vulnerable to both seasonal and economic fluctuations.

Sewing and other outwork gave women the opportunity to meet household needs much as they did in cottage industries. A high proportion of married and widowed women underlines their need for income and the probability that they had dependents. They could move in and out of the system, or they could be virtually permanent 'full-time' workers. Whether or not women undertook homework was highly dependent on the level and reliability of a husband's income; it could also determine what sort of homework they did. With urbanisation and the development of heavy industries that provided work for men, often little work was available in the same areas. In Glasgow, homeworkers clustered in locations where 'male' trades like heavy engineering, dock work and shipbuilding concentrated and where nearby work for women was limited.[18] Single women, widows, lone parents and wives with ill or unemployed husbands often took homework because it required little training. For example, Berlin, Glasgow and London clothing trades relied on wives and daughters of workers, employees and minor officials. Lower middle-class women were a significant hidden part of this workforce, often widows of clergymen or officials who worked at home precisely because it was socially more acceptable and easier to hide. French government investigations in 1905 and 1911 revealed that married women's earnings provided up to fifty per cent of total family income. The range and quality of outwork was vast: dressmakers, shirtmakers, seamers, tailors, milliners, fur-sewers, glove stitchers, almost anything that could be sewn, women did (docs. 36, 37). In 1850, an estimated 5,000 working-class women laboured stitching shirts by hand in New York City alone. Glasgow merchants put out flowering to thousands of seamstresses in Ayrshire; 20,000 to 30,000 worked for MacDonalds at the height of the trade.[19] Working mostly out of their homes, their pay and working hours were dismal. Building on the outwork system of domestic industries, employers put work out based on a factory or large workshop combined with a network of agents who put work out to women in rural communities and towns. Yet the system put women in a particularly vulnerable position since employers dictated pay and timescales, and fines were levied for 'unsatisfactory' work. Seamstresses usually had little recourse.

From the mid-nineteenth century the sewing machine altered the sewing trades. When women bought their own machines, they also absorbed the overheads, making them a more attractive workforce. While sometimes employers rented them out, it was common to gather them into workshops and run them from a single power source. Workshops introduced machines on a large scale, mechanising and centralising garmentmaking by 1860 (doc. 38). In the US, the Wheeler and Wilson 'manufactory' employed

> mechanics, salesmen, and agents, from six to seven thousand men and women. If we estimate, as is usually done, four persons to each family represented, we have a population of nearly . . . thirty thousand, a good-sized inland city . . . supported by this industry.[20]

This development facilitated the ready-made trade but simultaneously damaged the high-class fashion trades. Although initially seen as an advantage to women, sewing machines sped up work, raised production targets, and increased hours of work, stress and exhaustion (doc. 39, Image 6). They also split the production process so workers usually only sewed one part of an item rather than making a complete garment, so that the skill content and a sense of ownership deteriorated (doc. 40). Industrial homework expanded around the turn of the century, as retailing shifted to department stores, serving vast new markets of white-collar, skilled and semi-skilled workers. But by 1910, signs of decline had begun.

INDUSTRIAL ENTREPRENEURS

Running throughout industrial trades are entrepreneurial women who carved out specific spaces for themselves. This section is a snapshot into the types of trades and women who followed this route, like Ann Leslie and Miss Willson (docs. 41, 42). Milliners typified women's opportunities in the textile trades, and across Britain, women in many towns ran well-established firms catering to fashion. For example, Mary Gibbon, née Gainsborough, ran a successful millinery workshop first in Colchester then in Bath as a widow. Skill, reputation and position were important, so a woman had to be in the fashionable districts and to be where passing trade and exclusive customers would come. When she moved to Bath, where she had family connections, her location guaranteed a ready clientele, and the number of her apprentices confirms the activity of her firm. Gibbon's prominence was captured in the *New Bath Guide*, 1766, 'Whether thou in Lace and Ribbons/ Choose the Form of Mrs Gibbons'.[21] Margaret Cameron similarly used business acumen and fortitude to manage in a world dominated by male businesses. She was sequestered for bankruptcy twice but survived, 'testifying to remarkable business skills'.[22] Former slave Elizabeth Keckley also used millinery to shape a new life, and according to her autobiography, she became highly successful, working for both Mrs. Jefferson Davis and Mary Lincoln. Reviewers of her book, however, took a rather different view and she was caught up in criticisms of Mrs. Lincoln, as well as lambasted for 'making it up' (doc. 44). Entrepreneurial women could be found across the landscape and throughout the nineteenth century, and in the late eighteenth and early nineteenth centuries,

> 10 to 15% of western Europe's large trading firms were run by women. Historians have no difficulties finding women running important trading houses, presiding over the birth of manufacturing firms, acting as bankers, or conquering new markets for their products until the end of the eighteenth century.[23]

Representing the variety of these industrial firms are Eleanor Coade and Madame C.J. Walker, the name she promoted herself under. Coade took over and ran a highly successful artificial stone manufactory in eighteenth- and early nineteenth-century London, while Madame Walker invented, developed, distributed and sold hair products in the United States to care for Negro hair. Respected by contemporaries, Coade was praised for her statuary by the Royal Society of Artists and Walker, a former washwoman, became a millionaire and one of the wealthiest women in America (docs. 45, 46).

CASE STUDY: WOMEN IN THE PRINTING TRADES

Women had a long history as assistants in the printing trades, and across the period from 1750 to 1914, it was an important industry for women. Most women entered printing through family connections, frequently as widows. However, daughters and single women appeared from time to time. The John Johnson collection of trade ephemera held at the Bodleian includes numerous women printers, working with husbands and as widows, such as Susanna Burchett (later Miles) or Dorothy Mercier who advertised in the mid-century as printers and engravers, while Hannah Barker suggests that women comprised roughly eight per cent of the trade in the Northeast of England.[24] Numerous female printers worked in Scotland, since the trade was less restricted than in England and France. Agnes Campbell, in business for forty years, became the wealthiest Scottish bookseller in the early modern period, gaining public appointments and using law to protect her patents and restrict the trade of others.[25] Aberdeen appointed a succession of female printers as 'Printer to the Town' and in 1764, Susan Traill, partnering her son, was granted the position (doc. 47). In addition to women who clearly had the expertise and 'grit' to run a print shop, further down the social scale, women performed ancillary tasks, but they were also printers, engravers and bookbinders in print shops. Notably, the more public face of the shop owner is recorded on trade cards and in trade directory records, while many women in the shops were much less visible. Exeter printer Andrew Brice was noted for the large number of female printers he employed while in Paris, Mademoiselle de Silly, Madame Moria and Mademoiselle Ferriéres engraved and printed Haydn symphonies.[26] Almost a quarter of the plates produced by the Royal Academicians were engraved by women.[27] These were highly skilled women, and their presence demonstrates that it was not necessarily lack of skill or even ability that operated to shape the context of women in the print trades. Sharing another link with the feminist movement, Emily Faithfull set up the Victoria Press in 1860 (doc. 48 and Image 7) and trained and employed women.

Like many skilled trades, there was tension in the print shops, and printing challenged ideas of sex and gender at a type of work seen as belonging to men. Commentaries from the period show how women's perceived weakness and fragility was cited frequently (doc. 49). A gendered division labour certainly operated, but Margaret Irwin reported to the Royal Commission on Labour that women in the trades were 'healthy, well-paid and contented' (doc. 50), confirmed by women's testimonies (doc. 51). By the turn of the century, women were well entrenched in printing in the United States as well, and Edith Abbott echoed the point that it 'is important from the point of view of women's work, not merely because so many women are engaged in it, but because it is one of the old skilled hand trades' (docs. 52, 53). Yet she underlines that the men believed in their ownership of the trade.

THE SWEATED TRADES REVEALED

Criticism of sweated trades grew across the century as they became a more visible and dominant form of work for many women of the working classes. As an important source of income for both married and unmarried women, the system allowed women who worked in shops to continue in the same work, often for the same manufacturer, after childbirth. Defined as 'a system of subcontract wherein the work is let out to contractors to be done in small shops or homes', it was furthermore characterised 'by the working conditions that such a system engenders: long hours, low wages, and insanitary conditions'.[28] Women in homework were especially vulnerable to employers who dictated pay and completion dates and fined 'unsatisfactory' work. They were also subject to economic and seasonal cycles, fads and fashion. Subcontracting changed needlework from a trade that could earn a good living, as we saw with milliners, to one controlled by those with capital and an increased division of labour that undercut craft skills. From the middle of the century, women like Harriett Martineau critically reflected on 'slop work', its take-over of sewing (doc. 54), while in France, Julie-Victoire Daubié argued that women were undermined by convents and prisons who gave sewing work to women, impoverishing working woman who needed to make a living. A common refrain was that the system of subcontracting further handicapped women (doc. 55), while poor education and the gender division of labour meant men who took all the 'good' work because of women's lack of education (see also Vol. 3). Rates of pay were a particular concern of contemporaries (doc. 56). In 1907, the *Daily News* mounted an exhibition on sweated industries, producing an Exhibition Handbook of articles on specific trades and a lengthy appendix on stall workers. The preface to the handbook was used to specifically point to the 'suffering' of the worker and confront the public with them to lead to serious consideration of change for the whole system (docs. 57, 58).

The section concludes with Beatrice Webb, B.L. Hutchins and Jane Addams, who bring together an overview of sweating and link it to domestic homework, arguing why and how the system should be eradicated (docs. 59–61). These women represent the powerful voices of educated, forceful women of the latter part of the nineteenth and early twentieth century. In this they bring the discussion full circle. While they review women's industrial homework, their concern was both to raise awareness and suggest solutions. Providing examples, details and statistics – and using some of the material extracted in this volume – they implicated the nation in their critiques. As Beatrice Webb said,

> 'The sweater . . . is the whole nation,' for employer, shopkeeper, and purchaser all contribute to create and keep alive the system . . . and our guilt is not only that which attaches to the passive tolerance by us as citizens of any wrong or suffering in the state, but amounts to active, if ignorant, participation in oppression.
>
> (Image 8)

THE LAST WORD

The final word belongs to workers and their literary supporters. Ottilie Baader described the world of a sweated seamstress and the implications of the sewing machine (doc. 62, Image 9). One of the best-known critiques of the sweater system is Thomas Hood's *Song of the Shirt* (doc. 63), while Louise Otto-Peters, German feminist and reformer, depicted the world of the lacemakers at mid-century (doc. 64). Literature was deliberately used to emphasise the conditions of these workers, using emotion to evoke sympathy, and it played an important role in public awareness.

Notes

1 On definitions, see Sandra L. Albrecht, 'Industrial Homework in the United States: Historical Dimensions and Contemporary perspective', *Economic and Industrial Democracy*, vol. 3 (1982): 413–430.
2 Deborah Simonton, *The Education and Training of Eighteenth-Century English Girls, with special reference to the working classes*. PhD Thesis, University of Essex, 1988.
3 Ivy Pinchbeck, *Women Workers and the Industrial Revolution 1750–1850* (Routledge and Sons, Virago, 1930; 1981), 256. Simonton, *Education and Training*, 321.
4 For details of the trade, see Fredrik Guy Neville Sjögren, *Entrepreneurship and Technological Change: The Birmingham and District Cut-Nail Trade, c. 1811–1913*, PhD University of Birmingham, June 2019.
5 Amy Erickson, 'Clockmakers, Milliners and Mistresses: Women trading in the City of London companies 1700–1750', Working Paper, Cambridge Group for the study of Population, https://doi.org/10.17863/CAM.109861.
6 *Women in Industry, A Study in American Economic History* (D. Appleton and Company, 1909), 66–72.
7 Robert Campbell, *The London Tradesman, being a compendious view of all Trades, Professions and Arts . . . calculated for the information of Parents, and Instruction of Youth in their Choice of Business* (T. Gardner, 1747), 152.

8 Simonton, *The Education and Training of Eighteenth-Century English Girls, with special reference to the working classes.* PhD Thesis, University of Essex, 1988, chapter 5; O. J. Dunlop and R. D. Denman. *English Apprenticeship and Child Labour – A History* (Fisher Unwin, 1912), 150–51.

9 See Mary Prior, 'Women in the Urban Economy: Oxford, 1500–1800', in *Women in English Society, 1500–1800*, ed. Prior, Mary (Methuen and Co. Ltd, 1985), 104.

10 Data for Essex and Staffordshire, Simonton, *Education and Training*, chapter 5, and they comprised two per cent in Warwickshire and about five per cent in Wiltshire: Joan Lane, *Apprenticeship in Warwickshire, 1700–1834.* Ph. D. Thesis, University of Birmingham, 1977. 122; Christabel Dale, *Wiltshire Apprentices, and their Masters, 1710–1760*, (Devizes, 1961).

11 Marilyn J. Boxer, 'Women in Industrial Work: The Flowermakers of the Parisian Belle Epoque', *French Historical Studies*, 12, (1981): 404, 408, 417, 418, 422.

12 Caroline Milhaud, *L'Ouvriere en France: sa condition presente, les reformes necessaires* (Félix Alcan, Éditeur, Librairies Félix Alcan et Guillaumin Réunies, 1907).

13 Deborah Simonton. 'Milliners and *Marchandes de Modes*: Gender, Skill and Creativity in the Workplace', in *Luxury and Gender in European Towns, c.1700–1914,* Anne Montenach, Marjo Kaartinen and Deborah Simonton, eds. (Routledge, 2014), and '"Sister to the tailor": Guilds, gender and the needle trades in eighteenth-century Europe', in Johanna Ilmakunnas, Marjatta Rahikainen, Kirsi Vainio-Korhonen, eds. *Early Professional Women in Northern Europe, c. 1650 to the 1850s* (Routledge, 2017).

14 Campbell, *The London Tradesman*, 208; Joseph Collyer, *The Parents' and Guardians' Directory* (1761), 195.

15 Nicola Phillips, *Women in Business, 1700–1850* (Boydell, 2006), 220.

16 Simonton, *The Education and Training of Eighteenth-Century English Girls, with special reference to the working classes.* PhD Thesis, University of Essex, 1988.

17 *The Education and Training of Eighteenth-Century English Girls, with special reference to the working classes.* PhD Thesis, University of Essex, 1988, 138–48.

18 James McMillan, *Housewife or Harlot: The place of women in French Society, 1870–1940* (Saint Martin's Press, 1981), 66–67; Alice J. Albert, 'Fit Work for Women: Sweated Home-workers in Glasgow, c. 1875–1914', in *The World is Ill Divided: Women's Work in Scotland in the Nineteenth and Early Twentieth Centuries*. Eleanor Gordon and Esther Breitenbach, eds (Edinburgh University Press, 1990), 165 also 159, 163–66; M.J. Boxer, 'Protective Legislation and Home Industry. the Marginalization of Women Workers in late nineteenth century and early twentieth century France', *Journal of Social History*, (1986): 52, 54; James H. Treble, 'The Characteristics of the Female Unskilled Labour Market and the Formation of the Female Casual Labour Market in Glasgow, 1891–1914', *Scottish Economic and Social History,* 6, (1986): 39, 46.

19 T.C. Smout, *Century of the Scottish People,* (Fontana Press 1987), 20.

20 Wheeler and Wilson instruction manual, c. 1872, Windham Textile and History Museum.

21 Christopher Anstey, *The New Bath Guide: Or, Memoirs of the B – r – d Family, in a Series of Poetical Epistles* (5th ed, 1767), 97. See Deborah Simonton, *Gender in the European Town* (Routledge, 2023), 44, 107, and "Sister to the Taylor", 163ff, and Susan Legouix Sloman, 'Artists' Picture Rooms in Eighteenth-century Bath', *Bath History*, 6 (1996, 139–43.

22 Stana Nenadic, 'The Social Shaping of Business Behaviour in the Nineteenth-Century Women's Garment Trades'. *Journal of Social History*, 31, 3, (1998): 631. See also Edinburgh Post Office Directories, National Library of Scotland, https://digital.nls.uk/directories/browse/archive/91049051.

23 Beatrice Craig, *Women and Business since 1500. Invisible Presences in Europe and North America?* (Palgrave, 2016), 1.

24 Bodleian Library, 'The John Johnson Collection of Printed Ephemera', http://www.bodleian.ox.ac.uk/johnson; Hannah Barker, 'Women, work and the Industrial Revolution: Female involvement in the English Printing Trades', in *Gender in Eighteenth-century England,* Hannah Barker and Elaine Chalus, eds. (Longman 1997), 88–100.
25 Alistair J Mann (1999), 'Embroidery to Enterprise: the Role of Women in the Book Trade of Early Modern Scotland', in *Women in Scotland, c.1100–c.1750,* Elizabeth Ewan and Maureen Meikle, eds, (Tuckwell), 142–45.
26 T. N. Brushfield, *The Life and Bibliography of Andrew Brice* (Exeter, 1888), 43. H. C. Robbins, *Haydn: The Symphonies (36–48)* (Decca, 1972), 9.
27 Geraldine Sheridan, 'Views of Women at Work by the Royal Academicians: The Collection, *Descriptions des arts et metiers* (1761–1789)', *Studies in Eighteenth-century culture*, 32, (2003): 165–67.
28 John R. Commons, 'The Sweating System', in Leon Stein, ed., *Out of the Sweatshop*, Leon Stein ed., (Quadrangle., 1977), 44. Louis Levine, 'Sweat shops', in *America's Working Women*, Rosalyn Baxandall, Linda Gordon and Susan Reverby, eds. (Vintage, 1976), 101. See Albrecht, 'Industrial Homework in the United States', 421.

Part 1

DOMESTIC INDUSTRIES

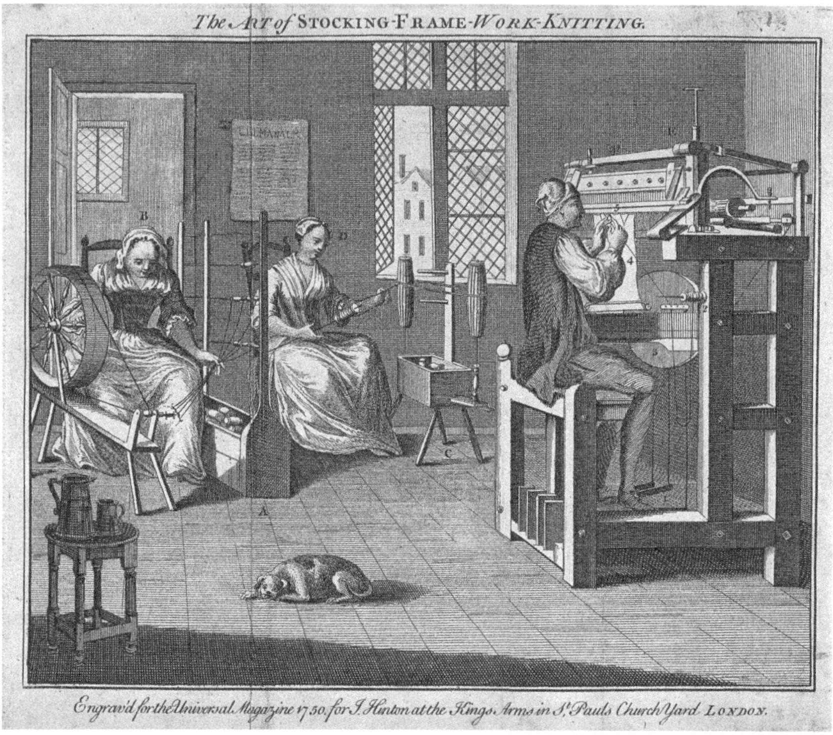

Image 1 Spinners and Stocking Making, 1750. Wellcome.

1

EMPLOYMENT OF WOMEN BEFORE THE INDUSTRIAL REVOLUTION, 1915

B. L. Hutchins

Source: B. L. Hutchins, *Women in Modern Industry* (G. Bell and Sons, Ltd., 1915), 1–2, 5, 9–14, 30.

EDITORIAL HEADNOTE

Elizabeth Leigh Hutchins (1858–1935), who published as B.L. Hutchins, was a social researcher as well as an activist. One of the first students at the London School of Economics, she was the daughter of a solicitor and his wife; privately educated, she attended King's College for Women in London and was one of the first women students at the London School of Economics from 1896 and was taught by Beatrice Webb (doc. 59). She was on the Women's Industrial Council, editor of its journal, *Women's Industrial News*, and a founding member of the Fabian Women's group in 1908. She was part of a wide network of social reformers working to improve the conditions of women's work, many of them, like her, feminists, social reformers and among the first generation of university-educated women, several of whom are included in this collection.

She published widely on women's work and wages. Her book, co-authored with Amy Harrison, *A History of Factory Legislation* (1903), is a classic study. Her main concerns were the contemporary issues of women's homework and sweated industries, and she contributed to publications from Europe to Australia on the topic.

'Employment of Women before the industrial Revolution' is the opening chapter in her *Women in Modern Industry* (1915), in which she looks back to the period of cottage homework and the putting-out system. The book was largely complete before the First World War, and she chose not to revise it before publication. Her intention was 'to give a sketch or outline of the position of working women, with special reference to the effects of

DOI: 10.4324/9781003676669-2

the industrial revolution on her employment, taking "industrial revolution" in its broader sense, not as an event of the late eighteenth century, but as a continuous process still actively at work.' While most of the book is contemporary, she followed this chapter with one on the Industrial Revolution and the two together form the backdrop to her wider discussion of women's work, wages and place in the unions.

SKETCH OF THE EMPLOYMENT OF WOMEN IN ENGLAND BEFORE THE INDUSTRIAL REVOLUTION

The traces of women in economic and industrial history are unmistakable, but the record of their work is so scattered, casual, and incoherent that it is difficult to derive a connected story therefrom. We know enough, however, to disprove the old misconception that women's industrial work is a phenomenon beginning with the nineteenth century.

It seems indeed not unlikely that textile industry, perhaps also agriculture and the taming of the smaller domestic animals, were originated by women, their dawning intelligence being stimulated to activity by the needs of children. Professor Karl Pearson in his interesting essay, *Woman as Witch*, shows that many of the folklore ceremonies connected with witchcraft associate the witch with symbols of agriculture, the pitchfork, and the plough, as well as with the broom and spindle, and are probably the fossil survivals, from a remote past, of a culture in which the activities of the women were relatively more prominent than they are now. The witch is a degraded form of the old priestess, cunning in the knowledge of herbs and medicine, and preserving in spells and incantations such wisdom as early civilisation possessed. . . .

Textiles. Wool and Linen. – No trace remains in history of the inventor of the loom, but no historical record remains of a time without some means of producing a texture by means of intertwining a loose thread across a fixed warp. Any such device, however rude, must involve a degree of culture much above mere savagery, and probably resulted from a long process of groping effort and invention. From this dim background hand-spinning and weaving emerge in tradition and history as the customary work of women, the type of their activity, and the norm of their duty and morals. The old Anglo-Saxon, Scandinavian, and German words for loom are certainly very ancient, and Pictet derives the word *wife* from the occupation of weaving. In the Northern Mythology the three stars in the Belt of Orion were called Frigga Rock, or Frigga's Distaff, which in the days of Christianity was changed to Maria Rock, rock being an old word for distaff.

Spinning, weaving, dyeing, and embroidering were special features of Anglo-Saxon industry, and were entirely confined to women. King Alfred in his will distinguished between the spear-half and spindle-half of his family; and in an old illustration of the Scripture, Adam is shown receiving the spade and Eve the distaff, after their expulsion from the Garden of Eden. This traditional distinction between the duties of the sexes was continued even to the grave, a spear or a spindle, according to sex, being often found buried with the dead in Anglo-Saxon tombs. . . .

It is evident from old accounts that a good deal of weaving was done outside by the piece for these great households, and of course spinning and weaving were largely carried on in cottages as a bye-industry in conjunction with agriculture. Bücher gives a very interesting account of spinning as an opportunity for social intercourse among primitive peoples. In Thibet, he says, there is a spinning-room in each village; the young people, men and girls, meet and spin and smoke together. Spinning in groups or parties is known to have obtained also in Germany in olden times, and girls who now meet to make lace together in the same sociable way still say that they "go spinning." Spinning-rooms exist in Russia. In Yorkshire spinning seems to have been done socially in the open air, in fine weather, down to the eve of the industrial revolution.

Spinning was one of the first works in which young girls were instructed, and thus spinster has become the legal designation of an unmarried woman, not that she always gave up spinning at marriage, but because it was looked upon as the young unmarried woman's chief occupation. Old manuscripts also show women weaving at the loom, illustrations of which can be found in the interesting works of Thomas Wright.

In 1372 a Yorkshire woman spinner was summoned for taking "too much wages, contrary to the Statute of Artificers." In 1437 John Notyngham, a rich grocer of Bury St. Edmunds, bequeathed to one of his daughters a spinning-wheel and a pair of cards (cards or carpayanum, an implement which is stated in the *Promptorum Parvulorum* to be especially a woman's instrument). In 1418 Agnes Stebbard in the same town bequeathed to two of her maids a pair of wool-combs each, one combing-stick, one wheel, and one pair of cards. An illuminated MS. of the well-known French *Boccace des Nobles Femmes* has a most interesting illustration showing a queen and two maidens; one maiden is spinning with a distaff, another combing wool, the queen sits at the loom weaving. Women often appear in old records as combers, carders, and spinners. . . .

Irish women were noted for their skill in dressing hemp and flax and making linen and woollen cloth. Sir William Temple said, in 1681, that no women were apter to spin flax well than the Irish, who, "labouring little in any kind with their hands have their fingers more supple and soft than other women of poorer condition among us."

In the old Shuttleworth Accounts, reprinted by the Chetham Society, there are minute directions to the housewife on the management and manipulation of her wool. "It is the office of a husbandman at the shearing of the sheep to bestow upon the housewife such a competent proportion of wool as shall be convenient for the clothing of his family; which wool, as soon as she hath received it, she shall open, and with a pair of shears cut away all the coarse locks, pitch, brands, tarred locks, and other feltrings, and lay them by themselves for coarse coverlets and the like. The rest she is to break in pieces and tease, lock by lock, with her hands open, and so divide the wool as not any part may be feltered or close together, but all open and loose. Then such of the wool as she intends to spin white she shall put by itself and the rest she shall weigh up and divide into several quantities, according to the proportion of the web she intends to make, and put every one of them into particular lays of netting, with tallies of wool fixed into them with privy marks thereon, for the weight, colour, and knowledge of the wool, when the first colour is altered. Then she shall if she please send them to the dyer to be dyed after her own fancy," or dye them herself (recipes for which are given).

After your wool is mixed, oiled and trimmed (carded), you shall then spin it upon great wool wheels, according to the order of good housewifery; the action whereof must be got by practice, and not by relation; only this you shall be carefull, to draw your thread according to nature and goodness of your wool, not according to your particular desire; for if you draw a fine thread from wool which is of a coarse staple, it will want substance . . . so, if you draw a coarse thread from fine wool, it will then be much overthick . . . to the disgrace of good housewifery and loss of much cloth.

Weaving and Spinning as a Woman's Trade. – The employments carried on by women in the household may have yielded money occasionally, as we have seen from some of the foregoing quotations, but the work appears in these Extracts to have been carried on rather as a bye-industry, as a means of utilising surplus produce, than as a recognised trade for gain or profit. Did women carry on the manufacture of woollen goods definitely as a craft or trade? The evidence on this head is not very clear. A statute of Edward III expressly exempts women from the ordinance, then in force, that men should not follow more than one craft. "It is ordained that Artificers Handicraft people hold them every one to one Mystery, which he will choose between this and the said feast of Candlemas; and Two of every craft shall be chosen to survey, that none use other craft than the same which he hath chosen. . . . But the intent of the King and of his Council is, that Women, that is to say, Brewers, Bakers, Carders and Spinners, and Workers as well of Wool as of Linen Cloth and of Silk, Brawdesters and Breakers of Wool and all other that do use and work all Handy Works may freely use and work as they have done before this time, without any impeachment or being restrained by this Ordinance." The meaning of this ordinance is rather obscure, but the greater liberty conferred on women would seem to imply that they were not carrying on the trades mentioned as organised workers competing with men, but that they performed the various useful works mentioned at odd times, incidentally to the work of the household. Miss Abram says women were sometimes cloth-makers (see 4 Edw. IV. c. 1), and often women cloth-makers, combers, carders, and spinners are mentioned in the Parliamentary Rolls. There were women amongst the tailors of Salisbury, and amongst the yeoman tailors of London, also among the dyers of Bristol and the drapers of London. Women might join the Merchant Gild of Totnes, and some belonged to the Gild Merchant of Lyons. . . .

Professor Unwin quotes a rule of the Clothworkers of London, in the second year of Edward VI., imposing a fine of 20 pence on any member employing even his own wife and daughter in his shop. At Hull, in 1490, women were forbidden working at the weaver's trade. But in 1564 the proviso was introduced that a widow might work at her husband's trade so long as she continued a widow and observed the orders of the company. The London Weavers clearly recognised women members, for they enacted that "no man or woman of the said craft shall entice any man's servant from him." But another rule prohibited taking a woman as apprentice. The statutes of the Weavers of Edinburgh in the sixteenth century provided that no woman be allowed to have looms of her own, *unless* she be a freeman's wife. Probably it was felt in practice to be impossible to prevent a woman helping her husband, or carrying on his trade after his death, although there was evidently a desire to keep women out of the craft as much as possible. By the seventeenth century Gervase Markham writes as if women did no weaving at all. "Now after your cloth is thus warped and delivered up into the hands of the Weaver, the Housewife hath finished her labour, for in the weaving, walking, and dressing thereof she can challenge no property more than to entreat them severally to discharge their duties with a good conscience." . . .

Records of rates of pay to journeymen weavers, tuckers, fullers, etc., 1651, ignore women as textile workers altogether; the only women mentioned in this assessment are agricultural workers and domestic servants. Nevertheless, old accounts of the seventeenth century do show payments to women, not only for spinning, but for weaving and "walking" woollen cloth, and we can only conclude that while the progress of technical improvements had made weaving largely a men's trade, it was yet also carried on by women to a considerable extent.

The Development of Capitalistic Industry. – The growth and development of a capitalistic system of industry can be traced from the fifteenth century, and forms one of the most interesting and dramatic episodes in economic history. It is, however, not very easy to determine in what way the change influenced women's employment. The more prosperous among the weavers gradually developed into clothiers, employing many hands, but the majority tended to become mere wage-earners. A petition of weavers in 1539 stated that the clothiers had their own looms and weavers and fullers in their own houses, so that the master weavers were rendered destitute. "For the rich men the clothiers be concluded and agreed among themselves to hold and pay one price for weaving, which price is too little to sustain households upon, working night and day, holy-day and work-day, and many weavers are therefore reduced to the position of servants." The Petition of Suffolk Clothiers, 1575, says that the custom of their country is "to carry our wool out . . . and put it to sundry spinners who have in their houses divers and sundry children and servants that do card and spin the same wool." In the north of England also large clothiers employing many hands were to be found as early as 1520. The subsequent development of the industry, Professor Unwin tells us, took place in a very marked degree in those districts which were exempt from the operation of the statutes forbidding clothiers to set up outside market-towns. In other parts of the country the struggle was acute. "The protection of industry from all competition was the first and last word of the crafts. To employers and dealers the monopoly of trade chiefly meant their own monopoly of production and sale, while the wage-earner's predominant anxiety was to keep surplus labour out of the craft, lest the regular worker might be deprived of his comfortable certainty of subsistence."

There was, however, a great expansion of trade and industry going on, and labour was needed. The master who had accumulated a little capital perhaps moved out to the valleys of Yorkshire or Gloucestershire in search of water-power for his fulling mills or finer wool for his weavers, or forsook the manufacturing town for some rural district where labour was plentiful and he could escape the heavy municipal dues which his business could ill afford to pay. The ordinances of Worcester, for instance, contain regulations intended to prevent the masters giving out wool to the weavers in other parts so long as there were people enough in the city to do the work, "in the hindering of the poor commonalty of the same."

The struggle between these two forms of industry, the craft carried on in the towns and the dispersed industry under a more definitely capitalistic organisation in the country, went on for centuries. From the earliest years of the reign of Henry VIII. to the accession of Elizabeth, a constantly increasing amount of legislation was devoted to the protection of the town manufacture against the competition of the country. This legislation was interpreted by Froude as a genuine endeavour to protect a highly skilled, highly organised industry of independent craftsmen against the evils of capitalism, but the closer researches of Professor Unwin show that this is idealism; the craftsmen were merely pawns in the hands of town merchants who dreaded to see some of the trade pass into the hands of a new class of country capitalists. This is an historical controversy too difficult to follow closely here; what we have to note is the part played by women in the change.

We may as well admit that women's work during this industrial transition appears mostly as part of the problem of cheap unorganised labour. "The spinners seem never to have had any organisation, and were liable to oppression by their employers, not only through low wages, but through payment in kind, and the exaction of arbitrary fines." Irregularity of employment was another trouble:

> To compensate their masters' greed and extortion they had recourse to petty dishonesties on their own part, and were frequently accused of keeping back part of the wool given out, or of making up the weight by the addition of oil or other moisture to the yarn. . . .

In the seventeenth century the rates of spinners' wages appear very low, even measured by contemporary standards. Mr. Hamilton has reproduced the wages assessed at Quarter Sessions by the Justices of Exeter in 1654. Weavers were to have 2½d. a day with food or 8d. without. It is difficult to guess whether these weavers were supposed to be men or women; the rates fixed are less than those for husbandry labourers (which were fixed at 3d. and 10d.), but rather more than those for women haymakers, which were 2d. and 6d. Spinsters, however, were to have "not above" 6d. a week with food or 1s. 4d. without. In 1713 at the same place spinsters were to have not above 1s. a week, or 2s. 6d. if without board, which again compares very unfavourably with the other rates mentioned. It is difficult to understand the extreme lowness of these rates of pay to spinsters, unless on the assumption that they were intended to apply to servants actually living and working in the clothiers' houses; or that spinning was supposed not to occupy a woman's whole time, which no doubt was often the case. But the rates fixed on that assumption should of course have been piece rates. . . .

No doubt the Poor Law helped in some degree to depress wages, for another form taken by this many-sided industry of wool was that of relief work under the Poor Law. Spinning was the main resource of those whose duty under the Poor Law was to find work for the unemployed, and in institutions such as Christ's Hospital, Ipswich, children were set to card and spin from their earliest years. Such instances might be multiplied indefinitely. A charitable workhouse in Bishopsgate used to give out wool and flax every Monday morning to be spun at home to "such poor people as desire it and are skilful in spinning thereof." . . .

A still more remarkable development of female employment, perhaps, was the beginning of the factory system in the sixteenth century. These were chiefly in the west of England industry, and in Wiltshire. Leland in his *Itinerary* mentions a man called Stumpe who had actually taken possession of the ancient Abbey of Malmesbury and filled it with looms, employing many hands. A still more celebrated instance was the factory of John Winchcomb, a prudent man who married his master's widow and had a fine business at Newbury, described in a ballad which shows him employing 200 men weaving, each with a boy helper, and 100 women carding wool:

> And in a chamber close beside
> Two hundred maydens did abide
> In petticoats of stammel red
> And milk-white kerchiefs on their head.
> . . . . . .
> These pretty maids did never lin
> But in that place all day did spin.

In 1567 the Weaver's Gild of Bristol prohibited its members from underselling one another in the prices of their work, and also forbade them to allow their wives to go for any work to clothiers' houses, which at least implies that there was some demand for their labour. Now, although the growth of capital may have seriously affected the position of the male craftsmen, as Professor Unwin tells us, and reduced them to be mere wage-earners, it seems not impossible that the economic position of women may have been improved by the opportunity of work for wages outside the home. Women had worked for the use and consumption of their own households, and, as wives of craftsmen, they had worked as helpers with their husbands. The new organisation of work by a capitalist employer opened up the possibility to women and girls of earning wages for themselves. The additional earnings of wife and children even if very small make a great difference in the comfort of a labourer's family. It is likely enough, indeed it is evident that their work was often grievously exploited, and the reduction of the craftsman to the position of a mere wage-earner may have diminished the spending power of the family. Of all this we know little or nothing definitely, but it seems probable that the supersession of handicraft by a quasi-capitalistic form of organisation affected women less adversely than men. In the eighteenth century, the palmy days of the domestic system, some women in the industrial centres were earning what were considered very good wages. Arthur Young says of the cloth trade round Leeds: "Some women earn by weaving as much as the men." Of Norwich he says: "The earnings of manufacturers (*i.e.* hand-workers) are various, but in general high," the men on an average earning 5s. a week, and many women earning as much.

It must be also remembered that each weaver kept several spinners employed, so that unless his family could supply him, he might easily be forced to have recourse to the services of women workers outside. Mr. Townsend Warner quotes an estimate that 25 weavers might require the services of 250 spinners to keep them fully supplied with yarn.

Mantoux thinks this excessive, though it has to be remembered, as Mr. Townsend Warner points out, that the spinners usually did not give their whole time. Again, the description of the organisation of the trade, end of eighteenth century, quoted by Bonwick, conveys the impression that women, in some cases at all events, were taking a responsible part.

> I went to York, to buy wool, and at that time it averaged about 1s. per pound. I then came home, sorted and combed it myself. After being combed, it was oiled and closed, that is, the long end of the wool and the short end were put together to form a skein. It took a number of skeins to make a top, each top making exactly a pound. Then I took it to hand-spinners 20 or 30 miles distant. The mother or head of the family plucked the tops into pieces the length of the wool, and gave it to the different branches of the family to spin, who could spin about 9 or 10 hanks per day; for the spinning I gave one half penny per hank, and sometimes ½d. for every 24 hanks over.

Another interesting account is given by Bamford:

> Farms were most cultivated for the production of milk, butter and cheese. . . . The farming was mostly of that kind which was soonest and most easily performed, and it was done by the husband and other males of the family, whilst the wife and daughters and maid servants, if

> there were any of the latter, attended to the churning, cheese-making, and household work, and when that was finished, they busied themselves in carding, slubbing, and spinning of wool and cotton, as well as forming it into warps for the loom. The husband and sons would next, at times when farm labour did not call them abroad, size the warp, dry it, and beam it in the loom, and either they or the females, whichever happened to be least otherwise employed, would weave the warp down. A farmer would generally have 3 or 4 looms in his house.

Of course it is not to be inferred that the women thus employed were always free to control or spend their own earnings; in law they undoubtedly were not, if married. The domestic system so picturesquely described by Defoe (in his *Tour*), under which the family worked together, each, from the oldest to the youngest, doing his or her part, no doubt often involved a quite patriarchal distribution and control of the resulting earnings. Still the mention of women as separate and individual earners that occurs often in eighteenth-century works on the subject must indicate that they were attaining a greater measure of individual recognition and self-determination than formerly.

It is interesting also to notice that the cloth industry was sometimes carried on socially in the eighteenth century. Bradford Dale was covered with weavers and spinners, and the women and children of Allerton, Thornton, and other villages in the valley, used to flock on sunny days with their spinning wheels to some favourite pleasant spot, and work in company.

Frame-Work Knitting. – The frame-work knitting trade has many points of resemblance with the woollen weaving trade. Hand-knitting, we are told by Felkin, was not introduced till the sixteenth century. It became extremely popular and was pursued by women in every class of life from the palace to the cottage. A kind of frame or hand-machine was invented in the seventeenth century by Lee. It is said that Lee invented this machine in a spirit of revenge and bitterness against a young lady he had fallen in love with, who was so intent on her knitting that she could never give him her attention when he made love to her. From watching her at work he acquired a mastery of the mesh or stitch, and anger at her being so engrossed with her employment impelled him to make a machine that would deprive her of her work.

The frame-work knitters were incorporated under Charles II, and the company made rather drastic rules, trying to exclude women from apprenticeship, though they might become members on widowhood, as in so many of the old guilds. Frame-work knitting also gave employment to women and children in seaming up the hose. In the eighteenth century the trade became sweated and underpaid. The hours of work were as much as fifteen a day. Women, however, were paid at the same rates per piece, and were subject to the same deductions, and some of them were good hands and could earn as much as men.

Silk. – The broad difference between linen and woollen on the one hand, and silk and cotton on the other, is that the two former, so ancient that their origins are lost to history, arose as household industries at the very early stage of civilisation in which the family is self-sufficient, or nearly so, providing for its own needs and consumption by the work of its own members; the two latter, on the contrary, appear chiefly as trades carried on not for use but for payment, and are also sharply differentiated from the more ancient industries by the fact that the raw materials – silk and cotton – are not indigenous to these islands, but have to be imported.

In the manufacture of silk, women early appear as independent producers and manufacturers, for in the fifteenth century they were sufficiently organised to be able collectively to petition Parliament for measures to check the importation of ribbons and wrought silk, and on their behalf was passed an Act (1455) 33 Hen. VI. c. 5, . . . The importation of silk, ribbons, etc., was forthwith prohibited, . . . Henry VII. dealt with several silk women for ribands, fringes, and so forth, as recorded in his accounts. A statute of Charles II. 14 Ch. II. c. 15 says many women in London were employed in working silk.

The manufacture of silk was introduced into Derbyshire at the beginning of the eighteenth century. John Lombe's silk mill was the first textile mill at work in that county. A rather considerable manufacture of piece silks and silk ribbons and braid grew up in Derby and Glossop, a large proportion of women and girls being employed. The numbers of operatives in this industry increased up to the census of 1851 and 1861, when about 6000 operatives were employed, after which it began to go down, reaching the low figure of 662 in the county in 1901; in 1911, 442.

In Macclesfield silk-throwing mills were erected in 1756, the manufacture of silk goods and mohair buttons having been already carried on for centuries. The silk throwsters of Macclesfield for many years worked for Spitalfields and supplied them with thrown silk through the London manufacturers. In 1776, it is recorded, the wages paid to the millmen and stewards were 7s. a week, the women doublers 3s. 6d., children 6d. to 1s. The manufacture of broad silk was established at Macclesfield in 1790. We know by inference that many women must have been employed, but information is unfortunately scanty in regard to the social conditions of this trade, so specially adapted to industrial women. It is evident, however, that women kept their place in it, for the apprenticeship rules laid before the Committee on Ribbon Weavers in 1818 expressly included women, both as apprentices and journeywomen.

The inherent delicacy of many of the processes, and the fact that silk as a luxury trade is especially susceptible to changes of fashion, have retarded the use of machinery and preserved the finer fabrics as an artistic handicraft. But this, in itself a development to be welcomed, must also indicate that capital and labour can be more advantageously employed in the industries that have evolved more fully on modern lines, for the silk trade is undoubtedly declining in England. . . .

In Birmingham trades, especially the making of buttons and other small articles, women were employed as far back as we can find any records. At Burslem, Young found women working in the potteries, earning 5s. to 8s. a week. Near Bristol he found women and girls employed in a copper works for melting copper ore, and making the metal into pins, pans, etc. At Gloucester he found great numbers of women working in the pin manufacture. In the Sheffield plated ware trade he found girls working, but does not mention women. Of the Sheffield trades generally he says that women and girls earn very good wages, "much more than by spinning wool in any part of the kingdom."

It is unfortunate that we have, so far, very little information in regard to women's work in non-textile trades previous to the industrial revolution. It is tolerably safe to infer that the above scattered hints indicate a state of things neither new nor exceptional. There can be little doubt that women constantly worked in these trades, either assisting the head of the family, or as a wage-worker for an outside employer. But we know so little that we cannot attempt to enlarge on the subject.

2

THE COLONIAL PERIOD, 1909

Edith Abbott

Source: Edith Abbott, 'The Colonial Period', in *Women in Industry: A Study in American Economic History* (D. Appleton and Company, 1909), 16–32.

EDITORIAL HEADNOTE

American Edith Abbott (1876–1957) was also the daughter of a lawyer, Lt Governor Abbott of Nebraska, and his wife, who were early woman suffrage supporters, and she was raised with progressive values and imbued with the need for social reform and rights for women. After boarding school in Omaha, she returned home to become a schoolteacher because of the financial downturn. Determined to continue studying, she took correspondence courses, attended summer schools and eventually attended the University of Nebraska, where she completed a BA degree. At a summer school at the University of Chicago, she attracted the attention of the faculty, especially Thorstein Veblen, and received a fellowship to work on her doctorate at the University of Chicago in 1903. Her dissertation on unskilled wage labour was published in June 1906 in the *Journal of Political Economy*. She moved to Boston, worked for the Women's Trade Union League, and carried out research on the issues women faced in wage-based industries at the Carnegie Institution, leading to a series of articles in the *Journal of Political Economy*. Earning a post-doctoral fellowship, she went to London to study at the London School of Economics and was taught by Beatrice and Sydney Webb, who impressed her with the need for reform, not charity. Returning to the US, she joined the staff of Jane Addams' Hull House in Chicago (see doc. 61), becoming assistant director of research and working with the Research Director of the Chicago School, Sophonisba P. Breckinridge, her mentor.

She developed an interest in the problems faced by immigrant women workers, promoting better accommodation, the ten-hour day, and union representation. Like many of her peers, she worked for women's voting rights. Together with Breckinridge, she pushed for professional social

DOI: 10.4324/9781003676669-3

work, and the two published together frequently (see Vol. 4). She became Dean of the Chicago School, helping it to relocate to the University of Chicago where they launched the first graduate-level programme in social work.

Her journal articles formed the basis for her book *Women in Industry: A Study in American Economic History* (1910) dedicated to Breckenridge. She saw the book as a contribution to understanding the problems of wage-earning women, acknowledged that depending on circumstances women might have real power, but also recognising the fact that women had not always worked for wages in a system where 'production was often so carried on as to allow the return for the labor of the entire family to be collected by the head of the family who had the legal right to the time and earnings both of his wife and of his minor children.' Unlike Hutchins, her book is a more fully developed history of American industrial women to demonstrate the contribution women made to the development of industry. This chapter included here is deliberately partnered with Hutchins as an opening foray into understanding industrial women in the domestic handwork era.

'THE COLONIAL PERIOD'

There remain, however, a number of instances, in which women were employed in and were even at the head of what might, strictly speaking, be called industrial establishments. A woman, for example, occasionally ran a mill, carried on a distillery, or even worked in a sawmill. The "Plymouth Colony Records" note in 1644 that "Mistress Jenny, upon the presentment against her, promiseth to amend the grinding at the mill, and to keep morters cleane, and baggs of come from spoyleing and looseing. "At Mason's settlement at Piscataqua," eight Danes and twenty two women" were employed in sawing lumber and making potash.[1] In 1693 a woman appears with two men on the pages of the "Boston Town Records" "desiring leave to build a slaughter house." But all of these seem to have been unusual employments. . . .

Although there is no doubt of the fact that women were gainfully employed away from home at this time, such employment was quite unimportant compared with work which they did in their own homes. In considering minor industrial occupations within the home we find that a few women were bakers[2] and some were engaged in similar work, such as making and selling of preserves or wine.[3] But the great majority of women in this group were employed in the manufacture of textiles, which in its broadest sense includes knitting, lacemaking, the making of cards for combing cotton and wool, as well as sewing, spinning and weaving.

Some women must have found knitting a profitable by-employment. Knit stockings sold for two shillings a pair, and occasionally for much more. One old account book records that "Ann" sold a "pare of stockens for 16s." Sewing and tailoring were standard occupations and were variously remunerated, – one woman made "shirts for the Indians" at eight-pence each, and "men's breeches" for a shilling and sixpence a pair, and in addition to this work of tailoring she taught school, did spinning and weaving for good pay, managed her house, was twice married and had fourteen children.[4]

Spinning and weaving, the processes upon which the making of cloth depended, absorbed a great deal of the time of the women and girls of the period. This work was not uniformly organized according to any one industrial system. In the seventeenth century, the work was household industry; the raw materials were furnished by the household and the finished product was for household use; but so far as any part of it was marketed or exchanged at the village store, the system became closely akin to handicraft. The commodity that was exchanged or sold belonged to the woman as a true craftswoman, the material had been hers and the product, until she disposed of it, was her own capital. When the article was sold directly to the consumer, as frequently happened, even the final characteristic of handicraft, the fact of its being "custom work," was present.[5]

With the expansion of the industry, especially in the latter half of the eighteenth century, a considerable part of the work was done more in the manner of what is known as the commission system. As yarn came to be in great demand, many women were regularly employed spinning at home for purchasers who were really commission merchants. These men sometimes sold the yarn but often they put it out again to be woven and then sold the cloth.

The most important occupations for women, therefore, before the establishment of the factory system, were spinning and weaving. It is impossible to make any estimate of the number of women who did such work, or of their earnings, of the proportion of homespun which went to market, or of what part of it, even when exchanged by the husband, was manufactured by the wife and daughters. But it is quite safe to say that spinning for the household was a universal occupation and that the number. of those who used this, and later, weaving also, as a "gainful employment" was very large. . . .

In the latter half of the eighteenth century, more persistent efforts were made to further the cloth-making industry, and much interest was manifested in the possibility of making children useful to this end. Two Boston newspapers announced in 1750 that it was proposed "to open several spinning schools in this Town where children may be taught *gratis.*" In the following year the "Society for Encouraging Industry and Employing the Poor" – was organized with the double purpose of promoting the manufacture of woolen and other cloth, and of employing "our own women and children who are now in a great measure idle."

The Province Laws of the session of 1753–54 provided for a tax on carriages for the support of a linen manufactory which, it was hoped, would provide employment for the poor. The preamble of the law recites that the "number of poor is greatly increased . . . and many persons, especially women, and children, are destitute of employment and in danger of becoming a public charge."

Although this scheme did not realize all the hopes of its promoters the policy was not abandoned. In 1770, Mr. William Molineux of Boston petitioned the legislature to assist him in his plan for "manufacturing the children's labour into wearing apparel" and "employing young females from eight years old and upward in earning their own support;" and the public opinion of his day commended him because, in the words of a contemporary, "The female children of this town . . . are not only useful to the community but the poorer sort are able in some measure to assist their parents in getting a livelihood."

It was claimed that, as a result of the work of the spinning schools, at least three hundred women and children had been thoroughly instructed in the art of spinning and that they had earned a large sum as wages. Domestic industries became increasingly important during this period, and children as well as women were employed in the various processes of manufacture carried on in the household. The report of Governor Moore of New York in 1767 to the Lords of Trade said with regard to his province, "every home swarms with children) who are set to "spin and card."

. . . In the eighteenth century, as the cloth manufacture developed, there was an increased and reasonably steady demand for yarn, so that the earnings of women spinners were by no means inconsiderable for those days. In some localities women were paid eight cents a day and their "keep" for spinning. In the Wyoming Valley, six shillings a week seems to have been the standard wage of a good spinner.

The best idea, however, of what home work in the different processes of cloth manufacture meant to the individual, can probably be gained by a study of some extracts from . . . old memorandum books. . . . The eighteenth century account which is selected . . . is one taken from the credit side of a merchant's book for 1781 and shows the earnings for the year of a "spinner," Theodora Orcutt, who was probably, judging from her purchases, a wife and mother.

Account of Theodora Orcutt[6]

1781.		£	*s.*	*d.*
September (1780?).	By spinning 11 Runs at 7/4-3 runs 7d.	0	9	1
February 11.	By-spinning 4 Runs for handkerchiefs................	0	2	4
March 2.	By spinning 8 Runs linen yarn at 7d................	0	4	8
	By spinning 5 Runs tow yarn................	0	2	8
"6.	By spinning 1 Run fine tow yarn at 7d................	0	0	7
"13.	By spinning 2 Runs woolen yarn................	0	1	4
April 8.	By spinning 13 Runs tow yarn at 8d................	0	6	11
	By spinning 14 Runs linen yarn................	0	9	4
"29.	By spinning 9½ Runs fine tow yarn at 8d................	0	6	4

May 13.	By spinning 2 Runs fine thread for stockings at 8d.....	0	1	4
"	By spinning 4 Runs tow yarn at 8d	0	1	4
"	By spinning 3 Runs coarse tow yarn at 4/ (O.T.)........	0	1	7
"	By spinning 3 Runs coarse linen yarn at 6d	0	1	6
June 19.	By spinning 8 Runs fine yarn for Lawn.......	0	8	0
"	By spinning 22 Runs coarse linen yarn at 6d........	0	11	0
"24.	By spinning 2 runs linen yarn at 8d.	0	1	4
July 5.	By spinning 10 Runs tow yarn at 4/ (O.T)	0	10	4
"9.	By spinning 3½ Runs tow yarn at 4/ (O.T)	0	1	10
"11.	By spinning 10 Runs tow yarn at 6d. (O. T.)........	0	5	0
July 25.	By spinning 3 Runs fine linen yarn at 8d.	0	2	0
"	By spinning 2 Runs coarse linen yarn at 6d........	0	1	0
"	By spinning 2 Runs fine tow yarn at 8d	0	1	4
"31.	By spinning 1 Run fine tow yarn at 8d.	0	0	8
August 24.	By spinning 19 Runs coarse linen chain............		9	6
September 11.	By spinning 9 Runs coarse tow yarn................		1	0
	By spinning 2 runs sent to Miss Graves			
	By spinning 4 tuns tow by Do, 8 runs tow}		6	5
TOTAL.............		4	8	5

This account of Theodora Orcutt is especially interesting because it shows how many different kinds of yarn had a marketable value at this time, and how much women must have earned by trading the product of their labor at country stores, as well as by selling it directly to the professional weavers and the small "manufactories."

Another interesting example of the way in which women exchanged the cloth which they made to purchase other articles is the list of goods which one Susannah Shepard of Wrentham tendered in part payment for a chaise. The contract and the credit were as follows[7]:

"Agreed with Mrs. Susannah Shepard, of Wrentham, to make her a chaise for £55, she finding the harness, the wheels, leather for top and lining, remainder to be had in goods, at wholesale cash price, of her manufacture.

"*(Signed)* STEPHEN OLNEY."
PROVIDENCE, November 13, 1795.

Received of Mrs. Shepard on account of chaise,

5½ yards of thick-set at 4s. 8*d*...............	£1 5s. 8*d.*
2t yards of velveret, at 4s. 8*d*	10s. 8*d.*
21 yards of satin bever, at 4s. 8*d*	12s. 10d.
1 yard & 2 nails of carpeting, at 3s.	4½d
13 yards carpeting....	£1 18s. 7½s.
2 handkerchiefs. 7s.	£4 18s. 2d.

There was, too, at this time no small amount of spinning and weaving done by women as custom work. In one New England community, near Northfield, Massachusetts, a weaver by the name of Olive Moffatt, who was a descendant of the early Scotch immigrants, was famous for such work. She was employed by most of the well-to-do families in town, and for many years her loom was considered indispensable for wedding outfits. Her linsey-woolsey cloth was considered inimitable for evenness of texture; and no one else in town could weave such patterns of linen damask. She also understood perfectly how to color fine lamb's wool yarns a beautiful shade of red with madder. The use of logwood on indigo was common enough, but a "good red" like Olive Moffatt's was difficult to obtain. Her earnings must have been very considerable for that period for she charged six pence and seven pence a skein for fine linen thread and three pence a skein or eight pence a "run" for fine woolen thread. In general the work of women spinners became more profitable after the early "manufactories" were started, . . .

In England, weaving was a man's occupation, but "spinning and the preliminary processes of cleaning, carding and roving were conducted in the early times by the women and children."[8] In this country, although professional weavers seem to have been most frequently men, yet it is clear that weaving was not an uncommon occupation for women even in the early days.[9] As the cloth manufacture developed, it became a very important one, and, . . . it continued to give employment to a great many women well into the nineteenth century.

It is perhaps scarcely necessary to say by way of summary, that the gainful employment of women in different processes of manufacture in their own homes,[10] was common enough in the seventeenth and eighteenth centuries. In so far as the early spinners and weavers furnished their own material and disposed of their own product as custom work, they were true craftswomen, belonging to a system that has not survived to any extent in modern industry. When the product was disposed of at a country store, one of the essential elements of handicraft, "custom work," was lacking. But under whatever system they worked, these "women in industry "were an important factor in the industrial life of the period.

As the gainful employment of women during this period grew so largely out of their household duties, such training as they received for their work was, in a sense, part of their general education. Although girls as well as boys were apprenticed when they were very young, the girl's indenture, unlike that of the boy, failed to specify that she was to be taught a trade. Early laws provided for the binding out of the children of the poor, and in some towns where the custom of bidding off the poor prevailed, children were put to live "with some suitable person" until they were fourteen, at which age they were to be bound until they became free by law, but it was especially specified that "if boys [they be] put to some useful trade."[11] The poor law of Connecticut provided that poor children whose parents allowed them to "live idly or misspend their time in loitering" were to be bound out, a "man child until he shall come to the age of twenty-one years; and a woman child to the age of eighteen years, or time of marriage."

The girl's indenture seems to have been for the most part a mere binding out to service. She was trained doubtless to perform the domestic tasks of the housewife, and sometimes it was agreed that she was to be taught "the trade, art, or mystery of spinning woollen and linen" or knitting and sewing as well. Her indenture might require, too, that she was to be "learned to read," which was again unlike that of the boy, who was also to be taught writing and occasionally even "cypering." The Province Laws of Massachusetts which provided that poor girls as well as boys were to be bound out contain the provision that "males [be taught] to read and write, females to read as they shall respectively be capable." It is of further interest with regard to the training of girls and boys that the General Court of Massachusetts desired that boys as well as girls be taught how to spin and that both girls and boys who were set to keep cattle in the various towns, should "bee set to some other impliment withall, as spinning up on the rock, kniting, weveing tape.[12]

It seems clear, however, that although girls were called apprentices during the colonial period, this did not mean that they were consciously given any industrial training.[13] But it should, perhaps, be repeated that the ordinary experience of the girl in the colonial household tended to make her skillful in spinning and probably in weaving as well, so that she received preparation for the two most important occupations of that time without any specialized training or the serving of a formal apprenticeship.

In concluding this discussion of the employment of women during the colonial period, some reference must be made to the attitude of the public opinion of that day toward their work. The early court orders providing for the employment of women and children were not prompted solely by a desire to promote the manufacture of cloth. There was, in the spirit of them, the Puritan belief in the virtue of industry and the sin of idleness. . . .

Perhaps the best expression of the prevailing attitude toward the employment of women at that time is to be found in one of the Province Laws of Massachusetts Bay for the session of 1692–93. The law ordered that every single person under twenty-one must live "under some orderly family government," but added the proviso that "this act shall not be construed to extend to hinder any single woman of good repute from the exercise of any lawful trade or employment for a livelihood, whereunto she shall have the allowance and approbation of the selectmen . . . any law, usage or custom to the contrary notwithstanding."

It is not, therefore, surprising to find that, in 1695, an act was passed which required single women who were self-supporting to pay a polltax as well as men.[14] That this attitude was preserved during the eighteenth century, the establishment of the spinning schools bears witness. There was, however, the further point that providing employment for poor women and children lessened the poor rates, and the first factories were welcomed because they offered a means of support to the women and children who might otherwise be "useless, if not burdensome, to society."

The colonial attitude toward women's work was in brief one of rigid insistence on their employment. Court orders, laws, and public subscriptions were re-sorted to in order that poor women might be saved from the sin of idleness and taught to be self-supporting.

Source Endnotes

1 Weeden, "Social and Economic History of New England," i, 168; and see p. 310 for note of a woman who bolted flour for her neighbors.

2 See, for example, Felt, "Annals of Salem," ii, 152; and see also the mention of Widow Gray in *Boston News Letter*, January 21, 1711.

3 The *New England Weekly Journal,* July 5, 1731, advertised a shop kept by a woman for the exclusive sale of preserves and similar products.

4 See Temple and Sheldon, "History of Northfield," p. 163.

5 This discussion of industrial systems follows in the main Bücher's analysis in his "Industrial Evolution" (Wickett's translation), Chap. IV; and the introductory chapter in Unwin, "Industrial Organization in the Sixteenth and Seventeenth Centuries," in which Bücher's interpretation is related to the industrial organization of to-day.

6 Temple, "History of Whately," pp. 71, 72. "A 'run' of yarn consisted of 20 knots. A 'knot' was composed of 40 threads, and a thread was 74 inches in length or once round the reel. A 'skein' of yarn consisted of 7 knots. An ordinary day's work was 4 skeins when the spinner carded her own wool; when the wool was carded by a merchant she could easily spin 6 in a day."

7 See Bagnall, "Textile Industries of the United States," p. 173–174.

8 Chapman, "The Lancashire Cotton Industry," p. 12.

9 An extract from an old account book, for example, shows a credit to "Sarah Badkuk (Babcock) for weven and coaming wistid," Weeden, i, 301; see also *ibid.,* ii, 855. Mrs. Holt's receipt for £1 51.Ud. for spinning is a relic in Bailey, "History of Andover," p. 578. In the Moravian settlement in Pennsylvania, the light weaving was entirely "woman's work" (Bagnall, i, 27), and Virginia cloth was described as "Having been made of cotton and woven with great taste by the women in the country parts." Bishop, "History of American Manufactures," i, 343.

10 Two other household manufactures of which mention might be made here, are the making of lace and the manufacture of the hand cards used for combing cotton and wool; that is, the preparing the fiber for spinning. . . .

11 Capen, "Historical Development of the Poor Law of Connecticut," p. 55.

12 Bee, "Massachusetts Colonial Records," i, 294; ii, 9.

13 Attention may be called in passing to the fact that after two hundred and fifty years the opportunity of an apprenticed girl has increased very slightly. An industrial

census today shows a very considerable number of girl apprentices, but the great proportion of them are in dressmaking or millinery shops where they are general service girls, learning only what will make them temporarily useful in the shop and not what is necessary to make them skilled workers in the trade. See, for example, the Bulletin "Sex and Industry," issued by the Massachusetts Bureau of Labor in 1903, which showed (p. 210) that only eighty-seven girls were serving any apprenticeship except in dressmakers' and milliners' shops. The number of apprenticed boys was 5,320.

14 "Province Laws," i, 213: "All single women that live at their own hand, at two shillings each, except such as through age, or extream poverty . . . are unable to contribute towards the publick charge." Men, however, of sixteen years or upwards were rated "at four shillings per poll."

3

A PLAN OF THE ENGLISH COMMERCE

Daniel Defoe

Source: Daniel Defoe, *A Plan of the English Commerce, Being a compleat prospect of the trade of this nation, as well the home trade as the foreign . . . Humbly offered to the consideration of the King and Parliament* (Charles Rivington, 1728), 48, 89–91, 288–89.

EDITORIAL HEADNOTE

Daniel Defoe (1660–1731) is well-known as a writer, businessman, sometime spy and commentator on a variety of public issues. Educated at the dissenting academy in Newington Green, he rejected the ministry to follow his father in business and politics. As a non-conformist, he was barred from political office and was a staunch supporter of religious freedom and freedoms of the press. He fought in the Monmouth Rebellion of 1685 against James II and VI but managed to escape after the defeat and was eventually pardoned. His political tracts followed. Struggling in trade, he was bankrupted, spent time in prison, and on release continued in trade but also worked as an accountant and began to write for money, suggesting projects to the government. He was acutely aware of social problems, and continually fought for freedom of the press, serving a sentence for libel. He turned novelist, poet and satirical writer. His interests in trade and commerce are apparent in his *A Tour thro' the Whole Island of Great Britain* (1724), *The Compleat English Tradesman* (1726) and *A Plan for the English Commerce* (1728) extracted here. In these books Defoe characterised the English people, identified their strengths and advantages and charted their course to greatness, arguing, 'Trade is the Foundation of Wealth, and Wealth of Power'. This flavour infuses the short extract here, chosen for its comments on the working family and women especially, whom he describes as unemployed until domestic industries made them useful.

DOI: 10.4324/9781003676669-4

As to the Country, the Revolution of Trade, brought a Revolution in the very Nature of Things; the Poor began to work, not for Cottages and Liveries, but, for Money, and to live, as we say, at their own Hands: The Women and Children learnt to spin and get Money for it, a Thing entirely new to them, and what they had never seen before. The Men left the Hedge and the Ditch, and were set at Work by the Manufacturers to be Wool-Combers, Weavers, Fullers, Clothworkers, Carriers, and innumerable happy Labours they perform'd, which they knew nothing of before; nay the Flemings came over (for Money) and taught them how to perform those things. . . .

In these unemploy'd counties [where no employment for women and children existed], you see the women and children idle, and out of business; these sitting at their doors, and those playing in the streets; even in the market towns, and the most populous villages, where they might be supposed to be employ'd, the poor by the rich, yet there 'tis the same, much more in the single scattering villages, where they have no business but their own.

Whereas, in the manufacturing counties, you see the wheel going almost at every door, the wool and the yarn hanging up at every window; the looms, the winders, the combers, the carders, the dyers, the dressers, all busy; and the very children, as well as women, constantly employed . . . a poor labouring man that goes abroad to his day work, and husbandry, hedging, ditching, threshing, carting, etc. and brings home his week's wages, suppose at eight pence to twelve pence a day, or in some counties less; if he has a wife and three or four children to feed, and who get little or nothing for themselves, must fare hard, and live poorly; 'tis easy to suppose it must be so.

But if this man's wife and children can at the same time get employment, if at next door, or at the next village there lives a clothier, or a bay-maker, or a stuff or drugget weaver; the manufacturer sends the poor woman comb'd wool or carded wool every week to spin and she gets eightpence or ninepence a day at home; the weaver sends for her two little children, and they work by the loom, winding, filling quills, etc., and the two bigger girls spin at home with their mother, and there earn threepence or fourpence a day each; so that put it together, the family at home gets as much as the father gets abroad and generally more.

This alters the case extremely the family feels it, they all feed better, are cloth'd warmer, and do not so easily nor so often fall into misery and distress. . . .

The Bone Lace Manufacture. It is true, that there was always, perhaps, for some Ages past, a Manufacture of Bone Lace carry'd on in England; but the Improvement and Encrease of it within about 20 to 30 Years past is such, and so visible, that he must be utterly ignorant of Trade that is not convinc'd of it. In former Times, the chief Place for this Manufacture was about Buckingham, Stony Stratford, and Newport Pagnaell, vulgarly Newport Pannel; you have it now spread, almost entirely over the Counties of Buckingham, Bedford and Oxford, and far into the Counties of Berks, Northampton, Cambridge, Hertford and Surrey, especially where any or all those Counties border on the first: It is also erected in the Weft, and especially in the Counties of Dorset and Wiltshire, where particularly at Blandford they make Lace of an exceeding high Price, and not outdone, Brussels Lace excepted, by any out of Flanders, France, or even Venice itself. In a word, this Manufacture is so much encreased in England, that it employs many Thousands of our People more than ever; and if I may credit the Report of the Country where 'tis chiefly made, where one was employ'd by it 30 Years ago, above 100 are employ'd by it now, and these of the most idle, useless and burdensome

Part of our People (I mean such as were so before) are the principal Hands employ'd, viz. the younger Women, and female Children. These were a real Charge upon the diligent laborious Poor, such as the Husbandmen, the Farmers, and the Handicrafts of other Trades; and are now made able to provide for themselves, and ease their Parents and Parishes of a dead Weight, which was in many Cafes insupportable; but I cannot dwell upon the Particulars, which otherwise would be profitably enquired into. In short, 'tis believ'd there are above an Hundred Thousand Women and Children employ'd, and who get their Bread by this Manufacture, more than did formerly; for 'tis the Encrease of it that I am now discoursing of; and this Encrease has an Effect upon the general Commerce of this Kingdom, very much to the Advantage of England . . .

4

A SIX WEEKS' TOUR THROUGH THE SOUTHERN COUNTIES OF ENGLAND AND WALES, 1768

Arthur Young

Source: Arthur Young, *A six weeks' tour through the southern counties of England and Wales* (W. Strahan . . . [and 4 others]), 1768; 70, 152.

EDITORIAL HEADNOTE

Arthur Young (1741–1820) was an agricultural reformer and writer from London. Educated at Lavenham, where his family originated, he claimed he received a poor education and then apprenticed to a wine merchant, which he thought a waste but completed. He later regretted his lack of a university education and found trade detestable. He started writing at seventeen and in 1761 attempted to start his own magazine, which failed. Having poor health, he turned down a commission in a cavalry regiment, and by twenty-two had few options, due to his health, lack of education and dislike of trade. His mother, a wealthy woman in her own right, then offered him the tenancy of a farm, which led him to focus on gaining a comprehensive knowledge of agriculture. Late in 1767, marital discord led him to give up the farm at Bradfield so he advertised for a new place, and his tours of inspection of potential farms led to *A Six Weeks' Tour through the Southern Counties of England and Wales* (1768), extracted here. His descriptions of the industries in these agricultural counties give a good account of the cottage industries in the counties through which he travelled and women's part in them.

From Hadleigh I continued my journey to Sudbury, an exceeding, dirty, but a great manufacturing town. I made such enquiries as were most likely to gain some good information relative to their manufactures; and my intelligence ran as follows; it contains a great number of hands, who earn their livelihood by

DOI: 10.4324/9781003676669-5

working up the wool from the Sheep's back to, the weaving it into says and burying-crape, which are their principal articles. The spinning is here a poor business; a Stout girl of 15 or 16, not being able to earn above 6 d. a day; but the combing is, the best of all their employments, yielding from 12s. to 14s, a week; the weavers of the fays and burying-crape earn from 7 s. to 9 s. but the first price the most common. Besides these articles they weave shipflags, which employ the women, and girls of seven or eight years of age, yielding the latter about 2 s. 6 d. or 3 s. a week. The whole manufactory works chiefly for the London markets; but some says go down their river (which is navigable from hence, to Maningtree) for exportation. . . .

[Crikley Hill] There is no manufacture nearer than Gloucester; the Staple of which city is pins, which employs near 400 hands, of whom a great number are women and children: good hands at pointing and Sticking earn from, 10 s. to 11s. and 15 s. a week: children of 9, 10, and 11 years old, earn 2 d. and 3 d. a day; but some journeymen do not get more than 7s. 8 s. and 9s. a week: the Wages in general are good. There are some glass-houses in this city; and a pretty brisk trade carried on by means; of the *Severne*, with *Shrewsbury, &c.* and *Bristol.*

5

A SIX MONTHS' TOUR THROUGH THE NORTH OF ENGLAND, 1770

Arthur Young

Source: Arthur Young, *A six months' tour through the north of England, containing, an account of the present state of agriculture, manufactures and population, in several counties of this kingdom* (W. Strahan, 1770), Vol 1, 49–50, 124–25; Vol. 2., 6–7, 64, 168.

EDITORIAL HEADNOTE

Continuing his writing, he turned his interests to agricultural reform and new ways of improving agriculture. With encouragement, he published *The farmer's letters to the people of England . . . to which are added Sylvae, or, Occasional tracts on husbandry and rural oeconomics* (1767). When he found himself without a farm, he returned to his pen as a parliamentary reporter for the *Morning Post*, as well as volumes on agriculture and further tours throughout England, Ireland and even France, Catalonia and Italy. He promoted his tours in advance, so he could meet with local farmers and discuss their ideas. In 1793, with the establishment of the Board of Agriculture, his career shifted again and he became Secretary of the board despite the opposition of William Marshall, whose idea the Board was. Young was not only the best-known agricultural reformer and publicist of his time, with an international reputation, but also a figure of importance in the political and social issues of the day. He was elected Fellow of the Royal Society in 1774.

This extract from the tour of the North is considered an important historical source, given its breadth and duration. Like Defoe, he noted the lack of work for women, rarely describing them as part of the agricultural workforce. Tea was becoming a fashionable drink amongst the elite and middling sort, so he was sensitive to the poor doing so.

DOI: 10.4324/9781003676669-6

The town of *Bedford* is noted for nothing but its lace manufactory, which employs above 500 women and girls. They make it of various sorts up to 25 s. a yard; women that are very good hands, earn 1 s. a day, but in common only 8d, 9 d., and 10d. Girls from eight to fifteen, earn 6d. 8d-. 10d. a day. This manufacture is of infinite use to the town, employing advantageously those who otherwise would have no employment at all. . . .

[Sheffield] Here is likewise a silk mill, a copy from the famous one at Derby, which employs 152 hands, chiefly women and children; the women earn 5 or 6 s. a week by the pound; girls at first are paid but 1 s. or 1 s. 5 d. a week, but rise gradually higher, till they arrive at the same wages as the women. It would be preposterous to attempt a description of this immense mechanism; but it is highly worthy of observation, that all the motions of this complicated system are set at work by one waterwheel, which communicates motion to others, and they to many different ones until many thousand wheels and powers are set at work from the original simple one. They use Bengal, China, Turkey, Piedmont, and American raw silk; the Italian costs them 35 s. a pound, but the American only 20 s. it is a good silk, though not equal to the Piedmont. This mill works up 150 lb. of raw silk a week all the year round, or 7800 per annum. The erection, of the whole building, with all the mechanism it contains, cost about 7000£ . . .

In this country [Boynton, near Cleveland] the poor have no other employment than that what results from a most imperfect agriculture; consequently three-fourths of the women and children were without employment. It was this induced Sir George to found a building large enough to contain on one side a row of looms of different sorts, and on the other a large space for women and children to spin. The undertaking was once carried so far as to employ 150 hands, who made very sufficient earnings for their maintenance; but the decay of the woollen exportation reduced them so much, that now those employed there are, I believe, under a dozen.

[East-Newton and Laystrope] Poor rates about 2d. in the pound real rents; this is extremely low, considering that the poor women and children have no manufacture for employing them; all, however, drink tea. . . .

[Shorton] The employment of the poor women is spinning of flax: A woman can earn from 3 d to 6 d. a day; but the children are generally idle till 12 years old; and all the poor drink tea.

[Rookby] Poor rates are 8 d. in the pound: the employment of the poor women and children is spinning a little flax and worsted: tea, to my great wonder, is but little drank here.

6

AN INQUIRY INTO THE NATURE AND CAUSES OF THE WEALTH OF NATIONS, 1776

Adam Smith

Source: Adam Smith, *An Inquiry into the nature and causes of the wealth of nations* (1776; Methuen, 1904).

EDITORIAL HEADNOTE

Adam Smith (1723–1790), moral philosopher and political economist from Kirkcaldy, Scotland, was raised by his mother, the daughter of a significant landowner, as his father died five months before his birth, with the support of influential relatives and friends named as guardians by his father. Following a grammar school education, he went to Glasgow College, where he was influenced by Francis Hutcheson, professor of moral philosophy. Enabled by a scholarship he moved to Balliol College Oxford, where his whig, Presbyterian and Hanoverian sympathies and being a Scot, set him apart from the Oxford of the day. He returned to Scotland to honour his scholarship, and was invited by Henry Home, Lord Kames, to give a series of lectures, the success of which led him to expand them. He also made friends with many who would shape his thinking and future, one of the closest of which was David Hume. He was offered the post of professor of logic combined with the professorship of moral philosophy at Glasgow College in 1751. The following year, he took the Chair of moral philosophy from Hutcheson. These years served as an apprenticeship as he developed his interests in ethics, rights and duties of man according to the laws of nature politics and economic. His writing was often the result of long gestation, and this is especially the case with *Wealth of Nations*, which only emerged twenty-five years later. In 1764 he resigned his Chair, aged forty, to act as travelling tutor to the third duke of Buccleuch. Though critical of this form of education,

DOI: 10.4324/9781003676669-7

he also recognised its perquisites, including a pension of £300 a year for life and a chance to travel, especially to France, to meet many of the Enlightenment authors whom he had read and taught on as well as key *salonistes*. At this time, he also began serious work on the *Wealth of Nations*. Hume predicted that such a closely reasoned work would not be an immediate success: 'But it has Depth and Solidity and Acuteness, and is so much illustrated by curious Facts, that it must at last take the public Attention' (Smith, *Corr.*, 186).

Notably, Smith had very little to say about women and made only brief comments on their role in the economy in *Wealth of Nations*. Clearly, they were not central in his imagination to the analysis he proposed. Nevertheless, continuing the theme of cottage industries, Smith's comments on the division of labour are an important statement on the working of these industries and the ways they subordinate the workers to the men of wealth. Although he does not identify the workers, the industries he described involved both men and women – spinners and pin makers, for example.

BOOK 1, CHAPTER 1

The greatest improvement in the productive powers of labour, and the greater part of the skill, dexterity, and judgment with which it is any where directed, or applied, seem to have been the effects of the division of labour.

The effects of the division of labour, in the general business of society, will be more easily understood, by considering in what manner it operates in some particular manufactures. It is commonly supposed to be carried furthest in some very trifling ones; not perhaps that it really is carried further in them than in others of more importance: but in those trifling manufactures which are destined to supply the small wants of but a small number of people, the whole number of workmen must necessarily be small; and those employed in every different branch of the work can often be collected into the same workhouse, and placed at once under the view of the spectator. In those great manufactures, on the contrary, which are destined to supply the great wants of the great body of the people, every different branch of the work employs so great a number of workmen, that it is impossible to collect them all into the same workhouse. We can seldom see more, at one time, than those employed in one single branch. Though in such manufactures, therefore, the work may really be divided into a much greater number of parts, than in those of a more trifling nature, the division is not near so obvious, and has accordingly been much less observed. . . .

BOOK IV, CHAPTER 8

In every other art and manufacture, the effects of the division of labour are similar to what they are in this very trifling one [pinmaking]; though, in many of them, the labour can neither be so much subdivided, nor reduced to so great a simplicity of operation. The division of labour, however, so far as it can be introduced, occasions, in every art, a proportionable increase of the productive powers of labour. The separation of different trades and employments from one another, seems to have taken place, in consequence of this advantage. This separation too is generally carried furthest in those countries which enjoy the highest degree of industry and improvement; what is the work of one man in a rude state of society, being generally that of several in an improved one. In every improved society, the farmer is generally nothing but a farmer; the manufacturer, nothing but a manufacturer. The labour too which is necessary to produce any one complete manufacture, is almost always divided among a great number of hands. How many different trades are employed in each branch of the linen and woollen manufactures, from the growers of the flax and the wool, to the bleachers and smoothers of the linen, or to the dyers and dressers of the cloth! . . .

In the different operations, however, which are necessary for the preparation of linen yarn, a good deal more industry is employed than in the subsequent operation of preparing linen cloth from linen yarn. To say nothing of the industry of the flax-growers and flax-dressers, three or four spinners, at least, are necessary in order to keep one weaver in constant employment; and more than four-fifths of the whole quantity of labour necessary for the preparation of linen cloth is employed in that of linen yarn; but our spinners are poor people, women commonly scattered about in all different parts of the country, without support or protection. It is not by the sale of their work, but by that of the complete work of the weavers, that our great master manufacturers make their profits. As it is their interest to sell the complete manufacture as dear, so is it to buy the materials as cheap as possible. By extorting from the legislature bounties upon the exportation of their own linen, high duties upon the importation of all foreign linen, and a total prohibition of the home consumption of some sorts of French linen, they endeavour to sell their own goods as dear as possible. By encouraging the importation of foreign linen yarn, and thereby bringing it into competition with that which is made by our own people, they endeavour to buy the work of the poor spinners as cheap as possible. They are as intent to keep down the wages of their own weavers as the earnings of the poor spinners, and it is by no means for the benefit of the workman that they endeavour either to raise the price of the complete work or to lower that of the rude materials. It is the industry which is carried on for the benefit of the rich and the powerful that is principally encouraged by our mercantile system. That which is carried on for the benefit of the poor and the indigent is too often either neglected or oppressed.

BOOK IV, 488

Three or four spinners, at least, are necessary in order to keep one weaver in constant employment; and more than four-fifths of the whole quantity of labour necessary for the preparation of linen cloth is employed in that of linen yarn; . . . It is not by the sale of their work, but by that of the complete work of the weavers, that our great master manufacturers make their profits.

7

ANNALS OF AGRICULTURE AND OTHER USEFUL ARTS, 1784, 1791

Arthur Young

Source: Arthur Young, *Annals of Agriculture and other useful arts*, extracts.

EDITORIAL HEADNOTE

As one of his many endeavours, in 1784 Young began the publication of the *Annals of Agriculture*, which ran for forty-five volumes. Young wrote many of the articles in the Annals himself; it was a labour of love and exhibited his belief in the importance of agriculture and the benefits of pursuing improvements. George III, nicknamed 'Farmer George', contributed writing under the pseudonym 'Ralph Robinson', and included others he considered model farmers. He intended it to put before the public the views and experience of the foremost agriculturists but was bitterly disappointed in its sales. It lasted until his eyesight failed in 1815. The two extracts here continue the theme of rural industries, with notes on the baize industry around Colchester and lacemaking, which was a distinctly woman's industry.

7.1. ARTHUR YOUNG, *ANNALS OF AGRICULTURE AND OTHER USEFUL ARTS*, VOL. 2 1784, 108–109

Source: Arthur Young, *Annals of Agriculture and other useful arts*, vol. 2 1784, 108–109.

At Colchester I made enquiries into the state of the baize manufactory, which is carried in that town to a great extent. This fabric, like that of Sudbury, flourishes very much at present, so that all hands are fully employed, and the masters can scarcely get their work done; but the American war was a great injury to it, and the Spanish much more, so that many hands were then out of employment for months together.

DOI: 10.4324/9781003676669-8

This declension was marked to me by the carriage of the manufactures to London, for at present four or five waggon loads go every week whereas in the Spanish war none went: each waggon is calculated to carry 250 pieces, worth 5£. each, or 1250 £. per waggon, or about 5000 £. a week: I apprehend there must be some error in this account, as 250,000 £. a year is very inconsiderable for such a town as this.

The weavers earn 10s. a week, besides finding employment for their wife and child at 4 s. a week more. They have several sorts of fabrics here, the chief of them are made mostly of short cloathing wool, of an inferior quality, mixed with some long combing wool. They make baize two yards wide in this manner, which sell undyed at 3 s a yard. Most, if not all their manufactures are for foreign consumption, especially for the Spanish American demand. A few for the Portuguese, but not in considerable quantity; but at Coggeshall they are entirely in that branch.

Great numbers of combers are here, who earn more than the weavers; the consequence of which is, that they will not work more than three or four days a week, and spend the rest at the alehouse.

The manufactory is exceedingly improved by means of a mechanical addition to the loom, which enables one weaver to do the business of two. In wide stuffs they formerly had two hands to a loom, now only one. The number of looms in the place guessed at 500. Many women weave and earn nearly as much as the men. Much lambs wool used. None of the manufacture ever goes to London by water.

7.2. ARTHUR YOUNG, *ANNALS OF AGRICULTURE AND OTHER USEFUL ARTS*, V. 16, 1791, 499

Source: Arthur Young, *Annals of Agriculture and other useful arts*, v. 16, 1791, 499.

The wives and children all employed in lace making; they begin at six or seven years old; women earn, on an average, 8d. a day, some even to 10d. and 1s. It is a great object to all the poor; the trade is now very brisk, and the dealers have made much money for four or five years past.

8

'LABOURING CLASSES', THE STATE OF THE POOR, 1797

Frederick Morton Eden

Source: Frederick Morton Eden, 'Labouring Classes', in *The state of the poor; or, an history of the labouring classes in England, from the conquests to the present period.* (B. & J. White [etc.], 1797), Vol. 1, 558–59.

EDITORIAL HEADNOTE

Frederick Morton Eden (1766–1809) brings a different perspective to our understanding of these industries. An insurance company manager and writer on the state of the poor, his ambitious and privately financed *The State of the Poor* was a pioneering piece of social investigation. Born the son of a baronet, later Governor of Maryland and related to Lord Baltimore, he attended Christ Church College, Oxford, and then went into the insurance business where he stayed the rest of his life, dying young at forty-three at the office of the Globe Insurance Company, of which he was a founder and Chairman. While at Oxford, he had succeeded to the baronetcy on his father's death in 1784.

His investigation into the poor was assisted by 'a few respectable clergymen' and an assistant, who travelled throughout the country for a year. His approach followed Adam Smith's concept of natural liberty in economic affairs. He rejected legislation as a solution and government regulation and praised self-improvement. But his detailed knowledge of the working of the poor laws meant he rejected Smith's criticisms of the Settlement laws and the social drawbacks of the division of labour. He saw enclosure as a means of improving employment and prosperity and questioned retention of the poor laws, in comments that presaged some of Thomas Malthus' views. He remained pro-populationist, though.

This extract, using Scotland as his exemplar, as opposed to the previous accounts which were English, further describes the work of labouring people in domestic industries, and praises their independence and lack of the need for any assistance.

DOI: 10.4324/9781003676669-9

In the Highlands of Scotland, every peasant makes his own shoes, of leather of his own tanning. They are sewed with thongs of calf-skin, instead of hemp; both because there grows very little hemp in the country, and because the leather is more durable than the thread of hemp, not being so liable to rot from being frequently wet. They are in general made with a strength, elegance, and lightness, which one who has never seen them will not be easily persuaded to believe. It is to be lamented, that, after two or three Highland cottagers have joined together in purchasing and dressing a hide, one of them would be often obliged to lose one or two days' work, besides tear and wear of cloaths, in going 20 or 30 miles to inform an excise-officer of it, and to pay him the stated duty; or to run the risk of being thrown in gaol, and severely fined, besides forfeiting the hide. No clogs are used in the North of Scotland. In a country where there is so much walking up and downhill, they would not answer. Few regular mechanics, of any kind, are employed by the labouring classes in the Highlands. Every man there is Jack of all trades; and yet, where *the good-man* of the house is but tolerably dexterous, so convenient, in general, and so well adapted to all really useful purposes, are their cloaths, furniture, and implements, that the want of regular tradesmen and mechanics seems to be but little felt. Many a shepherd and cotter, with his wife and children, appear at kirk and market, neat, tidy, and even fine, in cloaths which have been touched by no hand but their own, since they were shorn from the sheep, and sown in the flax-fields; except that the man has given 1s. 6d. (once in about three years) for his bonnet, and about a shilling to a tailor for making his *coat*. Nor has there, perhaps, been a single bought article used in preparing them, except the awl, needle, thimble, cauldron,[1] and a very few parts of iron-work in the weaving loom. The women extract the dyes from trees, shrubs, and herbs, of their own culling or rearing. The buds and tender twigs of the alder, heath, in different states of verdure, and woad, are very much used. They have no occasion for the assistance of fullers, shoemakers, masons, carpenters, turners, coopers, dyers, and very little for that of tailors and blacksmiths: weavers are more employed, because the women do not, in general, now work at the loom, as they formerly did. The only model which now remains in the Highlands, of the ancient *beart*, or loom, is that used for the weaving of broad garters and belts. It is much the same with the simplest kind of those we meet with on Grecian and Roman marbles, and not much adapted to expedition, though it did very well in a state of society in which women had little else to do, while the men were abroad at war or at the chase; and where it was reckoned a degradation to a man to pursue any such effeminate occupation. A few of the females still weave: but the loom now in use is of such a construction as in a great measure to preclude the sex from that useful, elegant, and venerable branch of female employment; as it obliges them to lean very much forward over a large beam, to which they must fit quite close. Spinning upon the *cuigil*, rock, or distaff, is still pretty much in use in the Highlands. It is slow, but makes an excellent thread, and is so easy an employment, that it seems peculiarly fit for children and feeble old women.

Any old woman that has the use of her hands, and can fit in an elbow chair, or on a low stool, may spin at the distaff; and accordingly we rarely meet with an old woman in the North of Scotland, that is not otherwise employed, but who has got a distaff stuck in her girdle, and a spindle in her hand.

Source Endnote

1 For dyeing.

9

SETTLEMENT EXAM FOR MARY HARRISON, WEAVER, LANCASHIRE, 1821

Source: 'Mary Harrison', in Settlement examinations for Culcheth parish.

EDITORIAL HEADNOTE

Settlement Examinations were fundamental to the English 'Old Poor Law' (43 Elizabeth c. 2) and codified with the Act of Settlement (An Act for the better reliefe of the Poor, 1662, 14 Charles II c. 12.). The Act defined a settlement according to place of birth, and its purpose was to restrain migration and vagrancy. Anyone seen as an 'incomer' to a parish who could not prove their financial probity by having rented a property worth at least £10 per year were required to notify the parish officers of their presence within forty days. If the parish officers deemed them to be liable to be likely to require poor relief, they could be removed and sent back to the parish of their birth. It could also be a means of removing anyone who was seen as undesirable in any way. Use of the legislation became more significant after amendments in 1691 and 1697. From the 1690s people could gain a settlement through birth, marriage, apprenticeship, regular employment for a period of a year, renting a house worth £10 per annum, paying parochial taxes or serving as a parish officer. Also, people could only be removed if they actually sought relief. The same legislation regularised the use of Settlement Certificates. As Mary Harrison's Examination shows, these interviews, recorded by the parish official, provide a sort of biography for working people. They can be formulaic, since the examinant had to answer certain questions, and claimants were generally aware of what officials wanted to hear. In Mary's case, it also tells us she was a weaver underlining that women did weave, but more often in the nineteenth century.

DOI: 10.4324/9781003676669-10

Mary Harrison of Hollins green weaver 17 November 1821. Born at Houghton near Winwick 1790. Parents both dead. Father left the family and was drowned at Weston. When he ran away, exam[inan]t left her mother's family and went to live with Peter Allen of Culcheth weavers as a winder of bobbins. She only went for meat and clothes [for] 7 months and then went to live with her grandmother for a week or two. Then with Thomas Marsh in Warrington weaver as a winder of bobbins and childs nurse [for] 9p. a week meat and clothes – less than a year. Then wove about 10 months for Josiah Smith of Culcheth at 1s. a week. Bound apprentice by Overseer of Houghton to David Caldwell of Croft weaver for 5years – stopped 1½ years then turned over to Thomas Taylor of Culcheth left Caldwell because he was a severe master.

3 months to Chorley to Taylor's daughter who married Thomas Crowther of Chorley miller worked as a batter and picker of cotton for 5 months and lodged with Crowther. She then went to her mothers in Warrington and worked as a weaver in her house until she died. Then went to live as a weaver with John Taylor of Caddishead Carter [for] 4 years. Then went to bat and pick cotton at Bolton at weekly wages – 18 months. She then went and wove a short time for John Stirrup of Croft at weekly wages. She then went to Warrington to her brother. She has wove ever since for herself. About 10 years ago she lived with her brother James in Sutton near St Helens and was pregnant. The Sutton overseer took her to Prescot to examine her as to her settlement. She was removed to Culcheth. William Roberts of Warrington brought her to Culcheth along with the order and delivered her to John Green who gave her an order to Aspull Workhouse where she lay in for four months.

10

DAVID LOCH'S TOUR IN SCOTLAND IN 1778

Source: Arthur Mitchell, 'David Loch's Tour in Scotland in 1778', *Proceedings of the Society of Antiquaries of Scotland* 32 (November 1898): 19–28.

EDITORIAL HEADNOTE

Little is known about David Loch (d. 1780), except that he moved from being a shipmaster at the port of Leith, Scotland, to becoming one of the leading merchants at the port. This gave him extensive knowledge of Scotland's trade. His essays from the 1770s were collected as *Essays on the Trade, Commerce, Manufactures and Fisheries of Scotland* (1778). The second volume comprised the *Tour through the trading villages of Scotland*, to which this extract refers. A detailed account of manufacturing in some 140 Scottish towns and burghs, from Alloa to Whitburn, its statistical detail in many respects anticipates that of Sir John Sinclair's *Statistical Account of Scotland* (doc. 11).

The source here is in two parts, the first being a summary of the contents and conclusions of Loch by Arthur Mitchell in 1898, and the second is selected extracts from the original *Tour* of 1778. Mitchell explained that Loch 'made this tour, and wrote an account of it, at the instance of the Hon. Board of Manufactures. No doubt he was chosen by the Board as a competent and trustworthy observer', which the extracts support. Mitchell's summary comments also on the change over time, offering a glimpse into the past, but also to the concerns of the late nineteenth century. Loch's extracts here are brief and provide a map of industries, but they also indicate that women were not always the subordinate, casual or ancillary worker that is often depicted.

In 1778, that is, 119 years ago, David Loch wrote a book entitled – *A Tour through most of the Trading Towns and Villages of Scotland; containing Notes and Observations concerning the Trade, Manufactures, Improvements, etc., of these Towns and Villages.*

DOI: 10.4324/9781003676669-11

Mr Loch made this tour, and wrote an account of it, at the instance of the Hon. Board of Manufactures. No doubt he was chosen by the Board as a competent and trustworthy observer. He made his tour with a special object, that is, his observations were to lie in a particular direction. Other books by Mr Loch show that this came easily to him, and that he was well fitted for the task which he undertook.

Tours more or less of this character, made in Scotland during the last, or early part of the present century, are somewhat numerous, and are often full of interest and instruction. . . . Good observers, however, in some one direction are usually found to observe well in other directions, and records of travel by them have often much more than a special interest, though the particular objects of such travellers may give the colour and chief value to the story they tell. They desire to see certain things, and they do see them, when they are to be seen, and their story is mainly a record of these observations, though other things are also seen and recorded. The story they write thus becomes an account of how the country, which they travelled over, stood in regard to some particular matter at the date of the visit, and so it becomes possible to compare that state with the corresponding state at a later date, by which changes of much interest may be disclosed. Mr Loch's notes, for instance, concerning trade and manufactures in the small towns and villages of Scotland in 1778 reveal many curious and important changes, which are not generally realised.

He visited and made notes regarding 132 towns and villages, and I have picked out 60 of these as the subject of the following remarks. . . . I leave out of consideration all the larger towns, such as Edinburgh, Leith, Glasgow, Paisley, Greenock, Dundee, Montrose, Dunfermline, Kirkcaldy, Aberdeen, Inverness, Hawick, etc. What Mr Loch says about trade in these larger places shows that a marvellous change has taken place in them, but my present object is to show the change which has taken place in the small towns and villages. I also omit many small towns, for the reason that Mr Loch has scarcely said anything about them. . . .

Perth, Ayr, and Kilmarnock are perhaps the largest of the 60 towns and villages which I have selected. I have not excluded them, because some things about them are interesting, as, for instance, (1) that Perth, 119 years ago, had a silk manufactory, had 600 looms employed in making silesias and sheeting, had a prosperous shoe-market, and had a trade in gloves that was famous; (2) that Ayr had 260 looms, of which 60 were employed in silk manufacture, while a few miles south of it there were about 190 looms, 55 being "in the silk way"; and (3) that Kilmarnock had 426 looms, of which 240 were employed in weaving silk, and the rest in making serges, shalloons, duffles, blankets, carpets, and linens, had also a great manufactory of shoes all for export, carried on a thriving trade in nightcaps with Holland, and sent its manufactures to all the ports then open for trade. The lady who started the manufacture of woollens in Kilmarnock in 1728 – Miss Maria Gardiner, "half aunt to the unfortunate Lord Kilmarnock" – was still alive when Loch made his tour, and we learn from him that she brought spinners and weavers from Dalkeith to teach the people of Kilmarnock. It would scarcely be to that town that one would go now in search of instructors in the arts of spinning and weaving.

In first reading Mr Loch's book, what most struck me was the change which has occurred in the small towns of the North-East of Scotland. In every one of these there was a considerable manufacture and trade in 1778. This consisted chiefly in weaving and spinning. Elgin, for instance, had about 80 looms at work, Forres 40, Nairn 46, Fochabers 50, Keith 100, Huntly 200, Cullen 120, Portsoy 30, Cromarty 61, Fortrose 32, and so on.

In an appendix to these remarks I give a short note regarding each of the 60 towns and villages, as nearly as possible in Mr Loch's own words. These notes show that weaving was far from being the only trade occupation. Spinning was, perhaps, a still more extensive employment, but it is not so easy to indicate the extent of the spinning, as it is the extent of the weaving – the latter being fairly measured by the number of looms employed. In the whole of the 60 small towns and villages there were, in those times of Home Industries, 5272 looms at work.

The materials used in weaving and spinning were wool, hemp, flax, silk, and cotton. Wool appears to have been the material chiefly used – flax and hemp following. But silk was also much used, as is shown by the fact that in the small towns, with which I am dealing, there were 754 looms employed in the manufacture of silk. Much of what was spun was sent south, largely to Nottingham, as yarn or thread.

The fabrics and objects manufactured were very varied in their character and designations. In these 60 towns and villages we hear of the manufacture of osnaburgs, shalloons, serges, duffles, dowlas, silesias, broad cloths, narrow cloths, blankets, plaids or mauds, carpets, flannels, lastings, mancoes, calimancoes, nightcaps, stockings by hand and frame, long lawn, diapers, damask, tykes, checks, plain linen, lunks, napkins, gauze lawn (flowered and striped), sheeting, inkle, canvas, sacking (for flour, bisquet, and hop bags, and for tarpaulin), tapes, silk stockings, silk knee-garters, mitts, breeches pieces, sewing thread, lace, hats, boots and shoes, nails, spades, soap, candles, and pottery.

These things were not made solely for home consumption. On the contrary, it is stated that to a very large extent they were exported to Glasgow, London, Nottingham, Darlington, Ireland, Holland, the West Indies, Halifax, Quebec, etc. Silk and flax were largely imported, and wool also to a considerable extent.

An interesting old-world picture is presented by the account of the daily waggons arriving at Selkirk with combed wool from Darlington, Manchester, Halifax, and Durham, and being loaded for the return journey with yarn spun by the people of the little Scottish town. This tells of an extensive business largely done in the homes of the people. We know, indeed, that it was very extensive, for we are told by Loch that "the number of people employed in the different branches of the woollen manufactory, in and about Haddington, was upwards of 800."

It is interesting to find Cromarty in 1778 with a large manufacture of sacking, to be spread nearly over the whole kingdom; but it is still more interesting to find that it had thriving naileries and spade manufactures. Naileries existed in some of the other small towns, as, for instance, in Pathhead, while spades and other implements for country use were extensively made at Sanquhar – "equal to any in Britain."

The lace-making at Renfrew and Hamilton seems to have been on a considerable scale. At Renfrew it is described as being after the manner of Mechlin and Brussels. It was carried on by a Mrs Pettau, whose husband was an early teacher of the art of making fine thread, in a district which has since become very famous for the thread it produces. . . .

It is curious to find a trade in silk stockings and in shoes for the London market in a little town as far north as Huntly, and we also find that fine silk knee-garters and mitts were made there, as well as gauze and lawn – flowered and striped.

Boots and shoes seem to have been made for export in many of the little towns, as, for instance, in Keith, Huntly, Peterhead, Dunse, Lanark, Forfar, Perth, and Kilmarnock.

The people of Gullane, Loch says, spin good yarn, and "are roused to industry by Mr and Mrs Cochran who are resident," but rabbits formed their chief export. The water, he says, "is soft and good," which raises a question as to the source of the supply at that time, since in our day it is notably hard.

The trade carried on in all these little towns and villages, 119 years ago, is now carried on in our large centres of population. These large cities or towns have grown vastly in population, and their manufactures and trade of all kinds have increased even more vastly. On the other hand, manufacturing, and trade that is not local, have all but ceased in the little towns and villages. This does not, however, involve their showing a diminished population. Most of them, in fact, show an increase, though the increase is very small as compared with that which has taken place in the large towns. This means that there are, in the small towns and villages of the North-East of Scotland, for example, to which reference has been made, more people now than there were in 1778, and they live without the aid of local industries, and do so, I hope, with greater ease, in more comfort, and in healthier surroundings. This may or may not be correct, but the thing that is certainly correct is that, within what may properly be called a short time, great changes have gradually and silently taken place in these communities, that these changes are already forgotten, and that they would probably be quite unknown were it not for some such chance record as that which we have been considering. It would be futile, I think, to ask whether there is in these changes a going forward or a going back. What has happened is in no sense the work of a mysterious evolution, though it probably exhibits the operation of that law of natural selection, in which everyone believes, and which tends to the survival of the strongest. In other words, the small home industries of the small towns appear to have been killed by competition with the large industries of the great towns.

EXTRACTS FROM MR LOCH'S TOUR

1. ELGIN. – Eighty looms are "employed in summer on the linen, and in winter on woolen." "Here are about £15,000 sterling's worth of yarn sold at London and Glasgow annually."
2. FORRES. – "There is a deal of yarn spun here for sale. Here are about 40 looms, partly for woolen, and partly for linen. The Glasgow market is their chief place of sale. There is about £20,000 sterling's worth, of yarn spun here in one year from Dutch flax."
3. NAIRN. – "There are about 46 looms employed partly on woolen and linen."
4. FOCHABERS. – "About 50 looms employed on piece-work, woollen and linen." "There is very good thread made here for stockings, most of which goes to Nottingham." . . .
6. HUNTLY. – "There are about 200 looms employed mostly on the long lawns, and fine linen diapers, and woolen." "About £50,000 sterling's worth is annually spun and manufactured here; taking all branches into the account." "Many shoes are made for sale, which are sent to London." "William and Alexander Forsyth make good silk stockings, from the coarse silk, which meets with ready sale. They make from the finest silk, knee-garters, mitts, and breeches-pieces. Mr Burnet manufactures brown-thread for the Nottingham market. Mr M'Vey manufactures plain linen, damask, diaper, and gauze lawn, flowered and striped. George Junken manufactures plain lawns, twisted, striped, and flowered." . . .
8. PORTSOY. – "Here are about 30 looms on long lawns, linen, and piece work, and a considerable thread manufactory for stocking-making, all of which go to Nottingham." "Mrs Mary Robertson makes sewing-thread, and employs 6 looms on gauze and flowered-lawns." "The importation of flax is considerable, about 4000 matts being annually brought from Holland to supply the manufactures at Huntly and the country round."
9. BANFF. – "Here is a very extensive manufacture carried on in the thread way, for stocking-making, white and brown, almost the whole of which goes to Nottingham." "George Robertson & Co. make thread to the amount of £40,000 sterling annually. They keep about 50 flax-dressers, import about 3500 matts of Dutch flax annually, pay about £70 sterling a day to spinners and all the different workpeople in that line." "Here are 28 looms employed in piece goods in the woolen and linen way."
10. PETERHEAD. – "Messrs James and Thomas Arbuthnots, junior, and Company carry on a considerable manufacture of coarse thin woolen stuffs, serges, calimancoes, shalloons, etc., to the amount of £50 sterling a-week." "Shoes are likewise made here for exportation. Messrs Kilgours, at Nether Kinmundie, manufacture, at an average weekly, 33 pieces of woolen cloth, of 26 yards each; they may amount in value to about £60 sterling."
11. ELLON. – "Here much is done in the knitting of stockings. About £100 sterling per week is paid by the Aberdeen merchants for this article alone." "Four looms are employed."

12. CROMARTY. – "A large manufacture for making sacking of the best kind, for flour sacks, and such other uses." "Here are 61 looms employed all in making from hemp yarn (for they use no flax) sacking of different fabrics for flour bags, bisquet bags, wool sacks, hop bags, hammock stuff, and tarpaulin stuff, and coarse stuffs for packages of every kind." "Here are two naileries and spade manufactures and both are very well employed."
13. FORTROSE. – "Here there is a deal of linen yarn spun for sale; there are 32 looms employed, about half in the coarse woolen and linen."
14. PERTH. – "A silk manufactory is here established by Mr Gloag, a sedate, sensible, enterprising man." "The skinners and glovers here are famous in their several branches of business." "The shoe-market or manufactory is in a prosperous way." "There are about 600 looms; the half of which is at present employed in silesias; the other in weaving sheeting, linen and woolen."
15. DUNKELD. – "There are at present about 100 looms employed on the woolen and linen branches, and a great deal of yarn spun, great part of which goes to London is manufactured." "Here are three tanneries, and a considerable quantity of shoes are made, for which they have a brisk demand."
16. SELKIRK. – "William Roger employs 8 large looms in the inkle manufacture, and has a great demand for that commodity. He makes broad and narrow tapes." "It is a thriving manufacture, and receives great encouragement from England." "There come down to this place considerable quantities of combed wool from Darlington, Manchester, Halifax, and Durham, daily by waggons, which is spun into yarn, and returned by the same conveyance. The sum paid weekly for spinning this wool may be about £55 sterling." . . .
19. KELSO. – "Here there are 70 looms employed in the woolen and linen." "The weavers here make 70 yards of flannel in two weeks on 2 looms occupied by a man and a boy." "They bring drest flax from Darlington and other places in Yorkshire, to be spun, then return it by land carriage to be manufactured." . . .
23. MOFFAT. – "Thomas, John, and Adam Keids at Moffat give an account of a particular kind of goods, made at this place, which are sold on the English side, and the demand is so great that it cannot be answered." "They also manufacture plaids or mauds, and blankets to a great extent, of which article they made 3000 yards last year. There is another article they manufacture, called checked serge. It is made into hunting coats, a light garb for summer wear, and answers very well for children's cloathes. They also make lastings, mancoes, flannels, and serges, which are mostly exported into Holland." "Here are about 50 looms all in the woolen branches. Serges, shalloons, duffles, blankets, coarse cloths of all denominations."
24. DALKEITH. – "The wool brought into Dalkeith in the year 1776 is about 7200 stones, tron weight, value £3240 sterling; of which there is exported about 6500 stones; so that there remains about 700 stones of said wool to be manufactured in Dalkeith and its neighbourhood, which is chiefly made into broad-cloths, from 4s. to 14s. per yard; narrow cloths from Is. 6d. to 6s. per yard; the amount

of the value of the whole manufactured woollen goods is computed to be about £3000 annually. Their chief markets are Edinburgh and Glasgow, and some to the north and south." "There are carpets made here of different patterns and pieces." "There are slaughtered in Dalkeith, at a medium, in one year, 100,000 sheep and lambs and about 2000 black cattle." "George Hislop, hat maker here, is a considerable dealer, and makes excellent goods." . . .

26. DUNBAR. – "Mrs Robert Fall employs many people in the spinning of wool, and in manufacturing it into carpets and other goods." "Sixty looms to manufacture canvas of all sorts." . . .
30. STIRLING. – "This town has long carried on a very extensive trade, in manufacturing shalloons and serges, Highland plaids, and carpets," for which last "demands are great at home, as well as from England, Ireland, and Holland." "Here are about 160 looms, 30 stocking frames, and 17 carpet looms." . . .
32. PATHHEAD. – "The manufacture of nails is carried on here to a great extent." "Here there are about 195 looms employed in manufacturing checks, tykes, napkins, and plain linen, all much in demand." . . .
34. COILINGSBUHGH. – "There are about 8 looms; a great deal of yarn is spun in and about this village." . . .
37. PITTENWEEM. – "Here there are about 20 looms, and spinning is carried on very briskly."
38. E. & W. ANSTRUTHER. – "There are about 36 looms in both towns." "A considerable thread manufactory is carried on. Their thread is much approved of – all coloured threads."
39. CBAIL. – "A great deal of yarn is spun." "Seventy-four looms in this town and Kingsbarns" – "mostly in the linen way and osnaburgs." . . .
41. AUCHTERMUCHTY. – "A good deal of coarse yarn is spun here; about 80 looms; a constant sale of coarse linens, about 30 pieces a day, 35 inches wide, and 80 yards long."
42. STRATHMIGLOW. – "There are about 33 looms employed." "A considerable quantity of ounce threads for the London market, frequently to the amount of 9000 spyndles in one year." . . .
44. SOUTH-FERRY. – "There are about 20 looms – mostly in the linen way." "There are hard soap and candles made, of good quality." . . .
46. PRESTONPANS, AND PORT-SETON. – "Two potteries – employ above 100 people. They make all sorts of the stone and flint kinds, both white and yellow, as is made at Stafford, as good in quality and full as good for the money." "Here are 20 looms." . . .
48. LANARK. – "Here there is a considerable manufacture of shoes and boots, mostly for the Glasgow market." "About 120 people employed in this branch." "Ninety-three looms, mostly in the brown linen way." "There is likewise a thread manufactory, for making white threads."
49. HAMILTON. – "There are about 110 looms, chiefly employed in working lunks, that is, linen warp and cotton waft." "The lace manufactory goes on with success and spirit." . . .

51. RENFREW. – "Mrs Pettau carries on a lace manufactory, after the manner of Mechlin and Brussels in Flanders." "Sixty looms are employed in the silk way, and 40 in long lawns and plain linen." . . .
53. KILMARNOCK. – "240 looms are employed in weaving silk; 66 in the carpet way; 40 in the linen branches; 30 for blankets; 30 for serges and shalloons; and 20 for duffles." "There are 6 frames for making stockings." "Kilmarnock nightcaps are a good article for the Holland market." "A great quantity of shoes are manufactured here, all for export." They send their goods to "the West Indies, Halifax, Quebec, and all the ports that are at present open for trade." "The woolen manufacture was introduced by Miss Maria Gardiner (half aunt to the unfortunate Lord Kilmarnock), who, observing the indolence of the people of that place, brought spinners and weavers of carpets from Dalkeith about the year 1728. From that time the woolen manufacture has been carried to a considerable extent: the lady is still alive" (1778). . . .
57. AYR. – Looms for woollen and linen are about 200, "and those employed in silk are about 60." "A few miles south of Ayr there are 55 looms in the silk way." "There are here about 190 looms, with 15 stocking frames."
58. SANQUHAR. – "There are about 30 looms, all employed in the woolen way." "Here are 5 frames in the stocking way." "A tilt mill is erected here for making spades, and all such implements for country use, in the iron way, equal to any in Britain." . . .
60. GULLANE. – "Spin good yarn." People "roused to industry by Mr and Mrs Cochran, who are resident." The water is "soft and good." Rabbits form the chief export.

11

'ABERDEEN', THE STATISTICAL ACCOUNT OF SCOTLAND, 1797

Source: 'Aberdeen, County of Aberdeen', Sir John Sinclair, (ed.) *The Statistical Account of Scotland*, Vol. XIX, 1797 (William Creech, 1791–1799), 200–208.

EDITORIAL HEADNOTE

Sir John Sinclair (1754–1835), from a family of Scottish nobility, was born at Thurso Castle, Caithness, educated at Edinburgh High School and the Universities of Edinburgh and Glasgow and as a gentleman commoner at Trinity College, Oxford. Although member of Lincoln's Inn in 1774, the Faculty of Advocates in 1775, and called to the English bar in 1782, he never practised either Scots or English law. At sixteen he had inherited substantial lands and income in Caithness and he later married well. He became MP for Caithness in 1790 and continued in politics and from a supporter of Lord North, being ignored, he moved to becoming independent. When his wife died in 1785, he was devastated and momentarily left politics, travelling abroad and making connections. From the 1780s, he published a vast array of massive books and pamphlets. His interest grew in politics and economy and his trip to Prussia and Russia stimulated his interest in agriculture, while travel boosted his enthusiasm for 'useful knowledge'.

In the 1790s, as an elder in the Church of Scotland, he proposed a survey of the state of the country, which became the twenty-one volumes of the *Statistical Account of Scotland*. To him, 'Statistics should reveal the quantum of happiness in a population', as well as 'the means of further improvement', reflecting perhaps the influence of Jeremy Bentham, his contemporary. In 1790, he sent out a questionnaire of 160 items and followed this up with another six and another five in 1791, which included education which he had overlooked. Initially intending to summarise the reports he received but appreciating their variety and individual flavour, he only made minor editorial changes. 'The important features of Sinclair's survey were its comprehensive range of topics and the fact that it was fully carried through. All 936 parishes were reported on in the following nine years, and the book as a whole is the most frequently quoted of all Scottish historical sources'. (ODNB)

The extract here on Aberdeen gives a flavour of the material he collected, and specifically a snapshot of domestic industry in Aberdeen and its environs. It points to the role of merchants who were putting out thread production and gradually introducing it to water-powered mills. He also reiterates a refrain that permeates the literature on women's industrial work: that women were restrained by the need to look after homes. Like most commentators, he saw women as married – he does not note single women.

ABERDEEN

The principal manufacture of Aberdeen, prior to the year 1745, was knitted stockings, which were mostly exported to Holland, and from thence dispersed through Germany. After that period the linen-manufacture was introduced, and brought to considerable perfection. The spinning of linen-yarn in this place, for manufactures, arose from a small beginning. Some patriotic gentlemen, a few years after the battle of Culloden, being desirous to spread this useful art more extensively in the northern district, applied to the Board of Trustees at Edinburgh, who sent a woman here qualified to instruct others in the art of spinning. She was accompanied with all the implements necessary for her purpose. As a proof that her exertions were crowned with success, it may be observed that the spinning of linen-yarn has arisen in this town to the extent of nearly 100,000 spindles per annum. This is accomplished mostly by the wives and daughters of mechanics and labourers, and procures them a yearly income of about £5000 Sterling. Much linen-yarn is besides brought to Aberdeen from the country round to a considerable extent. The quantity, however, of linen-cloth made here and in the neighbourhood is very small, owing, it is believed, to the Irish, who have engrossed the greater part of that branch of trade, both at the English and foreign markets, not on account of the superior quality of their goods, but of the encouragement given by their Parliament to the linen-manufacture, which enables them to undersell us even in our own country. A considerable quantity of the coarser kinds of this yarn is exported to Perth, Dunfermline, Glasgow, and other manufacturing places to the southward. Messrs Collison, Thomson and Company, of this place, lately began the manufacture of brown sheetings, osnaburghs, and sail-cloths, and are the only manufacturers of such goods here. They have already, by unremitting attention, brought their brown sheeting and osnaburghs, to as great perfection as any made in Scotland. Their sail-cloth manufactory only commenced in 1795, and what they have yet made has been sold to the sail-makers in this place, who acknowledge it equal in quality to the best that comes from the south country. The sheetings and osnaburghs are shipped for London, and from thence are chiefly sent to the West Indies and America. From the satisfaction there manufactures have given, they are greatly on the increase, and bid fair to be carried to a considerable extent. The flax used in the linen branches here is chiefly imported from Holland, and some from England. But the Baltic flax is used for brown sheetings, osnaburghs, and other coarse goods.

Thread Manufacture. – In the article of thread, particularly white and coloured pound threads, the Scotch stand unrivalled, and they must maintain their superiority by local advantages, which no other country at present can possess, and the manufacture is carried on to an extent equal to any demand. Aberdeen exceeds in quantity that of any other town in Scotland; and none have surpassed, if they have yet come up to, their fabric in quality. All the threads made here are sent to the English market, and for the greatest part direct to London, and from thence to many different places abroad. Besides pound thread there is made here a considerable quantity of the finer threads, called ounce or nun's thread, from their having been made by nuns in France and Flanders before the manufacture was introduced into this country. The principal thread manufacturers in Aberdeen are, Milne, Cruden and Company, for stitching and ounce threads; Leys, Masson and Company, for stitching and coloured threads; and Young and Walker, for coloured threads only.

These, with several less extensive adventurers in the same trade, and including a few who manufacture linen-yarn only, employ nearly 100 boys under 14 years of age, who earn each from 1s. 8d. to 2s. 6d. a-week; 600 men, earning from 5s. to 12s. a-week each; and not under 2000 women, who have constant employment, mostly in their own houses, in spinning yarn, doubling and twisting thread, etc. Many women, who work within the manufactures, will earn from 5s. to 6s. a-week; but those who work in their own houses cannot earn nearly so much, a considerable part of their time being taken up with family matters, and other avocations. But additional to the persons just now mentioned, who dwell in the city and suburbs, the thread-manufactures here give occasionally employment to at least 10,000 women in this and other northern counties in spinning linen-yarn. Their employment in spinning for manufactures can only be called occasional, because in summer they are generally employed in procuring fuel, and spinning wool and flax for family use. Their labour is also required in the field during harvest.

Woollen Manufactures, etc. – In the beginning of this century, the woollen manufactures of Aberdeenshire were chiefly coarse slight cloths, called plaidens and fingroms, which were sold from 5d. to 8d. per ell, and stockings from 8d. to 2s. 6d. per pair. These were manufactured by the farmers and cottagers from the wool of their own sheep, and by the citizens from the wool brought to the market from the higher parts of the country. The goods were bought up by the merchants of Aberdeen, at a weekly market held in town, and at stated periodical fairs held through the country, and which, in regard to manufacture, were under the regulation of the Dean of Guild of Aberdeen, who regularly attended, and who, being invested with legal authority, confiscated such goods brought for sale, as were deficient in quality, size, or measure. The chief market for exportation was Hamburgh, from which place was brought over, at the public charge, and placed in a public warehouse, a press or machine for packing of bale goods, by which 400 or 450 dozens of men's stockings may be put into a portable package; but are made seldom to contain above 300 dozens, forming, when packed, an oblong square, and measuring about 50 cubic feet, and weighing 15 cwt. gross.

Soon after the rebellion, anno 1745, a spirit of agricultural improvement, as well as of commercial enterprize, raw material, so that from £70,000 to £80,000 Sterling is laid out on labour for foreign consumpt[ion]. About 400 persons are employed in wool-combing, and 30,000 occasionally employed in spinning and knitting. It is said occasionally employed, because a great proportion of these are frequently otherwise occupied, particularly at harvest, at moss, and in the summer season, providing some pieces of clothing for themselves or families.

The advantages peculiar to this branch of manufacture are, that children at the age of ten, and people very far advanced in life, may, and often do, though in a scanty measure, maintain themselves by their labour at this work, and the knitting can be carried on while travelling or watching cattle or the like; nor does it require much, or at least not constant light, many carrying on their work throughout the winter evening, with the faintest light issuing from a few turfs, – a circumstance much in favour of a country where the nights are long, and the inhabitants poorly supplied with fuel or light. From these circumstances, perhaps, it is, that the stocking manufacture finds hands, and has its work done at a lower rate than some other branches of manufactures, a good knitter not being able to earn more than 2s. per week, and the average not exceeding 1s. 6d.

There are a few stocking-frames in Aberdeen, but nothing considerable is done in that way. When speaking of the extent of the stocking manufacture of Aberdeenshire, it must be understood, that what is manufactured in the adjacent parts of the shire of Mearns, to the distance of 12 or 15 miles on the coast, is included, as all that trade centers in the city of Aberdeen, and is carried on by the merchants and manufacturers residing there.

The wool used in the stocking-manufacture is brought from London and Newcastle. The whole quantity of wool imported annually into Aberdeen is not less than 2800 bags, of 240 lb. each.

If the value of the stockings exported is allowed to be £ 102,000, and the average price at the rate of 25 s. per dozen of mens stockings, the quantity of wool consumed in that article will be 2500 bags: the soap consumed in washing the wool and scouring the stockings will be about 37 tons, and about 35 tons of oil used in combing the wool . . .

It has been observed, that 300 dozens of mens stockings, when packed, weigh 15 cwt. and measure about 50 cubic feet; five feet go to a barrel bulk. The quantity manufactured would therefore afford lastage for no more than five vessels of a hundred tons burden, and the wool and other materials used in the manufacture, cargoes for 13 vessels of the same tonnage.

Allowing the linen-yarn manufacture to be of the same amount, it is presumed the lastage is much the same with the woollen, but the material of the former would not afford lastage for above seven vessels of an hundred tons. Hence both these branches of manufacture, which form the principal staple articles of export from the port of Aberdeen, would only employ 30 vessels, or rather afford 30 cargoes for a vessel of that tonnage; and hence it may be accounted for why the proportion of shipping belonging to the port of Aberdeen is so much inferior to places in Scotland of less trade and population.

When it is said above, that the stocking-manufacture is of superior quality now to what it was formerly, it is to be understood of the fabric in general: there were much higher priced worsted stockings made about 50 years ago than at present. They were the work of women of the better sort. We have heard of two or three guineas per pair having been paid; but there were but few of such quality knitted; and such, it is apprehended, were more for curiosity than use, and the value more imaginary than real. There were, till of late, a good many made, which brought from 60s. to 90s. per dozen, and were both a neat and comfortable wear; but the silk manufacture has lessened the demand for these at present, and they are only sought for by those who seek for convenience, rather than follow fashion.

In the year 1789, a water-mill was first erected near Aberdeen, with machinery for teasing, scrubbling, carding, and rowing of wool, and jennies for spinning the same to manufacture into cloth. Previous to this period the manufacturer was obliged to import his warp-yarns from the north of England. The woft was chiefly spun by old women, and that only from backings or nails, as they were not able to card the wool. . . .

The country people, 10 miles round Aberdeen, manufacture about 900 stone a-year of Scotch wool, mostly for their own use. . . .

The only inconvenience that the woollen-manufacturers in Aberdeen labour under is the want of weavers, particularly for broad cloths, which indeed is the only bar why they do not extend their manufacture of cloths, of the quality of the Yorkshire broads and Rachdale baizes, for exportation.

12

THE BRITISH LINEN COMPANY CORRESPONDENCE

Source: Alastair J. Durie (ed.), *The British Linen Company 1745–1775*, (Scottish History Society and Pillans & Wilson Ltd., 1996), Scottish History Society, Fifth Series, Vol. 929–30, 34–36, 49–50, 73–74, 113–114, 121–22, 133–34, 225–26.

EDITORIAL HEADNOTE

The linen industry had a long pedigree in Scotland and had achieved a fairly substantial toehold in the English market by the later seventeenth century. Not surprisingly, therefore, linen featured prominently in the economic arguments of the pamphleteers in the debate over the question of union with England.

As Alastair Durie explained in the introduction to this collection, the British Linen Company was a significant factor in the growth of the linen industry (1746), along with the Board of Trustees for Fisheries and Manufactures, (1727), which devoted most of its time and limited resources to assisting the industry through regulation, instruction and promotion, and government policy which helped local producers against overseas competition. For twenty years or so, it was a major force within the industry and in the development of what was becoming Scotland's premier industry. At the peak of its operations in the 1750s, it was probably not just the largest single firm in the whole of the Scottish economy, handling every stage of manufacture from the importation of flax to the bleaching of the finished cloth. As a classic protoindustrial organisation, it employed thousands of weavers and spinners in the east and north of Scotland and marketed hundreds of thousands of yards of cloth annually.

The uneven quality of Scots yarn, and the tendency of prices to rise in the Lowlands as demand increased, led to an ambitious scheme to establish a number of spinning agencies in the North of Scotland. Many of the workers there had to be trained from scratch, and while no clear data exists, one of the master-spinners in the north claimed in August

DOI: 10.4324/9781003676669-13

1754 to have over 1,400 spinners under his control. The development of putting out of protoindustries has been historically described as using an underemployed skilled workforce, normally women who were experienced spinners. Here, however, the company spent time and money recruiting and training workers in an area where there was little other employment. Durie says they he selected about one-fifth of the available material; this extract further reduces that, focusing partly on the practices of the company but especially on the relation of women to the company.

To Mr George Chalmers, Dunfermline

10 October 1746

After inspecting the 1000 cloth you left here, we find the yarn pretty well boiled but so unevenly sorted and wrought that we cannot put it to your account till we have the pleasure of seeing you here. We doubt not such pieces you make for the future will be free from such faults and that you endeavour to introduce in the country such a creeks [sic] of linen as may be saleable and lasting. Pray cannot you introduce the Osnaburgs with you? If you have spinners we will send you a woman for ten days to teach your spinners and will pay you for these goods all your charges in manufacturing and 5 per cent more for your trouble, or if you think sending a woman here would do better, she will be taught in eight days and may teach these with you when she returns and a weaver, if sent here, might be taught the working in two days as there is no difficulty in it.

. . .

To Thomas Shairp of Houston, Esquire, one of the Proprietors

25 April 1747

The British Linen Company being informed that the town and barony of Leadhills belonging to the Right Honorable the Earl of Hopeton contains about 400 families where the women are quite idle and depend solely upon the labour of the men for their subsistence.

The Company therefore in order to promote industry and extend the linen manufacture thro' the Kingdom propose to send there a person skilled in the heckling of flax who will give out dressed lint to those women to be spun into yarn for the Osnaburg manufacture and pay them weekly for what yarn they shall return at the rates usually paid in other places for spinning. Provided my Lord Hopeton will countenance to the undertaking and particularly that he would cause a woman to be sent from Leadhills to be instructed at Edinburgh in the method of spinning this kind of yarn which will cost no more than her maintenance for two or three weeks at most as in that time any experienced woman will learn it and be capable to instruct her neighbours at home. And further that My Lord would allow his factor to lay out the money for the wheels which will cost about 4/6 per piece and distribute them amongst the miners who should be obliged to take a wheel for every woman, (or if that shall be thought too much) for every two women in his family betwixt the age of 10 and sixty years and this advance can easily be replaced to his Lordship by ordering the factor to deduct the value of the wheels out of the first payment that shall be made to the workmen.

We judge it will be quite proper at first to get my Lord to interest himself in this affair as above. But are of opinion that in a few months practice the people will need no authority to be interposed or any other spur to industry than the benefits accruing from their labour as they will be able (in conformity to their industry and application) to earn from 16d to 2/4 per week. So that if the town have 400 families and each to produce only one spinner who we shall suppose makes at a medium 20d per week or £ 4 6/8 per annum, the returns in general for spinning to Leadhills will be £1733 6/8.

From the experiments made by the Company in the Osnaburg manufactures, we have the pleasure to acquaint you that they have not only given satisfaction to our own West India merchants in Scotland but what is much more material to both the West India merchants and linen drapers at London. Now the Company is resolved to push that branch of the linen as far as it's possible. And for that end the Court of Directors have ordered us to ask your assistance in procuring an answer to the enclosed proposal from my Lord Hopeton who you see (if we are rightly informed) will have it in his power at a very small expence to make all of his people at Leadhills very useful to themselves, the Company and their country.

. . .

To Mr David Stiven, weaver, Dunfermline

22 April 1747

You have but small reason to complain of our returning you the linens you call Huggabags, as they were not only ill manufactured but made of the worst tow yarn we ever saw and no sort of care had been taken to boil the yarn with ashes before they were wove. We desired you to make some Huggabag of either 3/4, 6 quarter or 2 yards broad of good sufficient yarn, and we should be determined by the price at which you could afford the samples if or not we might give you an order to go on and enlarge your trade in that way. But surely you cannot say we desired you to rake together all the trash of ill made linen of that sort in your town?

The great fault of all your town made diapers is that the figures are by no means square, being much longer waft ways than they are by the warp. Pray mend that on your next pieces you send us which will encourage a future correspondence.

Court of Directors

8 February 1748

The Managers acquainted the Court that as the season for bleaching both fine and coarse linens draws near, they had wrote to Mr William Gray at Glasgow and Mr William Colvin at Denovan in order to know at what rates they would bleach the Company's linens, but as yet had received no return. The Court approved of the same, and directed the Managers further to write Mr Andrew Wight at Ormiston, Mr Andrew Dickson at Haddington and Mr William Neilson at Roslin to the same effect and communicate their returns to the Court.

The Managers informed the Court that through the increase of the Company's affairs it would be absolutely necessary to hire a much larger warehouse than that which the Company presently had, and one better situate so as both to give access for carriages and if possible to have it disjoined from any neighbouring houses, that thereby the Company's effects might be in less hazard from fire. And as the Earl of Murray's house in the Canongate seemed in every way well adapted for a warehouse for the Company where at the same time there would be as much spare room as would lodge the Managers, and perhaps more of the Company's servants under the same roof with their effects, they had wrote a letter to Mr John McKenzie of Delvin, agent for the Earl, offering him a rent of £50 stg yearly for the use of his house and gardens, upon his lordship's agreeing to enter in to tack for some few years.

. . .

To Alexander McKenzie, Dingwall

19 May 1748

Mr John Dingwall, writer in this place, having proposed to the Court of Directors that you should be constituted and appointed the Company's agent or factor for carrying on the spinning of Osnaburg yarn at Dingwall on the same footing with Mr John Reid at Tain, please know that the Court have agreed to the same upon Mr Dingwall's joining with you in a bond of security to the Company for a faithful account and reckoning being made of all goods and cash that shall be entrusted to your management. And for which purpose have extended a bond for your and Mr Dingwall's signing which he will transmit you.

The conditions of employing Mr Reid are; the Company keeps him supplied for flax fit for that manufacture, the sea hazard, freight, charges of unloading, heckling and spinning together with the charges of reshipping the yarn when made and all the other risks and expences of bringing the yarn to Leith being entirely on the Company's account. And further the Company allows him to draw on us for what cash is necessary to carry on the spinning. The premium allowed him in full for his trouble is at the rate of one penny stg for each spindle of yarn he shall so spin.

The Company has allowed Mr Reid to lay out some of the Company's cash on spinning wheels in order to enlarge the spinning more expeditiously. But then this money is to be recovered from spinners how soon they are capable from their work to repay the same. It will certainly be necessary for you to go to Tain for some days to observe their method of carrying on the spinning which will be of much more service than any instructions that can be communicate to you in a letter, and therefore have enclosed you a letter to Mr Reid which you see will procure you a spinning mistress, or the opportunity of teaching one there, as you shall like best. And at the same time by looking through their affairs and Mr Reid's advice will be able to judge what flax & utensils will be necessary for you to begin with.

. . .

To Nathaniel Child, London

28 April 1752

. . . We are extremely sensible of what you write concerning the yarn. It has been our close application since the erection of this Company to promote and enlarge the spinning of all sorts of yarn from our own flax, and at present have got a good deal done, and in a year or two hence hope to have most if not all of our goods made from yarns of our own spinning and suitably proportioned to the quality and fineness of the cloth. In the Highlands and Islands we have at present about 2500 spinners at work and daily increasing, and as these people were totally ignorant of the business, you will easily judge the attempt has cost a great deal of expence and trouble, and will yet take time to finish it. The Company had pushed the spinning in the low countries, considering their demands for yarn would have heightened the price beyond what the London and Manchester people give at present, and therefore in order to preserve ourselves are obliged to go on cautiously. We think your proposal of laying a duty on yam exported to Ireland in proportion to what they charge upon yam exported from thence to Britain is very reasonable, and we hope something that way may be attempted next session.

To Mr William Tod, London

24 February 1753

Mr Doig is to keep all his good yarn from 4 hanks per lb downwards upon hand until you give further directions or are satisfied that the bounty is to be continued.[1] We do not well know what to make of the undertakers for spinning in the North. Mr Forsyth says that the spinning is decreasing. Mr McKay of Tordarroch says that he loses £10 stg [sterling] on every ton manufactured. Both of which accounts seem to me void of truth; because in every other part of Scotland from the high price that provisions are giving a good deal of spinning is carrying on now and it would not seem probable that anyone but a downright fool (of which I will not accuse Mr McKay) would carry on our trade at such disadvantage as £40 per cent loss.

There is great demand at Glasgow for Edinburgs of which article we are like to be run out altogether for want of yarns, and yet from the former accounts from the North do not well know what quantity to order from the Baltic for next year and now is the right time. The flax on hand here and at Dundee may in all probability be disposed of before the next comes home, but you know we have 80 tons locked up at St Petersburg. Mr Doig and I have been talking of this matter and we think that at present 150 tons may be commissioned from Riga to be bought at such price as the market will admit of vizt 50 tons Cutt Marienburg, 70 tons Lithuania and 30 tons Drujaner flax; but it is my opinion that even that quantity might be doubled if the last year's crop be good and the price under 18 Rix Dollars per shippound for Lithuania and so in proportion for others. You will therefore take the affair under consideration and write Mr Mudie according to what you think best and let us have a copy of the letter you write in order to be registrated in our letter book. Below is a note of the sales, Glasgow and London included. Amount of Sales tot. 23rd February, 1753 £32,409 9/6.

. . .

To William Duff, sheriff of Ayr

24 January 1756

There's a fabric of linen in your county that's commonly known by the name of Irvine linen which if a little improved and altered from what is usually brought to the market would in time and especially if the bounty is renewed be of general demand for export to Spain for their West Indies. I have for time past employed Mr Brown the stampmaster at Irvine to buy up the cloth brown which was found fault with abroad on account of its not being equally alike broad and being rather too thin. This year I desired him to employ 6 or 8 looms in making that sort of cloth of yarn well sorted and boiled to be full 29 inches in breadth out of the loom and set a little thicker than the usual run of country cloths which are bought from 9 1/2 d to 11 d per yard and the Company would take all these looms' produce for one year by way of trial. He has wrote me that he cannot get any of the country people to alter their method. I'm therefore at a loss whom to employ or how to get another proper person to correspond with on that head. I therefore presumed to give you this trouble. I desire you to show this letter to anyone you think proper and if too high profits are not insisted upon, in time that branch might be extended considerably in your country.

To John Brown, Ayr

20 March 1756

Yours of the 10th with three pieces of linen are safe come to hand. We have narrowly inspected them and compared them with some of the common country make and find that they are better made both in point of colour and of the yarn, sorting and weaving. But they are still to be amended both in the thickness of the cloth and making them of equal lengths. They ought to be full 56 yards or 56 ½ yards after lying some days in a loose manner when out of the loom. The thin setting of the yarn in the reed and the rubbing by the weaver together with the stretching the piece must have in the loom, requiring the cloth to be laid loose so as to return to its true length and breadth. You will see by the subjoined note of the lengths of these 3 pieces how much such a precaution is necessary. What goods of the like kinds we have had bought up for us in your neighbourhood have usually been paid for with a discount of 5 per cent for measure. At least we think you should allow the Scots ell brown to hold out the yard when bleached.

As to what you say about contracting with you for 16 looms and our agreeing to give a higher price if yarn shall rise above its present rate, these cannot at present be replied to. For if your magistrates and town of Ayr shall succeed in what they have in their great wisdom thought fit to petition the Parliament for; vizt not to grant a bounty on our own manufacture's exports or to take off the duty on foreign yarn, this Company cannot give you any employment because the allies and friends of your good town who carry on this individual species of manufacture in Silesia and other parts in Germany have a drawback on all their linens exported from Britain. We cannot therefore export them on equal terms without a bounty or the drawback being taken off. And unless our yarns be kept at a price equal with the foreign will that bounty be of any general good to the nation? We say therefore that if your towns of Ayr, Irvine, Glasgow and Paisley shall succeed in their opposition to the linen manufactures of Great Britain in conjunction with the dealers in foreign linen, you can have no contracts made for greater or lesser number of looms.

. . .

To Joseph Forsyth, Dingwall

28 July 1759

There is no doubt every person would chose [sic] to have as little trouble and as great profit on his business as possible, but that may be drove too far as the undertakers for the Trustees' stations are likely to experience. The Board of Trustees are now heartily tired of house building and giving salaries in the Highlands. It will therefore be unnecessary to make me any proposals for building houses or giving salaries other than what a premium for executing the work will bring in proportion to the extent of the spinning. The present year is merely a trial at what rate of expence the business can be carried on, for this purpose the Trustees will allow 2d per spindle above the price paid the spinner and pay all charges of transport to and again. This you know is double the rate it can be done for in this country. The method Mr Scott takes is to cause erect houses made of turf with a ditch thrown round to keep out ground dampness, and to employ a woman both to teach the ignorant and give out his lint and receive in his yarns. By this method he will get business done on cheaper terms than the way you propose and I hope make something to himself Against another year I propose to deliver him the flax rough and receive the yarns when spun upon a price stipulated, as is now done with the white flax for coarse grists. But the Trustees must first know the charge of transport before a fair and honest allowance can be made on that account. If you are pleased upon these terms to make a trial I shall order so much flax to be delivered you. If not, I am sorry for it but can propose no other terms than what Mr Scott asked when here, and Mr Mackay has since approved of and accepted himself.

To Hector Scott, Inverness

21 August 1759

I come now to reply more particularly to your letter of the 15th. I agree with you that the wheels and reels should be inspected, marked and numbered as quickly as they are made so that they may be distributed early in the season to the spinners and for that purpose you should get some of the magistrates to direct the inspection of the wheels and reels and to attest them by 50 or even half of that number. With regard to Mr Shaw's refusing you access to your own house, you may be certain he will use every method in his power to disappoint one he imagines will supplant him and therefore if you cannot force him to quit his possession, you must do the best in your power without him. I dare say you will find difficulties (as must happen in all new undertakings) in establishing colonies of spinners in the different parts but these you must endeavour to surmount. If you yourself think it proper to carry on a spinning at Lochaber, do so and let me know the name of the distributing places, as I must get it marked in the Trustees' books. And from what you say about the Governor of Fort Augustus, I suppose Lochaber must come in the room of Fort Augustus for a spinning station. I apprehend the behaviour of the Governor to be owing to his connection with Mr Shaw; however you may do without them. Only let me know the whole particulars in a letter such as may be shown. As I have an entire confidence in your integrity and application to business I have no difficulty to assure you that I shall take my hazard of being reimbursed, and thereby agree to allow you for this year upon any extraordinary expences for house building or spinning mistresses' fees that has not hitherto been allowed for in your agreement and proposals to the amount of £20 stg more upon your instructing such to be really necessary. I hope there will now nothing happen to retard your going on with spirit. I desire you may write me from time to time as to your success therein. I hope you will not lose time in fighting with Shaw or the Governor but cultivate a friendship with the McDonalds and Frazers and establish yourself there on a firm footing. Mr Mackay of Tordarroch who carries on the spinning on the same footing with you at the head of Lochurchqull [sic] and Assynt assures me of this year of 5000 sp[indle]s of yarn.

...

To David Flint, Edinburgh

11 January 1760

In consequence of the letters I had wrote to the sundry agents employed by this Company for promoting the spinning of linen yarns in the several stations of Loch Broom, Loch Carron and Glenmoriston, I was in hopes that before this time I should have received an exact state of the charges attending the spinning, together with a note of what wheels and reels would be annually wanted with the premiums to be paid for teaching the ignorant and prize money to the best spinners, but as yet I have received no answer from them. By what I have hitherto been able to learn concerning the expence of land carriage etc for spinning in the interior parts of the Highlands, I am persuaded that nothing less than 5d per spindle will prove to be a saving bargain with anyone who contracts with the Honorable Board. This seemingly extravagant demand arises from the high charge of land transport, and that the first undertakers of those stations having begun and their continuing to give the price of l0d per spl to the spinner, being the same that is given in the Lothians where expence of living is higher and almost no risk or charge attends the trade whereas for the same grists of yarns spun in Orkney, the sea coasts of Sutherland, Caithness, Cromarty, Ross and Inverness shires no more is paid the spinner than 8d per spi[ndle] and out of the difference which is 2d persp[indle] the undertaker has a handsome reward for his trouble and is enabled to furnish his employer with yarns in quantities upon reasonable terms.

If therefore the Honorable Board shall think it proper I shall adventure on behalf of the British Linen Company to contract for the spinning of 100,000 and not less than 60,000 spindles linen yarns to be performed in the space of four or five years from this date, to be spun in the above stations of Lochbroom, Lochcarron, Glenmoriston Sutherland towards the Bay of Tongue and other interior parts of the Highlands and in the Isle of Skye at the rate of 5d per spl amounting in the highest to £2083 6/8 of l00,000 spindles and for 60,000 to the sum of £1250. It being always understood the Board will allow the necessary sums for teaching, for prize money and for wheels and reels. And I hereby pledge myself that if any thing lower can be done how soon I have received the final answers from the agents employed in the spinning in these parts, I shall communicate it to the Board and deduct accordingly from my proposition of 5d per sp[indle] But I apprehend it were prudent for the Board as well as the Company to know what shall be further done in those Highland stations, that so the necessary provisions on both sides may be prepared in time for executing what may be agreed on. By my last accounts from the agent employed for carrying on the spinning in Assynt, and to the head of Strathurehill in consequence of my agreement with the Board last year, I was made to hope for 5000 sp[indles] of yarn against next May or June, and from Stratherrick, Beauly, Laggan, Auchindrame etc. I am told above 100 girls have been taught that never saw such a machine as a spinning wheel before, and a demand is made for liberty to teach more and desiring I would allow him for these 5/ – per head as well as for those stipulated in our agreement.

To John Anderson, Perth

24 January 1760

One Mr Richard Neilson from this place, a very knowing and experienced manufacturer having lately gone to Dundee to settle there, he is now employing many hands in the county about in some new branches of the linen manufacture. This it seems, and an opinion that Company are to deprive them of their trade as the man comes from Edinburgh and is a near relation of Mr Tod at London, has exasperated the merchants so much that they are trying to stop the progress of the Company's notes there and at Coupar Angus, and I dare say everywhere else. I must therefore beg of you to aid the Company in this matter by satisfying the ignorant and showing others the bad consequences of hurting the credit of particulars and the trade of the Nation.

It's a pity that the people in Dundee did not see farther into things. While there is two million stg. of foreign linens annually imported, it must surely be a blessing to the Company to employ our own poor rather than Germans or French. No man can say his trade is diminished since the commencement of the Company. If these things are true can a man of skills settling in a place be a hurt to it in particular, or could it be a hurt supposing this Company had settled him there as their agent? On the contrary I think the place and country about are greatly obliged. I shall detain you no longer, only to beg you would write any of your friends at Dundee to befriend Mr Neilson instead of distressing him and to show the error of attempting to hurt the Company's circulation.

. . .

To David Flint, Board of Trustees, [Edinburgh]

14 July 1760

Having lately received sundry letters complaining of the undertakers for the stations of Glenmoriston and Lochbroom from Hector Scott at Inverness who I had employed to introduce and carry on the spinning of flax at Lagan, Auchindrome, Stratherrick, Strathglass, Beauly etc as also from Mr John Mckay at Cyderhall who I had employed to do the same at Strathorde, Assynt etc. In consequence of the agreement made with the Honorable Board of date the 30th of March 1759 I hereby transmit you one of these letters from Mr McKay dated the 17th of May last, together with one from Mr Mcleod of Ledmore to him for your perusal; from which, and from what Mr Scott the bearer can vouch, you will be convinced of the unfair dealings of these undertakers and of the impossibility of a frugal scheme's succeeding at the same time, and in competition with one by much more liberal in its appointments. Mr Scott by living at Inverness, where wheelwrights are at hand, by his knowledge of the country and the language, got his part of the scheme in a great measure executed before Mr Shaw had time to counteract him, and in fact has taught 100 girls to spin in these parts, who were ignorant of that art. The part Mr Shaw had then to act, was only that of giving more money to the people employed which indeed he has done to the extent of no less than 2d per spindle, over and above the high price formerly paid of 10d per spyl. In this extravagant folly of Mr Shaw's, I have been obliged to follow him by giving the same rate for spinning, because otherwise I must have given up the plan, after all the flax was sent there and the people employed to carry it on. And in this way Mr Scott has spun up about 2000 spindles of yarn, whereof 930 spindles have been delivered me of very well made yarn considering the short time the spinners have had to learn the art. Of these yarns 395 spindles were spun at Stratherrick, 225 at Laggan & Auchindrome, & 310 at Beauly. Mr Mckay at Cyderhall in Sutherland, at the date of writing me his letter as above, sent up 1521 spindles of yarn which are now all examined, and found to be every way as well done as those by Mr Scott.

The cause of Mr Mckay's not having taught many more hands the art of spinning in the mountainous, and more interior parts of Sutherlands is that in winter these countries are inaccessible, and when he set about, early in this summer, he was prevented in the manner set forth in his and Mr McLeod's letter, and besides the fault of throwing away the public money in unnecessary expences for teaching spinning, Mr Ross at Lochbroom had added another of giving away wheels and reels to those already instructed and that have long been in the employment of the said Mr Mckay, thinking by that means to hurt him, and by such unfair methods to make a figure in the eyes of the Board by thus increasing the quantity of yarns made at his station, tho' in fact far distant from Lochbroom, and instead of raising new hands, he is only decoying the old experienced spinners with the public's utensils and money.

All of which I beg you will please to lay before the Honorable Board of Trustees and when considered you will be so good as to let me know what shall be done with the flax I have already prepared conform to agreement in March 1759, that can now be got spun up with the agents, and their spinning mistresses engaged, and with the wheels and reels not disposed of.

APPENDIX

NOTE ON THE MANUFACTURE OF LINEN

It may be helpful to sketch the key steps in the manufacture of linen, an industry now virtually extinct in Scotland. There were five main steps from raw material to finished product.

Flax was harvested by pulling. Though it could be and was grown in Scotland on some scale, most flax used in the industry was imported, either from Holland or Russia. Scottish farmers disliked flax as a scourging crop, and one with uncertain yields: despite frequent attempts to encourage the growth of more flax in Scotland, these had little long-term significance.[2]

The next stage was to prepare the flax for spinning. The seed had to be 'rippled' out of the heads, and then the flax was loosely retied, and taken for steeping under water in river backwaters or in lint pots, specially-made pits. The purpose of retting, the name of this process, was to allow the outer bark to begin to separate. The flax was then taken out, dried, and beaten with mallets ('scutching') so as to remove the bark entirely. The final exercise was that of 'heckling', the combing of the stem so as to release the fibres, a dusty, demanding task.

When the fibre was ready, it was spun up on a spinning-wheel, the yarn being measured by winding on a reel, and then sold for manufacture into thread or cloth. This was exclusively a female task, some spinners working full-time, others not, but an activity in which many households were involved. Sometimes the finished yarn was sold in an open market to weavers and manufacturers, but increasingly the latter gave out flax and then collected the yarn back, the spinner being paid for her spinning rather than the yarn. To prevent embezzlement, the yarn received back was weighed to make sure that it tallied with the weight of the flax given out.

The yarn was then woven into cloth on a handloom. Whereas spinning was a female occupation in the eighteenth century, handloom weaving was a male preserve. If the weaver were an aspirant to better-quality work, he took the precaution of boiling the yarn to remove the dirt which the spinners' fingers had imparted. He also made sure that the yarn he used, whatever the type of fabric he was to weave, was of a consistent quality and free from knots. The cloth from his loom could be sold brown (unbleached) or white (bleached).

It had first to be inspected for a small fee by an official (the 'stampmaster') of the Board of Trustees for Fisheries and Manufactures, who checked for the consistency of weave, it being a well-known malpractice to put the best work on the outside of the folded web. The stampmaster also measured the length and breadth of the cloth, which were marked on the end of the cloth, and stamped it with a thistle stamp showing his name and the location of his office. Should a buyer find deficiencies, he was entitled to compensation not from the weaver but from the stampmaster himself, which was intended as an incentive to the official to do his duty carefully.

The final stage was the bleaching and finishing of the cloth. At its simplest, bleaching involved a programme of steeping of the cloth in an alkaline solution, washing it out in clean water, and then applying a dilute acid, this being repeated until the cloth was thoroughly clean and 'white'. This process could take, depending on the weather, as many as five to eight weeks. The cloth was then either beaten with mallets ('beetling') or put through the cylinder (a species of mangle), to get the surface as smooth as possible.

Source Endnotes

1 The question of whether the bounty would be renewed was becoming of pressing concern. Tod reported in Mar. that there were 'many unforeseen difficulties . . . [and] that

the last resolution of the Ministry seemed to be that the Bounty on Irish linen [exported] should be discontinued and the Bounty on British reduced to 1d per yard and that no other fund could be given for the whole British than the Scots window tax': SRO, NG1/1/12, BOTM 26 Mar. 1753.

2 Flax from the Baltic was imported in bundles of 12, 9 or 6 heads. The best was generally reckoned to be the growth of the province of Marienburg (Marienburg Clean), followed by Drujaniar Rakitzer, with the lowest quality known as Badstup or paternoster.

13

HOME INDUSTRIES IN THE HIGHLANDS AND ISLANDS, REPORT TO THE BOARD OF AGRICULTURE, 1914

Source: William Robert Scott, *Report to the Board of agriculture for Scotland on home industries in the Highlands and Islands 1914* (H.M. Stationary off., Neil & Co., 1914), 77–86, 106, 190.

EDITORIAL HEADNOTE

William Robert Scott's *Report to the Board of Agriculture*, just before the First World War, is a detailed snapshot of Scotland's 'traditional' industries. Scott, from the Economic History department at St Andrews University, declared the efforts of the British Linen Company a failure, suggesting that there was relatively little enthusiasm for a scheme dedicated to the Highlands. His key interest was in 'native' industries, and he suggests linen was imposed on the north and east of Scotland. He was far more enthusiastic about knitting, tweed, wool, hosiery and kelp. In this extract, however, he analyses some of the issues of the linen industry, which acts as a complement to doc. 12, nevertheless concluding that despite the problems, women could support themselves and pay off husbands' and sons' debts. The remainder of the extract focuses on the traditional industries and their successes and situates women in the workforce of these industries.

D. LABOUR IN THE MAKING OF TWEED

The accounts in the foregoing pages of the methods of producing tweed and of the organisation of the industry will have afforded glimpses of the condition of the workers. This aspect of the industry is of such interest that it is worthy of more detailed treatment. From the point of view of employment, tweedmaking is an occupation for women. It is only in weaving, save in exceptional cases, that male labour is used. Sometimes old men, or those who are unable to do other work, help in the preliminary processes, such as teasing the wool. In St Kilda able-bodied men assist the women in this work. Spinning is women's work. Weaving,

DOI: 10.4324/9781003676669-14

on the other hand, is divided between the sexes. In Harris, nine out of ten weavers are women; while in Lewis, in Shetland, and on the mainland most of the weavers are men.

The nominal earnings are all reducible to a piecework basis. Weavers receive a rate per "long yard," per yard or per foot in different districts. In the Long Island, they can make 15s. for a week of about sixty hours. In the other processes a woman of average skill can earn 10s. in the same time. When the wool comes from the croft, and its value is deducted from the selling price of the tweed, the balance which remains, after the payment of expenses, would give 11s. 6d. a week under similar conditions. These are the figures for Harris; they are lower in Uist and Lewis, and considerably less in Shetland. In the latter case they seem to conform to the rates in the hosiery trade.

. . . Mechanical production has become so general that people think in terms of the factory system. To realise the position of the tweed worker, it is incumbent on the inquirer to think himself into the conditions of the domestic system. Home work in cities has acquired an evil reputation, but that is due to the city, not to the work in itself. If the house of a crofter or cottar is of some degree of comfort, there is no reason why some humble industry should not be carried on in it. In very many cases, the land cannot give full employment to those who live on it. Thus the women have time to spare beyond that required for their household duties. Without home industries or industries in the vicinity of their homes, there would be a waste of human energy, and it is at least as important to economise this as mechanical powers or raw materials.

Women in the lower ranks of industry in towns tend to suffer. If they work in factories, those of them who have young children cannot attend to them themselves; and, in spite of crèches and other agencies, one is inclined to think that the children suffer, and hence the State in the next generation. On the other hand, the female home worker in a town is too often deprived of light and air. She has to work long hours, her remuneration is low, and her surroundings are bad. The female factory worker is better paid – as far as merely nominal wages go-as compared with the Highland spinner. In the Dundee jute factories, during a fifty-five hours' week, women make 11s., 12s., 14s., 16s., and sometimes 20s. a week. The average rate all over is said to be 15s. a week, that is 25 per cent. more than the Harris spinner. The purchasing power differs greatly. Necessaries are cheap in the Hebrides, but the simple luxuries are relatively dear. There is a great difference, in favour of the Highlander, in rent. No doubt this expense is usually regarded as falling on the husband or son, but the truer view, especially where the women contribute materially to the income of the household, is to regard the family earnings as the unit. Then, again, the woman worker in a town has to spend small sums, which come to an appreciable aggregate amount, in various ways which are not required in the Highlands. So that, though on the whole it may not be possible to make an exact comparison of real wages of women workers in the Highlands and in the towns, it may be concluded that those of the former are of considerable value to them in their situation. Apart from the question of earnings, the tweed-worker has some advantages from her occupation. Her surroundings are healthful. In the older type of cottage she had an abundance of air, even though it was mixed with peat smoke. Her occupation was interesting in itself, and of such a nature that it could be interrupted to permit of attention being given to any household task that required it. In the long winter evenings work could be carried on while any neighbour talked or sang or told interminable Gaelic tales. For those who are able to appreciate the simple and satisfying things in life, an occupation of this kind has much to recommend it. In it there is not the pressure and the speeding up of the factory, while there is a sufficient element of skill and artistic work in some of the processes to enable the tweed-maker to take a pride and a pleasure in what she produces. No doubt she suffers from what Professor Marshall calls "monotony of life," but here one has to distinguish between two different things. To a person brought up in a city, Highland life would be unbearably monotonous; but to the people themselves there is a wide range of interests, arising out of the varied life of the township, which they find pleasant and even exciting. Then, too, they preserve the almost lost art – at least in this country of introducing what Schiller called "the play-instinct" into their work. Thus, in tweed-making, "the waulking party" is not only the finishing of the web—it is also a social gathering of great interest to those who participate in it.

There are, however, signs that the younger women are feeling the insistent call of the great centres of population. Some go to domestic service, and many take part in fish-curing. During the years 1909 to 1911, 6736 women and girls were employed regularly in the latter occupation for periods varying between five weeks and twenty-nine weeks. This work brings high money earnings to those who are skilled at it, and it provides variety and change of scene, since the herring-gutters follow the shoals of fish. This employment cannot be described as an agreeable one, and it requires good physique to stand the exposure to the weather which it involves. Tweed-making, on the other hand, is more suited to those who have home ties, and it can be continued by workers far past middle life. In some quarters it is thought that spinning is not a healthy occupation. Possibly this might be so, if women worked at it for long hours all the year round. As a rule, tweed-making is a winter occupation, and the workers would be a good deal in their houses in any case. Most of them have duties which take them out of doors for a short time almost daily; and, in the industry itself, if vegetable dyes are used, these must be gathered, and in all cases dyeing and waulking take place in the open air. If work is continued into the spring and summer, other processes can be performed outside, when the weather permits it. The chief dangers arise in an old cottage which may be insanitary, or in an improved one where the windows are kept closed. It seems a great pity that these workers, in the latter type of house, should lose the great advantage they could have in pure air, by refusing to admit it. An "open-window" campaign to be needed in some districts where the cottages are good.

The quite exceptionably protracted period of the efficient working life has a bearing both on the social condition of the people and on their real earnings. It is not uncommon to find women well over seventy years of age still busy at the making of tweed, and the Lochbroom Home Industries received webs from workers of ninety years of age. A decline in the amount received by this Association during the last few years is attributed to the effect of Old Age Pensions, which shows that a considerable proportion of those who sent tweeds for sale were able to benefit, and they worked shorter hours. Weaving, too, shows a remarkably long working life. There are several at work who are well over seventy years of age, and one who is more than eighty produces a special cloth, which is in demand. for summer wear by ladies. A remarkable case, relating to a woman weaver in Yorkshire, was recorded in the Press. She was ninety years of age, and had helped in the woollen industry in her own home since she was four years old – if this account is correct, a working life of eighty-six years is extraordinary. While the hand-made tweed trade is clearly an occupation at which people can work till very late in life, the prevalence of elderly workers suggests the reflection that as these become incapacitated their places may not be taken by others, and thus the supply of labour will gradually become exhausted. The future demand for labour cannot be predicted with any degree of precision, since it will depend on the advantages offered by all other occupations in a certain district or even over a wide area. It appears that what has weighed with younger persons, who refrained from taking up tweed-making, were the various uncertainties grouped together under "inconstancy of employment." Of late there has been a tendency for young people to begin tweed-making – thus one hears of girls in their teens spinning regularly and of youths learning weaving.

Another aspect of the condition of labour in tweed-making deserves mention chiefly in relation to a remark of Adam Smith. In a well-known passage he states that "the advantage which is gained by saving the time commonly lost in passing from one sort of work to another is much greater than we should at first view be apt to imagine it. It is impossible to pass very quickly from one kind of work to another that is carried on in a different place, and with quite different tools. A country weaver who cultivates a small farm must lose a good deal of time in passing from his loom to the field, and from the field to his loom." Whatever may have been the conditions in Adam Smith's time, the modern tweed-worker who has some land is able to make a better division of his time than that in the example in the Wealth of Nations. Tweed-making is done either by those who have little land to cultivate, or else by others who own a croft, during the winter. In most cases, if the labour were not employed in this way it would not be used at all, since there is no demand for it in the districts where the people live. Most of them are not able to seek work in the Lowlands. Besides, as J. S. Mill shows, there appear to be some people who can change from one occupation to another and who seem to need change. This appears to be so in the Celtic temperament, at least in its present environment. It seems to want that inertia which starts slowly but continues long rather it begins quickly; and, while for a short period it can work long hours most intensely, a time comes before long when a change of occupation is needed. It is for these reasons that specialisation need not be expected to occupy a large place in Highland labour economy.

In view of the relatively high price of Shetland wool, the question of preserving its characteristics becomes one of considerable consequence. . . . Certainly, as far as the hosiery trade is concerned, any measures which would maintain and improve the quality of the wool would be beneficial to the industry. On the other hand, a deterioration in the character of the fleeces would have serious consequences for this industry, and also for that of Shetland tweed, since much of the reputation of both depends on the softness and fineness of the wool.

In Shetland it is the custom to pluck the wool from the sheep. This is known as "rowing." It is then washed, and afterwards it is either sent to the mainland to be spun at a mill or it is hand-carded and hand-spun at home. Shetland wool is comparatively easy to card by hand, and this process introduces certain social peculiarities which have important consequences when an attempt is made to calculate the earnings of the workers in the hosiery trade. On the western side of the largest island ("the mainland") the function, known as a "cairdin'," occupies an important place in the life of the younger members of the community. In fact, the faces of the spinners always brighten when "a cairdin" is mentioned – those of the more youthful knitters with pleasant anticipations, those of older workers with kindly recollections. The manner of conducting this combination of work and play is as follows: – When a family has wool ready for carding, "a cairdin'" is announced. Women gather at the cottage about four o'clock in the afternoon. They have tea, and then work together at carding till suppertime, which is usually at eleven o'clock. Then the young men arrive and dancing begins, which is continued till the early hours of the following morning.

It must be noted, however, that besides machine-carding and machine-spinning, and hand-carding and hand-spinning, there is a third alternative, namely, machine-carding of the wool in Shetland and its subsequent spinning by hand. This operation is performed at Voe in the parish of Delting, where a small but complete plant, consisting of a teaser and carding-machine driven by a small engine, has been erected by Messrs Thos. M. Adie & Sons. There are arguments both in favour and against the carding of native Shetland wool by machinery. Messrs Adie urge that the starting of this mill has enabled them to obtain more hand-spinning than had been the case previously. On the other side, it is contended by many experienced workers that the fibre of the wool is cut or otherwise injured by machine carding, and that some of the finer filaments are lost. Certainly there appears to be a disposition amongst the most careful spinners to avoid machine-carding as being detrimental to the character and quality of their work . . .

After the wool has been hand-carded or machine-carded at Voe, it is spun, and is then ready for knitting. Some knitters use all hand-spun yarn, others all mill-spun, or, again, others change from one to another according to circumstances or to the type of garment they are making. The mill-spun yarn is of two kinds: one is obtained by the crofter sending his own wool to be spun; the other is bought from a mill by the merchant in Shetland who gives it out to be knitted by the women.

The prevalence of the industry is most striking. In 1901, out of 7445 females of ten years of age and upwards who were returned as engaged in occupations, no less than 5045 were working at hosiery. These, it must be remembered, were the women who were working with the object of obtaining a sale for their knitting; there were very many more who worked primarily for their own use or for that of their families, a considerable number of whom no doubt sold some articles occasionally. Again, there are subsidiary industries, dependent on the hosiery trade. One of these is that known as "the dressing of Shetland hosiery." When the goods have been knitted, they require to be washed before being offered for sale to the public. This is sometimes done by the maker, sometimes by the merchant who has bought the goods. Again, after a Shetland shawl or other knitted article has been in use, it requires to be cleaned from time to time; and, if it is washed in the usual way, it is liable to shrink-or, as the knitters graphically describe it, to jump.

. . . It seems that, with the hearty co-operation of the knitters in Fair Isle, a prosperous little industry could be built up there. The women have a speciality out of which a good deal could be made. One can see in the designs and colours of Fair Isle hosiery that the workers just fail to secure rich and harmonious effects. Provided they were willing to accept teaching, it would, in my opinion, be worth investigating the characteristics of the continental wool-work of the sixteenth century, in order to discover what was best and most artistic in the original type from which Fair Isle hosiery was derived. This should be modified by any subsequent real improvements. In this way designs and colouring could be taught for which there should be a good market. Such teaching would be of little use unless the knitting was made into articles for which there is a demand. If what is really distinctive in the present designs were preserved; and, at the same time, these were modified to the uses of the present day, and made in rich and harmonious colours, there would be a good sale for such knitted goods amongst ladies and children. . . . In this scheme the question of design is essential. It would be necessary to improve the present type without an abrupt breach of continuity. What, it appears to me, is required is such instruction as would enable the workers to continue to produce a speciality; but one for which there would be a demand on the ground of its picturesqueness, not merely on that of its singularity. Finally, what has already been said regarding the improvement of the breed of sheep in Shetland also applies to Fair Isle.

Returning to the consideration of Shetland hosiery proper, the articles made are very numerous. The most artistic work is the knitting of fine lace shawls and scarves. The wool of these is spun very finely and great skill is shown in the variety of patterns. It is remarkable that the design develops during the progress of the work. Many of the most skilled knitters cannot give details of the pattern they intend to make it simply grows under their hand as they knit; and yet, at the end, when it is examined, it will be found to be well balanced and satisfying. This uniqueness in each piece of good work is the best guarantee that these fine shawls will not be supplanted by machine-made imitations. Some of the best of these fine shawls command high prices. They sell, retail, at £20 to £30.

[Lace]. The impediment to progress arises from the delay that may elapse in the securing of orders. Hence the workers suffer from "inconstancy of employment."

This characteristic is even more marked in the Tarbert lace school. A woman makes a piece of lace, and she has to wait for payment till it is sold. If a long period elapses, this is disheartening, especially where the money is required. Thus there is a certain waste of the training given, since the girls tend to take up other occupations where there is greater certainty of pay and where the amount earned is paid when it has become due. For instance, last year one girl made lace worth £16 in six months, but gave up lace-making to go into domestic service. . . .

The real problem in the lace industry is the prompt payment of the worker. This requires capital. In Ireland the same difficulty was experienced. Up to 1893 the market for Irish lace was described as "irregular and uncertain." In that year Her Excellency the Countess of Aberdeen purchased a business for the sale of lace which had been established in 1847. Capital was provided by the formation of a company (which was not to pay dividends) through an overdraft from the bank. With these funds the managers were able to pay promptly for lace, and also what is of almost equal importance-to improve designs and to keep in touch with the market. A plan of this kind seems worthy the consideration of those who are interested in the existing Scottish lace industries. The guarantee of a sufficient amount of working capital, in the form of a loan from a bank, would not involve a serious responsibility, if divided amongst several persons. But it would be necessary that someone who had business experience should be ready to advise, since allowance would have to be made for the risk of unsaleable stock and for the charge for interest during the time which would elapse between the payment of the workers and the date at which the school received cash for the lace they made. In this way the women who were trained would have an inducement to continue at work; they could count on early payment for good work, and they would be encouraged to make the most of their time. . . .

With regard to St Kilda tweed, Mr A. G. Ferguson, 93 Hope Street, Glasgow, calculates that a man and his wife working together would make a web of St Kilda tweed of 30 yards in 5 weeks. The woman works 12 hours a day, that is, 360 hours, while the man does all the weaving (which takes 48 hours), and helps in the teasing and carding. Thus, as regards time, the St Kilda figures agree with those of Shetland, when hand-carding is included in both places. . . .

THE CENSUS AND HOME INDUSTRIES

In so far as the census records the numbers of those engaged in home industries and in rural industries, the figures are of great interest and importance. Interpretation of the data is likely to err unless it is remembered that some of these occupations are carried on in conjunction with others. Thus the worker who spends his time on two or more industries should record as his occupation that one which is his main employment, and thus there is no trace of his other work in the figures. . . .

Omitting the kelp industry (as to which the census supplies no particulars), the occupations in which the people work at home are the hosiery manufacture and tweed-making. Comparing the returns for the former in 1901 and 1911, a great decline in the number of workers is shown. This occurs in Shetland, Orkney, Sutherland, Ross and Cromarty, and Inverness. On the other hand, there is an increase in Caithness and Argyll, but the figures are small-being only 10 in 1901 and 31 in 1911 for the two counties. It is in Shetland that the falling off is most remarkable from the numbers affected. The total number of women returned as working at hosiery in 1901 was 5045; in 1911 there were 2782, a decrease of 2263. A part of this sum is no doubt represented by the increase of 1009 in female relatives working on farms and crofts," and by another increase of 210 in female fishcurers. It is far from easy to judge of the significance of these figures. The decline is certainly not a positive one (for almost the whole female population still works at hosiery), rather it indicates that, at the time the census was taken, a number of women who employed themselves at hosiery and another occupation expressed a preference for the latter in making their return.

No doubt the natural tendency of a woman who makes hosiery, and who works on a croft, is to enter herself under that industry on which she has been occupied for a few days before she fills her census form. Thus a late season would tend to increase the number returned as hosiery workers, while, conversely, an early one would reduce it. Or, activity in the hosiery trade in March would augment the total; a dull period then would reduce it. If one attempts to form a rough estimate of the number of women in Shetland who make hosiery for sale, Mr Anderson (of Anderson & Co., Lerwick, who has been in this trade for sixty-one years) calculates the whole number of knitters at 90 per cent. of the female population. This estimate is no doubt too high, but it is extraordinary at what an early age girls begin to knit goods for the market. As far as can be judged, the output in 1911 showed some increase as compared with that of 1901. This does not, however, involve an increase in the amount of labour at the later date, since the larger use of machine-spun yarn would dispense with a certain quantity of hand-work in spinning.

14

HUMBLE PETITION OF THE POOR SPINNERS, LEICESTER, 1788

Source: Humble Petition of the Poor Spinners, which on a very moderate calculation consist of Eighteen Thousand, Five Hundred, employed in the Town and Country aforesaid. Leicester, 1788, British Museum Tracts, B544; reprinted in B. L. Hutchins, *Women in Modern Industry*, (G. Bell and Sons, 1915), 270–71.

EDITORIAL HEADNOTE

The Humble Petition is a brief critique on spinning, women's special employment, being gradually moved to spinning mills. While these are covered in Vol. 2, it is useful to mention that women went to the mills as the first labour force. This did not help those who could not move, like the elderly, probably the poor who could lose settlement, and many wives and mothers. If men could find agricultural or other craftwork, moving was a challenging dilemma to families.

Sheweth, that the business of *Spinning,* in all its branches, hath ever been, time out of mind, the peculiar employment of women; insomuch that every single woman is called in law a *Spinster*; to which employment your Petitioners have been brought up, and by which they have hitherto earned their maintenance. That this employment above all others is suited to the condition and circumstances of the *Female Poor;* inasmuch as not only single women, but married ones also, can be employed in it consistently with the necessary cares of their families; for, the business being carried on in their own houses, they can at any time leave it when the care of their families requires their attendance, and can re-assume the work when family duty permits it; nay, they can, in many instances, carry on their work and perform their domestic duty at the same time; particularly in the case of attending a sick husband or child, or an aged parent . . .

It is therefore with great concern your Petitioners see that this antient employment is likely to be taken from them – an employment so consistent with civil liberty, so full of domestic comfort, and so favourable to a religious course of life. This we apprehend will be the consequences of so many spinning mills, now erecting after the model of the cotton mills. The work of the poor will be done by these engines, and they left without employment. . . .

DOI: 10.4324/9781003676669-15

The proprietors of the spinning mills do indeed tell your Petitioners that their children shall be employed after the manner of the children at the cotton mills. Your Petitioners have enquired what that manner is; and with grief of heart they find that a vast number of poor children are crowded together in an unhealthy place, have no time allowed them for recreation and exercise, are kept to work for ten or twelve hours together, and that in the night-time as well as by day; hereby they become cripples and emaciated beyond measure. That no care is taken of their morals, as your Petitioners can learn; though these very children are the means by which their masters are raised to wealth and honours too; for we have heard that a certain great *mill-monger* is newly *created* a knight though he was not *born* a gentleman. . . .

The adventurers are turning their cotton mills into jersey mills, and new ones are daily erecting; and our masters show what their expectations are by undervaluing our work and beating down our wages.

15

OBSERVATIONS ON THE LOSS OF WOOLLEN SPINNING, 1794

Source: A.B., Observations on the detriment that it is supposed must arise to the family of every cottager throughout the kingdom from the loss of woollen spinning by the introduction of machines for that work (np., 1794), 3–8, 10–11, 13, 14.

EDITORIAL HEADNOTE

The anonymous *Observations on Loss of Woollen Spinning*, published six years after doc. 14, continues the concern with the introduction of machines. A more detailed critique, it offers a description of women's work in the domestic system and illustrates the implications of the shift to machine spinning.

But neither the Wool-Combers nor the Manufacturers state the great Grievance of the Machines for spinning Wool which is most deeply felt by every day labourer, whose wife and children return home from the next market town with sad tidings, that the Wool-man puts out no more handwork (in many places they call it Jazy-work) or that they have carried their spinning home to the Wool-man who has set off seven-pence in a shilling.

This method of computing the pay for Jazy-work which is universal with the spinners, requires some explanation to those who are not conversant with it: Formerly every skain a spinner could run her wool to, she was paid one penny for it; of what the Comber calls coarse work, by spinning a pound weight; a moderate hand could make twelve skains, consequently her pay was then twelve-pence: many could run this pound to fourteen or fifteen skanes, when in proportion, she received her additional penny per skain, what the Comber calls fine Work, is paid much in the same proportion, for though they receive more if they spin tat wool to a greater number of skains, yet the time it takes brings it to nearly the same pay as the coarse work. The skain is measured by a reel round which the yarn winds a certain number of times. The woman puts on a table the number of skains she has spun to a pound; the Wool-man counts off seven, and pays her for the remaining five, six or seven skains that weigh into the pound: this he calls setting off

DOI: 10.4324/9781003676669-16

seven-pence in a shilling, thus receiving only five, six or seven-pence at most for what she knows when provisions were only half their present price, she used to receive one penny per skain. This deduction varies according to the demand for yarn, and sometimes pay is reduced to three-pence and the set-off is nine pence.

The Combers being men and boys may possibly turn to some other work, but it is not so with the wife and daughters of the day-labourer, whose occupation in a country parish where no particular manufactory is carried on, must be in their own dwelling; who deprived of the Woollen Spinning have non other employment, (except when they can go into the fields) to bring in any money towards support of the Family. To tell a poor woman with three, four, or five children, all under age at which farmers will employ them to set her children at work, where no Wool is to be had is a mockery of misery, and if it is in a neighbourhood distant from Machines, where some hand-work is still put out, the low price that is paid for her unwearied labour, of running with her children all day at the Wheel, disheartens her. The scanty fare it enables them to eat when the day's work is done, with want of firing makes her at length prefer breaking a hedge for her own fuel, and often for sale to the Village Tradesman, and bringing up her children to the same idle habits.

Many things combine to make the Hand Spinning of Wool, the most desirable work for the cottager's wife and children. – A Wooden Wheel costing 2s. for each person, and with one Reel costing 3 s. set up the family. The Wool-man either supplies the with Wool by the pound or more at a time, as he can depend on their care, or they take it on his account from the chandler's shop, where they buy their food and raiment. No stock is required, and when they carry back their pound of Wool spun, they have no further concern in it. Children from five years old can run at the Wheel, it is a very wholesome employment for them, keeps them in constant exercise, and upright: persons can work at it till a very advanced age.

But from the establishment of the Spinning Machines in many Counties where I was last Summer, no Hand Work could be had, the consequence of which is the whole maintenance of the family devolves on the father, and instead of six or seven shillings a-week, which a wife and four children could add by their wheels, his weekly pay is all they have to depend upon. The children are trained to perfect idleness there being no work in which to employ them. The end of this is theft and a train of vices when grown up, for they never after like a quiet house and continued occupation; another advantage of this work was that until these Machines were introduced, it was equally to be obtained in every County, unlike every manufactory, a child with a Wheel was never thrown absolutely out of bread, by change of place when grown up. – But all this is altered. I went into a very neat Work House in a Town in Wiltshire, (where Weaving was carried on in the town and found all hands idle. I expressed my surprise, the Master said it was much to be lamented, but that a Wool-Combing and a Spinning Machine, had been lately put up, since which the Parish found it more to their interest, to let the people in the house be perfectly idle, than to let them spin Wool, which used to be their employment. In the cottages I heard the same thing. I then walked to the Machines, and with some difficulty gained admittance: there I saw both the Combing Machine and Spinning Jenny.[1] The Combing Machine was put in motion by a Wheel turned either by water or steam. The frames were supplies by a child with Wool, and as the wheel turned, flakes of ready combed Wool dropped off a cylinder into a trough, these were taken up by a girl of about fourteen years old, who placed them on the Spinning Jenny, which has a number of horizontal beams of wood, on each of which may be fifty bobbins. One such girl sets these bobbins all in motion by turning a wheel at the end of the beam, a wire then catches up a flake of Wool, spins it, and gathers it upon each bobbin. The girl again turns the wheel, and another fifty flakes are taken up and Spun. This is done every minute without intermission, so that probably one girl turning that wheel, may do the work of One Hundred Hands at the Wheel at least. About twenty of these sets of bobbins, were I judge at work in one room. Most of these Manufactories are many stories high, and the rooms much larger than this I was in. Struck with the impropriety of even so many as the twenty girls I saw, without any woman presiding over them, I enquired of the master if he was married, why his Wife was not present? He said he was not a married man, and that many parents did object to send their girls, but that the poverty of others, and not having any work to set them to, left him not at any loss for hands. I must do all the parties justice to say, that these girls appeared neat and orderly[2]: yet at best, I cannot but fear the taking of such young persons from the eyes of their parents, and thus herding them together with men and boys, must bring up a dissolute race of poor.

These Machines then once set up, and the expence of them does not appear very great, 20 Girls do the work of 2,000 Women and Children, and when these girls are of age to go into a Farmer's Service, how can they endure the fatigue and exposure to weather, necessary to their situation. Numbers confined together in one room cannot make them so hardy and strong, as running at the wheel in a cold cottage, and frequently at the outside of their door in the open air. – If they marry, they can neither teach their children to work, or spin, or bring in any earnings to maintain them. Who then shall patch the cloaths, mend the shoes, and oeconomize their little store?

Shut up from morning till night, except when they are sent home for their meals, these girls are ignorant of, and unhandy at every domestic employment, whereas if at her wheel in her mother's cottage, the girl assist in every occupation of the family. She lights the faggots, nurses the young children, gleans in the harvest, takes charge of the house in her mother's necessary absence to the shop, or when she can get work at neighbouring house, becoming an assistant to her parents in sickness and old age, in her turn a good wife to a day labourer, a fit mother for his family she lives with those to whom she will feel an affection towards them: but a girl taken from six years old to sixteen, and employed at the machines, can know none of these habits; at her return to meals, she will bring to the surrounding listeners of their frugal board, all the evil she has learnt, and doubtless evil she will learn, for unlike a school, where at least the mistress will not teach the girl vice, and numbers frequently emulate to good; here, numbers who are solely collected to do their task, and whose morals are in no way an object to their employer, must have their natural tendency to corrupt. In this state of mind, and debility of constitution as fifteen or sixteen, these girls are dismissed to the cottage of their parents, for it no longer suits the manufacturer to employ them; younger children will answer his purpose at a cheaper rate. – Now – What are they fit for? – Thus it appears that the wife and daughter of a cottager are likely by the introduction of these Machines to become enervated and depraved, idle and pilfering.

But should it not be the case, and their mind and health be unimpaired, the loss of Hand Spinning to the cottage obliges the labourer to press for an increase of his wages to maintain the family. – This once obtained, perhaps an increase only adequate to his real wants: – will he stop there? – No, – his success in this attempt will make him hope to go further, and having once gained by shrinking from his work, he will try it again and again, until Farmers and Labourers become at perpetual variance. . . .

If these are the miseries that result from the Machines to the day-labourer's wife and children during his life, what must be their lot when deprived by his death of all support, but the pittance their own industry affords them. A widow could assist to maintain herself and children by her spinning when she was paid 1 d. for every skain; but now, she must become a parish pauper, a wretched inhabitant of a Work-house, if one is established in her parish. – I say, wretched, not from the nature of the Work-house in itself, for I should deem it, if well attended to, the best general mode of relieving the poor. But left solely to the care of farmers, and neglected as they almost universally are in country parishes, I fear they are instruments of oppression instead of relief. By many persons even of information who have not well considered the nature of a Work-house, it is held forth as a terror to the poor, and turned into a House of Correction. . . . Now as this method of relieving the poor is becoming daily more general, I must observe, that if such houses are well regulated, there is no work to which the objects proper to inhabit them can be put so eligible as the Hand Wheel. These Houses should be a receptacle only for the widow and infant orphan, the aged and infirm. . . . The Woollen Wheel would for these hours not employed in the domestic concerns of the family, afford the real poor the most wholesome and useful work. . . .

Where Lace making prevails in parishes, the Family of a Spinner, may always be distinguished by their superiorly neat and healthy appearance. The wretched Objects of Lace-making, would deter any feeling mind from wishing to establish this work in the place of Jazey. Sedentary and always leaning over a pillow they exist on Gin and Opium, snuff and Tea; half the children they have die infants, from the close attention they are obliged to pay to their bobbins, and those who live, are destitute of health and energy. Even this miserable occupation, from the recent Importation of Lace and Patent Loom Work in imitation, produces but a trifling gain.

Source Endnotes

1 AS I had not any view but my own information at the time I saw these Machines, I did not take such accurate notice as I now wish I had done, of the number of bobbins at work to One Girl's Wheel, therefore I do not pretend to be exact in my calculation, but only state the numbers from memory.

2 It is to be wished that some favourable account could be given of all such Manufactories, but in some it is very far otherwise, as is too well-known to many enquirers to need anything further to be said on the subject.

Part 2

INDUSTRY AND WORKSHOPS

16

APPRENTICESHIP INDENTURE IN THE METAL TRADES, 1781

Sarah Osbourne

Source: Sarah Osbourne, apprenticeship indenture in the metal trades, Overseers of the Poor, Harborne, Warwickshire, 1781. DRO 61/7/8. Harborne Parish Apprenticeship Indentures.

EDITORIAL HEADNOTE

This section looks first at the metal trades where women worked across the spectrum, and girls like Sarah Osbourne were placed as apprentices by parish officials in the English Black Country to learn a trade in these industries. Like many (see doc. 24) she was sent to learn both housewifery and chapefiling, both of which could have stood her in good stead on completion as a wife and metal worker. The image of her apprenticeship is typical of many, using a printed form and requiring the master to keep her from becoming a charge on the poor law.

DOI: 10.4324/9781003676669-18

THIS Indenture, made the [illegible] Day of [illegible] in the [illegible] Year of the Reign of our Sovereign Lord [illegible] by the Grace of God, of Great-Britain, France, and Ireland, King, Defender of the Faith, and ſo forth; and in the Year of our Lord One thouſand ſeven Hundred and [illegible] Witneſſeth That [illegible] Church-Wardens of the Pariſh of [illegible] in the [illegible] And [illegible] Overſeers of the Poor of the ſaid Pariſh, by and with the conſent of his Majeſty's Juſtices of the Peace for the ſaid [illegible] whoſe Names are hereunto ſubſcribed, have put and placed, and by theſe Preſents do put and place [illegible] a poor Child of the ſaid Pariſh, Apprentice to [illegible] with h[illegible] to dwell and ſerve from the Day of the Date of theſe Preſents, until the ſaid Apprentice ſhall accompliſh h[illegible] full Age of [illegible] according to the Statute in that Caſe made and provided. During all which Term the ſaid Apprentice h[illegible] ſaid M[illegible] faithfully ſhall ſerve in all lawful Buſineſs, according to h[illegible] Power, Wit, and Ability; and honeſtly, orderly, and obediently, in all things demean and behave h[illegible] ſelf towards h[illegible] ſaid M[illegible] and all h[illegible] during the ſaid Term. And the ſaid [illegible] for h[illegible]ſelf, h[illegible] Executors, and Adminiſtrators, doth Covenant and Grant, to and with the ſaid Church-Wardens and Overſeers, and every of them, their and every of their Executors and Adminiſtrators, and their and every of their Succeſſors, for the Time being, by theſe Preſents, That the ſaid [illegible] the ſaid Apprentice in [illegible] And ſhall and will during all the Term aforeſaid, find, provide, and allow, unto the ſaid Apprentice, meet, competent, and ſufficient Meat, Drink, and Apparel, Lodging, Waſhing, and all other Things, neceſſary and fit for an Apprentice. And alſo ſhall and will ſo provide for the ſaid Apprentice, that ſhe be not any way a Charge to the ſaid Pariſh, or Pariſhioners of the ſame; but of and from all Charge ſhall and will ſave the ſaid Pariſh and Pariſhioners harmleſs and indemnified during the ſaid Term. In witneſs whereof, the Parties abovesaid to theſe preſent Indentures, interchangeably have put their Hands and Seals, the Day and Year above-written.

Sealed and deliver'd in the Preſence of

WE whoſe Names are ſubſcribed, Juſtices of the Peace for the [illegible] aforeſaid, [illegible] conſent to the putting forth of the aboveſaid Apprentice, according to the intent and Meaning of the above Indenture.

Image 2 Sarah Osbourne apprenticeship indenture. 781. DRO 61/7/8. Harborne Parish Apprenticeship Indentures.

This indenture made the twenty-fifth day of October in the Twenty-first Year of the Reign of our Sovereign Lord George the Third by the Grace of God of Great-Britain, France, and Ireland, King, Defender of the Faith, and so forth, in the Year of our Lord One thousand seven hundred and eighty-one. Witnesseth that William Sibboth and George Stansby, Churchwardens of the parish of Harbourne In the County of Stafford and James Joyner and Thomas Eliot Overseers of the Poor of the said Parish, by and with the consent of His Majesty's Justices of the Peace for the said County whose Names are heretunto subscribed, have put and placed, and by these Presents do put and place Sarah Osbourne a poor child of the said parish, Apprentice to Mark Pearsall of the County of Warwick Bucklechapemaker with him to dwell and serve from the Day of the Date of these Presents, until the said Apprentice shall accomplish her full age of twenty-one years according to the Statute in that Case made and provided. During all which Term the said apprentice her Master faithfully shall serve in all lawful Business, according to her Power, Wit, and Ability; and honestly, orderly, and obediently in all things demean and behave herself towards her said master and all his during the said Term. And the said Mark Pearsall for himself, his Executors and Administrators doth Covenant and Grant, to and with the said Overseers and Churchwardens . . . That the said Mark Pearsall for himself, his Executors and Administrators and every of their Successors, for the Time being doth covenant and grant, to and with the said Church-wardens and Overseers, and everyone of them and their Executors and Administrators, and their and every of their Successors in the arts of housewifery and chapefiling and polishing shall Teach and Instruct or cause to be taught and instructed in the best way and manner that he can. And shall and will during the Term aforsesaid, find, provide and allow unto the said Apprentice, meet, competent Meat, Drink and Apparel, Lodging, Washing, and all other Things, necessary and fit for an Apprentice. And also shall and will provide for the said Apprentice, that she be not in any way a Charge to the said Parish, or the parishioners of the same; but of and from all Charge shall and will save the said Parish and Parishioners harmless and indemnify during said Term. In witness whereof, the Parties abovesaid to these present Indentures interchangeably have put their Hands and Seals, the Day and Year above written.

(all signed except Sarah Osbourne)

17

ON PINS AND NAILS, BIRMINGHAM, 1783

William Hutton

Source: William Hutton, 'On Pins and Nails', in *The History of Birmingham*, 1783, 6th ed. (James Gunn: 1836), 190–92.

EDITORIAL HEADNOTE

William Hutton (1723–1815), best known for his *History of Birmingham*, arrived in Birmingham in 1750 having served an apprenticeship in a Derby silk mill and then another to a stocking maker, where he stayed, unhappily, as a journeyman for a few years. Poorly educated, he lived with his sister Catherine, who had been in service with Calvinist ministers and was well-read and resourceful. She stimulated his interest in reading, and he took up learning the trade of a bookbinder. He started selling books at Nottingham market, then in 1750 moved to Birmingham to set up as a bookseller, stationer and bookbinder, where he flourished. At age fifty-six he took up writing, and his *History* (1782) was the first book he published. He became a consummate authority on his adopted town and fondly recounted: 'Birmingham, like a compassionate nurse, not only draws our persons, but our esteem, from the place of our nativity, and fixes it upon herself: I might add, I was hungry, and she fed me; thirsty, and she gave me drink; a stranger, and she took me in. I approached her with reluctance, because I did not know her; I shall leave her with reluctance, because I do' (*History*, iv). These extracts describe the pin and needle trades, and like many sources, assume the man is the maker, although women were an integral part of these and other metal trades.

PINS

Are made from the best brass wire, which is drawn by steam power, by being passed successively through a set of holes in a steel plate, each hole being less than the preceding one. The wire goes through many annealings in the course

DOI: 10.4324/9781003676669-19

of this process, and is cleaned with aquafortis. The heads are formed of fine wire, much less in proportion to the weight of the pin. It is wound into ringlets, similar to a brace spring. They are cut off with shears, to the proper length. This is a nice operation, and requires much skill to perform with the required precision. A man will earn £2 per week at this simple operation, and although several of the wires are cut at once, he will rarely miss cutting them exact. The wire to form the body, is drawn out into straight lengths from the coil, and is then cut into other lengths for the pointer. A circular file, turned by steam power, is used to form the point; this is also a nice operation. As many as can be held conveniently, are pointed at once, and cut off to a guage [sic] the length the pin is to be, both ends being pointed first. The wire is again pointed, and again cut, till the length is exhausted and a new one taken. Children are employed in putting on the heads, mostly under the superintendence of women. It is performed by a simple process, and the head is made secure by being struck by a small stamp. The pin then passes through the process of cleaning in aquafortis, and is then boiled in a solution of tin, which gives them the white appearance they have when bought. They are afterwards dried in bran, and are then weighed, or put upon paper ready for sale.

NAILS

In most occupations, the profit of the master and the journeyman bear a proportion. If the former is able to figure in genteel life, the latter is able to figure in silk stockings. If the master can afford to allow upon his goods ten per cent discount for money, the servant can afford to squander half his wages. In a worn-down trade, where the tides of profit are reduced to a low ebb, and where imprudence sets her foot upon the premises, the master and the man starve together. Only half this is our present case. The art of nail-making is one of the most ancient among us; we safely charge its antiquity with four figures. We cannot consider it a trade in, so much as of Birmingham; for we have but few nailmakers left in the town; our nailers are chiefly masters, and rather opulent. The manufacturers are so scattered round the country, that we cannot travel far, in any direction, out of the sound of the nail-hammer. But Birmingham, like a powerful magnet, draws the produce of the anvil to herself.

When I first approached her [Birmingham], from Walsall, in 1741, I was surprised at the number of blacksmiths' shops upon the road; and could not conceive how a country, though populous, could support so many people of the same occupation. In some of these shops I observed one or more females, stripped of their upper garment, and not overcharged with their lower, wielding the hammer with all the grace of the sex. The beauties of their face were rather eclipsed by the smut of the anvil; or, in poetical phrase, the tincture of the forge had taken possession of those lips, which might have been taken by the kiss. Struck with the novelty, I inquired, "Whether the ladies in this country shod horses?" but was answered, with a smile, "They are nailers."

A fire without heat, a nailer of a fair complexion, or one who despises the tankard, are equally rare among them. His whole system of faith may be comprised in one article. That the slender twopenny mug, used in a public-house, is deceitful above all things, and desperately wicked.

While the master reaps the harvest of plenty, the work man submits to the scanty gleanings of penury, a thin habit, an early old age, and a figure bending towards the earth. Plenty comes not near his dwelling, except of rags, and of children. But few recruits arise from his nail shop, except for the army. His hammer is worn into deep hollows, fitting the fingers of a dark and plump hand, hard as the timber it wears. His face, like the moon, is often seen through a cloud.

18

THE NAILMAKERS OF BROMSGROVE, 1896

Robert H. Sherard

Source: Robert H. Sherard, 'The Nailmakers of Bromsgrove' in 'White Slaves of England', *Pearson's Magazine*, vol. 2, (1896, July-Dec.): 167–73.

EDITORIAL HEADNOTE

Virtually a hundred years later, Robert Sherard commented on the metal trades more widely. Close friend, first biographer and staunch defender of Oscar Wilde, he was a widely published novelist, journalist and social commentator. He took some unpopular positions, such as supporting anti-Dreyfusards in France and writing xenophobhic and antisemitic articles about immigration to England. He was resourceful and tenacious in his journalism. Living mainly by his journalism, his investigative reports for *Pearson's* and for *The London Magazine* resulted in the *White Slaves of England* (1897) amongst others. Visiting Bromsgrove in the Black Country, he describes the relationship of masters to men and again referred to women only briefly, yet what he says about the workers largely applied to them too, as their testimony indicated.

THE sadness of the lives of the nailmakers of Bromsgrove and district is accentuated by the fact that there at least, unlike the murky towns which have been described, there are many simple, natural things which would make even a poor life happy, given a humble and contented nature, such as is the prime characteristic of these workers. The little town is bright and sweet and clean, with many picturesque old houses and a fine old church, and all round it, within two minutes' walk from the long, principal street, is some of the prettiest country in the Midlands; trees and meadows and brooks and undulating slopes, with lovers' lanes for long walks to many sites, historical and picturesque.

A simple man, a God-fearing man[a] – and the Bromsgrove nailmaker is both God-fearing and simple – might be very happy here where what is best in town

DOI: 10.4324/9781003676669-20

and country is combined, did not an imminent and terrible danger at all times overcast his life with the blackest of shadows; the imminent and terrible danger called clamming. Now, the plain English for clamming is starvation.

"Nailmaking," said to me Mr. J. Powell, formerly secretary of the now disbanded Nailmakers' Union, "is one of the worst trades in the kingdom. There are scores of men in this parish who are not earning nine shillings a week for seventy, eighty, or ninety hours' work, and out of these earnings have to pay from one shilling to eighteen pence a week for firing, and about sixpence for keeping their tools in order."

On investigation the fact becomes patent, that in this idyllic scene is laid the action of one of the cruellest industrial tragedies in England, a tragedy all the more poignant. because the sufferers are simple, defenceless men, admirably yet pitifully resigned, who would be very happy with very little, the little which, in spite of unceasing lifelong toil, they are never able to obtain. The industry of nailmaking is profitable only to those who do not make them; to this the luxurious houses and carriages of the nailmasters eloquently testify. And to become a nailmaster requires neither knowledge, nor brains, nor capital. Anybody with a few pounds to start with can enter this business, for success in which apparently nothing is needed. except an entire absence of the altruistic sense. All that has to be done is to rent a small warehouse, to purchase a weighing-machine, and to engage at, say, fourteen shillings a week a man to look after the ware-house, weigh the nails, and keep the accounts.

A little writing of business letters at home and an occasional trip to neighbouring markets will keep the nailmaster pleasantly employed. The nailers will do all the rest. They will find the workshops, the tools, the firing, and even the iron, and each week will bring the nails to the warehouse to be weighed and paid for. There is no risk, and there is a certain profit, because for certain classes of nails there is a steady and increasing demand. Formerly the masters used to supply the bundles of iron to the workers, receiving them back in the form of nails, and allowing for a certain amount of waste (about 14lb. to each bundle of 60lb.) Now it is customary to refuse to a would-be worker the advance of even one bundle, so that unless he can find the 3s. 6d. necessary for its purchase, he must just forego nailing. And there are hundreds of men and women in the Bromsgrove district who never have 3s. 6d. to lay out in this way from one year's end to another.

"We have to buy our iron at 3s. 6d. the bundle," said a woman to me, "and after we have worked one in, they give we another out." But they never advance the first bundle. Speaking of this hardship, one woman told of better days long past. "In them days," she said, we usen't to have to stand still for want of iron. Nowadays, at most factories, it's: You won't get no iron here.' Why, they wouldn't trust you for a bundle of iron, not if you clammed a week."

To each cottage in Bromsgrove, Sidemoor, and the district is attached a nailing shed, the rent for which is included in that of the cottage. Each of these sheds is fitted with a forge and bellows, provided by the landlord. The nailer has to find his own bench and set of tools, at an outlay of from five to ten pounds. The bench is fitted with a peg, or miniature anvil, on which the red hot iron is pointed, a hardy, or fixed chisel, over which the iron is bent and partially cut, a bore into which the severed length is inserted previous to the fashioning of the head of the nail. This is effected by means of the Oliver, which is a heavy hammer worked by a treadle, and restored to its upright position by a simple system of leverage. The completed nail is ejected from the bore by means of a lever, operating on a tit or tiny steel rod, which, jerked up-wards, expels the nail.

In some of the nailing sheds may be seen at work as many as four nailers, each provided with his bench. Of these one is the tenant of the shed, and the others are "stallers." The "stallers" are working, each on his own account, contributing to the rent and the firing. It is cheaper for them to co-operate in this manner than for each to rent his own shed and supply his own firing. . . .

The persistent laboriousness of these men was my first impression. Not for one second did they interrupt their mechanical movements, undisturbed by our advent, indifferent to all but the maximum to be effected. They answered my questions, they even made comments, but their weary eyes never deflected from their work, their hands and feet busy in one monotonous jig. Now it was working the bellows, now stoking the fire, now turning the irons, and now fashioning them on the bench, a series of brusque, jerky, harassed movements, not for one second suspended; perpetual motion, under the whip of hunger, as long as nerves could direct and muscles fulfil.

These men were making Flemish tacks, and one of them, speaking for all, told me that even by working fifteen hours a day, he could not earn 12s. a week. "Out of this, I have to pay stalling and breeze (the name given to the firing). To earn 12s. a week, he would have to make over 20,000 Flemish tacks, and that was beyond his powers. He could make 20,000 Flemish tacks in one week, but not more. . . .

Thus, 20,000 Flemish tacks means 24,000. Each 1000 (1200) tacks are paid for with 6d. "The right price on them," said the man, "is 7 d., but we is paid 6d. because we've nothing to do." This man admitted his inability to make more than twenty thousand (24,000) of these nails in one week. His work would consequently produce 20 X 6 d. = 10s. 10d. From this he would have to deduct 6d. for stalling and 9d. for breeze, leaving (10s. 10d.-IS. 3d.) 9s. 7d. Thus, for making 24,000 tacks he would receive 9s. 7d., less 6d. for wear and tear of his tools, leaving 9s. 1d. This means that he has to make 220 tacks for 1d.

The manufacture of each tack involves, besides the accessories of working the bellows, turning the irons, stoking, the following labour: The red-hot iron is laid on the peg, and with from four to six blows of the hand-hammer, whilst the rod is turned with the other hand, the point of the nail is fashioned. The now pointed bar is laid on the hardy, the point touching a gauge by which the length of the nail is regulated. A blow with the hand-hammer cuts the nail length almost off the bar and bends it, thus almost severed at right angles. This length is now inserted in the bore; the cold iron is twisted away from it, and with a movement of the foot, Oliver is brought down, flattening the protruding mass and forming the head of the tack. Sometimes Oliver has to be brought down twice, and usually, at least, two blows with the hand-hammer are necessary to properly fashion the head. Then the lever ejecting the nail from the bore has to be worked. This completes the operation. . . . On the other hand, as the men always work two rods at the same time, a little time is saved in the matter of bellows-blowing, turning, and the stoking, although each tack exacts separate and repeated operations described. These operations have to be carried out 220 times in their entirety to earn the wage of 1d.

Flemish tacks can, I believe, be made by machinery, but this cannot be said of brush nails, which were being made by a cadaverous-looking man in the next shed visited. Brush nails are bought at the warehouses at 1s. 3d. the thousand (1200), and this man was earning 7s. a week at the making of them. He works from 7 a.m. till 10. p.m., and turns out about 11 lb. of these nails in a week. "I could make more if I were stouter," he said, "but I got ill by clamming and going short on my belly." He was paying 8d. a week for stalling and 1s. 2d. a cwt. for breeze. "I pays more than I burns," he said. It was a very draughty shed, and the man coughed terribly.

In the next place there were working side by side an old man of sixty and his wife. The shed was filled with poultry, hens were roosting over the forge, hens were brooding in packing-cases in the corners. The man had been at the trade all his life, and said: "It's never been worse in price." He was making clout nails at 8d. for 3lb. He could make about 30lb. in a week, and could earn at it about 7s. His wife made tacks at 6d. the 1000, and could earn about 1s. a day, working nine hours.

I begged a few words of her. She told me that formerly "when nailing was better, we made 20s. a week between us. My old man has told you the outside farthing that he earns. His average is 6s. 3d. a week, and when Saturday comes it is hard to lay it out. I have to turn it over very often. And my old man is the hardest working man in Bromsgrove, and has never been on the beer in his life."

Out of their wages she had to pay 2s. 6d. a week rent for cottage and workshop, 1s. for repair of tools, and 1s. 1d. for fuel. Tea, bread, and margarine, was the staple food; bread and cheese was an occasional treat; sixpenny worth of meat came once a week.

Clothes were out of the question. "I has been married twenty-three years," she said, "and I has never had a new dress since I were married." "Amusement?" she added. "There is none for me; bed and work is all we get." This woman has brought up six children.

Amongst the lamentable documents which I brought home with me from Bromsgrove, I find a written statement showing how a nailer, his wife, and five children live on the 15s. a week which by their joint efforts the parents can earn.

This is the budget: Rent, 2s. 6d.; firing, 1s. 6d. repair of tools and kitchen fuel, 1s. 6d.; bread, 4s. 6d.; bacon, 9 d.; meat, 9d.; margarine, 1s.; cheese, 5d.; sugar, 7d.; tea, 4d.; tobacco, 3d.; lamp-oil, 2d.; candles, 1d.; soap, 3d.; sundries, 3d. Sundries may be supposed to include such luxuries as clothing, milk, potatoes, literature, amusements, doctor, medicines, and so on. . . .

Were it not for their poultry and what they can earn as agricultural labourers in the summer, the nail-makers would undoubtedly starve. However, what with a pig (reared either in the shed or the kitchen, *à la mode d'Irlande*) and fowls and ducks, and odd jobs on the neighbouring farms in the season, they manage during the fine weather to save a pound or two to help them over the winter.

I then came upon an unhappy family hammering away for dear life. There were the father, the mother, the son and the daughter. The shed was dark but for the glare of the forge. The father said that all together "we don't get up to 13s. a week." I should explain that the daughter was a child of three, who was sitting on the forge, warming her naked little toes at the comfortable blaze, and hammering them in pure enjoyment on the brick-laid hearth, and that the son, a lad of about thirteen, who had passed the sixth standard, could only "do a few nails after school-time," perhaps 2000 (2400) a week, and earn 10d. The mother said that often on Saturdays, after all debts were paid, she had not one shilling "to go to town with to buy a bit of meat for Sunday's boiling." As to clothes, she had had two new dresses since she was married, sixteen years ago, and one of these was, thanks to a subscription which was raised at her chapel, when she buried her eldest child and a black dress seemed necessary.

Next door I found a man of about sixty-five, who had been working at the trade for fifty years, and, without interruption, from 7 a.m. till 10 p.m. per diem. He couldn't earn a shilling a day and "mostly earned tenpence." His aged mother and another old man were working in the same shop. Each nail that he made involved two blows with the Oliver and three with the handhammer.

As we were returning from Sidemoor that evening, Mr. Powell told me of the malpractices of the "fogger." The fogger is the middleman, usually a small storekeeper, who flourishes in the Bromsgrove district in spite of the Truck Act and Her Majesty's Commissioners for Oyer and Terminer. He contracts with the masters to supply such quantities of nails, and obtains these nails from the makers at about 30 per cent less than the tariff price.

He pays for the nails, sometimes in money, but more often in goods from his shop, bread, iron, breeze, and so on, which he sells at least 30 per cent dearer than the non fogging tradesmen of the town. But then he gives credit. He is liable to the penalties of the Truck Act, no doubt, but, as Mr Powell says, the men dare not give evidence against him. One fogger was, however, recently prosecuted by Mr. Powell and heavily fined.

Amongst the many sad and haggard faces which the mere name of Bromsgrove evokes, I think the one that haunts me most is that of a very old man, with whom I conversed on the last morning of my stay in that idyllic He was a man of eighty-five, who started nailing at the age of seven. . . . working six or seven hours a day, he could only earn 1s. 6d. (less 6d. for stalling) in the whole week. This was very much less than he earned before he was eight years of age, when, as he told me, he could make his 1s. a day, working from 7 a.m. till 8 p.m. "Times were then half as good again as now." . . . But, he admits, nailing has been going down steadily for forty years. "It's the foggers ruins such as we," said his daughter. "Aye, foggers charge such outdashus [audacious] prices," said the old man. He added: "It's not because there's no work.

. . . One grievance of the workers, a very comprehensible grievance, is that often a whole week's work is rejected at the warehouse, on one pretext or another, as unsatisfactory. Possibly the master has ordered more than he can place. The men have to bear the loss and toil back home under their parcels "to do the best they can" with the nails, to sell them for what they will fetch, as waste iron or otherwise. Again, even to earn a bare subsistence many men work all night for several nights in the week.

Yet in spite of all these woes and worries, the Bromsgrove nailers are a contented, resigned, and God-fearing race. . . . The Bible thrown into the scale makes their lot seem happy to these heroic Christians. As they toil at their anvils they sing hymns. The "Doxology" is a favourite anthem. The last sound I heard as I left Bromsgrove was the voice of a poor old woman, bowed and almost blind, who was working at her forge. She was singing in an enthusiasm of hope and fervour, "The Lord will provide."

Editorial Endnote

a Although Sherard refers regularly to men, women also were a key part of the workforce.

19

VARIOUS TRADES FROM THE LONDON TRADESMAN, 1747

Robert Campbell

Source: Robert Campbell, *The London Tradesman, being a compendious view of all Trades, Professions and Arts . . . calculated for the information of Parents, and Instruction of Youth in their Choice of Business* (T. Gardner, 1747), 124–26, 149–54, 170–71, 206, 211–13, 244, 250–51, 260–61, 300.

EDITORIAL HEADNOTE

The London Tradesman (1747) is a detailed account of the various trades and professions in London during the eighteenth century and aimed at parents wishing to put their children into apprenticeship. He draws on his own experience as a tradesman to provide practical advice and insights into the workings of different industries. Within each chapter, Campbell provides a detailed description of the work involved, the tools and equipment used, and the skills required. He also offers advice on how to succeed in each trade, including tips on managing finances, dealing with customers, and navigating the complex world of London's guilds and trade associations. This first extract (see also doc. 30) focuses on trades in which women were employed, outside of millinery and related trades; in several they were assistants, though occasionally the primary workers. Of nearly 400 trades mentioned, women figured in very few, most of which are described in the extract.

CHAP. XXX

Of the Gold and Silver-Lace Man . . .

The Business of a Wire-Drawer is purely mechanical; a Hobby Horse is capable to execute their Business, since the whole of their Work is performed by the Engine, which they have nothing to do but turn round; nor are their Engines costly; their chief Care is in preserving the Colour of the Metal, to which a moist Hand is a

DOI: 10.4324/9781003676669-21

very great Enemy. They are paid so much an Ounce for their Labour by the Lace-Man, who furnishes them with the Plate. They employ but few Hands, and give but small Wages.

The Wire being once drawn to a proper Fineness is sent to the Flatting-Mills, where it is made flat by passing between two Rollers.

The Silver by being flatted is made ready for Spinning, which is performed by Spinners brought up to that Business: It is done in a long Room; at the one End of which stands their Wheel, made of Steel; the Spindles are placed on this Wheel in the same Manner as those us'd in Rope-Walks, or for spinning Thread for Sail-Cloth; a Thread of Silk is fastened to the End of one of the Spindles; one Person turns the Wheel, while another holding the Thread of Silk in one Hand, and the flatted Silver in the other, allows the Silver to wind gently about the Silk as it is turn'd round by the Wheel: In this Manner the wholly Thread of Silk is covered, which is rolled upon a Bottom, and is now called Silver or Gold Sleysy. A moist Hand cannot be employ'd in this Work; and it requires much Care to preserve it from tarnishing, and much Experience to compleat the Workman. Women are employed in this as well as Men, and may earn Twelve or Fifteen Shillings a Week honestly; but they are much given to pilfering the Stuff and have a trick of moistening the silk to make up the deficiency in weight. The Master is paid by the Lace-Man at so much an ounce, who generally furnishes him with materials.

The Bone-Lace Maker is another Servant of the Lace-Man. Their Work is not performed in the Loom, but wrought by Hand in different Parts, and put together on a Pillow, in the Manner that Thread-Lace is made. The Ground Work of some of their Patterns are made by Orrice-Weavers, and afterwards ornamented by the Bone-Lace Maker. He ought to be a good Pattern-Draughts-Man, as the Beauty of his Work depends upon the Richness and Variety of the Figures. . . .

The Button-Maker, I mean the Silver and The Silver Gold Button-Maker, is the next humble Servant of the Lace-Man; the Lace-Man furnishes him with all Materials for his Buttons, except Moulds, and buys them off him when done. The Silver and Gold Button-Maker is a pretty ingenious Business: He must have a Fancy and Genius for inventing new Fashions; a good Eye, as his Business is poreing, and a clean dry Hand. It requires no great Strength, and is follow'd by Women as well as Men, which has reduced the Trade to small Profits, and a small Share of Reputation; the Women are generally Gin Drinkers, and consequently bad Wives; this makes them poor, and to get something to keep Soul and Body together, work for a mere Trifle, and hawk their Work about to the Trade at an Under-Price, after they have cheated the Lace-Man of his Stuff. This has reduced the Craft to a very low Ebb; however, a good Workman, if he can get Employ among the Crowd, may earn Twelve or Fifteen Shillings a Week.

The Fringe, Frog, and Tassel-Maker is likewise employ'd by the Lace-Man. Some of the Button-Makers perform the Work; but it is chiefly done by Women, upon the Hand, who make a very handsome Livelihood of it, if they are not initiated into the Mystery of Gin-Drinking.

Embroiderers may be reckon'd among the Dependants of the Lace-Man; as in his Shop the greatest Part of their rich Work is vended, and he furnishes them with all Materials for their Business. It is chiefly perform'd by Women, is an ingenious Art, requires a nice Taste in Drawing, a bold Fancy to invent new Patterns, and a clean Hand to save their Work from tarnishing. – Few of the Workers at present can Draw, they have their Patterns from the Pattern-Drawer, who must likewise draw the Work itself, which they only fill up, with Gold and Silver, Silks or Worsteds, according to its Use and Nature. We are far from excelling in this Branch of Business in England: The Nuns in Foreign Countries far exceed anything we can perform. We make some good Work, but fall short of the bold Fancy in French and Italian Embroidery: This I take to be chiefly owing to the Want of a Taste for Drawing in the Performers; they may go on in a dull beaten Tract, or servily imitate a Foreign Pattern, but know not how to advance the Beauty of the old, or strike out any new Invention worth Notice. An Embroiderer ought to have a Taste for Designing, and a just Notion of the Principles of Light and Shade, to know how to range their Colours in a natural Order, make them reflect upon one another, and the whole to represent the Figure in its proper shade.

CHAP. XXXIII

Of the UPHOLDER, and the trades employed by him . . .

The Upholder, according to this description of his Business, must be no Fool; and have a considerable Stock to set up with: However, a young Man who has a Mind only to be a mere Upholder, and has no Prospect of setting up in the Undertaking Way, does not require such an universal Genius as I have been speaking of: He must handle the Needle so alertly as to sew a plain Seam, and sew on the Lace without puckers; and he must use his Sheers so dextrously as to cut a Valence or Counterpain [sic] with a genteel Sweep, according to a Pattern he has before him. All this Part of the Work is performed by Women, who never served an Apprenticeship to the Mystery, as well as Men. The stuffing and covering a Chair or Settee-Bed is indeed the nicest Part of this Branch; but it may be acquired without any remarkable Genius. All the Wooden-Work they use is done by the Joiner, Cabinet-Maker and Carver. A Tradesman who is a good Hand in the Upholder's own Branch is paid Twelve or Fifteen Shillings a Week; and the Women, if good for anything, get a Shilling a Day.

CHAP. XXXVIII

Of the BARBER and PERUKE-MAKER . . .

The Wigg-Maker employs the Net-Worker for Cauls to his Wiggs: They are generally made in the Country by Women, and bought up by the Haberdasher, who furnishes the Wigg-Maker with them, and Silk for weaving his Hair on, and

Ribbons for mounting his Wiggs. He buys his Blocks from the Turner; but I shall defer mentioning that Trade, till I can range it under a more proper Head.

[CHAP. XXXIX. *Of the Milliner (see section 3. These are subsidiary trades)*]

If I am not mistaken I placed the Hoop-Petticoat-Maker as an Article in the Milliner's Branch; but, upon Recollection, I chuse to afford seven-fold Fence a Section by itself, since I am bound to do Houour to every Thing that concerns the Fair; and if I had lumped it with the rest of their Wardrobe, I might be suspected an Enemy to this Female Entrenchment. – The Materials are striped Holland Silk, or Check, according to the Quality of the Fair, to be inclosed, and supported with Rows of Wale-Bone or Rattan. . . .

As to their Use, I dare not divulge the Secrets of the Fair; they have kept it inviolably, nay, better than we have kept the FreeMason's Sign; for I defy all the Male Creation to discover the secret Use the Ladies designed them for: Some apparent Advantages flow from them, which every one may see, but they have a cabalistical Meaning, which none but such as are within the Circle can fathom: We see they are Friends to Men, for they have let us into all the Secrets of the Ladies Legs, which we might have been ignorant of to Eternity without their Help; they discover to us indeed a Sample of what we wish to purchase, yet serve as a Fence to keep us at an awful Distance. They encourage the Consumption of our Manufactures in a prodigious Degree, and the great Demand we have for Whale-Bone renders them truly beneficial to our good Allies the Dutch; in short, they are a public Good, and as such I recommend them.

They are chiefly made by Women: They must not be polluted by the unhallowed Hands of a rude Male. These Women make a tolerable Living by it: The Work is harder than most Needle-Work, and requires Girls of Strength. A Mistress must have a pretty kind of Genius to make them fit well and adjust them to the reigning Mode; but in the main, it is not necessary she should be a Witch.

Since I am so bold as to make free with the Ladies Hoop-Petticoat, I must just peep under the Quilted-Petticoat. Every one knows the Materials they are made of: They are made mostly by Women, and some Men, who are employ'd by the Shops and earn but little. They quilt likewise Quilts for Beds for the Upholder. This they make more of than of the Petticoats, but not very considerable, nothing to get rich by, unless they are able to purchase the Materials and sell them finished to the Shops, which few of them do. They rarely take Apprentices, and the Women they employ to help them, earn Three or Four Shillings a Week and their Diet.

CHAP. XLIV

Of the Stay-Maker

THE Stay-Maker is employed in making Stays, Jumps, and Bodice for the Ladies: He ought to be a very polite Tradesman, as he approaches the Ladies so nearly;

and possessed of a tolerable Share of Assurance and Command of Temper to approach their delicate Persons in fitting on their Stays, without being moved or put out of Countenance. He is obliged to inviolable Secrecy in many Instances, where he is obliged by Art to mend a crooked Shape, to bolder up a fallen Hip, or distorted Shoulder: The delicate easy Shape we so much admire in *Miranda* is intirely the workmanship of the Stay-Maker; to him she reveals all her natural Deformity, which she industriously conceals from the fond Lord, who was caught by her slender Waist: Her Shape she owes to Steel and Whalebone, her Black Locks to the Tire-Woman, and her florid Complexion to Paint and Pomatum: She is like the Jack-Daw in the Fable, dressed out in borrowed Plumes, and her natural Self, when deposited in the Bridal-Bed, is a mere Lump of animated Deformity, fitter far for the Undertaker than to be initiated in the Mysteries of Connubial Joy. How necessary a Qualification is it in that kind of Tradesmen to keep the Deformed secret? and how dangerous to the Repose of the Fair Sex would it be to blab the misshapen Truth? I am surprised the Ladies have not found out a Way to employ Women Stay-Makers rather than trull our Sex with what should be kept as inviolable as Free-Masonry. But the Work is too hard for Women, it requires more Strength than they are capable of to raise Walls of Defence about a Lady's Shape, which is liable to be spoiled by so many Accidents.

The Materials in Stays are Tabby, Canvass, and Whale-Fin, commonly called Whale-Bone: The Stay-Maker takes the Lady's Shape as nicely as he can, if it is natural, and where it is not, he supplies the Deficiency; then he cuts out the Tabby and Canvass by the Shape in Quarters, which are given out to Women to be stitched, at so much the Pair of Stays: This Part of the Stay-making Trade is but poor Bread; a Woman cannot earn above a Crown or Six Shillings a Week, let her sit as close as she pleases. . . .

There are a Species of Tradesmen who make nothing else but Bodice, which every Woman knows differ from Stays; but Women are chiefly employ'd. They are made, if I mistake not, of Pack-Thread instead of Whale-Bone; and those employ'd, either as Master or Journey People, earn a tolerable Subsistence: Women that can apply themselves, and refrain from Gin, may get from Five to Eight Shillings a Week.

CHAP. L

Of the **TURNER in Wood, Ivory,** *and* **Silver,** *and sever other Trades depending on the Turner's Shop . . .*

There are several sorts of Basket-Makers; some who make Baskets of Green-Willows for coarse Uses, others that make yet a fine sort, that are stript, split, shaved and died: Those who make the coarser sort for the Gardener's Use carry on the most considerable Trade, and their Apprentices must have some Robustness but not much Ingenuity; and the Workers in the finer sort of Baskets to be met with in the Turner's Shops require less Strength but a better Genius. There are Numbers of

Women employed in all the Classes, and all things considered earn as much Money as at Trades that make a greater Figure in the World: Journeymen have from Nine to Fifteen Shillings a Week.

CHAP. LIV

Of the WATCH-MAKER, *and those he employs. . . .*

The Springs are made by a Tradesman who does nothing else, and the Chains by another: These last are frequently made by Women, in the Country about London and sold to the Watch-Maker by the Dozen for a very small Price. It requires no great Ingenuity to learn to make Watch-Chains, the Instruments made for that Use renders the Work quite easy which to the eye would appear very difficult.

CHAP. LIX

Of the WEAVERS *in general . . .*

The Silk-Throwster, by a Mill calculated for that Purpose, throws the Silk, and prepares it for the various Uses of the Weaver; he employs mostly Women, to whom he gives but small Wages: It is a very profitable Business for the Matter, and requires but a small Share of Ingenuity. Spinning the hard Silk and winding it employs a great Number of Female Hands, who may make good Bread of it, if they refrain from the common Vice of Drinking and Sotting away their Time and Senses.

CHAP. LXXII

Of the SHIP-BUILDER, and those employed under him. . . .

Yarn for Sail-Cloth is made of dressed Hemp, and spun in the self-same Manner that Rope-Yarn Sail Cloth is spun. The Thread is the direct Length of the Web, and the House in which it is spun is as long, and resembles a small Rope-Walk. The Spinners make very good Bread of it, and Women are as much employed as Men. As to the Weaving, it is done the same Way as other Linen Cloth: The Journeymen are paid by the Yard, according to the Fineness of the Sail Cloth.

20

VARIOUS TRADES, FROM JOSEPH COLLYER, THE PARENTS' AND GUARDIANS' DIRECTORY

Source: Joseph Collyer, *The Parents' and Guardians' Directory and the Youth's Guide in the Choice of a Profession or Trade* (R. Griffiths, 1761), 60–61, 67, 80, 84–85, 93, 113–14, 152 53, 234, 236–37, 248–49, 263, 273–74, 286–87, 292.

EDITORIAL HEADNOTE

The Parents' and Guardians' Directory (1761, see also doc. 31) is the same sort of guide for parents to placing out their children. Following Campbell, Joseph Collyer noticeably draws on many of Robert Campbell's descriptions, sometimes with virtually identical descriptions. His gender-neutral introduction on education reflects some of the 'best practice' of contemporary educational theory, showing real regard for the child. However, it is obvious that the main intent is to consider boys' options. Having said that, he includes more trades for girls, and the tone of the work is more sympathetic to the female sex.

OF THE BASKET-MAKERS

THERE are several sorts of Basket-makers: Some who form Baskets of green oziers, chiefly for the use of the gardeners. These are the most considerable branches; for some of the masters employ many hands, and also rent large ozer plantations; which not only produce sufficient for themselves, but many to spare. This part of the work requires no other abilities but strength and application; and a journeyman may earn from 10 or 15s. a week. About 100£. will setup a master very handsomely; but some of them employ much more.

Another sort of Basket-makers make finer works with rods tripped, split, shaved, and dyed; or with cane split, or straw dyed of various colours. The workers in these finer sort of baskets, which are chiefly to be found in the turner's shops, require less strength and more ingenuity. Many women are employed in these making smaller wares; . . .

DOI: 10.4324/9781003676669-22

OF THE BODICE-MAKER

THIS was once a trade of universal use; but now Bodice are worn by none but the poorer sort of women and girls in the country. They are made of canvas and whale-bone, or cane, and sometimes of leather; but these last are almost out of use. Women are principally employed in making them; they can get six or seven shillings a week, and require no great qualifications. Their apprentices are generally parish children, whom they take with little or nothing. As their dealings are mostly in the country, they require a pretty large stock; most of them now deal also in ordinary stays, by which means they make a handsome livelihood.

OF THE BROOM-MAKER

THE Makers of Birch or Heath Brooms are confined to about half a dozen masters who live in Kent-street, Southwark, and return several hundreds a year in this trifling article; some of them having upwards of 500£. stock constantly by them, deposited in their yards in great sacks of brooms of a prodigious height. I do not find that they take apprentices: Their work is done by men and poor women who it is said get from 8 to 16s. a week.

OF THE BUTTON-MAKER

THE greatest part of the Mohair, Silk, and Horse-hair Buttons are made in the country, and sent up to the shops in town; those made here are chiefly Livery Buttons, or some patterns particularly bespoke. Those who work at this branch are chiefly women, who are paid by the dozen, and are able to get but a poor living.

The boy or girl designed for the business of making Gold and Silver Buttons, ought to have some fancy and genius, that they may be able to invent new fashions; they should also have good eyes and a dry hand. The laceman furnishes them with all the materials for his Buttons, except the moulds, and pays him for the work when done. They take with apprentices 5 or 10£ and may earn 12 or 15s a week. Women and girls are principally employed. . . .

OF CARPET-MAKING

THERE are a species of Carpets made of lit of various colours; and mostly used by the sides of beds. These are sold at the turners shops; and are made by people who do nothing else. This work, which is but a late invention, is mostly performed by women, who earn from 5 to 8s. a week.

OF THE CONEY-WOOL-CUTTER

THIS is a very profitable business to the master; though it requires no extraordinary genius; but he ought to be versed in accounts, and have at least 3 or 400£. to begin trade for himself, which is the more necessary as there is business but for few journeymen. The Coney-wool-cutter buys not only rabbit skins, but the furs of beavers, &c. and employs women first to pluck off the long straggling hairs, and then to cut off the fine wool that grows underneath; which is done with such dexterity that the wool of every rabbit adheres together as if it was still joined to the skin. They in the same manner cut off the fur of beavers, &c. The fine wool or fur of these beasts is sold in sacks to the hatters at so much a pound for making hats. The masters take from 20 to 40£. with an apprentice.

OF THE EMBROIDERERS

Business is performed by women, and is an ingenious art. The girl, who is to be put apprentice to it, ought to have a dry clean hand, and a genius for drawing. She should be taught not only to draw flowers, &c. with great facility, but to have a just notion of the principles of light and shade, that she may range the colours in a natural order, and make them reflect a beauty on each other. As few of the present workers can draw, the pattern-drawer makes the pattern for the work itself, which the Embroiderer fills up with gold and silver thread, silks, or worsteds. They take 5 or 10£, with an apprentice; who, when out of her time, may setup mistress, if she has a good interest with the great, or with the saddlers, taylors, and milliners who work for them.

OF THE FAN-PAINTER

FAN painting is an ingenious business, and requires skill in drawing, in perspective, in the proper disposition of the lights and shades, and in laying on the colours. This business is however almost ruined, by the introduction of printed Fan Mounts; and therefore it would be a pity that any ingenious girl, who has a taste for drawing, should be put apprentice to it.

OF THE FAN SHOP

IN these shops nothing is sold but Fans and Mounts; they are generally kept by women, who employ themselves in inventing and colouring printed Fan-Mounts, and in mounting these fluttering implements of the ladies. They sell fans brought from China, and some of them export considerable quantities of all kinds of Fans. They take about 10£. with an apprentice; but there is but little employment for the journeywomen, who may earn, when they get a good shop, 12 or 15s. a week.

OF THE GILDER

THE Gilding of metals is a very profitable, and at the same time a dangerous business: with respect to those who perform the work, occasioned by the quick-silver used in this art, which is apt to affect their nerves, and render their lives a burthen to them; whence the trade is but in few hands, and some of them women. Gilding is performed with the following amalgama of gold and quicksilver: the gold in thin plates is heated in a crucible, and when just ready to flow, three or four times the weight of quick silver is poured upon it, and being immediately quenched in water, both together become a soft substance like butter. When the artist intends to gild, he rubs the piece to be gilt with aqua fortis, and then covers it with the amalgama. When it is all covered over and smooth, he holds it over a charcoal fire, by which means the mercury evaporates, and the gold remains upon the piece; the artist then rubs off all the roughnesses, and at the same time spreads the gold with an instrument called a scratch-brush; he then burnishes the work, and this gives it the colour wanted. The gilders take from 5 to 10£ with an apprentice. A journeyman may earn from 15s. to a guinea a week; and a master may setup with about 60£.

OF THE GLOVER

THIS is a very good shop-keeping business. Those, who have a great trade, deal for many hundreds, if not thousands, a year. The leather of Gloves is not tanned, but cured with alum; which renders it soft and pliable, and therefore more proper for gloves, &c. The master cuts out the work and gives it out to the makers, who are generally women; and, if quick hands, can get nine or ten shillings a week; but most part of the Gloves, worn in London, are made in the country, where labour is cheaper than it is in the city. . . . The Glovers take with an apprentice from 10 to 30£. A journeyman to a shop may get 20 or 30£. A year and his board, or use, in setting up for himself, from 100 to 1000£.

OF THE QUILTERS

Quilting is chiefly performed by the women; but there are some masters, who employ a number of women and girls in making Bed Quilts for the Upholsterers. The women of this business not only make Bed Quilts, but quilted Petticoats, &c. They either take poor girls apprentices, whom they keep for the sake of their work, or have a small sum for learning those grown up, whom they afterwards pay about 10 or 12s. a week.

OF THE RIBBON-WEAVER

THIS is a pretty light easy trade, and fit for lads of a slender make, or even for girls. The silk for the warp, or long way of the Ribbon, which is generally of the finest kind, is wound round a machine called a warping-frame, and then taken off on a wheel, which is fixed at the end of the loom, and kept at a proper breadth by what is called a sley; which is not very unlike a fine comb, the silk threads going between the teeth. The Weaver then winds a coarser sort of silk on little quills, which are put into the shuttle. When some of the threads that are round the sley are, by means of a treadle, which are long pieces of wood fixed to the tackle of the loom, pulled lower than the rest, and the shuttle put through the vacancy. The Weaver then putting his foot on the other treadle, pulls down those threads that were before uppermost, and returns the shuttle back with his other hand; and this is repeated with astonishing quickness. In this manner all plain weaving is performed; the only difference being in the strength and breadth of the looms, and the labour required to throw the shuttle. A quick hand may earn ten or twelve shillings a week, by making ribbons. They take from 5 to 10£. with an apprentice, whose working hours are from six to nine. A very little will setup a master, and honesty and industry will hardly fail of increasing his flock, if he is not burthened with a great family.

OF THE SHOE-MAKER

THIS is a business that requires no very extraordinary abilities, nor any learning, besides reading, writing, and accounts. . . . The principal business of these Shoemakers, and of their journeymen and apprentices, is cutting out Shoes, delivering them to the makers, receiving them when finished, fitting them on the feet of their customers; and keeping their books. . . . The men, who really make the Shoes, are considered as journeymen; though they take apprentices. . . . The journeymen and the women, who bind the Shoes, and sew the quarters together, when they are made of silk, velvet, callimanco, &c. get but small wages. These journeymen take about 5£. with an apprentice; who, when out of his time, may get about 9 or 10s. a week; or, if he has a little money, and some acquaintance, he may setup as a chambermaster and work for his own customers.

OF THE SILVER AND GOLD THREAD-SPINNERS

THE most necessary qualifications in this business, in which both men and women are employed, is a dry hand. The silver or gold wire being drawn to the utmost fineness by the Wiredrawer, and then flatted, it is spun, or, in other words, twisted round a thread of silk. This is done in a long room, at the end of which is a wheel of steel, on which are spindles placed in the same manner as in the wheel of a rope-walk. To one of the spindles is fastened the silk together with the slatted wise; one person turns the wheel, while another holding the thread of silk in one hand, and the slatted silver or gold wire in the other, allows it to wind gently about the silk, as it is turned round by the wheel: In this manner the silk is covered; after which it is rolled upon a bottom, and is now called silver or gold slesy. The persons employed in this work may earn twelve or fourteen shillings a week. The master is paid by the Laceman, who generally furnishes him with the materials. He takes from 5 to 10£. with an apprentice; who, when his time is expired, may set up with 50£

OF THE SLOP-SHOP

THIS business requires no great skill, ingenuity, or learning, to become master of it; writing a good hand and accounts are all the qualifications necessary for a young man before he is put apprentice. In the Slop-shop are sold all kinds Jackets, Shirts, Trouzers, and other wearing apparel belonging to sailors, ready made. It is a very profitable business. The masters take about 20£ with an apprentice; who, when out of his time; may have 20£. a year and his board as a journeyman, for cutting out the cloth, giving it to the workwomen, and attending the other business of the shop. Some of the masters, and particularly those who contract to serve the royal navy, employ several thousand pounds in trade.

OF THE STAY-MAKER

HIS business requires of some genius, but no extraordinary education. The boy who is to be put apprentice to a Stay-maker ought however to be naturally polite, to be possessed of a tolerable assurance, an easy address, and the power of keeping secret those defects which it is frequently his business to conceal, by bolstering up a fallen hip, or distorted shoulder. The materials in Stays are tabby, canvas, and whalebone. The Stay-maker takes the lady's shape, if it be a fine one, as nicely as he can; and where it is uneven or deformed, endeavours to conceal every defect; he cuts out the tabby and canvas by the shape in quarters, which are given out to be stitched by women, who are able to earn only 5 or 6s. a week. After this, having prepared the whalebone, he thrusts it between the rows of stitching, which requires a good deal of strength, and is the nicest part of Stay-making. The Stays being boned are loosely sewed together, and fitted on the lady, when, if they answer according to expectation, they are bound, the braiding laid along the seams, the lacing put down the stomacher, and finished so as to be the fit for the lady's use. The masters take from 5 to 10£. with an apprentice; who when out of his time, will have the common wages of a Taylor, by working as a journeyman; or, if he has 50 or 60£. he may setup for himself.

OF THE TASSEL-MAKERS

THESE are more frequently women than men. They make Tassels for pulpit cushions, window-curtain cords, and for a variety of other uses. These Tassels are made of gold or silver thread, silk, mohair, or worsted, worked over a mould. When Tassels were worn by the ladies to their manteels, this was an exceeding good employment, and many families got a genteel maintenance by it; but now, I believe, it is hardly worth learning. The makers take girls out of the schools, and parish children with little or no money; who, if good hands, may, when out of their time, be able to get fix or eight shillings a week as journeywomen; or may setup with a very little; all materials being found by the Lace or Worsted-men, their employers.

OF THE UPHOLSTERER, OR UPHOLDER

THE boy, who is disposed to be of this business, requires no very extraordinary genius, nor any uncommon education. The Upholsterer makes beds with all their furniture, as the Valence, Tester, &c. though all the wood work is performed by the Bed-stead-maker, Carver, &c. They stuff and cover Easy Chairs and Settee Beds, and make all kinds of Curtains both for Beds and Windows. . . . They take from 20 to 50£. with an apprentice; who, when out of his time, will be able to get 12 or 15s. a week. They employ women, who earn a shilling or eighteen pence a day; . . .

OF THE WATCH CHAIN-MAKER

THE only qualifications, necessary for this seemingly curious art, are a nice hand and good eyes. The links of these chains are easily made by an engine used for that purpose; after which they are rivetted together. In this business women are employed as well as men. They take about 10£. with an apprentice; and about the same sum will enable a young man to setup for himself.

OF THE WATCH-SPRINGER AND LINER

THIS business requires no very uncommon abilities or learning; and is very often performed by women. It is entirely confined to the cases, which he polishes, springs, and lines. The Springer and Liner takes about 5£. with an apprentice; who when his time is expired, may setup with about 10£, and earn from 15 to 25s. a week.

21

VARIOUS TRADES, FROM THE BOOK OF TRADES OR LIBRARY OF USEFUL ARTS, 1806

Source: Anon., *The Book of Trades or Library of Useful Arts*, 3rd ed. (Tabart and Co., 1806), Part 1: 7–13, 27–28, Part II: 46–49, 51–56.

EDITORIAL HEADNOTE

Half a century later, the anonymous *Book of Trades* is more limited than both its predecessors and tended to include trades that needed no apprenticeship for girls. The extracts are included here for comparison with the two mid-eighteenth-century volumes.

PART I

THE WOOL-COMBER

. . . A pack of wool weighs 240lbs., and, it is said, will employ more than sixty, persons a week to manufacture it into cloths, viz. three men to sort, dry, mix, and make it ready for the carder; five to scribble it; thirty-five women and girls to card and spin it; eight men to weave it; four to spole it; and eight to scour, mill, pack, and press it. . . .

THE SPINNER

In many country villages the art of spinning is carried on by women and children in the open air, as it is represented in the plate. Spinning is applied to the reducing of silk, flax, hemp, wool, hair, &c., into thread. Spinning by hand is performed either with the distaff and spindle, or on the wheel: in the former case the person sits to her work; in the latter she stands, or rather runs backwards and forwards. We shall describe both methods. When the distaff and spindle are used, the flax or other substance is tied or fixed on a long stick: the spinner draws out a thread, which she fixes to her spindle; then with her left hand she turns the wheel, and

DOI: 10.4324/9781003676669-23

with her right guides the thread drawn from the flax, &c., round the spindle, or rather round a spole which goes on the spindle. When a sufficient quantity is wound on the spole, it is taken off, thrown into the basket, and replaced by an empty one.

Spinning of wool is managed by a different process. Here the wool, in those fine slivers taken from the wool-comber, is held in the hand; a thread of it is fastened to the wheel, which the spinner. turns with velocity, and runs backward from it, thereby drawing out the thread to a considerable length. In either mode of spinning, when the spindle is filled, its thread is wound upon a reel, and taken off in the form of a skain or hank. The wool is delivered out to the spinner by weight, and when she returns it it is again weighed. Women must be very expert who can earn at this business one shilling in a day. Children at an early age are taught the art, and will soon earn from six-pence to one and six-pence a week.

Besides the above mode of spinning wool upon the wheel, a more antient method is still practised in the county of Norfolk, with the distaff and spindle, which may be used either sitting, or walking while the spinner tends on cows, poultry, & c. The sliver of wool is braided round the distaff (or *rock* as it is called by the Norfolk spinners), from the slit end of which a thread is drawn and fastened to the slender spindle, which receives a whirling motion by being quickly rolled upon a piece of smooth leather called the trip-skin, fastened upon the thigh of the spinner, who with one hand gently draws a few hairs from the tail of the sliver, while the other winds up the spindle and renews its whirling motion. – In this way finer yarn is made than by any other method, but more than six-pence per day can seldom be earned.

Spinners are employed by the master & wool-combers, the whole of whose trade may be properly described in this article. The act of combing the wool has been already noticed. Spinning the wool into skains is the next process: these are afterwards put into the hands of other women, called *winders*, whose business is, by means of a wheel and other simple apparatus, to wind two, three, or more of these skains together, so as to make a compound thread of them. This thread is wound on to spoles or bobbins, for the convenience of having them fixed on spindles, which are turned round by millwork in order to twist the threads thus combined into a firm substance. When a taken from the mill, the worsted is washed, dyed, and dried; it is then done up in crewels, and fit for sale. . . .

Sometimes the worsted is required to be very white: in that case, before it is dry, after washing, it is hung up in a close room, in which a charcoal fire is burning; on the fire some finely powdered roll-brimstone is thrown and the room made air-tight, so as neither to admit the external air, nor suffer the vapour from the sulphur to escape.

The variety and importance of those branches of our manufactures which are produced from cotton, wool, flax, spun into yarn, have occasioned many attempts to render spinning more easy, cheap, and expeditious, by means of complicated machinery. Several of these have been very successful; particularly those for cotton by Sir Richard Arkwright; but the spinning-mill has not as yet been able to afford worsted yarn so cheap as that which is spun by hand. . . .

THE HAT-MAKER

Hats are made either of wool, or hair of different animals, particularly of the beaver, rabbit, and camel. The process is nearly the same in all; it will therefore be sufficient if we describe the method made use of in the manufacture of beaver hats.

The skin of the beaver is covered with two kinds of hair, the one long, stiff and glossy; the other is short, thick and soft, and is alone used for hats. To tear off one of these kinds of hair, and cut the other, women are employed, who make use of two knives: a large one something like a shoe-maker's knife, for the long hair; and a smaller one nearly in the form of a pruning knife, with which they shave or scrape off the shorter hair.

When the hair is off, they mix and card it; they then place it on a table having slits in it lengthwise: on this table they mix the hair together, the dust and filth falling through the chinks or slits. In this manner they form gores, as they are called, of an oval shape, and with the stuff that remains they supply and strengthen the parts that may be slighter than they should be. In that part of the brim which is next the crown, the substance is thicker than in the other parts of the hat.

The gores thus finished, the workman goes on to harden them into closer or more consistent flakes by pressure; [the man then continues the process of making the hat]. . . .

PART II

THE LACE-MAKER

The LACE-MAKER is . . . busily engaged in her work in the open air, which even in this country is no uncommon sight during the summer months.

Lace is not woven, and of course it requires in the operation neither warp nor woof. It is made of silk or of thread, which is wound on little bobbins, made of bone or ivory, about the thickness of a skewer: hence the name bone-lace. The pattern, to which the lace is to be made, is drawn on paper or parchment, pricked with pin-holes, and then put on the pad or cushion which the woman holds on her knees. All the ends of the thread are first fastened together, and the lace-maker twists them variously, over and under each other, round the pins, which are stuck into the holes in the pattern: these pins they remove from one part to another, as their work goes on; and by these means are produced that multiplicity of eyes, or openings, which give to lace the desired figures.

For this operation much art and ingenuity are not necessary: it is, however, very tedious work; and when the thread is fine, and the pattern full and complex, it requires a degree of patience which can rarely be expected in persons of easy circumstances. Lace-making, therefore, is consigned to the hands of indigent women and young girls, who, by their skill and dexterity, raise the value of materials, originally of little worth, to almost any sum. But the time required to produce this beautiful manufacture is always in proportion to the value of the work; so that after all, little money is earned in the business.

The origin of the art of lace-making cannot be distinctly traced: by some it has been supposed to be the same as that which is called in Latin authors the *Phrygian art;* but this probably consisted rather in needle-work, than in that sort of netting used in the making of bone-lace. Borders sewed upon cloths and tapestry, which are mentioned by antient writers, were a kind of lace worked with a needle: this lace is undoubtedly of much older date than that made by netting. Of the former kind much is still extant among old church furniture, which was probably the work of nuns, or ladies of fortune, who devoted their time to the business on religious motives: but had it been manufactured as an article of commerce, something more would have been found concerning it in contemporary authors.

A lace manufactory was established in Paris, under the auspices of the celebrated Colbert, in the year 1666; but this was done by the needle, and was similar to what is called *point.*

The Germans, however, claim the honour of having invented the art of lace-making by means of the cushion and bobbins: they ascribe the invention to Barbara, the wife of Christopher Uttmann, who died about the year 1575. At this period the mines in Germany were become much less productive than they had been for centuries: the wives and daughters therefore, of the miners, were induced to turn their hands to the making of lace, which, owing to the low price of labour, they were enabled to sell so cheap, that it became fashionable, in opposition to the Italian lace worked with the needle, and even supplanted it in commerce.

The best laces are now made at Mechlin, Brussels, Ghent, Antwerp, and Valenciennes, which still enrich the country around, and induce the farmers to cultivate flax on the poorest soils. In France, lace was made in large quantities in the convents.

In our own country, the manufacture of lace is carried on to a greater extent and perfection in Buckinghamshire than in any other part of the United Kingdom, particularly in the town and neighbourhood of Newport-Pagnel, which is a sort of mart for that article, and flourishes considerably by its means.

[From THE MILLINER, see section 3]

Crapes when made into court dresses are ornamented in a thousand different ways: sometimes as caps, or turbans, they are ornamented with *spangles*, *artificial flowers*, and with *diamonds*. Spangles are small thin round leaves of metal pierced in the middle, which are sewed on as ornaments to a dress. They are made in the following manner: a wire is twisted in the form- of a screw; it is then cut into single spiral rings, like those used by pin-makers; and these rings, being placed on a very smooth anvil, are flatted, and spread by a smart blow of the hammer, so that a small hole remains in the middle; and the ends of the wire, which lie over each other, are closely united. Spangles were first made in the gold and silver manufactories of France, and the method was long kept a secret: at length, however, they were successfully imitated in Germany and other parts.

Artificial flowers are made, sometimes of very fine coloured paper, sometimes of the inside linings upon which the silk-worm spins its silk, but principally of cambric, which is a kind of linen made of flax, first manufactured at Cambray, in France; of which great quantities were imported into this country: but now, persons convicted of wearing, or selling, or making up for hire, any cambric or French lawns are liable to a penalty of 5l. The cambrics chiefly in use here are manufactured in Scotland and Ireland.

Ribands used by the milliners are woven: of these there are several sorts, distinguished by different names; as the China, the sarsenet, and the satin riband. Muffs and fur tippets are sold by the milliner, but the manufacture of them from the skin is a distinct business.

Velvet is used by milliners, and is now much in fashion. Velvet is a sort of stuff or silk, the nap of which is formed of part of the threads of the warp, which the workman puts on a channelled ruler, and then cuts, by drawing a sharp steel tool along the channel of the ruler to the end of the warp.

THE FEATHER-WORKER

THIS is another business in which women are chiefly employed. The person represented in the plate is at work on a military feather; but the feathers which are represented as in the shop window for show, are those which ladies wear in full dress. Within these few years, the trade for feathers, especially for those worn by the military, has very greatly increased.

Before the feathers come into the hands of the person who makes them up for sale, they undergo several operations. They are curled, either by being baked, or by means of hot irons; and when necessary, they are also dyed. The feathers principally in use are those of the ostrich, heron, the common cock, swan, peacock, and goose: of these, some are adapted to plumes with which hearses and horses are decorated at the funerals of the great; others are fitted for ornaments to the human head to some we are indebted for the beds on which we lie, and to others for the pens with which we write.

Geese are plucked in some parts of Great Britain five times in a year: the first plucking is at Lady-day for feathers and quills, and four other pluckings are made between that time and Michaelmas for feathers only. In cold seasons many geese die by this barbarous custom. The fens in Lincolnshire abound with geese; and the produce of feathers is so great, that frequently three hundred bags, each containing one hundred weight and a half, are sent away in a year. Military feathers are chiefly made of the hackle feathers, as they are; called these are plucked from the neck of the cock. The feathers of this bird are in great demand: his neck and back are clothed with long streaming feathers, intermixed with orange, black, and yellow; his tail is made up of stiff feathers, with two large ones waving over the rest in form of a sickle.

The plumage of the *wonderful Indian cock* is very beautiful, and consists of five different colours, viz. the black, white, green, red, and blue; and the tail is made up of twelve very beautiful feathers. But ostrich feathers are the most valuable: they are such as are represented in the plate. In their natural state they are mostly black and white: the largest feathers are at the extremeties [sic] of their wings and tails. The feathers of the ostrich require dying and dressing before they can be used as ornaments in ladies' head dresses. The spoils of this bird are so valuable, that it is no wonder the human race, who reside in the vicinity of his resorts, have ever been his declared enemies, and constant pursuers. The Arabs are so sensible of the value of the ostrich, that they train their fleetest horses for the purpose of hunting them. When the ostrich perceives that he is pursued, he sets off at first in a gentle pace, as if insensible of his danger, or sure of escaping. In running, he keeps his wings, like arms, in constant motion, corresponding exactly with that of his legs. At length, when he is worn out with fatigue and hunger, he resolves to conceal himself; for which purpose he covers his head with the sand, or forces it into the first thicket he comes near, where he patiently waits until he is taken by his pursuers. The hunters always avoid killing their prey, because those feathers that are taken from the ostrich while he is alive are the most valuable; the others are dry, light, and liable to be spoiled by worms. Many tribes hunt and take them for the purpose of rendering them tame, that they may thereby obtain a supply or feathers, which is accomplished with very little trouble.

Round feathers, . . . are composed of a number of smaller ones: if they are taken from the cock's neck, they are neatly tied on wire with thread; but if they are small ostrich feathers, they are twisted round an upright wire. The single ostrich feathers have usually a small piece of wire at the end, for the purpose of fixing into the cap, turban, or hair. Women that work at this business can earn two shillings a day.

Feathers make a considerable article of commerce, being used for beds, writing-pens, &c. Those imported from foreign countries pay a heavy duty to the revenue. There is also a duty upon ostrich feathers, both in the undressed as well as in the dressed state.

22

APPRENTICES IN THE EIGHTEENTH CENTURY

Source: Apprentices in the Eighteenth Century.

EDITORIAL HEADNOTE

The following sources are included to illustrate the ways girls and women might come into a variety of industries. The apprenticeship indentures are legal documents laying out the conditions, trade, period of service and frequently the fee paid, and none appear to be or have been parish apprentices, which are included here (doc. 24). They are drawn from different sources, which shape the contents and testimony, and rarely do we hear the woman's voice. They also illustrate the way some women came into contact with the administrative world of the eighteenth century and suggest that they knew how to use and understand the systems.

22.1. ANNE JARVOIS PUTS HERSELF APPRENTICE

Source: Anne Jarvois puts herself apprentice, Birmingham DRO 61/7/8, Harborne Parish, 1717.

EDITORIAL HEADNOTE

Private or trade apprentices, i.e. not parish or charity-funded apprenticeships, were girls' best chances of entering a trade other than though family workshops and connections. Bundled with the parish records of Harborne in the Black Country, this indenture is distinct in that she puts herself apprentice, although with the agreement of her mother. It also names no trade but gives her guarantees that she would be taught 'in all sorts of business'. It is typical also that she was indentured until twenty-one and would not marry without permission. The payment, however, was low compared to most fees (£2 10s.), and even parish apprentices were commonly placed with £5.

DOI: 10.4324/9781003676669-24

This Indenture Witnesseth that Anne Jarvois Daughter of Sarah Jarvois of the parish of Harborne in the County of Stafford by and with the consent of her Mother Testifying the same by her signing and sealing Herself doth put and place her self apprentice to Hillary Wattmore of the parish of Feckenham in the County of Worcester with him after the manner of an apprentice to serve from the Day of the Date hereof until she shall accomplish the age of one and twenty years During which Term the said Apprentice her said master faithfully shall and will serve his Secrets keep his lawfull Commands Every where gladly so. She shall do no damage to her said Master nor let it be done of others but to her power shall lett or forthwith Give notice to her the said Master of the Same his Goods of her said Master. She shall waste nor lend them unlawfully to any harm to her said Master She shall not do Cause or procure to be Don. She shall nither buy nor sell without her Masters Leave Matrimony she shall not Contract nor from the services of her said Master Day nor Night shall absent herself but in all things as an honest and faithfull Apprentice Shall and will . . . behave herself Towards her said Maters and all his During all the said Term and the said Hillary Whattmore in Consideration of the Sum of fifty shillings of Lawfull money of Great Britain to him in hand well and truly paid by said Sarah Jervis (the Receipt thereof is [unreadable] of this Covenant and promis to Teach or Cause to be Taught and Instructed his said Apprentice in all sorts of Business the best way and manner that he can finding and allowing unto his said apprentice Sufficient Meat and Drink washing Lodging and all other necessaries During the said Term and also shall and will at the End of the said Term find and afford unto his said apprentice Two suits of apparel one for Working Days and another for Holydays and for the true performance of all and Every the Covenants and agreements aforesaid and Either of the parties Binds Themselves unto the other firmly by these presents. In Witness whereof the parties first above Named to these Indentures Interchangeably have set their hands and seals the sixth day of December anno dom, 1717.

Sarah and Anne made their mark, Hillary signed

22.2 MARTHA PILLAH, APPRENTICE, CHARGED WITH THEFT, MAKES AND MENDS MEN'S CLOTHES 1717

Source: Martha Pillah, apprentice, charged with theft, makes and mends men's clothes 1717, *Old Bailey Proceedings Online, Ordinary of Newgate's Account*, May 1717 (OA17170520).

EDITORIAL HEADNOTE

Martha Pillah appeared in the records, charged with theft, in 1717. She said she had been an apprentice, served her whole time and was working for herself at the time of her arrest. The record was written by the chaplain of Newgate prison, where she was held, and who commented on her character. Through him we have a glimpse of her voice as he acknowledged her confession and admissions of bad behaviour.

Martha Pillah, alias Pillow, condemn'd for stealing 6 Guinea's, and 15 Shillings, from Mrs Elizabeth White, on the 16th of April last. She said, she was about 18 years of age, born of very honest Parents in Brewers-yard, in the Parish of St. Margaret, Westminster: That her Friends put her out Apprentice to a Taylor, and when the Time of her Service with him was expir'd, she work'd for herself, whose chief Business then was, the making and mending Men's Cloaths. She confess'd the Fact she was to suffer for; and also own'd, That she had been a very lewd and lascivious Woman, concern'd in many wicked things, and had once before now, taken her Tryal at the Old-baily, for a Fact of which she was Guilty, but (for want of sufficient Proof) acquitted. I found her ignorant to the last degree in any thing that was either Pious or Good; and 'twas no small Difficulty for me to bring her to a sense of Religion, of her miserable Condition, and thereby to a State of Repentance.

22.3 ELIZABETH COCK, BASKETWEAVER, 1756

Source: Elizabeth Cock, basketweaver, 1756, 'Examinations, 1750–1766: no 331', in *Chelsea Settlement and Bastardy Examinations, 1733–1766*, Tim Hitchcock and John Black (eds.), (London, 1999), pp. 102–106. *British History Online* http://www.british-history.ac.uk/london-record-soc/vol33/pp102-106

EDITORIAL HEADNOTE

Elizabeth Cock's settlement exam (see doc. 9 for explanation) gives a good account of how women moved through the worlds of industrial work. Although apprenticed and following her master into another parish, she was abandoned and left to deal with her situation as best she could. Applying to the poor law, she was probably chargeable to Chelsea as she had lived there and indeed was currently living there.

331. [p. 116] Middlesex, to wit. The examination of Elizabeth Cock, who on her oath says that she is about 16 years of age and was born in the parish of Chelsea, and apprenticed to Robert Ellis, a basket maker in the parish of St George Hanover Square, with whom she lived for some time until her said master removed into the parish of Chelsea. And there this examinant lived with her said master about one

year and a half, and until that her said master went away and left her. Then this examinant went and lived with her own sister, a lodger in the parish of Fulham, without any hiring for a year, or any wages. And lived with her about one year and a half, and then came and applied herself to the overseers of the poor in the said parish of Chelsea. The mark of Elizabeth Cock. Sworn before me, 22 Dec. 1756, Samuel Bever.

22.4 MARY SHREWSBURY, STOCKING TRIMMER

Source: Mary Shrewsbury, 'Stocking Trimmer. Ordinary's Account', *Newgate's Account*, 3 March 1737 (OA17370303). *Old Bailey Proceedings Online* (www.oldbaileyonline.org, Version 8.0, 17 May 2023). See also the trial account: https://www.oldbaileyonline.org/record/T17370216-21?TEXT=MARY%20 SHREWSBURY.

EDITORIAL HEADNOTE

Mary Shrewsbury's story was a familiar if not common one. She was well-brought-up, apprenticed and successfully worked as a stocking trimmer until she became pregnant. The detail of the ensuing infanticide follows other stories from the Old Bailey cases. Narrated again by the Chaplain at Newgate, her story shows the fragility of working women's situation in this period.

Mary Shrewsbury, alias Threwsbury, 23 Years of Age, of honest Parents, who gave her good Education at School, and instructed her in the Christian Religion. Her Father was a Stocking-Weaver, and when she was of Age, put her Apprentice to a Stocking-Trimmer in Wapping; she serv'd out her Time honestly, and with approbation, and she till she was taken up, wrought at her Business and kept herself very well, and maintain'd a good Character, not being addicted to any Vices, or a loose Life; 'till of late she grew intimate with a Man in Spittlefields, who seduc'd and debauch'd her, and by whom she prov'd with Child of that miserable male Infant, whom she Butcher'd and Murder'd in a most barbarous Manner. She told nobody of her being with Child, and had provided nothing for it; and when her full Time was come, being in Lodgeings by herself, she was deliver'd of the Child, and in the dark with a Knife cut its Throat. Her Landlady coming up, carried away some Things which she threw in the Vault; then another Woman came up, who amaz'd at what she saw, she said to her that she had miscarry'd, and was a Quarter gone. After this, Suspicions encreasing in the Neighbourhood, the Overseer of the Poor came to her and enquir'd into the Matter, she alledged that the Child was thrown into the Vault, which they search'd thoroughly, but could not find: The Overseer setting a Guard upon her for that Night, next Morning brought an expert Midwife, after much searching through the House and Room, and about the Bed, and they found a great many stain'd Clouts; at last going into a Closet by the Fire, she found the Child with it's Throat cut, and the Head almost off. Mary seeing this swoon'd away, when she recover'd, the Midwife asking her how she could treat her own Child, of a good Growth, and come to its full Time so barbarously? Mary took the whole Blame upon herself, because some suspected the other Woman to be too much concern'd in the Affair. She was kept secure 'till her Recovery, and then sent to Newgate, and at the ensuing Sessions at the Old-Bailey, this Murder was fully prov'd upon her. I representted to her the Atrociousness of such a horrid Cruelty, which she did not disown, but acknowledg'd that she was punish'd most deservedly and justly. While under Sentence she behav'd very well, and to outward Appearance was penitent, and on several Occasions, particularly when she receiv'd the Sacrament, wept and cried most bitterly. She declar'd that she hop'd for Salvation thro' the Merits of Christ's Blood and Sufferings; was sincerely penitent for all her Sins, especially the heinous Crime of Murder and Blood-shedding, and in Peace with all the World. . . .

Guilty, sentenced to death.

23

HIRING AGREEMENTS

Source: Hiring Agreements.

23.1 ANN KEELING. ARTICLES OF AGREEMENT

Source: Ann Keeling. Articles of Agreement. Wedgwood archives, 266316–133, 28 February 1781.

EDITORIAL HEADNOTE

Hiring agreements could resemble an apprenticeship, like Ann Keeling's, which put her on a graduated pay scale as she learned her trade at Wedgwood's pottery as a 'paintress' (doc. 23.1). Women were frequently hired as paintresses, mainly edging and decorating the pottery. Wedgwood hired skilled painters and notable artists, like George Stubbs and John Flaxman. But he also hired numerous women, and artists like Lady Diana Beauclerk, Elizabeth, Lady Templeton and Emma Crewe who were used exclusively to decorate his jasperware. Factory records show that he hired at least half a dozen women to work on the Frog Service for Catherine the Great; the highest-paid paintress, a Mrs. Willcox, was paid half of the highest-paid man. Little else is known about Ann, but she may have been related to one of Wedgwood's key modelers, Anthony Keeling, a potter in his own right running A&E Pottery. Thus, in a sense, she may have been joining the family business.

These articles of agreement made and fully agreed upon this day the 28th day of Feby 1781

Witnesseth that Ann Keeling of Hanley, in the county of Safford with her fathers consent doth hire herself with Josiah Wedgwood of Etruria in the said county potter, to serve the said Josiah Wedgwood in the business of painting at his London works to the full extent and term of 3 years from the date therof. And the said Josiah Wedgwood the master in consideration of the service of his said servant, shall find said servant, sufficient meat, drink and apparel, lodging and all other necessaries during the said term, and also shall pay unto the said servant for the first year and for the first year the sum of three pounds, for the second year, the

DOI: 10.4324/9781003676669-25

sum of 4 pounds, and for the third and last year the sum of five pounds. – Witness the parties hands

The witnesses named Josiah Wedgwood & Wm Keeling signed in the presence of Peter Swift: [both signed]

Signed by the within named Anne Keeling – in the presence of Thomas Bryerly: [she made her mark]

23.2 HIRING OF TIREUSES, LYON 1722

Source: Hiring of Tireuses, Lyon 1722, Order from the Consulate of September 3, 1722, prohibiting any master from employing any girl as a daily *tireuse* if they are not hired out. Municipal archives of Lyon, HH 514.

EDITORIAL HEADNOTE

Hiring agreements could be carefully regulated and gave the young women a standing in law. This one is from Lyon and prohibits silk manufacturers makers from hiring *tireuses* without them being properly hired out. The intention was to protect employers who wanted to hire women long-term, and who found it difficult to find employees as some manufacturers only hired them on a daily basis but depleted the supply. The knock-on effect of the regulations was to give the women some security of employment and protections.

To the Provost of Merchants and Aldermen of the city of Lyon, judges of the consular jurisdiction of the arts and crafts police.

The masters and guards in charge of the merchants and master workers in gold, silver and silk fabrics of this city humbly supplicate and show you that they take some care to prevent the abuses which are introduced into the factory, they receive frequent complaints, that several masters interfered in employing *tireuses* as day labourers, against the prohibitions of the consular ordinances of August fifth, seventeen hundred and four, and of February fifteen, seventeen hundred and eighteen this year, which brings considerable harm to those who, following the regulations, want to hire them for years, who cannot find any by the bad practices that several workers use of removing them from each other, which causes great disorder, to which we are obliged to resort to you.

May it please you, Gentlemen, to order that the said ordinances of August fifth, seventeen hundred and four, and February fifteen, seventeen hundred and eighteen, will be executed according to their form and tenor, and in addition to better obviate all these abuses than the masters will be obliged to write or have written in a book the hiring of the said female printers, the date of the day and the agreed price of which they will have a duplicate written in the same hand which they will be required to represent to the master's guards during their visit to penalty of twenty pounds fine applicable half to the two hospitals of this city and the other half to the master's guards, and require in addition that prohibitions be made for all merchants, masters or mistresses in the future from taking the said *tireuses* or others, without having previously informed themselves of those of whom they left, if they have fulfilled the said commitments, which will be proven by a consent note given by the masters for whom they last worked, and where there would be masters who would occupied without their having finished their time, they would also be condemned to the same fine of twenty pounds, applicable as above, and will be your order read published and displayed by all where necessary will be and executed as for fact of police and regulation notwithstanding oppositions or designations whatsoever and without prejudice to them and will do justice.

Signed J. G. Roze, Denis, Reverony, Borde, Bequey and Delafont.

The provost of merchants and aldermen of the city of Lyon.

Seen by us, the request must be written, as well as the consular orders set out therein, all communicated to Alexandre Prost, esquire, lord of Grangeblanche, lawyer and attorney general of the city and community of Lyon, advisor and prosecutor of the King in the consular jurisdiction of the arts and crafts police of the said city, which was agreed in its conclusions.

The said sir provost of merchants and aldermen have ordered and now order, that the consular orders of August five thousand seven hundred and four, and February fifteen thousand seven hundred and eighteen, will be executed, according to their form and tenor, in doing so and adding thereto as necessary, that in the future and from the day of the publication of these presents, the merchants and masters or mistresses of the art of workers in silk fabrics of this city, who will employ girls to pull the threads of their trades will be required to have a book of which they will give a copy to the printer, on which will be written in the same hand the day that the girl will have entered the service of the master, the time for which she will have been hired or engaged, the sum which will have been promised to him per year, and will also be written on the said books subsequently and dates the sums which will be paid to the said drawers so that the said books will then serve as a rule and proof in the event of difficulties which may arise between the parties.

During the visits which will be made by the masters and guards, both the masters of their community and the rope pullers will each be required to represent double their book to justify in what capacity the girls who will be found working with the said master silk workers work.

The hirings or commitments of the said girl *tireuses* cannot be made for less time than one year, during which the said *tireuses* will be required to work faithfully and assiduously without being able to leave the service of the masters during the year which will have been started, nor be able to be removed from it, except for legitimate cause, or with the consent of the parties, with the exception, however, of the wives or widows of masters who will be able to work as in the past as day laborers by providing proof of their quality;

24

PARISH APPRENTICES

Source: Parish Apprentices.

24.1 PARISH APPRENTICES. HACKNEY PETTY SESSIONS BOOK, EXTRACTS: 1734

Source: Parish Apprentices. Hackney Petty Sessions Book, 1734, in *Justice in Eighteenth-Century Hackney: The Justicing Notebook of Henry Norris and the Hackney Petty Sessions Book*, ed. Ruth Paley (London: London Record Society, 1991), 117–129. British History Online, http://www.british-history.ac.uk/london-record-soc/vol28/pp117-129

EDITORIAL HEADNOTE

While 30 per cent of pauper apprentices were girls, 60 per cent of female apprentices were placed out by poor law officials. Commonly, families were refused support from their parish if they had resident children who could be apprentices to someone else in the parish, including kin. These children could be put to a trade, although many girls went to housewifery, and they were frequently found in domestic industries. Nevertheless, a girl placed in a workshop trade, perhaps associated with housewifery could become an important producer in a domestic industry alongside a husband or family members. A key difference was that girls apprenticed by their families would serve a specified term, and in the more prosperous trades like millinery this was between two and four years, while parish apprentices usually served until they reached the age of twenty-one or marriage. The Overseers of the poor negotiated with local ratepayers, and sometimes with those from neighbouring parishes, to take a child, and as the examples from Hackney show, they paid a premium to the new master and often had to clothe or otherwise provide for a girl before she could be placed out. Most of these examples were placed in industries that required little training, and only Elizabeth Johnston found herself with a milliner, which could have been a promising opportunity.

DOI: 10.4324/9781003676669-26

397. Ordered That Mary Pegram aged 13 years a poor Child of this Parish be bound apprentice to Joseph French of the parish of S^{t}. Mary at Newington in the County of Surry pin maker for the usual Term and that M^{r}. Thomas Wood the Churchwarden do pay to him the sume of forty shillings with her.

596. Ordered That Sarah Silvester aged 14 years a poor Child belonging to this parish be bound apprentice to W^{m}. Bradley of the parish of St George in Bloomsbury in the County of Middlesex Labourer and that Mr John Davis the Churchwarden do pay him the usual allowance of Forty shillings.

614. Allowed an Indenture whereby Elizabeth Johnson aged fourteen Years a poor Child of the Parish of St John at Hackney was bound apprentice to Elizabeth Emerton of the Parish of St Mary Islington in the County of Middlesex milliner.

650. Ordered That Susannah Holbrook aged ten years a poor Child of this parish be forthwith bound apprentice to Joseph French of the parish of Saint Mary Overes in the County of Surry pin maker and that M^{r}. John Davis the Churchwarden do pay forty shillings with her and Six shillings towards providing some Clothes for her she being almost naked and having had the meazles since she hath been upon liveing with him.

The Mermaid Tavern: Monday, 18 February 1734, Justices present: Stephen Ram, Henry Norris

705. Ordered That Susannah Twitchell aged 13 years a poor Child of the Parish of S^{t}. John at Hackney in the County of Middlesex be bound apprentice to Joseph French of the parish of S^{t}. Saviour in Southwark Pin Maker and that M^{r}. John Davis the Churchwarden do pay forty shillings with her and also twenty shillings towards cureing her of a Scorbutical Humour and that she have the usual Clothing.

711. Ordered That Sarah Cavennough aged [sixteen *deleted*] fourteen years a Poor Child of the Parish of Hackney be bound apprentice to Randall Burr of Bacon Street in the Hamlet of Bethnal Green in the County of Middlesex Stocking maker and that Mr John Davis the Churchwarden do pay to him forty shillings with her and also twenty shillings to be laid out in necessary Clothing for her. [*See* 735]

730. Ordered That Ann Inott aged thirteen years a Poor Child of this Parish be forthwith bound apprentice to Daniel Loiseauz of the Hamlet of Mile End new Towne in the County of Middlesex weaver and that Mr Morgan Bynon the Churchwarden do pay forty shillings with her and also that he lay out twelve shillings in Clothing for her she being almost naked.

735. Allowed an Indenture of apprenticeship whereby Sarah Cavennough aged fourteen years a poor Child of this parish was bound to Randall Burr of the Hamlet of Bethnal Green Stocking maker. [*See* 711].

24.2 MARY WILKINSON, APPRENTICED TO WEAVING, 1760

Source: Mary Wilkinson, apprenticed to weaving, 1760, 'Examinations, 1750–1766: no 395', in *Chelsea Settlement and Bastardy Examinations, 1733–1766*, ed. Tim Hitchcock and John Black (London, 1999), pp. 102–106. *British History Online* http://www.british-history.ac.uk/london-record-soc/vol33/pp102-106

EDITORIAL HEADNOTE

Mary Wilkinson's story comes again from the settlement and bastardy exams, and despite having been apprenticed to a good trade, it is not clear whether she continued to work after her apprenticeship. But like Mary Shrewsbury, she found herself pregnant. She clearly knew who the father was and they had cohabited, but she applied for relief when she found herself unable to support herself.

395. [p. 173] Middlesex, to wit. The examination of Mary Wilkinson, lodging in the parish of Chelsea in the county of Middlesex, taken upon oath this [blank] Nov. 1760. This examinant, upon her oath saith that she is near 23 years of age, that she was born in the parish of Walton-on-Thames in the county of Surrey. That she was put out by the said parish of Walton as an apprentice to one Richard Henley, a weaver at Addlestone in the parish of Chertsey in the said county of Surrey. That she continued with her said master between six and seven years. That she never was married, that she never kept a house, or tenement of £10 by the year, paid any parish taxes, nor hath been a yearly hired servant in any one place for twelve months together since. This examinant upon her voluntary oath further says that she is now great with child or children which are likely to be born a bastard or bastards, and to become chargeable to the parish of Chelsea. And that Thomas Rayner, an in pensioner belonging to the sixth ward in his Majesty's Royal Hospital in the said parish of Chelsea had carnal knowledge of her body (and he only). That he and the examinant cohabited together going on three years, lastly in the house of one Richard Angier in or near Turk's Row in Chelsea aforesaid. By whom, the said Thomas Rayner, she now is great with child or children, she now goeth with and is pregnant of. And that he, the said Thomas Rayner, is the true and only father thereof, and no man else. [Blank]. Sworn the day and year above written. [The above statement is crossed out in the original.]

25

MISS CLARA COLLET ON THE CONDITIONS OF WORK IN BIRMINGHAM, WALSALL, DUDLEY, AND THE STAFFORDSHIRE POTTERIES, 1893

Source: Miss Clara Collet, 'On the Conditions of Work in Birmingham, Walsall, Dudley, and the Staffordshire Potteries', in Miss Eliza Orme, Miss Clara E. Collet, Miss May Abraham, and Miss Margaret H. Irwin, *Reports, The Employment of Women*, Royal Commission on Labour Presented to both Houses of Parliament by Command of Her Majesty, February 1893, 49–55, 60–63.

EDITORIAL HEADNOTE

Clara Collet (1860–1948) was a University College London (UCL) graduate, as was Elizabeth Orme, with whom she testified to the Royal Commission on Labour in 1893. Born into a north London family of radical inclinations and friendly during childhood with the Marx family, she went to the North London Collegiate School, and with Frances Buss' recommendation she taught in Leicester from 1878 until 1885 while studying as an external student of UCL. In 1885 she enrolled for an MA in political economy at UCL which she completed in 1888, having been awarded the department's Joseph Hume scholarship in 1886, possibly the first woman to achieve an MA at a British university. She continued studying mathematics, lecturing to supplement her scholarship, before joining the pioneering statistical project of Charles Booth to map social conditions in London, living in the East end to facilitate her work. After working for the Royal Commission, she joined the Labour Department of the Board of Trade, where her statistical work on labour conditions influenced policy until her retirement in 1920 and beyond. In 1894 she was elected to Fellowship of the Royal Statistical Society and later served on its Council; in 1896 she was the first woman to be awarded a UCL Fellowship and in 1902 delivered a series of lectures on 'economic questions requiring medical answers', the first woman to lecture in the department.

The Royal Commission findings viewed wage-labour as beneficial for women, arguing that they were however underpaid and required to endure

DOI: 10.4324/9781003676669-27

unhealthy conditions, and encouraged unionisation. The detailed collection of data on pay and employment was a hallmark of Collet's work which she used effectively in a succession of publications. Her interest was not only poor women, and she also addressed the economic conditions of middling women. The extract here continues the theme of the metal and pottery trades of the Midlands and illustrates her approach to this research, as well as bringing women in late nineteenth-century industries to the forefront.

I. – BIRMINGHAM

1 Wages. . . . Buttons are also in many cases made in fairly large workshops or factories, and to these it was not so difficult to obtain admission, but facts as to wages were stated vaguely by the employers, and in the one case in which the wages for one department were given me exactly the wage books were not shown.

Witness 300, belonging to a firm of button makers, said that he employed over 200 women and girls and about 60 men; 15 children were half-timers. The hours of work were from 8 a.m. to 6 p.m. with 15 minutes for lunch and one hour for dinner, making 48½ hours per week excluding meal times. Linen cutters earned from 14s. to 16s., linen coverers earned about 14s., out of which they paid 1s. 6d. to the half timers helping them, in addition to 9d. paid by the firm. The majority in the factory would earn about 10s. . . .

Witness 348 gave me the wages earned in his factory in which metal caps, rings, and "runners" for umbrellas are made. The factory is in a poor part of the town. I had been previously informed by ladies managing evening classes that "umbrella girls" and "screw girls" were the roughest in Birmingham. The long fringes hanging over the eyes and the heavy and somewhat dissipated faces of the women bore out these statements; but the neat dresses of the majority of the girls, and the good order maintained were all the more noticeable. Several of the hands were married women, but a large number were girls under 16. . . .

Witness 351, secretary of the Bedstead Makers Association, said that about 800 women belonged to the women's trade union, of which he was also secretary; there were altogether about 2,000 women in the bedstead trade in Birmingham, of whom quite one-third were married women who were able to earn good wages. He considered that they averaged about 15s. a week in most cases, and that the wages ranged from 7s. to 25s. . . .

In the jewellery trade witness 420, Secretary of the Jewellers' Trade Union, said that average gilds would earn from 8s. to 11s.; polishers would start at about 5s. or 6s., and if skilled might earn as much as 15s.

Very few married women worked in these workshops.

The wage book of witness 354, who employed 13 girls in making rings, showed that in an ordinary week –

1 earned under 6s.
4 "from 6s. to 8s.
1 "8s. to 10s.
4 "10s. to 12s.
3 "over 15s.

There were no married women in this workshop, and no one over 25 years of age. The girls worked 52½ hours a week.

The only statistics given to me referring to a sufficiently large number of girls to be at all satisfactory as a test of the rate of wages in Birmingham as compared with that in other towns are those relating to the cocoa and chocolate works at Bournville, 4 miles from Birmingham. The principles in which this factory is managed are very similar to those adopted in the cocoa factory at Bristol, the numbers employed are nearly equal, no married women are employed in either, both firms are careful as to the character of the girls they employ, both have the reputation of paying the best average of wages in their respective districts, meaning by this expression that the average wage of the majority of the girls employed is higher than that of the majority of girls in any other factory. Such difference, therefore, as may be found in the wages caused by the girls in the two factories would very fairly represent the difference in the general rate of earnings in Bristol and in Birmingham, and would also to some extent, but not so exactly, represent the superiority in skill and energy of the latter place over the former. To compare the tables of wages of the two would be misleading, as the distribution according to age is not the same in the two factories. It may, therefore, be best to proceed on the hypothesis that the lower earnings are received by the younger girls, and on this hypothetical basis, leaving out girls under 16 and women over 25 years of age, . . . The higher wages in Birmingham are slightly due to the fact that the Bristol firm have a considerable quantity of their ornamental boxes made elsewhere, whereas in Birmingham the highest wages earned are for this work. In Bristol it would probably be impossible to find a sufficient number of girls skilled enough for this special branch. Again the percentages of girls under 16 years and of women over 25 are both higher in the Birmingham than in the Bristol firm, which seems to indicate that in Bristol girls go to the factory later and leave it earlier in life than in Birmingham. It may be noted, here that the standard Trade Union wages of iron founders in Birmingham in 1891 were 36s., and in Bristol 32s.

Of course, as the girls have nothing to do with buying or mixing the ingredients of the cocoa or chocolate, the above table has no bearing on the question of the quality of goods sold by the two firms.

2. CONDITION OF WORKSHOPS

Every assistance that could be given by the local shops was most willingly offered, and the prompt action taken by the Health Committee with a view to carrying out the Factory Act, 1891, has made it possible to give a statement of the condition of workshops in Birmingham which may fairly be regarded as representative. An additional inspector had been appointed to supervise workshops, and a house to house inspection had been begun by the ordinary sanitary inspectors, to discover all workshops and to ascertain their condition. At the time of my visit full particulars of 419 workshops had been entered in their Workshops' Register. In this register are entered the number of rooms used as a workshop, the dimensions, the number of gas jets and fireplaces or stoves, the methods of ventilation, the condition of the rooms, whether the Workshops' Abstract is posted up. the means of escape in case of fire, the water supply, the number and kind of privies, the provision or absence of separate privy accommodation for women, the numbers of men, women, boys, and girls found at work at the time of the visit, structural defects, and sanitary improvements requisite.

On analysing these records I found that in 193 of these workshops women or girls were employed. Of these 30 were tailors' workshops, 44 were workshops of dressmakers, mantle-makers or milliners, and 119 were workshops principally used for the manufacture of hardware of various kinds. Of these 193 workshops 55 had no Workshop Abstract posted up, and may, therefore, be regarded as having escaped inspection.

Of these –

21 were workshops of dress or mantle makers or milliners, with an average of 3.2 women and 1.2 girls to a workshop.

14 were tailors' workshops, with an average of 3.6 women and 2 girls to a workshop and of 3 men and boys to every workshop, exclusive of the rooms in which only men were employed.

20 were workshops used for the manufacture of horse collars, boots, gas stoves, bridles, hooks, jewellery, gilt chains, coffins, trunks, brass knobs, paper boxes, hair brushes, furniture, fancy leather and japanned goods, with an average of 2.5 women and 1.5 girls to each workshop, and 15 men and boys to every workshop, exclusive of the rooms in which only men were employed.

Of the 35 tailors' and dressmakers' workshops in the above list –

15 were in a satisfactory condition.
12 needed limewashing.
3 were without separate privy accommodation for
5 needed reconstruction of privies, &c.

Of the 20 other workshops –
7 were in a satisfactory condition.
6 only needed limewashing.
5 were without separate privy accommodation for the sexes.
2 needed reconstruction of privies, &c.

Of the 193 workshops taken together –
82 were in a satisfactory condition.

49 only needed limewashing.
37 were without separate privy accommodation for the sexes.

25 needed considerable sanitary improvement.
In 2 cases no privy accommodation whatever was provided.

In 55 cases the rooms of the workshops were reported as "dirty," 8 of these being the workrooms of dressmakers and milliners, and 7 being those of tailors.

In 29 cases workshops were reported as having one or more rooms without fireplace or stove; of these 8 were workrooms of dressmakers and 5 of tailors. In several other cases the nature of the occupation requiring an excessive number of gas jets explained the absence of any heating apparatus. . . .

The workshops' sanitary inspector, with whom I visited several workshops, stated that in some cases where employers had been ordered to provide separate accommodation, although only one man or one woman was employed, they had got over the difficulty by dismissing the man or woman. Some employers had moved to other workshops where the necessary accommodation was provided. At one workshop where the employer had the day previous to our visit been ordered to remove a bed from a workroom, the shutters were up, the man having moved within 24 hours of receiving the order. At another the mistress of the house, who worked with her husband and another man in a bedroom at the top of the house, and had been told that either the bed or the work must be moved from the room, gave a most satisfactory account of the prompt removal of the bed; she ended by inviting us to go upstairs and see for ourselves, and having accepted the invitation we found that nothing had been done. With much reluctance she decided that in future they would do their boot finishing in the kitchen.

. . . The suspicion with which visits are received by the small masters, and the very short time that it is possible for anyone to stay on the premises without permission of the occupier, render it difficult to notice with accuracy all the points deserving attention. . . . [six places were listed as workshops] although they come under the legal definition of a factory. They are in a building in which workrooms are let out to small employers, who each pay an additional rent for the use of steam power. This place seemed to me in a most dangerous condition; wide holes were in the floors, and the staircases were narrow and dilapidated and difficult of access. If fire broke out in any part of the building the consequences might be very serious.

It may also be worth while to draw attention here to the fact that the Factory and Workshops Acts, while making provision for protection from fire in the case of factories in which more than 40 persons are employed, makes no provision for the safety of persons in workshops in which more than 40 persons are employed, nor for small factories or small workshops congregated in one large building. . . .

Notwithstanding the great variety of articles made on health in Birmingham, there is not a corresponding variety in the work done by the women. Many of the machines used are merely different applications of the same mechanical principle.

So far as an outsider could judge, a knowledge of "press work" in the pen trade would enable a girl to do press work in the button trade or umbrella furniture trade.

(e.) Lead

The women and girls employed in iron enamelling undoubtedly suffer from the inhalation of lead dust. The wages are rather high in proportion to the skill required, and this must be in consequence of the painful results of the work. The manager of one of these enamel works said that undoubtedly the work was injurious, nearly all the girls suffered from attacks of colic and severe illness. The particular operation which has the worst effects is brushing the lead powder from the part of the enamelled iron plate not covered with foil. The only precaution taken, (beyond good ventilation) was the provision of a damp sponge on which the girl puts her brush before using it; by this means the dust is prevented from rising.

Two girls had neglected to use their sponges and had to be sent to damp them when I visited the workroom. Such carelessness seemed less excusable than the refusal of the women to wear respirators. One of the women hearing the manager blame them for refusing to wear respirators turned round rather indignantly and said that she wanted to breathe and not have her mouth and nose stuffed up all day. There was a small cloak-room here but no dining-room, and the manager thought it very probable that if any woman did not go home she would have her dinner in the workroom, a most objectionable proceeding. There was no sick club here, but the somewhat heavy fines were used as a relief fund. A fine of 3d. for singing was said to be imposed in order to prevent the women from getting more lead dust in their mouths than was unavoidable.

The resident superintendent of a home for working girls said that one of them was a dipper in an enamel shop. She was aged 17, had only been in the trade four months, and began with 5s., since raised to 6s. Her health was being ruined by the work, but she refused to give it up because "she liked the work and she liked the girls." Another girl of the same age went to the same factory and was never in the least affected by the work.

Since my visit detailed rules have been issued from the Home Office with regard to iron enamel works, requiring occupiers to provide adequate washing conveniences, suitable respirators, overalls, and head coverings, and to adopt measures for the removal of all superfluous dust, to provide a sufficient supply of sulphuric acid drink or other approved sanitary drink, to provide medical attendance and medicine for persons suffering from illness contracted in the process of manufacture and to take care that no food shall be eaten in the works except in an apartment specially provided for the purpose.

Several ladies informed me that the "screw girls" at Smethwick had a reputation for coarse language and immorality, and believed that it must in some way be due to the conditions of work. This I feel absolutely certain is not the case. The screw machine-room, in which some hundreds of women and girls are employed, is very large and extremely lofty with a ground glass roof. Each girl was tending 16 machines (except those who worked at machines somewhat different from the majority in use) standing between two rows of eight.

Their work was to see that no part of the machine was clogged up so as to prevent it from acting; they used pincers to put the machine right and so far as I could see the only danger that could arise would be in the case of a girl carelessly using her fingers instead of her pincers. The machines themselves struck me as being positively graceful in their action, and the effect on the eye was refreshing after seeing the monotonous working of the presses in the Birmingham factories.

The manager stated that no one under 17 years of age was engaged for the screw machine room, so that nearly all had previously been employed in other factories, principally at press work. He also stated that quite half were married and from their appearance I should expect that this calculation would prove considerably under the mark if a census were taken. The managing director maintained that the women were not at all addicted to drink and that their attendance on Mondays and the day after holidays was always regular. If this is true, the faces of some of the women gave very false testimony. But although there seemed to me a large enough number of coarse-looking women to bring discredit on "screw girls" generally, yet the majority were very respectable-looking women whose appearance in neat dresses and white aprons with bibs and shoulder straps produced a very favourable impression. Here, as elsewhere in Birmingham, exact information as to wages was refused. The lavatory and cloakroom accommodation seemed to me good.

The employment in factories and workshops of married women whose husbands are well able to support them seemed to me the worst feature in the women in industrial life of Birmingham. There is hardly any home work for married women in the city. Nearly all the tailoring given out by the Birmingham clothiers is done in tailors' workshops. The chief industries of the place necessitate the employment of girls in processes absolutely useless to them in home life. After marriage they miss not only the cheerful society (for it is cheerful) of the factory, but also the steady work to which they have been accustomed, and for both reasons many of them persist in going to the factory. They are not, generally speaking, engaged on work which would otherwise be done by men, and therefore there seems remarkably little of the opposition to married women's labour invariably displayed by men when they consider that their own labour is being displaced by women, but the evils exist none the less. The rate of infant mortality in Birmingham is very high, and were it possible to obtain particulars of the occupations of the mothers of the infants who have died under the age of five years, medical testimony points to the probability that an abnormal proportion of them would be found in factories or workshops. As there is so little home work in Birmingham, I have had no opportunity of seeing workers in their homes; but one witness, a doctor, stated that a comfortable home was an exception. It is also very doubtful whether the married women in factories ever save any part of their earnings. At the same time it may be questioned whether there is any town in England where the evils are so clearly recognised and efforts to remove them so vigorously and sensibly made.

Percentage of Women and Girls in Bourneville Works.

Under 16 years.	26.6
16 to 18.	29.51
18 to 25.	32.1
25 and upwards.	11.8

There seems ground for believing that the girls in these works knowing that they will not be kept on after marriage do not marry so early as most factory girls, and are less liable to be married by men in search of a wife to support them.

Bourneville Cocoa and Chocolate Works

This factory was moved from Birmingham 11 years and six times as many persons are now employed in it. Arrangements were made with the railway company for cheap tickets for the workpeople. The majority of the men moved from Birmingham and settled down near the factory, but the girls used to come in by train. But their numbers, since the migration to Bourneville, have been largely recruited from the outlying villages, and barely 10 per cent, actually come from the city. The hours of labour when busy, viz., from September to December, are 6 a.m. to 5.30 p.m. A cup of warm tea and a tea biscuit are given to every girl when she comes in the morning; half an hour is allowed for breakfast, a quarter of an hour for lunch, and one hour for dinner. During this season they leave off at 1 p.m. on Wednesday and 12.30 p.m. on Saturday. For nine months in the year the hours are 8.45 a.m. to 5.30 p.m. and till 1.30 p.m. on Saturday.

The girls change their boots if damp, and place them on racks in the cloak rooms above hot water pipes. For the sake of cleanliness, they have to wear white holland dresses at their work, taken off before they go home; they are charged two-thirds of the cost of the holland, and make the dresses themselves. They must have a clean dress every Monday.

A playground of about ¾ acre is provided for the girls, shut in by trees, and with benches all round it, several of which are under cover.

Fines for lateness go to the Hospital Saturday Fund: other fines to the sick club. The cloakroom is large and well fitted, and lukewarm water is laid on for washing. The dining-room is fitted with seats, with backs reversible into tables, and the room is frequently used as a lecture hall. Formerly hot joints were provided from the kitchen, but this practice was abandoned because "all the girls wanted the best cut." Now the girls bring their meat, and have it cooked for them, and only cold meat and different kinds of pies and puddings are sold to them. . . .

The factory is lighted with electric light. The ventilation is excellent, and the fresh air warmed by hot pipes as it comes in. A dust collector was provided in the starch mould room, but was not acting quite satisfactorily. The women work entirely apart from the men, and are superintended by forewomen. It is the special business of a district nurse to visit the girls who are ill, and a committee of forewomen meets once a week to give out tickets that may be required for hospitals, &c. About 36 cottages, which might be described as semi-detached villas, with five rooms and a scullery and a good garden to each, are let at 5s. to 6s. a week.

Although, in the majority of factories and workshops, in Birmingham there is but little provision for dining in comfort, the city itself is well supplied with good and cheap eating-houses; and so far as public effort is concerned, it may be safely said that, in Birmingham, if any scheme can be proved worth carrying out, it will be undertaken.

The evidence of factory girls has been tabulated, but a very noticeable feature of it is the absence of any of serious discontent. This is not due to the fact that they may have been peculiarly well situated. The superintendent of a home and club for working girls, nearly all of whom earned very low wages, confirmed the evidence of other club managers, that the girls complained very little about their work. Their troubles were nearly all domestic or social rather than industrial. It is noteworthy that in the Bourneville Works, where no married women are employed, the percentage of single women over 25 is unusually high. . . .

IV. – THE STAFFORDSHIRE POTTERIES

The conditions of work and the system of wages prevailing in the Staffordshire Potteries (Stoke-on-Trent, Hanley, Burslem, Tunstall, Fenton, Longton) are strikingly different from those under which women work in other industries. It seems best to describe in detail the work done, but the numerous technical terms in use and the difficulty of observing correctly without any practical acquaintance with the work, give much cause for diffidence in undertaking the task.

In the first factory inspected about 500 people were employed in making "useful" earthenware (such as dinner, tea, and toilet services) for the home and foreign trade. No women were in the room where the clay is made. In the next room work was being carried on at benches separated from each other by partitions. At one of these compartments a man was "throwing" coffee cups, and a woman "attendant" was weighing the clay and preparing it for the thrower. In the next compartment a man was "turning" the cups at a lathe driven by steam power. It was stated that the lathe used to be worked by a girl attendant with a treadle, and that this was still done in some places. Here the girl only sponges the edges of the cup after it has been turned, and she was therefore assisting the lathe turners in two compartments instead of one only as was customary when she treadled. It was stated that each of the men paid her 2d. in every 1s. earned, so that if each man made 30s. gross in the week the girl would have 10s. and the men would each have 25s. net. This payment is known as "scorage."

The men doing "flat" work each had an attendant, a woman or a girl who sponged and fettled the plates after the men had done their part of the work. These spongers were paid 1s. 8d. the day; others who were also putting handles on to basins were paid 2s. 2d. a day. One girl was preparing the clay for saucers, "batting" it out with a heavy mallet. It was stated that most of the spongers and fettlers were married women, men in several cases bringing their own wives to work with them. Half-timers, both boys and girls, were being employed as "mould runners," carrying the moulds to and from the drying stoves.

Girls here were making cups with the "jolly;" one girl fettled for the "jollyer" and another girl was mould runner.

The most noteworthy process was that of "towing" the plates. This was introduced within the last 10 years and is substituted for sponging. The plate is put on a "whirler" which revolves (by steam power) while the girl cuts round the edges and rubs the plate with tow. At this factory the whirler was placed in a kennel-shaped hutch with a chimney, a fan carried off the clay dust through a funnel into a chimney outside the factory. I was informed by persons unconnected with the firm, that this factory had the newest and best system of carrying off the dust caused by towing. Spongers and fettlers sponge the ware while it is damp, the "towers" cut and rub it after it has been dried, the work being, therefore, much more dusty.

In the "biscuit warehouse" women were sorting the faulty work from the good. The head women are warehouse, paid so much an "oven" of ware, and they pay their assistants on day-work.

Girls in a room by themselves were sorting out "stilts," "thimbles," and "spurs" (small pieces of ware placed between the articles in the "saggers" to keep them apart from each other when fired), picking out those good enough to be used again.

In the "printing room" the work was being done in groups. The printer, a man, passes the paper pattern which he has printed to the journeywoman "transferrer" or to her "cutter" who cuts out the plain part of the paper; the journeywoman then "transfers" the pattern to the biscuit, a process requiring considerable care and skill; another girl, an "apprentice," rubs the paper into the biscuit and afterwards puts the plate, &c. into water and washes off the paper. According to the information given me the printer receives 5 ½d. the "dozen" and keeps 3d., he pays 2 ½d. to the journeywoman who pays the apprentice 1d.; the cutter receives 4s. 6d. a week "and 6d. pocket money," 2s. 6d. of this being paid by the journeywoman and 2s. 6d. by the apprentice. Then out of every 1s. that the journeywoman earns she pays back 1d. to the printer. The printer has to pay the "mixer" (a man) 6d. a "score of dozens."

(G.) Glazing. . . .

In the dipping-room men were dipping the ware in the liquid glaze which contains lead. In an adjoining room, cups, &c., which had been dipped and dried, were being rubbed together tops to tops and bottoms to bottoms. The rough glaze powder which comes off, and which contains lead, was stated by the employer to be injurious to health.

After the glazing process the ware is fired a second time, and after this second firing bits of "spurs," etc. have to be knocked off with a metal scraper. Women and girls were doing this, the sparks flying as they chipped the bits off. In this department two women were paid a fixed quantity, out of which they paid their assistants as in the biscuit warehouse.

The burnishers and "paintresses" seemed drawn from a rather different class; they were working entirely separate from the men.

Witness 386 showed me over his earthenware factory in which white granite ware was being made. Here also several half-timers were at work. It was stated that they were engaged by the women and paid by them, and were frequently their children.

Here women were making cups with the "jolly," each had two girls to sponge and fettle, and two mould runners. Another wages custom was illustrated in this department. The women who make cups without handles are paid direct; but those who make cups which have to be sent up to the "handlers," receive their money from the latter. In the wage-books, therefore, the cup-makers sometimes seem to be earning very little, and the handlers seem to have abnormally high wages, whereas the money put down to them includes money to be paid to the cup makers and their assistants.

The "whirlers" at which the "towers" were working, were here also driven by steam; but the whirlers were not under cover of hutches. There was a grating close to each whirler, down which the dust was supposed to be sucked by means of a fan; but the women's hair was covered with dust, showing pretty conclusively that this was not properly carried off. One whirler was not even near a grating. The seven women engaged in towing were all married. It was stated that hatches had been made for them, but the women, a very rough independent set, had refused to work with them.

No women were in the dipping department; the rough edges of the ware were being rubbed off by boys.

Witness 386 slated that where women were employed in making cups or saucers, no men would be found making them. The women would be paid a lower rate, just as it was common for apprentices, when put to journeymen's work, to receive two-thirds of a journeyman's pay. . . .

In some parts of this [another] factory there were sheds with a man "jollyer," and a woman attendant in each. The factory was an old and large one, with rooms in unexpected places, which seemed to me to render supervision both difficult and necessary. The rooms were also badly ventilated, although the dust in these factories or "banks" are so great as to make ventilation of the utmost importance. The room in which the girls were brushing off the glaze from the ware that had been dipped and dried was very dark, badly ventilated, and by the manager's own admission, unnecessarily hot.

In another factory "throwing" was more common than "jollying." The thrower's attendant was paid from the office and not by the thrower.

The lathes were turned by women, working at the treadle. It was stated that with steam it was difficult to regulate the different speeds required. The woman was paid 4d. for every 1s. earned by the turner, not 4d. out of every 1s.

Towing was being done over a grid; the dust was really being carried down by a fan, and the hair and dress of the women were quite free from dust.

The printers here received 6 ½d. a dozen, of which 3d. goes to the journey-woman and her apprentice.

Girls were rubbing off glaze, and a very small boy was helping the dipper, taking the wet cups from him.

A large number of "paintresses" were employed here. The ventilating holes in their room were all stuffed up. The "paintresses" serve a seven years' apprenticeship, no half-timers being employed in this department; they receive 2s. the first year, and then two-thirds of the full rate of pay; journey-women earn about 12s. to 14s. here.

The men in these factories struck me as looking much more unhealthy than the women. In some cases, the girls in the glazing department looked very white and ill; the "towers" looked very rough, and were said to be hard drinkers; with these exceptions it would be difficult elsewhere to find so many good-looking girls as are to be seen in any one of these factories. The most objectionable feature seemed to me to be the employment of half-timers, obliged to carry rather heavy trays to and from hot drying closets in the midst of so much clay dust.

A "ware cleaner" (as the girls are called who rub the glaze off the ware) said that she had been 15 weeks in the infirmary through lead poisoning, The ware cleaners earned from 10s. to 12s. She was paid nothing when she was ill. There was no sick club for girls, although there was one for men. They would never think of applying to their employer when ill, but if absent long the other work-people would subscribe to help them.

Witness 395 said she was a "wheel turner and taker-off" in a china "bank" in Longton. She was paid so much a dozen by the man for whom she worked, and made on an average 1s. 10d. a day. She generally only worked half a day on Monday. There was no overlooker where the men and women worked together.

The women had nothing to do with the employer. She herself had been very wretched at one place because the man under whom she worked was so disagreeable.

She had worked at several "banks" in her time. In some places there used to be no privy accommodation at all, but she knew of no place at the present time where this was the case.

Witness 396 said that she was a majolica paintress at Longton. Her husband married her on his 17th birthday, and she was a little older. She had worked at two banks. The hours were from 9 to 6, but some of the unmarried women went at 8. About three years ago they had 3d. in the 1s. taken off, and even then she earned 11s. a week. The girls objected to the reduction, but were not united enough to hold out. Some of them had since had 1d. in the 1s. back. Lead was used in all the colours, and it was most unhealthy. In one of the banks an extra quantity was used and the girls were always ill. She herself did not suffer so much as her sister, who was very dirty and was constantly ill through not washing her hands, &c. Many of the girls ate their meals in the paint-room. At one bank they ought to have gone to the "glost" warehouse to eat their dinner, but in the other there was no place but the workroom in which to eat it if they came from a distance. There was no sick club for girls in either of the banks. The girls subscribed sometimes if any one were ill a long time.

Witness 398 said her daughter had worked at a "bank" in Tunstall. She was 15 when she died. She had been 18 months in the dipping-room altogether. At first she used to put the ware on the boards for the dipper, and was paid 6s. 6d. She was tempted by higher wages to become a "ware cleaner," brushing off the glaze from the dried ware; for this she was paid 5s. the "oven." Two months ago her sister, aged 18, had joined her in this; they each made 12s. 6d. a week by it, but it was too much for both of them. The younger one was taken ill on Friday, but insisted on going to the "bank" on Saturday to pay the girls under her. She came back and died the next day of lead poisoning. Her elder sister had already left the work and was "putting up" for the dipper at 6s. 6d. a week. The employers had been much concerned about the matter. The girls in the "glost" room were now provided with big gowns to go over their dresses, hoods for their heads and respirators. A place had been found for the elder sister in the biscuit warehouse. They had contributed 3£. 3s. to funeral expenses

The Secretary of the National Order of Potters believed that about 400 women were members of one or other of the men's unions. He did not think the system of men employing women and women employing assistants was a bad one, although it might be objectionable if many people were under one foreman who could engage or dismiss at will. As it was he considered there was such competition for competent women that if a man did not treat his attendant properly she would leave him and go to another man. In many cases husband and wife or child worked together. The transferrers were very independent, and when the printers' price was lowered refused to lose more than their fair share. In reply to a question as to whether the arrangement of one journeywoman and one apprentice to one printer did not sometimes leave one of them with too little work, this witness stated that this proportion had been the custom from time immemorial. Formerly there used to be a great deal, of "heavy" printing (with the pattern all over the paper, as in the willow pattern), and this was easy for the transferrers and more difficult for the printers; now the "light" patterns were in vogue, this was easier for the printer, but required more skill from the transferrer. He considered it rather a good thing to have only one transferrer and one apprentice, notwithstanding this change, as it prevented the printer from doing too much.

Witness 393, manager of girls' clubs, who had had opportunities of becoming acquainted with women and girls working in the potteries, said that so far as she could gather from what they told her the girls had nothing to do with their employers, and if anyone complained to the employer of the man under whom she worked the man would pay her out for doing so. The absence of any one of a group of workers very much hindered all the others in the group. Very often after the "wakes" (a special week's holiday), if the head man was a drunkard, the boys and girls assisting him could do nothing until he had recovered from his drinking bout, and were without work for days. Assistants in the printing room had occasionally complained that the transferrers were not fair to them when paying them their money. The paintresses worked in large rooms, and were under supervision. This was not the case with the attendants working "at the clay bank." Both Church of England and Nonconformist workers had failed to attract the latter class of girls to their evening classes and clubs. There were few leisured people in the district; the employers all lived at a considerable distance, and if asked to subscribe to any movement, often excused themselves on the ground that they had to subscribe to philanthropic efforts in the places where they lived. She did not consider that there was so much immorality amongst the girls at the potteries as amongst the servant girls at the small houses in the place. Early marriages were very common.

Witness 383, living at Stoke, stated that she heard very little about insanitary conditions in the factories, but there was much to complain about as to the houses. There were several cottages with only two rooms and several courts with only one closet for all the inhabitants. She came across a considerable number of cases of immoral conduct, but had never heard of one case in a factory nor of immoral relations between men and women working together in the factory. But she continually heard complaints about the indecent conversation of married women in the factories.

Witness 391 did not consider that the charges of immorality frequently made with regard to the pottery workers were justified. The worst girls she knew of in Stoke were not those who lived in the town but those who came from a considerable distance, particularly from Newcastle. She believed that the walk was the cause of the evil; the girls when quite little, some of them even when half-timers, got into the habit of starting together with boys and men walking in the same direction, and their behaviour and language were disgraceful.

The usual hours are from 7 a m. to 6 p.m., with half-an-hour for breakfast and one hour for dinner. The "paintresses" work shorter hours.

I am, Sir,
Your obedient servant,
(Signed) Clara E. Collet.

26

TESTIMONY OF RICHARD JUGGINS ON METAL WORKSHOPS, LORDS SELECT COMMITTEE ON SWEATING, 1889

Source: Testimony of Richard Juggins on Metal Workshops, Select Committee of The House of Lords on The Sweating System, 4 May 1889. (Printed by Henry Hansard and Sons and Published by Eyre and Spottiswoode, 1889), 233–310.

EDITORIAL HEADNOTE

Parliamentary enquiries figured large in identifying working conditions and the structure of industries during the nineteenth century. Virtually from the beginning on the century, legislation following from these enquiries began to reshape industries in Britain and were often cited by those in North America wishing to promote changes there. Much of the concern related to children and then women; the concentration was on factories and is dealt with further in Vols. 2 and especially 4. Workshops were only moderately regulated before 1867, but later legislation increasingly controlled them as well. The Lords Select Committee on Sweating was originally designed to study the East End of London, but it was extended to provincial towns like the area around Birmingham. Despite rumours of dissention and conflict, the report which emerged was one of good sense and helpful suggestions. While much of the press focused on sewing and textiles, the Committee also considered the metal trades.

Richard Juggins (1843–1895) was first secretary to the Midlands Counties Trades Association, 1886 to 1895, when he died. The aim of the federation was to embrace as large a number of the craftsmen in the small metal trades as possible, in order to redress the balance between employers and small isolated groups of workers. He was a nut and bolt maker and trade unionist who helped form the Nut and Bolt Makers' Association. Sacked from his job for organising a strike, he became the full-time secretary. He continued these activities, ultimately creating the Midland Counties Trades

DOI: 10.4324/9781003676669-28

Federation in 1886, and he worked to develop conciliation mechanisms across the metal trades. In addition to testifying to the Lords' Committee, three years later he was called to testify to the royal commission on labour. He supported direct labour representation in Parliament but was never selected as a candidate. In this extract, he was called back to testify further and to elaborate on the testimony of some of the workers, whose testimony follows. Well-respected, his testimony is largely descriptive and clarifying since the committee members had little knowledge of the industry.

MINUTES OF EVIDENCE 14TH MARCH 1889

Mr. RICHARD JUGGINS, having been re-called; is further Examined, as follows:

20658. Chairman] I want to refer you to some of your evidence to clear up one or two points. Will you look at page 31, Question 17655, and the following questions. You were speaking of the way in which work was done whether in factories or workshops, and you say that you divide the work into work that is done in factories and work that is done in domestic workshops; and then I ask you whether you mean that all the workshops are domestic workshops, and you say Yes; then I ask you whether all the persons working in the work-shop are members of the same family, and you say No; and then at Question 17659, 1 asked you whether you drew a distinction between a domestic workshop and a family workshop, and you said Yes; I do not clearly understand about these factories and workshops; perhaps you will explain it a little more? The only difference is that one is a family domestic workshop, and the other is a domestic workshop.

20659. A general domestic workshop, you mean? Yes; they are both based on exactly the same principles; the only difference is that members of one family work in the one shop, and in the other case, working under exactly the same conditions, they have a mixed number of people working in a shop of the same dimensions.

20660. Then in speaking generally, when you speak of a domestic workshop, you might mean either a shop where all members of the same family were working, or a shop where outsiders were working? Yes.

20661. Do you know whether the fact that outsiders were working in a shop, or members of the same family only would make any difference as to the workshop coming under the Factory and Workshop Act? According to the present Factory Act it makes a difference.

20662. Then with regard to many of these shops, in fact I think the generality of these shops, that were spoken of, the witnesses said that they were under the Factory Act, and were visited by factory inspectors? Where the people working in the small domestic workshops are not all of one family; and our contention is that, whether they be one Family, or whether they be two or three families, the same law should apply.

20063. You have not got a copy of the Factory Act with you, have you? No.

20064. Section 16, dealing with the period of employment and time for meals for children and young persons in domestic workshops, says: Where persons are employed at home, that is to say, in a private house, room, or place which, though used as a dwelling, is by reason of the work carried on there a factory or workshop within the meaning of this Act and so on. Now in these trades that you have been speaking of the work is never carried on in the dwellings? No; so that that part of the Factory Act could not apply; they are all apart from the house, not adjoining or connected with the house.

20665. Then, in your opinion, would it be necessary that the Act should be amended as regards these trades that you have been speaking of in order to bring them within the spirit of the Act? Yes, it is.

20666. On account of the fact that the work is never carried on in the actual dwelling room? Yes.

20667. Now I want you to look at page 49, Question 17967; there I say to you: "then am I to understand from you that the principal remedy, in your opinion, lies in the abolition by some means or other of the whole system of working in domestic or family workshops? and you say, Yes; is that what you meant the Committee to understand, that you would do away with these domestic workshops altogether, or only that you would have those that do not come under the Act placed under the Act? I would do away with them as far as practicable, and I would in place of them substitute factories specially adapted for carrying on work of the same kind.

20668. Now I want to call your attention for a moment to Section 98 of the Act, where it says: The exercise in a private house or private room by the family dwelling therein, or by any of them, of manual labour for the purposes of gain in or incidental to some of the purposes in this Act in that behalf mentioned, shall not of itself constitute such house or room a workshop where the labour is exercised at irregular intervals, and does not furnish the whole or principal means of living to such family; do you know whether the term private house or private room would apply to these workshops which are not dwelling rooms? It would not apply at all. It would apply more in the tailoring trade or such trades as are carried on inside the house, but not to the iron trades.

20669. Will you look now at page 41 of the Evidence at No. 17824 and the following questions; you speak there of children and young women under 18 years of age working 12 or 14 hours; you mean, I suppose, inclusive of the hours for meals? Yes; inclusive of the hours for meals.

20670. Do you know what the hours for meals are? Half-an-hour for breakfast, an hour for dinner, and in some cases they get half-an-hour for tea, but not in every case.

20671. those are the hours that you referred to in the answers to which I have called your attention? Yes.

20672. Do you mean to say, then, that children would be working 10 or 12 hours a day? Yes.

20673. Do you know what the legal limit is for children? I believe it is about 10½ hours according to the Factory Act. You see where the Factory Act does not apply, these children work excessive hours because there is no inspection.

20674. Will you refer to page 165, Question 19618; Lord Thring says: Do I understand you that women work in these spike-nail factories and you say, No; then the next question is, Not at all? and you say, None. You told us you would wish as far as possible to substitute factories for workshops? Yes, I have said that.

20675. And you have said that women do not work in spike-nail factories? No, they do not.

20676. Do you mean that you would not allow women to work at any kind of spike-nails in factories? No; I am quite willing for women to work in factories on spike-nails on the same conditions that women are employed in other factories, namely, that women are employed alone by themselves, and not mixed up with the male operatives; and that the sizes of work which they should make should be limited by an Act of Parliament, according to the strength of the female. At present there is no limit; they are at liberty to make any size, whether they are strong enough or not; and as a consequence it often brings on premature death.

20677. I think you gave us some limit that you would propose; was that as to the chains? In both trades, chain and nail, no higher than a quarter inch diameter. . . .

20679. Is there any other kind of middleman who is not a fogger? A fogger is a man who takes out the work from the master, works between the operatives and the master, and makes his profit from the operatives and not from the master.

20680. What would you call a factor? A factor would be a gentleman who would buy largely and send it into the open market; a fogger does not.

20681. Do you mean that the factor would not sell to large masters? No, the factor would buy from large masters.

20682. And sell to the merchants? And sell to the merchants. . . .

20685. This is what I understand you to say, there would be first of all the operatives, the men or women working? Yes.

20686. They would be working for the occupier of the shop, the head of the shop, would they not? Yes.

20687. He might be working for a fogger; that is to say, selling his goods to a fogger? Yes.

206S8. The fogger, you say, would sell them to a master? Yes.

20689. And the master to a factor? Yes.

20690. And the factor to the merchant? Yes.

20691. Does that apply equally to chains and nails? Yes.

20692. Are chains made in Walsall as well as in the district you are speaking: of? Yes, they are better.

20693. A better kind of chain? Yes.

20694. The same description of chain and a better quality? The same description of chain, and other descriptions of chains; curbchains, bridle-chains, and saddle-chains.

20695. But is the quality better of the same description of chain? Yes; it is all made by men at Walsall; there is no female labour employed.

20696. All made in factories? All made in factories.

20697. Do you know what the wages are at Walsall? I could not give you an exact list, but I suppose they would be about 20 per cent, higher wages in Walsall than in Cradley.

20698. How is it that they are all made in factories by men there, and that no women are employed? I cannot explain why they do not employ women there, unless it is for the same reason as in other parts of the country where chains are made, and no women are employed. Cradley Heath and district is the only place in England where women are employed. In all the chain factories in England the chain is made by men and not by women except in the district I refer to.

20699. Do they make the smaller kinds at Walsall too? Yes, they make the smallest chains at Walsall, as small as anywhere else.

20700. Is any quantity of the chain made at Cradley Heath, and in that district, sold at Walsall? Yes, large quantities are made at Cradley Heath by females, purchased by the Walsall manufacturers, and sent out as Walsall chain, simply because it is purchased cheaper on account of being made by the females than if it were made by the males in Walsall.

20701. Do you mean that it goes out as Walsall chain, and commands a better price? Yes, I do.

20702. Is it marked in any way? No.

20703. Would that be contrary to the Merchandise Marks Act, do you know? Yes, quite contrary.

20704. So that the women working at Cradley Heath are working; in competition with the men at Walsall? Yes.

20705. Does that have the effect, of cutting down the prices at Walsall? It has had a very material effect, inasmuch as the prices at Walsall are now reduced at least 25 per cent, compared to what they were some years ago.

20706. And your contention is that the master sells that chain as Walsall chain at a higher price, and yet gets it made much cheaper by women at Cradley Heath? Yes. I might add here, if you would allow me, that since I have been in London, we have inquired about the sale price of a dog chain that is made by these women for, at the most three farthings; and they are asking 1 s., or 1 s. 3 d. for it in London.

20707. Dog chains, you say? Yes.

20708. What would be the value of the material? About 2d.

20709. Twopence, and three farthings for the work? Yes.

20710. Do you remember a witness, I think it was Mrs. Hackett [below], who spoke of her husband complaining of only getting the lower price, the old price, for work for which he got the order after notice had been given and accepted of an increase in wages; and you explained to the Committee what the custom was.

I want to ask you whether there is any equivalent to that in factory working? No, none whatever; the case has never occurred. At times, when conferences of employers have been held at which I have attended, the time or date has been fixed when the advance should take place, and if it has been necessary to consider present orders they have always been considered at the conference and agreed upon; but no advantage has ever been taken at the factories of the factory operatives, not to my knowledge.

27

TESTIMONY OF FEMALE NAILMAKERS, LORDS SELECT COMMITTEE ON SWEATING, 1889

Source: Testimony of Female Nailmakers, Select Committee on The Sweating System, Select Committee of The House of Lords on The Sweating System, 4 May 1889. (Printed by Henry Hansard and Sons and Published by Eyre and Spottiswoode, 1889), 211–26.

EDITORIAL HEADNOTE

Mrs. Sarah Hackett worked with her husband in making nails, while Caroline Cox worked with others in a workshop among a cluster of nailmaking workshops. Their testimony is representative of women's work in the industry and elaborates on the structure, conditions and expectations of nailmaking (see doc. 26 introduction).

12 March 1889

Mrs SARAH HACKETT, is called in; and, having been sworn, is examined, as follows:

20283. Chairman.] Are you a spike-nail maker? Yes.

20284. Does your husband work at the same trade? Yes.

20285. Do you work in your own shop? Yes.

20286. You and your husband together? Yes.

20287. Is there anybody else in the shop? No.

20288. Then you can work at whatever time you please, and as long as you like? Yes.

20289. What are your general hours of work? From 7 in the morning till 9 at night.

20290. And what do you make; these large spike nails? These (pointing to a nail).

20291. I suppose you allow yourself an hour for dinner? I have not any time on account of there being no one in the house to do the work besides myself. My husband has half-an-hour for his breakfast, an hour for dinner, and half-an-hour for tea.

DOI: 10.4324/9781003676669-29

20292. Do you do the heading and pointing, both? No, the pointing.

20293. Your husband does the heading? My husband does the heading and I do the pointing.

20294. How do you cut the iron? Cut it down on the cutters, cold.

20295. Do you do that work, or your husband? I and my husband.

20296. Both together? Yes.

20297. And then he does the heading and you do the pointing? Yes.

20298. How much can you and your husband earn at that work? From 18s. to a 1£ a week, both of us.

20299. Have you anything to pay out of that? Yes, the breezes.

20300. What would that come to? Two shillings and threepence per week.

20301. Have you anything to pay for carriage? Twopence per bundle for carriage.

20302. Anything else; what do you allow for tools and so on? They are our own tools.

20303. What do you allow for the wear of them to keep them in repair? My husband does them himself.

20304. Then you take out of your 18s. or 20s. 4d. a cwt. [hundred weight] for carriage? Yes.

20305. And 2s. 3d. a week for firing? Yes.

20306. And how many cwt. can you make in a day? I could not say in a day; we make from 14 to 15 cwt. in a week.

20307. How far have you got to take the nails? About half-a-mile from our house to the warehouse.

20308. Then you get the iron delivered to you and the nails taken back over that distance of half-a-mile for 2d. a bundle? Yes.

20309. So that you pay somewhere about 5 s. in the week for this carriage? Yes.

20310. Do you think you could do it cheaper yourselves? Yes; they will not allow us to do our own carriage.

20311. Do you mean that you would not get any work unless you agreed to this payment for carriage? No, we should not.

20312. That would make your earnings only about 13s. a week clear? Yes.

20313. Could you earn that clear right round the year? Not round the year; some weeks we do not get work at all.

20314. You cannot get work some weeks? No.

20315. What do you pay for your house and shop? Two shillings and sixpence a week.

20316. How much iron do you generally get at a time? Sometimes one ton, sometimes two, sometimes three.

20317. Then do you take in the nails before it is all worked up, or do you have to wait till it is all worked up? Sometimes we send them in a fair order before the iron is worked up, and sometimes they stop till the iron is worked up.

20318. In that case, where you have to work up, say, three or four tons, do you get any money on account from the master? Sometimes.

20319. He would make you some little advance of money. What I mean is, supposing you get our tons, for instance, it would take you some time to make it up, would it not? Yes.

20320. How long about would it take you, do you suppose? It would take us six or seven weeks.

20321. Then, supposing you did not send in the nails till the four tons was all worked up, and you did not get the price for them for six or seven weeks, how would you manage to live in the meantime? They allow us something on Saturdays sometimes, but not always.

20322. And if they do allow you anything, do they charge you anything for it? No.

20323. What would happen if you had an order that took you four or five, or six weeks, and if the prices changed in the meanwhile; the price might go up or it might go down? If he wanted to leave four or five tons on our ground, and the price was to go up, he would expect us to work on it at the old price.

20324. Does that often happen? Yes.

20325. Then I suppose, if the master thought that prices were likely to go up, it would be to his advantage to give you a large order? Yes; he sent us a ton of iron the Saturday after this last notice was given for us to work up at the old price, and my husband is at play now before he will work the iron up at the old price.

20326. When did he get this ton of iron? The Saturday after the notice was given out

20327. What do you mean by "the notice"? That (handing in a letter) is the letter that my husband wrote to me.

20328. Would you like to read a part of it to the Committee? "I am still at play; I have had orders to work up the iron at the old price, but it breaks my heart to do it; I have not commenced yet. We are all right at home."

203.9. That order was given a week after the notice was given, you say? Yes; and we had no order at all with the iron.

20330. I do not quite understand what the notice is. What do you mean by the notice; do you mean that this ton was given you a week after the notice for advance, but you were to work at the old price? Yes

20331. And what your husband says is that it would break his heart to work at that price? Yes.

20332. What is the old price, do you know? No, I could not say.

20333. Do you know what the price according to the notice is? No, I do not.

20334. Have you any children? My husband has three.

20335. Are they living with you? Yes

20336. How old are they? There is one 15 in September, and one is 10 on the 10th of December, and the other eight on the 5th of May.

20337. Are they working any of them? No.

20338. Are they girls or boys? Two girls and a boy; the eldest is a girl and the youngest is a girl.

20339. Are they at school any of them? Yes, two.

20340. What does that cost you? Sixpence a week.

20341. [Duke of *Norfolk.*] You said that your tools were your own? Yes.

20342. Do you remember what you had to pay when you first bought them? I could not say; my husband bought them before I was married to him.

20343. Were they bought second-hand, or did he get them new? He would get them new.

20344. You do not know what they cost? No.

20345. [*Chairman.*] Do you employ anybody to take care of the house for you? No, only myself.

20346. [Earl Brownlow.] Does your husband repair his tools during hours, or after hours; does he repair a tool whenever it goes wrong, or after the day's work is over? He repairs the tools before he can work; he has to stop and repair his tools because sometimes they break in his work, and then he has to stop work and do them.

20347. Can you give us any idea how much time your husband spends in the week at that? Sometimes he is doing it half a day, and sometimes a day at a time in the week.

20348. Therefore every week he loses from half a day to a day at a time for that? Yes.

20349. When you receive the iron do you see it weighed? No, it comes in in hundred-weights

20350. And you have to take it on trust as being fair weight? Yes.

20351. When it goes back do you see the nails weighed? My husband sees them weighed.

20352. [Lord *Clifford of Chudleigh.*] Do you generally have much charge for these under weights? We have to pay for all weights that we lose,

20353. But does it amount to much in the week or not? Sometimes it amounts to 6d. and sometimes 9d.

20354. |Lord *Monkswell.*] You say that a notice of advance has been given; do these advances generally date back to the notice; when a notice of advance is given the masters do not necessarily give in to that I suppose, but it only means that some conference is about to take place between the masters and the men? Yes.

20355. It means not that it has been agreed, but that the men have sent notice that they wish for higher wages? Yes.

20356. Supposing higher wages were settled a week or a fortnight after the notice was sent in, would a master consider that he was bound to give a man a higher price for the work immediately after the notice was given, or only after the master had agreed to the notice? After the master had agreed to the notice.

20357. Had the masters agreed to this latest notice which the men have sent in before the iron was sent in? No.

20358. Therefore, you had the iron sent in between the time of sending in the notice and the time of the masters agreeing to the advance? Yes.

20359. But your husband, nevertheless, considers it unfair that he should be called upon to work at the old price now, after the masters have agreed to the notice, I suppose? Yes.

20360. Supposing prices went down; supposing you had four or five tons of iron to work, and before you had finished working them prices went down, would you expect to get a higher price for the whole of the iron you did? No.

20361. Directly the reduction in price was agreed upon you would think it fair that you should be asked to work for less? Yes.

20362. [*Chairman.*] Do you know whether your nails are weighed in bags? Yes, they are weighed in bags.

20363. Is a proper allowance made for the weight of the bag by the master, do you know? I do not know that.

20364. You have nothing to do with that yourself? No.

20365. And you can say nothing at all about the weighing? No.

20366. What I think you mean by the notice is that the iron was received by you after the notice was given? Yes.

20367. Since then the advance in price has been agreed to, and, therefore, your husband thinks he ought to get the advanced price now? Yes.

20368. Where his master insists upon it that he shall work up the iron for the old price? Yes.

20369. And that you do not think is right? No. . . .

20377. Would you think it a good plan if women were not allowed to make these heavy spike nails at all? Yes.

20378. You think it is too hard work for women? Yes.

20379. Would you as soon work in a factory as work in your own shop? I would sooner work in my own shop with factory hours.

20380. You would like to have the factory hours, but work in your own shop? Yes.

20381. What you would like would be to work as you do now with your husband, but to have the same hours as in the factory? Yes.

20382. And to have the size of work that women should do limited? Yes.

20383. I suppose you live much the same as other witnesses have told us they do; you get tea, and bread and bacon? Yes.

20384. Butter? Yes.

20385. Where do you buy your things? At the Co-operative Society.

20386. Can you tell us what prices you pay? I pay 10d. a pound for the butter, 6 d. for the bacon, and 3 d. the sugar, and other provisions according to the prices.

203S7. Do you buy bread, or do you buy the flour? Buy the flour.

20388. What do you pay for the flour? Six shillings and eightpence.

20389. [Duke of *Norfolk.*] If the making of the spike nails were forbidden to women you would lose a good deal of the work you do now? Yes.

20390. But could you get work in the lighter branches which would enable you to earn as much each week as you do now? Yes.

20391. So that you would not lose anything even if the spike nail-making was forbidden to women? No.

20392. [Lord *Monkswell.*] You are obliged, I suppose, to work long hours; it is your own wish; that is to say, you work in order to get the money, I suppose? Yes.

20393. You are not obliged to work in order to get a particular task done by a particular day, I suppose? No.

20394. What you mean is that you want to get the same wage for factory hours as you now get for longer hours? Yes.

20395. [Chairman.] I suppose you would think it probable that if women are not allowed to make these larger sizes of nails the men would get more for them? Yes.

20396. So that altogether the two of you could earn quite as much as you do now? Yes.

The Witness is directed to withdraw.

MINUTES OF EVIDENCE 12th March 1889.

CAROLINE COX is called in; and, having been sworn, is Examined, as follows:

20410. [Chairman.] Can you tell the Committee how old you are? Going 16.

20411. You will be 16 next birthday? Yes.

20412. Do you know when your birthday is? No, I do not.

20413. When was your last birthday? Last Thursday week.

20414. Were you 16 last Thursday week, or 15? Fifteen last Thursday week.

20415. Are your father and mother alive? Yes.

20416. How many are you altogether in family? Ten of us altogether.

20417. Are you making these spike nails? Yes.

20418. What sort of nails do you make? This sort (pointing to a nail).

20419 What kind of nail do you call that? A "dog-ear."

20420. Do you make the whole of it, the heading and pointing and all? No, I only point them.

20421. Is that the largest kind of nail that you make? No.

20422. What is the largest? That (producing one).

20423. Do you know what that size is called? Half-inch.

20424. And you do the pointing of that? Yes.

20425. You do not cut it, do you? Yes.

20426. You do the cutting too? Yes.

20427. By yourself? No, another with me.

20428. Is your father working at this trade? No, he makes little nails.

20429. How many of you are working at this? Only one beside me; my other sister.

20430. Who does the shop belong to that you are working at? Mr. Homer.

20431. How many are there in the shop? Six in one shop.

20432. Does your mother work in the shop? No.

20433. She does not work at all? No.

20434. Are any of your family working in the same shop with you? Not in this shop; over the other side.

20435. But nobody in this shop? No.

20436. And how many shops has Mr. Homer got? There are eight in one, and two in another, and two in another, and six in another.

20437. That will be four shops? Yes.

20438. All in the same yard? All in the same yard.

20439. And some of the people belonging to you, some of your sisters, work in the other shop? Yes; only one sister.

20440. Have you any sisters younger than yourself? Yes, there are six younger than me.

20441. And I suppose all your mother's time is taken up at home: Yes.

20442. Have you any brothers? Yes, there are six younger than me with the boys and girls.

20443. Any older than you? One older than me.

20444. A brother? A sister.

20445. And she is working? Yes.

20446. In one of these other shops belonging to Mr. Homer? Yes.

20447. Who would work with you in cutting the iron for that nail? Mr. Homer's son.

20448. You two? Yes.

20449. Is that very hard work? Yes.

20450. Makes you very tired? Yes.

20451. I suppose that is much harder than the pointing? Yes, it is much harder than the pointing.

20452. How long can you work without resting cutting the iron? About half-an-hour.

20453. And then you have to have a little rest? Then we stop while we open some more bundles and then we go on again.

20454. What time do you generally go to work? Seven in the morning and knock off at eight at night.

20455. How long do they give you for meals? Half-an hour for breakfast, an hour for dinner, and half-an-hour for tea.

20456. How far is the shop from where you live; how long does it take you to walk backwards and forwards? Perhaps five minutes.

20457. I suppose you go home to breakfast, and to dinner, and tea? Yes.

20458. Do you never work longer than that? No.

20459. You never go to work earlier? Yes, on Saturday morning; we go about four or five o'clock on Saturday morning and knock off at eleven.

20460. Winter time too, do you go at four or five o'clock on Saturday? Winter and summer.

20461. And how about Monday? We go at breakfast time and knock off at tea time on Monday?

20462. And Tuesday, Wednesday, Thursday, and, Friday you go at seven and stay till eight? Yes.

20463. How many girls are working in the shop with you? Only one besides me; there are boys and Mr. Homer.

20464. Who is the girl who works with you? Sarah Jane Eden.

20465. How many boys? Besides the two girls, three boys and Mr. Homer.

20466. Do you ever go earlier than four o'clock in the morning: No.

20467. Did you ever find anybody working at the shop when you got there? That girl.

20468. You found her working? Yes.

20469. Do you know what time she got there? She said she had come in earlier to blow the fire up.

20470. Mr. Homer's son and three boys you say work in the place? There are two of Mr. Homer's sons in the shop.

20471. Do you know at all what you earn in a week? Between 4s. and 5s., and 6d. off for the stalling and tools.

20472. Does anything else come off? No, that is all.

20473. Who sells the nails for you? Mr. Homer.

20474. Does he give you the money for them? Yes.

20475. Does he weigh them? Yes.

20476. Do you ever see them weighed? Yes.

20477. Do you think it is all right? Yes.

20478. I suppose you would not know very well whether it was right or not? Yes, I can tell the weight.

20479. What price does he pay you? He pays us 4 d. per bundle for three eighths 3-inch brobs [dog-spikes or wall hooks].

20480. Is that what you are making now? Yes.

20481. How long have you been working there? I started just after I was 12 years old.

20482. And have been working ever since? Yes.

20483. I suppose you could not earn so much at the beginning? No.

20484. What did you earn, do you suppose? About 2s. a week, or 1s. 6d.

20485. And what kind of work did you do at first? The same work; I had five-sixteenths brobs and three eighths.

20486. Were you cutting this iron when you were just 12 years old? Yes.

20487. Did you work all the year round like that? Yes.

20488. Lord *Monkswell*. How old is young Homer, the eldest? He is 17.

20489. He is the eldest boy that works in your shop? Yes.

20490. And how old is the other girl that works in the shop? I do not know; 14, I think.

20491. *Chairman*.] What do you have to eat? Sometimes we have some bacon, sometimes we have some potatoes with a bit of salt on.

20492. That is for your dinner; what for tea? Sometimes we have a bit of bread-and-butter, and sometimes dry bread.

20493. Do you ever have any meat? We should be glad if we got a pound of meat for Sunday's dinner.

20494. You do not very often get it? No.

20495. I suppose you pay your wages over to your mother, do you? Yes.

20496. You went to school up to 12 years of age? Yes.

20497. Lord *Monkswell*. Do you have as much as you can eat of this bread and potatoes, or do you have a portion served out to you? No, we do not have as much as we can eat.

20498. Not as much as you would like to eat? No.

20499. *Chairman*] Do you know whether the Inspector has ever been in the shop? Yes, he has.

The Witness is directed to withdraw.

ALICE BRETTLE is called in; and having been sworn, is Examined, as follows:

20500. *Chairman.*] Are you making spike nails? Yes.

20501. What size; what are the largest you make? I have pointed some like that (pointing to a nail), half-inch, and some like that (pointing to another) five-eighths.

20502. Do you cut the iron too? Yes.

20503. Cut the iron and do the pointing? I pointed them, but now I head, and I put the heads on these sorts of nails (pointing to some nails).

20504. How many people work in the shop with you? Four; three besides myself; one man and three females, with myself.

20505. Whom does the shop belong so? Mr. Parsons.

20506. Has it ever been visited by a factory inspector, do you know? Yes.

20507. How long have you worked there? Hardly a twelvemonth.

20508. You can earn, I suppose, more doing the heading than you could do in the pointing? Not much.

20509. You get paid a better price for that, do you not? For some of them; when you do some sorts. For these (pointing to them) you get 1s. 5d. for 3½ by ¼ "rose"; then you have to give the pointer 6 d. a bundle out of that.

20510. Who is doing the pointing for you? A girl of fifteen.

20511. What can you earn a week now in nail-making? Of a regular thing, both of us, from 15s. to 16s. a week, the pair of us.

20512. Between you, you can earn that? Yes.

20513. Is that clear, or does anything come out of it? A shilling for tools.

20514. And the firing? No; he has so much a bundle allowed off these for his firing.

20515. You mean about 15 s. or 16 s. a week, with a shilling allowed out for fuel? Yes, both of; I and the pointer get from 15 s. to 16 s. a week, and I have to pay a shilling a week myself for tools.

20516. How do you divide that between you and the pointer? I give her 6 d. a bundle for pointing them, and I take the other.

20517. How many bundles do you make in the week? About 10 bundles.

20518. Then she will earn about 5s. Yes.

20519. And you would earn about 9s.? Yes; I have to pay a shilling out of mine for tools.

20520. I suppose the owner of the shop weighs the nails? Yes.

20521. Do you know what price he gives for them? He gets the list price.

20522. You do not know what the difference is between what he pays you and what the list price is? I could tell you if I had the list. (A list is shown to the Witness.) Beginning with the 3-in. by ¼, he takes 2s. 3d. a bundle for them; for the 3½ by ¼ he gets 2s. 1d.; for the 4½ by ¼, 2s.; for the 4 by 9–32, 1s. 10d.; for the 4 by 9–32 he gets 1s. 8d.; for the 5 by 5–16, 1s. 4½d. for the 5½ by 11–32 he gets 1s. 2d.

20523. Are you making all those kinds of nails? Yes. And for by 6 by 3/8 he gets 1 ½ d for 7 by 13–32, 10½ d.

20524. You are not making all those kinds of nails, too, are you? I have made as high as 6-inch.

20525. I want to find out the difference between the price you get and the list price? On my list for the 3 by ¼, I get 1s. 8d. a bundle; and for 3½ by ¼, 1s. 6½d.; and for 4 by ¼ get 1s. 6d.; for 4 by 9–32, 1s. 4d.; for 4 ½ by 9–32, 1s. 3d.; for 5 by 5–16, 1s.; for 5 ½ by 11–32, 10½d.; for 6 by 3/8, 8d.; that is the highest I have made, heading them.

20526. Do you have anything taken off for waste? When we get our iron he gives us a 56-lbs. bundle, and he looks for us to take 54 lbs. back again, and then the bags should be 2 lbs.; but we have weighed them and they have only been 1lb., and reckoning that and the nails together 56 lbs., we lose a pound of iron; the bags are short, and we reckon that we lose a pound of iron.

20527. The bags you say only weigh a pound? Yes.

20528. And he says they weigh 2 lbs.? Yes; then he keeps a penny off me for the pound of waste heavier.

20529. He says you are a pound short, and that the bag is a pound heavier? Yes; we have proved it and weighed it before his eyes.

20530. What does he say then? He begins to swear and walk away; he does not say any more then.

20531. But you do not get any satisfaction out of him? No.

20532. Is that a common thing; is it often done? Yes, you generally get a bother over your bags; we have weighed many a lot, and there has not been the right weight.

20533. But otherwise, with that exception of the bag, they do not charge you too much for the waste? They charge me 1 d. a pound for the waste; the bags and nails should weigh 56 lbs., and he says they only weigh 55 lbs.; the bag only weighs a pound weight, and that is where the mistake is, that we should weigh 56 lbs. instead of 55 lbs.; then he keeps the penny off me for the pound of waste iron.

20534. What are your hours of work? From seven in the morning to seven at night.

20535. Do you go to work earlier on Saturday? No, the usual hour; that is, from six in the morning till two; that is the factory hours.

20536. Do you take your own iron; do you carry it yourself? Yes; I carry 112 lbs. of iron myself.

20537. Do you carry back the nails? Yes.

20538. How far have you got to carry it? From 20 to 30 yards.

20539. He does not charge you anything more for carriage? He is allowed so much a bundle of the nails for carriage and firing.

20540. You have to carry it, you say? Yes.

20541. That is to say, he charges you so much; takes so much off? He has so much off the master's list, different to what there is on our list.

20542. For carriage and firing? Yes.

20543. Besides that, you have to carry 112 lbs. of iron and the nails? Yes.

20544. Do you find the work very hard work? Yes; I do not think that a woman ought to do it; they are too big for a woman to make. I think if they made nothing but that sort (pointing to some nails) they would be hard enough then for them.

20545. What do you call those? Three-and a-half by ½ rose.

20546. I forget whether you said there were some more shops in the same ground? Ten people besides us; four who are in that one shop; 14 people altogether.

20547. All close together? Yes.

20548. Does he work himself? No.

20549. Any of his family? One son-in-law, and one of his own sons.

20550. Are there any others of your family working in the same trade? My brother is working in the same trade; my father makes the little nails.

20551. How long have you been working? I began to point when I was between 11 and 12 years old.

20552. And you have been working ever since? Yes!

20553. How old are you? Nineteen the 28th of October.

20554. Lord *Clifford of Chudleigh.*] Is it harder work making the head than pointing? You have to work harder at heading, and it is much harder to knock them down than it is to draw the nails out.

20555. What is the weight of the hammer you use? From 2 ½ to 3 lbs.

20556. Lord Monkswell.] Do you carry a cwt. at one time? Yes.

20557. You prefer to do that, I suppose; of course, you could carry it at different times? They are only in hundredweights, and as we cut the iron we have to carry them one after the other, or carry them all together, which you prefer.

20558. You prefer to wait until you have got a cwt., and carry it? Yes, if you like that you can do it that way.

20559. You find it very hard work? Yes.

20560. Not so hard, I suppose, as in cutting the iron? There is not much difference; it is as hard to carry 112 lbs. as it is to cut the iron, and it is hard enough to cut the iron.

20561. You carry it from 20 to 30 yards? Yes.

20562. Yourself? Yes.

20563. *Chairman.* Is the shop very hot? Yes, in the summer time we have to strip to one skirt and a pair of stays; you cannot work with your body on because it is too hot.

20564. Is there anything else you would like to say to the Committee? I know one man who said he would never pay the women so much as the men for their work; when he had to pay the women so much as the men he should knock all the women off, and if they stayed on his ground they would have 1 s. 6 d. a week to pay for the tools, and a penny for every pound of iron for the waste.

20565. Is not that the usual charge, a penny for every pound of iron? Yes.

50566. There is nothing different in that then from the usual course? No; he said he never intended to pay the women so much for their work as he does the men.

20567. Lord *Clifford of Chudleigh.*] Do you think if you only worked at the small nails, at this 3 ½ by ¾ "rose," if those were the largest nails you made, you would be able to get as much work as you do now, or do you think you would have any difficulty in getting work; would you still be able to get work; do you think you could get as much work? Yes.

20568. Chairman] Do you think your hours are too long? You have to stand a good while at the blocks.

The Witness is directed to withdraw.

28

ON CHINA PAINTERS, ENGLISHWOMAN'S REVIEW, 1876

Source: 'Employment', [On China Painters], *Englishwoman's Review of Social and Industrial Questions*, Vol II, 15 April 1876, 170–72.

Image 3 Emma Meyer (1859–1921), Women decorating Porcelain at Den Kgl Porcelain Fabrik [Royal Porcelain Workshop], 1895. Public Domain.

DOI: 10.4324/9781003676669-30

EDITORIAL HEADNOTE

The Englishwoman's Review, which published from 1866 to 1910, participated in and recorded a great change in the range of possibilities open to women. The ideal of the magazine was the idea of the emerging emancipated middle-class woman: economic independence from men, choice of occupation, participation in the male enterprises of commerce and government, access to higher education, admittance to the male professions, particularly medicine, and, of course, the power of suffrage equal to that of men. This extract reprints a letter from *Lord Aberdare*, a former Home Secretary and Lord President of the Council. By 1876 he was engaged in a series of social educational and economic causes. The letter which is repeated here speaks for itself, but importantly demonstrates the tensions between women and men in the painting of china, a situation that was common in a number of industries where men's and women's work came into conflict and where men were jealous of women doing the same or similar work.

EMPLOYMENT . . .

Letter from Lord Aberdare. – It will be remembered that Lord Aberdare, on the occasion of a deputation to the Duke of Richmond on March 2nd, reminded the Lord President that some years ago a room near the South Kensington Museum, on the property of the Exhibition Commissioners, had been set apart for the reception of female painters on china, who were prevented by the jealousy of the men from pursuing their work at Stoke on equal terms. "To this statement," he says, in a letter to the Daily News: –

> Mr. Copeland and Mr. Campbell give a distinct contradiction. Mr. Campbell, in a courteous letter, informs me that the premises at South Kensington were erected by his firm, at the suggestion of Sir H. Cole, "for the purpose of affording technical instruction in china painting to students at the South Kensington School of Art, and most assuredly not in consequence of the tyranny of the men, &c." He adds that when he joined the establishment of Messrs. Minton, more than 30 years ago, he remembers his uncle, the late Mr. Herbert Minton, saying that the men objected to the women using a "rest," or piece of wood fixed to the table, on which the arm could be rested; but Mr. Campbell is strongly of opinion that "although at that time it may have been the idea that the men objected to the use of it on the part of the women, such a rest could not have been required by them; "and states that for more than 20 years, during which

he has had the entire management, he can most conscientiously assert that there has been no such oppression on the part of the painters and decorators; and that, on the destruction by fire of the premises at South Kensington, he offered employment at Stoke to the female artists, who, for various reasons, declined it, but who, he assures me, would have been treated by their fellow workmen with the utmost courtesy and consideration. Nothing can be more satisfactory than this contradiction to my statement; and although I regret having made a charge thus proved to be erroneous, I am glad to have given Mr. Campbell the opportunity of removing a misapprehension which I find to prevail widely, even among persons usually well informed on such subjects.

Perhaps, sir, you would kindly allow me space to explain the reasons for believing in the prevalence of the shameful – I wish I could say unmanly – custom to which I referred. In 1849 a Select Committee on Schools of Design was appointed by the House of Commons, and sat under the presidency of Mr. Milner Gibson. One of the most important witnesses examined was Mr. Herbert Minton, of Stoke-upon-Trent. I extract his answers to questions put to him by Mr. Beresford Hope:

Question 2.801. Am I correct in the information I have had that in painting flowers the females are not allowed to use a rest for the arm? – Yes; the men have the rest, the women not.

2.802. Can you give the Committee any reason for that? – It is an arbitrary rule; just the same as another rule, that the women are not allowed to use gold to gild.

2.803. By whom is that arbitrary rule enforced? – By the workmen entirely.

2,804. (Mr. Milner Gibson): What has suggested such an ungallant proceeding? – I cannot say. It is a most tyrannical thing, but such is the fact.

And Mr. Minton adds, in answer to question 2,805, "In years gone by there has been an attempt [on the part of the masters] to upset this arbitrary rule, and the men have turned out, and people [i.e., masters], considering their own private interests, have rather given way than contest the point. There has not been any attempt for the last fifteen or twenty years to renew the question; the women are so accustomed to it that they never think of using the rest; they are not brought up to it.

But this, it will be said, was so long ago as 1849. True, but Sir H. Cole assures me, and I have his authority to use his information, that such was his conviction of the continued prevalence of this arbitrary rule, that he has frequently, in comparatively recent times, referred to its existence in terms of condemnation at public meetings at Stoke, which he attended as representing the science and art schools, and that his statement was never disputed. Such being the case it is no wonder that the charge has been generally believed. I do not for a moment wish to set up this merely presumptive evidence of the continuance of a disgraceful custom against the clear and positive statements of such competent authorities as Mr. Campbell and Mr. Copeland. But even these gentlemen will see that the charge was not altogether unfounded, and will understand why I, in common with others, believed in the existence of a custom which all will rejoice to hear has become obsolete.

29

ARTIFICIAL FLOWERMAKING, DAILY NEWS SWEATED INDUSTRIES EXHIBITION HANDBOOK, 1907

Source: Thomas Holmes, 'Flowermaking', in Richard Mudie Smith, Compiler, *Sweated Industries Being a Handbook of the "Daily News" Exhibition*. Part PP, Worker's Section. May 1906. (Bradbury, Agnew & Co., Ltd.), 27–29.

Fig. 14.—Artificial-flower Makers: Blighting the Buds.

Image 4 An overcrowded artificial flower maker's workshop, Oxford Street. Wellcome Collection.

DOI: 10.4324/9781003676669-31

EDITORIAL HEADNOTE

Thomas Holmes, 'Flowermaking', in Richard Mudie Smith, Compiler, *Sweated Industries Being a Handbook of the "Daily News" Exhibition.* Part PP, Worker's Section. May 1906. (Bradbury, Agnew & Co., Ltd.), 27–29.

In 1907, the *Daily News* (1846–1930) mounted an exhibition on sweated industries, discussed more fully in the following (docs. 57, 58). The paper, founded by Charles Dickens, was intended as a radical rival to the right-wing *Morning Chronicle.* Many reformist writers contributed to the paper during its life, including George Bernard Shaw and Harriett Martineau. It continued its radical liberal voice, and the sponsorship of the exhibition on sweated trades was seen as a boon to the women's suffrage movement. This excerpt on flowermakers is a contrast to the view of flowermakers in the eighteenth century as skilled craftswomen with a milieu and a good trade, a cut above many other handworkers. Included among the sweated trades, flowermaking also replicated the deterioration in women's skilled handwork industries through the nineteenth century.

ARTIFICIAL Flower Making is one of the most interesting of London Home Industries.

It is also one of the worst paid. Great skill and a natural aptitude, combined with intense application, will enable a worker to earn twopence *per* hour. Few workers, however, combine all these characteristics, so three-halfpence per hour may be considered a liberal average of the earnings of the ordinary home-worker, though many fall below this standard.

Physical strength and endurance play no unimportant part in making of roses and other flowers, whose petals have to be subjected to great pressure that they may assume and retain the requisite concave form. This is necessary that the flowers may present a natural appearance, whether it be bud, half-blown, or full-blown flower.

The worker obtains from the factory all the material for flower making excepting gum, paste, or glue. These consist of spiral coils of thin wire, which has to be drawn and cut into suitable lengths; a special kind of paper, which has to be cut into various strips and wrapped tightly round the wire to form a stem, little rubber tubes to slip over the wire stem to give the necessary gloss and thickness for the stalk of the flower petals flat, hard and dry, in cakes that have been stamped out by machinery at great pressure; and little green things made of composition that represent the calyx of the flower.

Drawing and cutting the wire is not altogether pleasant, for the thin wire is liable to cut the band, unless the worker is well protected, but shaping the petals is really hard work. Sitting hour after hour at a table, a stiff rubber pad in front her, a small gas stove beside her, in which she warms her steel tool, the worker proceeds to separate the cakes of petals, and subject them all to pressure of the warm tool upon the rubber pad until they assume the necessary contour.

This work makes a great strain on the wrist, the arm, and the chest. Having her stems ready to hand, her thousands of petals are pressed, her paste or dextrine pot handy, the worker now proceeds to flower-making.

The centre of the flower is first made; for upon this the whole flower is built. In the creation of the centre the skill of the artist is apparent, for this gives the character of the flower. This centre is firmly fixed on one of the wire stems, the under side being coated with paste that the petals may adhere to it. One by one sufficient petals are added, the calyx is slipped along the wire stem and firmly glued into position, the little rubber tube is slipped along the wire then and firmly joined to the calyx, a few deft touches from clever fingers press the petals into the required position, the warm curling tongs are skilfully applied to the edges of the petals, and, hey presto! the flower is finished, and has become "a thing of beauty" if not "joy for ever".

The prices paid for making roses vary from *3s. 6d.* per gross for the best down to *1s. 4d.* per gross for button roses, but in the latter case a gross of small buds has to be included for the *1s. 4d.*

Confirmation Wreaths. – Beautiful Parma violets, now so popular, are made for *7d.* per gross, scarlet geraniums at a similar price, buttercups at *3d.* per gross do not touch the lowest limit, for in the making of beautiful confirmation wreaths less money is earned. These wreaths, which are largely for the export trade, contain about a gross of small white flowers. Each flower has to be made separately, and the wire stem has to be covered with white lawn, then intertwined with silver leaves, which are supplied to the worker, and the whole shaped into a complete and beautiful chaplet; *1s. 9d.* per dozen is the price paid for completed wreaths. One need not enquire the average earnings of the worker.

Part 3

CASE STUDY: MILLINERS AND SEAMSTRESSES

30

'SEWING TRADES' FROM THE LONDON TRADESMAN, 1747

Robert Campbell

Source: Robert Campbell, 'Of the Milliner', 'Of the Mantua-Maker' and 'the Cap-Maker', *The London Tradesman, being a compendious view of all Trades, Professions and Arts . . . calculated for the information of Parents, and Instruction of Youth in their Choice of Business* (T. Gardner, 1747), 206–10, 227–29.

Image 5 Les Marchandes de Modes, J.D. Bertaux. Musée Carnavalet. Public Domain.

DOI: 10.4324/9781003676669-33

EDITORIAL HEADNOTE

Following on from Campbell's entries on trades where women were found, here we bring together his comments on female trades, specifically milliners, mantua makers and cap-makers, trades seen as particularly female and related to the fashion industries. Despite these trades being highly recommended for girls from good families, he was notoriously scathing about their prospects and the morality of the trades.

OF THE MILLINER

The Milliner, though no Male Trade, has a just Claim to a Place on this Occasion, as the Fair sex, who are generally bound to this business, may have as much Curiosity to know the Nature of their Employment before they engage in it, and stand as-much in need of sound Advice in the Choice of an Occupation, as the Youth of our own Sex.

The Milliner is concerned in making and providing the Ladies with Linen of all sorts, for wearing Apparel, from the Holland smock to the Tippit and Commode; but as we are got into the Lady's Articles, which are so very numerous, the Reader is not to expect that we are to give an exact List of every thing belonging to them; let it suffice in general, that the Milliner furnishes them with Holland, Cambrick, Lawn and Lace of all sorts, and makes these Materials into Smocks, Aprons, Tippits, Handerchiefs, Neckaties, Ruffles, Mobs, Caps, Dressed-Heads, with as many *Etceteras* as would reach from *Charing-Cross* to the *Royal Exchange.*

They make up Cloaks, Mantels, Mantelets, Cheens and Capucheens, of Silk, Velvet, plain or brocaded, and trim them with Silver and Gold Lace, or Black Lace: They make up and sell Hats, Hoods, and Caps of all Sorts and Materials; they find the in Gloves, Muffs, and Ribbons; they sell quilted petticoats, and Hoops of all sizes, *&c.* and lastly, some of them, deal in Habits for Riding, and Dresses for the Masquerade: In a word, they furnish every thing to the Ladies, that can Contribute to set off their beauty, increase their vanity or render them ridiculous.

The Milliner must be a neat Needle-Woman in all its Branches, and a perfect Connoisseur in Dress and Fashion: She imports new Whims from *Paris* every Post, and puts the Ladies Heads In as many different shapes in one Month as there are different Appearances of the Moon in that Space. The most noted of them keep an Agent at *Paris,* who have nothing else to do but to watch the Motions of Fashions, and procure Intelligence of their Changes which she signifies to her Principals, with as much Zeal and Secrecy as an Ambassador, or Plenipo, would the important Discovery of some political Intrigue. They have vast Profits on every Article they deal in; yet give, but poor, mean Wages to very Person, they employ under them: Tough a young Woman can work neatly in, all manner of Needle-Work, yet she cannot earn more than Five or Six Shilling a Week, out of which she is to find herself in Board and Lodging. Therefore, out of Regard to the Fair Sex, I must caution Parents, not to bind their daughters to this Business: The vast resort of young Beaus and Rakes to Milliner's Shops, exposes young Creatures to many Temptations, and insensibly debauches their Morals before they are capable of Vice. A young Coxcomb no sooner is Master of an Estate, and a small Share of Brains, but he affects to deal with the most noted Milliner: If he chances to meet in her Shop any thing that has the Appearance of Youth, and the simple Behaviour of undesigning Innocence, he immediately accosts the young Sempstress with all the little Raillery he is Master of, talks loosely, and thinks himself most witty, when he has cracked some obscene Jest upon the young Creature. The Mistress, tho' honest, is obliged to bear the Wretch's Ribaldry, out of Regard to his Custom, and Respect to some undeserved Title of Quality he wears, and is forced to lay her Commands upon the Apprentice to answer all his Rudeness with civility and Complaisance. Thus the young Creature is obliged every Day to hear a Language, that by degrees undermines her Virtue, deprives her of that modest Delicacy of Thought, which is the constant Companion of uncorrupted Innocence, and makes Vice become familiar to the Ear, from whence there is but a small Transition to the grosser Gratification of the Appetite.

I am far from charging all Milliners with the Crime of Connivance at the Ruin of their Apprentice; but fatal Experience must convince the Public, that nine out of ten of the young Creatures that are obliged to serve in these Shops, are ruined and undone: Take a Survey of all the common Women of the Town, who take their Walks between *Charing-Cross* and *Fleet-Ditch,* and, I am persuaded, more than one Half of them have been bred Milliners, have been debauched in their Houses, and are obliged to throw themselves upon the Town for Want of Bread, after they have left them. Whether then it is owing to the Milliners, or to the Nature of the Business, or to whatever Cause it is owing, the Facts are so clear, and the Misfortunes attending their Apprentices so manifest, that it ought to be the last Shift a young Creature is driven to.

But if Parents will needs give their Daughters this kind of Education, let them avoid your private Hedge Milliners; those who pretend to deal only with a few select Customers, who scorn to keep open: Shop, but live in some remote Corner: These are Decoys for the Unwary; they are but Places for Assignations, and take the Title of Milliner, a more polite Name for a Bawd, a Procuress, a Wretch who lives upon the Spoils of Virtue, and supports her Pride by robbing the Innocent, of Health, Fame, and Reputation: They are the Ruin, of private Families, Enemies to conjugal Affection, promote nothing but Vice, and live by Lust. . . .

Cap-Makers are employed in making Velvet Caps, and Women's Hoods; and a Species of them make Leather Caps for Horsemen; These are of kin to the Shoe-Maker, and but few in the Business. The others are a kind of Milliners, and, generally speaking, deal in their Commodities, or some kind of Haberdashery Ware and those they employ, either as Apprentices or to work journeywork, are Women, and earn from Nine to Twelve Shillings a Week.

OF THE MANTUA-MAKER

The Mantua-Maker, as she is a Servant of the Ladies, may take it amiss if she is not allowed a Place among the many Arts and Mysteries we are treating of. Her Business is to make Night-Gowns, Mantuas, and Petticoats, *Robe de Chambres*, &c. for the Ladies. She is Sister to the Taylor and like him, must be a perfect Connoisseur in Dress and Fashion; and like the Stay-Maker, she must keep the Secrets she is intrusted with, as much as a Woman can: For, though the Stay-Maker does his Business as nicely as possible, and conceals all Deformities with the greatest Art, yet the Mantua-Maker must discover them at some times; she must see them, and pretend to be blind, and at all times she must swear herself to an inviolable Secrecy: she must leant to flatter all Complexions, praise all Shapes; and, in a Word, ought to be compleat Mistress of the Art of Dissimulation. It requires a vast Stock of Patience to bear the Tempers of most of their Customers, and no small Share of Ingenuity to execute their innumerable Whims. Their Profits are but inconsiderable, and the Wages they give their Journey women small in proportion; they may make a shift, With great Sobriety and Economy, to live upon their Allowance; but their Want of Prudence, and general Poverty, has brought the business into small Reputation: If a young Creature, when out of her Time, has no friend to advise with, or be a Check upon her Conduct, it is more than ten to one but she takes some idle, if not vicious Course, by the many Temptations to which her Sex and narrow Circumstances subject her. It is a Misfortune to the Fair Sex, when they are left young to their own Management, that they can scarce avoid falling into the many Snares laid for them by designing Men: Even their Virtues contribute to their Undoing; Men pride themselves in debauching such as betray any Marks of modest Virtue; their natural Innocence and Good-nature make them credulous, and too soon yields them a Prey to the affected Sighs and perjured Oaths of those who have no other View but their Ruin. In short, nothing can properly save them from falling but their Pride, which the servile Condition of a Journey woman too often humbles: I would conclude from this, that Parents, who bind their Daughters to this Business, must not think they have done their Duty, when, according to the Phrase, they have put a Trade into their Hands; they must instil into them early Principles of Piety, and inspire them with a virtuous Pride, and a delicate Concern for their Reputation: They ought to watch their Motions, and assist their unexperienced Years with good Advice; and never think themselves discharged of their Parental Duty, till they have settled them in the World under the Protection of some Man of Sagacity, Industry, and Good-nature: A Woman is always under Age till she comes (in the Law Phrase) to be under Cover. A Youth may be set a-float in the World as soon as he has got a Trade in his Head, without much Danger of spoiling; but a Girl is such a tender, ticklish Plant to rear, thar there is no permitting her out of Leading-strings till she is bound to a Husband. His Genius and Wages.

31

'SEWING TRADES' FROM THE PARENTS' AND GUARDIANS' DIRECTORY, 1761

Joseph Collyer

Source: Joseph Collyer, Joseph, 'Of the Cap-Makers', 'Of the Child's coat-maker', 'Of the Milliner', *The Parents' and Guardians' Directory and the Youth's Guide in the Choice of a Profession or Trade* (R. Griffiths: 1761), 90, 100–101, 194–96.

EDITORIAL HEADNOTE

Joseph Collyer, like Robert Campbell, also took up the 'female' trades, including milliners. He recognised the potential problems encountering women entering the fashion trades, but was more sensitive to the issues and dangers, and was less likely to lay blame on the girls themselves and more on social interpretations of women workers.

OF THE CAP-MAKERS

These are shop-keepers who make and sell velvet caps for men or women to travel in; as also men's mourning caps. They deal in many sorts of millinery goods, as ladies hats, bonnets, cloaks, cardinals, short aprons, hoods, handkerchiefs, or almost. thing made of black silk or velvet. Their apprentices ought to be smart girls of a genteel appearance; they should work well at their needles, and be ready accomptants. Their friends must give with them from 10 to 30£. in proportion to the trade carried on by the mistress. They serve only five years; and are kept the first part of their time close to the needle. Those, who cannot setup, may get 15 or 20£. a year and their board as journeywomen; they being qualified not only to serve Cap-makers, but may be shop-women to the milliners, the haberdashers, or to any buying and selling trade proper for women.

OF THE CHILD'S-COAT-MAKER

THIS branch of business is generally performed by women, and is a pretty profitable employ.

DOI: 10.4324/9781003676669-34

They take 10 or 15£ with a girl; who ought to be ingenious, handy, and a tolerable needle-woman. The boning part is hard work for the fingers; but the rest is easy enough. As the apprentice must appear neat and genteel, and, when out of her time, must depend on a good acquaintance, this trade is not fit for the children of people in low circumstances; but for those a little above the vulgar it is a very proper one. A journey-woman may get 1s. a day in summer; but they are generally out of business some of the winter months.

OF THE MILLINER

THE girl, designed for this employment, ought to have a genteel person, and be capable of a ready address; she too should write a tolerable hand, understand the first rules of arithmetic, work quick and well at her needle, and have some fancy and imagination. These qualifications, joined to strict modesty and justice, will hardly fail of pro-curing, in this branch of business, a comfortable and genteel support; and I know none fitter for the daughters of numerous families, where the parents live handsomely, yet have no fortunes to leave their children: But the young women put to this employ should have their minds strongly tinctured with a high idea of the dignity of chastity; for in this, as in almost: all shop-keeping businesses, they will be exposed to the attempts of designing men; many of whom glory in one of the most shameful acts of baseness, that of betraying to ruin heedless and unwary innocence. Women's best defence is private life; but where circumstances oblige them to come into the world young, the utmost care ought to be taken of their morals; and they should be taught to revere themselves, or, in other words, not to render themselves cheap, by little coquettish compliances. The girl that will patiently listen to, or join in the laugh with the young spark who makes loose allusions or impudent jests, is not far from falling a prey to the first artful seducer who shall take it in his head to seem enamoured with her beauty or wit.

The Milliner deals in a great variety of articles principally for ladies wear; such as all manner of Head Dresses, Ruffles, Handkerchiefs, Tuckers, Tippits, Gloves, Necklaces, Earings [sic], Flowers, Pompoons, Egrets, Cambricks, Lawns, Laces, Ribbons, &c. But this trade is not wholly confined to women, since the beau and fine gentleman has his Solitaire or Stock, his Watch or Canestring from the pretty Milliner; perhaps for nothing but that he may have an opportunity to stare the modest girl out of countenance, or to tempt her, by soft insinuations, to add one to the number of those he has betrayed to infamy and ruin. It is these pests of society that oblige us to give the above cautions. A Milliner, in good business, will not take an apprentice with less than 40 or 50£. but one, in a lesser way, will take with a girl 20 or 30£. Their friends find them in apparel during their apprenticeship; which is commonly only five years: To set up genteely will take 400 or 500£. but there are many who get a very good subsistance [sic] by being what are called Chamber-milliners, and keep no shops. They require a large acquaintance among people in genteel life; who frequently find their own materials, and give them to the workwoman to make up: But the Shop-milliner, who sells the goods of which their dresses are made, has greatly the advantage in point of profit. As journey-women they may get from 15 to 30£ a year and their board, according to their abilities and appearance.

32

LES MARCHANDES DE MODES, 1781

Louis Sébastien Mercier

Source: Louis Sébastien Mercier, 'Les Marchandes de Modes', *Le tableau de Paris* (Virchaux & Compagnie: 1781), Part I, 290–93.

EDITORIAL HEADNOTE

Louis Sébastien Mercier (1740–1814) was a dramatist and writer of a prodigious number of plays, pamphlets and novels. A political moderate and member of the National Assembly he voted against the execution of Louis XVI and was imprisoned during the Reign of Terror but released on the fall of Robespierre. The Tableau was a twelve-volume commentary on the Parisian working classes, originally published anonymously. The writing, tone and texture of the work is one of its key strengths, setting it apart from a simple guide to Paris as suggested by the title, which translates in English as a Painting of Paris. Heavily critical of the French *ancien régime*, he left France for Switzerland to complete the work. The extract here describes the fashion merchants, allowing some comparison with Campbell and Collyer (docs. 30, 31).

LES MARCHANDES DE MODES

There is no one as serious as a fashion shopkeeper, selling puffs and putting hundredfold meanings into flowers and gauzes. Every week you can see a new form and shape of hats. In this line of business, the invention makes its author famous. Hems and seams receive a profound and heartfelt respect for the happy geniuses that make the advantages of their beauty and figure vary. What is spent on fashion today exceeds the expenses of the table and that for horses and carriages. The unfortunate husband can never calculate to what price these changing fantasies will climb; & he will need swift resources to fight off these unexpected whims.

DOI: 10.4324/9781003676669-35

He thinks he will be singled out and pointed at, if he does not pay these trifles/superficial people just as precisely as he pays the butcher or the baker.

It is in Paris that the prosonde inventors in this area decide the laws of the universe. The infamous doll, the precious model, deck themselves out in the newest fashions; finally, the inspiring prototype passes from Paris to London every month; & from there it will spread its grace to all of Europe. It will go to the North and to the Mediterranean; it will penetrate as far as Constantinople & Petersburg; & the fold that a French hand has folded will be repeated by all the nations, who are but mere observants of the taste displayed in the Rue Saint-Honoré! All this indeed very silly! But custom, carrying an unwavering scepter, decides everything, orders everything, there is no answer to these words; one says, one does, one thinks, one is clothed as it says.

Fashion is a very extensive trade. It is only the vivid genius of the French that can rejuvenate even the most common things, as they can. Neighboring nations have tried to imitate us, but in vain, the light glory of taste will stay ours. It is not even considered that our superiority in this area could be contestable.

33

THE MILLINER, 1806

Source: Anon., 'The Milliner', *The Book of Trades or Library of Useful Arts*, 3rd ed. (Tabart and Co.: 1806), Part II: 45–50.

EDITORIAL HEADNOTE

Writing half a century later, Tabart's publication, like Campbell, Collyer and Mercier, similarly described the trade of millinery. Notably this publication presented a brief description of the trade without the moralising of earlier authors.

THE MILLINER

The business of a MILLINER, and the articles which she makes up for sale, are very well displayed in the plate. In the window of the shop are exhibited hats, caps, and bonnets; a cloak, a muff, and a fur tippet; while the milliner herself is busily employed at her counter in making up a hat. The boxes on the floor are intended either to send home her work when finished, or they are meant to hold some of the articles belonging to her trade; as feathers, artificial flowers, muslin, gauze, crape, &c. The drawers in the counter are usually devoted to ribands of different widths, colours, and prices; thread, laces, &c.

In the milliner taste and fancy are required, with a quickness in discerning, imitating, and improving upon the various fashions, which are perpetually changing among the higher circles. *Muslin*, which is one of the chief articles in the millinery business, is a very fine substance, made wholly of cotton; and it takes its name from the soft downy nap on its surface resembling moss, or in French mousse.[1] There are various kinds of muslins brought from the East-Indies: the best is said to come from Bengal. They are subject to a heavy duty upon importation, which is returned if exported into foreign countries.

Gauze is a very thin, slight, transparent kind of stuff, woven sometimes of silk, and sometimes only of thread. The gauze-loom does not differ very much from the common weaver's loom, but it has some appendages which are peculiar to it. There are a great variety of gauzes; some with flowers on a silk ground, some wrought with gold and silver. Gauze is chiefly made in this country, but part of what is used here is brought from China.

DOI: 10.4324/9781003676669-36

Crape is a very light transparent stuff, in some respects like gauze; but it is made of raw silk, gummed and twisted on the mill, and woven without crossing. It is used for mourning, and is now a very fashionable article in court dresses. Crapes used for mourning are either *crisped* or *smooth*: the first is *double*, and denotes the deeper mourning; the *single* or smooth crape is for the slighter. Crapes are of different colours, but the silk is always dyed in its raw state. The chief manufacture for this article of dress is at Lyons, but a great deal is made in various parts of this kingdom.

Source Endnote

1 For the use of milliners and mantua-makers who reside in the country, and also to gratify the curiosity of ladies in general in the country, and also to gratify the curiosity of ladies in general, a work is published in London every month, entitled 'The Monthly Fashions of London and Paris;' containing from ten to fifteen fashionable dresses in each number, drawn from real life, in the first circles. Price 1s. 6d. each number.

34

INVESTIGATION INTO THE SITUATION OF HAT WORKERS, 1841

Source: ENQUÊTE. Situation des ouvriers chapeliers [Situation of the hatmakers]. *L'Atelier*, n° 1, deuxième année, septembre 1841, 6–7.

EDITORIAL HEADNOTE

The investigation into Parisian hat workers at the mid-nineteenth century reminds us that women's industrial handwork crossed borders, and though the hat workers retained some sense of their skill and identity they too were under the pressure of changing systems, and the demand for more work at less pay. They also operated mutual societies to protect themselves from the vagaries of the system, and these organisations are discussed more fully in Vol. 3. *L'atelier* was founded in 1840 and proclaimed itself as a special voice of the working classes, written by workers, and much of its energy was in aid of cultural production and to insist on the rights of workers to express their point of view on contemporary production.

The hat industry employs 2,000 workers in Paris, divided into three very distinct groups: the fullers, the appropriators and the formers; all work in the factory, and are paid on a piece-rate basis.

Although the workers making up this part of Parisian industry are not as unhappy as those employed in many other parts, they are nevertheless not (especially the crushers) as happy as the public generally believes.

We will therefore expose, as exactly as possible, the position of each of these bodies.

The Fullers. – There are around 700 of them, some of whom form, through an annual subscription, a company called *Bourse auxiliaire des Fouleurs-Chapeliers de Paris* [Auxiliary Exchange of the Fullers-Hatters of Paris]. This society founded in 1817, with the permission of the authority and the consent of the masters, has constantly helped its members against unemployment, so frequent in this quarter since the manufacture of silk hats, and against the masters, who, able to make the members agree to a reduction in the prices fixed by them and the members, created workshops outside the barrier, and there, speculating on the misery

DOI: 10.4324/9781003676669-37

of poor fathers, who could not bear long unemployment, and on the isolation of those who remained outside of society made them work at prices much lower than those set by the tariff. . . . The price of craftsmanship allowed the fulling worker, about ten years ago, to earn a reasonable salary: but this has been declining every day since the manufacture of silk hats, the masters, by a false calculation, and with the intention however of preventing this part from being lost, two terrible competitions took place: first that of better workmanship which increases the work of the worker without increasing his salary, then that of the cheaper one, which forced the crushing workers, not yet a month ago, to reduce this already insufficient salary. So that the crushing worker earns on average, and if he is busy all year round, only 2fr. 25c. at 2fr. 50c. per day, still only the members; for the dissidents cannot gain this, the manners being paid to them half as much. For example, the way a hat costs 3fr. in Paris, costs 1fr. 50c. outside the barrier. Finally, the position of the crushing workers, especially those who work outside the company, and who consequently have no guarantee against unemployment, is so miserable that they often cannot go out for lack of shoes or clothes the most necessary. Many are occupied by licensed workers who themselves work for other masters, and we know how unhappy the worker is who resorts to those who make people work like this in all areas.

The Appropriators. – The appropriators are in Paris, numbering approximately 1200; 350 of them form, like the fullers, through a weekly contribution, a mutual aid association under the name of Bourse auxiliaire des Approprieurs-Chapeliers de Paris [Auxiliary Exchange of the Appropriators-Hatters of Paris]. Founded in 1820, its mission, like that of the fullers, is to protect the worker against unemployment and against illnesses caused by difficult, unhealthy and irregular work; because there are in this part, as in all millinery, seven months of the year, at least, where we work only three or four days a week, and five months, approximately, where we works sixteen hours a day. The appropriator, the one who works all year round, earns on average 3fr. 25c. at 4fr. 25c., our calculation established on different houses and different workers, more or less active. . . . We point out the unemployment in this part of the industry, because the hatter worker generally goes among the public to regularly earn 7 or 8 francs per day; moreover, which the masters have propagated and exploited for their profit: . . .

The spinners. – There are many in retail houses, their specialty being turning the brim of the hat. They find work at the retailer as well as at the manufacturer; However, as the remuneration is not the same, and it would be difficult to give the figure for those employed in retail, we will only talk about those employed in factories. There are around 100 to 150 of them, the number varies according to the seasons. Those who work there all year earn on average 4fr. at 4fr. 50c. per day.

The workers. – The hat industry also employs around 500 workers, almost all of whom work at home. They are divided into four very distinct bodies, which are: the hair cutters and trimmers who only work on felt hats; the seamstresses, who only work on silk hats, and the trimmers, who work on felts and silks. They are all paid on a piece-rate basis. Cutters and squarers earn on average 1fr. 25c. at

1fr. 50c.; the sewers of 1fr. at 1fr. 25c., and garnishes of 1fr. 25c. at 1fr. 50c. The workers working in the millinery are subject to the same unemployment as the men, and they have, moreover, that in the season when they could well work, they must lose precious time which requires the postponement of their work, and this three or four times a day. . . .

In this survey, as in all those given previously, we only considered the position of workers who are employed in Paris; we will return to this subject, and we will talk about all millinery in France.

35

MILLINERY WORKERS, 1910

Alice P. Barrows

Source: Alice P. Barrows, 'The Training of Millinery Workers', in *Economic Position of Women, Proceedings of The Academy of Political Science in The City of New York*, Henry Raymond Mussey (ed.), (Columbia University, 1910), 41–45.

EDITORIAL HEADNOTE

By the turn of the century, sewing had become a *cause célèbre* and in the United States, like in Britain and France, educated middle-class women turned to revealing and addressing the situation of seamstresses. This extract explicitly illustrates how millinery had shifted from a prestige industry to one that was ill-defined with far less promise than in 1761. Alice Barrows was born in Lowell, Massachusetts. She graduated from Vassar College in 1900 and became a teacher. In 1909 she became an investigator for the Russell Sage Foundation, which collaborated with the Committee on Women's Work in producing investigations, including one into millinery with Mary van Kleeck, later director of the Department of Industrial Studies. She later devoted forty-one years to the cause of education, twenty-three of them in the U.S. Office of Education.

Henry Raymond Mussey, introducing this volume of articles on women's work, wrote:

> Of all the problems that have come in the train of the industrial revolution none are more perplexing than those that concern women. It is a wearisome commonplace that the factory has taken over much of the industrial work of the home, and that women have followed their work into the factory; but the fundamental change thus introduced into their life has not always been clearly seen. Formerly home and industry were synonymous terms for them; training for industry was training in household management. To-day industrial work is sharply separated from the management of the

DOI: 10.4324/9781003676669-38

> home, and there has come into the occupation of women a dualism that finds no parallel in the life of men. Most of the difficulties of women in industry relate themselves in some way to this fact.

A number of chapters from this volume are also included in this collection and again illustrate the networks and connections of educated and socially concerned women at the turn of the century.

It is not easy to describe the millinery trade clearly because the essence of the description is to show that it cannot be made clear. If the next few paragraphs leave the reader with an impression of chaos then the description has been successful. "The millinery trade is about twenty-five different trades," said one employer. This statement does not give a true impression because it does not show that each branch overlaps and penetrates into every other in a most confusing manner. Millinery shops are of all types, in all parts of the city, with all kinds of work. Broadly speaking, the establishments can be divided into wholesale and retail, and in general it may be said that in wholesale shops it's speed we want, and in retail, careful, neat hand workers." Actually, such definitions of the trade are not true to fact. Every variety of hat is made in all kinds of ways whether manufactured at wholesale or retail. There are "trimmed hats" and "untrimmed hats," "ready-to-wear hats," "artistic millinery," "home-made hats," and "tailor hats." At first glance, it would seem that the trade is an excellent example of the subdivision of labor. The important point to the worker, however, is that sometimes it illustrates this subdivision of labor and sometimes it does not. Trimmed hats are found in the same establishments with untrimmed and ready-to-wear hats, or with only one or with neither. Artistic millinery is found in exclusive private shops and in sweatshops. Tailor hats are made in the same establishments with trimmed and untrimmed hats or in shops by themselves. Home-made hats are found to be contract work for great factories, or "neighborhood work for a few friends."

Naturally, this lack of system and standard is reflected in the demands made upon workers. In general, it may be said that there are four stages in making a hat, – designing it, making the frame, covering the frame, and trimming it. And in general it may be stated that there are seven kinds of positions open to a girl looking for work in millinery. She may be a learner, an improver, a preparer, a milliner, a copyist, a trimmer, or a designer. But when a girl starts to look for work as preparer, for example, she may turn toward a Fifth avenue shop where she must be a "neat worker" who can make frames accurately by hand, and have an eye for color and form"; here she may advance from preparer to designer; or she may find her way into a shop a few doors away where she does not need to make frames because they have two girls who make all the frames; or she may apply at a department store where in one department she will have an opportunity to do all the kinds of work found in the Fifth avenue shop, "only not so particular"; or she may go into the ready-to-wear department where "you never make a frame but cover with straw and stick on a rosette"; or she may join the throng of girls pouring into a Broadway wholesale house, and as she walks up the stairs she may stop at any one of the five floors and enter a "millinery establishment." But in one she will be asked to do straw operating all day; in another to make dozens of wire frames a day; in another to trim hats by the dozen and never make frames; in another to work at nothing but millinery ornaments. In the autumn of 1908 she finds it difficult to get a position as preparer because "the machines are driving them out"; and in the spring of 1909 preparers are in great demand because "the styles have changed this season, and hand work has come back this month." In any case, she thinks herself fortunate if she works more than six months a year at $5 a week in not more than three or four positions. No prophecy can be made about the kind of skill which will be demanded in any shop. . . .

If these facts about conditions in the millinery trade prove anything they prove that "learning to make hats" is a very different thing from "learning the millinery trade." The experiences of millinery workers would seem to suggest that in modern times, perhaps even more than in the days when industrial conditions were less complex, apprenticeship must include learning the trade as well as one process in it, if the workers are to be efficient. A milliner who does not know that millinery means machine work and hand work, speed work and careful work, that the seasons are irregular, that the wages are unstandardized, and that conditions are constantly changing, is in no position to become efficient. Such knowledge is part of her job, and it is as necessary that she should understand her various relations to the trade in which she is working as that she should master the technique of the machine that she is operating. Power to adapt to different types of establishments, to varied kinds of work, and to fluctuating seasons, rather than specialization in a particular process, is a practical necessity for the girl who would earn her own living. According to the testimony of both workers and employers she does not get this power in the trade itself; employers have no time for learners, and the girl finds that learning is nothing but running errands." According to the same testimony, the schools do not know the trade and do not prepare their pupils to do any one thing well.

36

ONE OF THE FUR-SEWERS, 1886

Helen Campbell

Source: Helen Campbell, 'One of the Fur-sewers', *Prisoners of Poverty: Women Wage-Workers, Their Trades And Their Lives*, (1886, Little, Brown, And Company, 1900), 139–49.

EDITORIAL HEADNOTE

Helen Campbell's chapters from *Prisoners of Poverty* continue the theme of the character of hand sewing work at the turn of the twentieth century. Initially a children's writer and novelist, she turned to non-fiction in the late 1870s, writing for newspapers and magazines, and from 1881 to 1884, she served as literary editor of Philadelphia-based *Our Continent*. Turning to the situation of women workers, she published her best-known work, *Prisoners of Poverty*, in which she addressed the difficulty of women meeting their financial needs because of their poor wages. Throughout her writing she documented that women's wages were virtually half of men's, and she contended that this dysfunction forced women into a position of vulnerability relative to men. Writing in an era of the emergence of social science, her work was often considered too emotional rather than statistically based, yet she won a prize from the American Economic Association in 1891 for her investigative work.

I told him [Leander, her boyfriend] from the time we went to school together that I was bound to get to New York, an' that sort of fired him up, an' we've talked hours to time about what it was like, an' what we'd do if we ever got there. My folks were set against the notion, an' so were his, but he went after a while, with some man that was up in the summer an' that gave him a place in a store. I couldn't go on account of father's dying sudden an' mother's holdin' on harder'n ever to me, but she was took within the year, an' there I was, free enough, an' not a soul in the world but Leander's folks that seemed to think much one way or another how I was likely to come out.

There was a mortgage on the farm, an' Dr. Grayson foreclosed an' had most of the money for his bill; an' when things were all settled I had forty dollars in cash

DOI: 10.4324/9781003676669-39

an' the old furniture. Leander's folks was dreadful short for things, for they'd been burned out once, an' so I just turned everything over to them but some small things I could pack in my trunk, mother's teaspoons an' such, an' walked down to the village an' took the stage for Portsmouth. I wasn't scared. I didn't care nor think how I looked. It was heaven to think I was on the way to folks an' the things folks do. I ain't given to crying, but that day I sat back in the stage an' cried just for joy to think I was going to have something different.

All this time I hadn't thought much what I'd do. Forty dollars seemed a big lot, enough for weeks ahead. I'd done most everything about a house, an' I could make everything I wore. I had only to look at a pattern an' I could go home an cut out one like it. The dress I had on was cheap stuff, but when I looked at other folks's I saw it wasn't so much out o' the way. So I said, most likely some dressmaker would take me, an' I'd try my luck that way. This was before I got to Boston, an' I went round there all the afternoon before it was time to take the train, for the conductor told me just what to do, an' I hadn't a mite of trouble. I never do going to a strange place. I was half a mind to stay in Boston when I saw the Common an' the crowds of folks. I sat still there an' just looked at 'em, an' cried again for joy to think I'd got where there were so many. 'But there'll be more in New York,' I said, 'an' there'll be sure to be plenty ready to do a good turn.' I could have hugged 'em all. I didn't think then the time would ever come that I'd hate the sight of faces an' wish myself on top of the hill in the cobble-stones, but it did, an' it does now sometimes.

I went on board the boat that night sort of crazy. I'd gone an' got some sandwiches an' things at a place the conductor told me, an' I sat on the deck in the moonlight an' ate my supper. I'd been too happy to eat before, an' I was so happy then I could hardly keep still. There was a girl not far off, a kind of nice-looking girl, an' she watched me, an' at last she began to talk. In half an hour I knew all about her an' she about me. She was a Rhode Island girl an' had worked in a mill near Providence, an' gone to New York at last an' learned fur-sewing. She said it was a good trade, an' she made ten an' twelve dollars a week while the season lasted an' never less than five. This seemed a mint of money, an' when she said one of their old hands had died, an' she could take me right in as her friend an' teach me herself, I felt as if my fortune was made.

Well, I went with her next day. She had a room in Spring Street, near Hudson, – an old-fashioned house that belonged to two maiden sisters, an' I went in with her the first night, an' afterward for a while had the hall bedroom. It didn't take me long to learn. It was a Jew place an' there were thirty girls, but he treated us well. For my part I've fared just as well with Jews as ever I did with Christians, an' sometimes better. I'd taken to Hattie so that I couldn't bear to think of leaving her, an' so I let my dressmaking plan go. But I'll tell you what I found out in time. These skins are all dressed with arsenic. The dealers say there's nothing poisonous about them, but of course they lie. Every pelt has more or less in it, an' the girls show it just as the artificial-flower girls show it. Your eyelids get red an' the lids all puffy, an' you're white as chalk. The dealers say the red eyes come from the flying hairs. Perhaps they do, but the lids don't, an' every fur-sewer is poisoned a little with every prick of her needle. What the flying hair does is just to get into your throat an' nose and everywhere, an' tickle till you cough all the time, an' a girl with weak lungs hasn't a chance. The air is full of fur, an' then the work-room is kept tight shut for fear of moths getting in. The work is easy enough. It's just an everlasting patchwork, for you're always sewing together little bits, hundreds of them, that you have to match. You sew over an' over with linen thread, an' you're always piecing out an' altering shapes. It's nothing to sew up a thing when you've once got it pieced together. If it's beaver, all the long hairs must be picked out, an' it's the same with sealskin. We made up everything; sable an' Siberian squirrel, bear, fox, marten, mink, otter, an' all the rest. There were some girls very slow in learning that only got a dollar a week, an' in the end four, but most of them can average about five. I was seventeen when I began, an' in a year I had caught all the knack there is to it, an' was an expert, certain of ten dollars in the season an' about six in between. It's generally piece-work, with five or six months when you can earn ten or twelve dollars even, an' the rest of the time five or six dollars. In the busiest times there'd be fifty girls perhaps, but this was only for two or three months, an' then they discharged them. 'Tisn't a trade I'd ever let a girl take up if I could help it; I suppose somebody's got to do it, but there ought to be higher wages for those that do.

This went on five years. I won't take time telling about Leander, but he'd got to be a clerk at Ridley's an' had eight hundred dollars a year, an' we'd been engaged for two years, an' just waiting to see if he wouldn't get another rise. I knew we could manage on that. Leander was more ambitious than me. He said we ought to live in a showy boarding-house an' make our money tell that way, but I told him I was used to the Spring Street house, an' we could have a whole floor an' be snug as could be an' Hattie board with us. He gave in, an' it's well he did; for we hadn't been married six months before he had a hemorrhage an' just went into quick consumption. I'd kept right on with my trade, but I was pulled down myself an' my eyelids so swollen sometimes I could hardly see out of 'em. But I got a sewing-machine from money I'd saved, an' I took in work from a place on Canal Street, – a good one, too, that always paid fair. The trouble was my eyes. I'd used 'em up, an' they got so I couldn't see the needle nor sew straight, an' had to give up the sewing, an' then I didn't know which way to turn, for there was Leander. The old folks were up there still, wrastling with the stones, but poorer every year, an' I couldn't get him up there. Leander was patient as a saint, but he fretted over me an' how I was to get along.

'You're not to worry,' says I. 'There's more ways than one of earning, an' if my eyes is bad, I've got two hands an' know how to use 'em. I'll take a place an' do housework if I can't do nothing else.'

You'd never believe how the thought o' that weighed on him. He'd wake me up in the night to say, 'Now, Almiry, jest give up that thought an' promise me you'll try something else. I think I'd turn in my grave if I had to know you was slavin' in anybody's kitchen.'

"'What's the odds?' I said. 'You have to be under orders whatever you do. I think it won't be a bad change from the shop.'

He took on so, though, that to quiet him I promised him I wouldn't do it unless I had to, an' 'twasn't long after that that he died. Between the doctor's bill – an' he was a kind man, I will say, an' didn't charge a tenth of what he had ought to – an' the funeral an' all, I was cleaned out of everything. I'd had to pawn a month before he died, an' was just stripped. Sewing was no good. My eyes went back on me like everything else, an' in a fortnight I knew there wasn't anything for it but getting a place. I left such things as I had in charge of the old ladies an' answered an advertisement for 'a capable girl willing to work.'

37

THE CASE OF ROSE HAGGERTY, 1886

Helen Campbell

Source: Helen Campbell, 'The Case of Rose Haggerty', *Prisoners of Poverty: Women Wage-Workers, Their Trades And Their Lives*, (Little, Brown, And Company, 1900), 18–29.

EDITORIAL HEADNOTE

Another chapter from Helen Campbell's volume *Prisoners of Poverty*, 'The Case of Rose Haggerty' gives an emotional account of a young girl who took up the responsibility of looking after a brood of her siblings when her parent's died, struggling to find work and manage the household. Taking up sewing for a sweater, even that ultimately failed her as it did many women in her position.

"THE case of Rose Haggerty." So it stands on the little record-book in which long ago certain facts began to have place, each one a count in the indictment of the civilization of to-day, and each one the story not only of Rose but of many another in like case. For the student of conditions among working-women soon discovers that workers divide themselves naturally into four classes: (1) those who have made deliberate choice of a trade, fitted themselves carefully for it, and in time become experts, certain of employment and often of becoming themselves employers; (2) those who by death of relatives or other accident of fortune have been thrown upon their own resources and accept blindly the first means of support that offers, sometimes developing unexpected power and meeting with the same success as the first class; (3) those who have known no other life but that of work, and who accept that to which they most incline with neither energy nor ability enough to rise beyond a certain level; and (4) those who would not work at all save for the pressure of poverty, and who make no effort to gain more knowledge or to improve conditions. But the ebb and flow in this great sea of toiling humanity wipes out all dividing lines, and each class so shades into the next that formal division becomes impossible, but is rather a series of interchanges with no

DOI: 10.4324/9781003676669-40

confinement to fixed limits. Often in passing from one trade to another, chance brings about much the same result for each class, and no energy or patience of effort is sufficient to check the inevitable descent into the valley of the shadow, where despair walks forever hand in hand with endeavor.

This time had by no means come for Rose, with just enough of her happy-go-lucky father's nature to make her essentially optimistic. Born in a Cherry Street tenement-house, she had refused to be killed by semi-starvation or foul smells, or dirt of any nature whatsoever. Dennis Haggerty, longshoreman professionally, and doer of all odd jobs in the intervals of his discharges and re-engagements, explained the situation to his own satisfaction, if not to that of Rose and the five other small Haggertys remaining from the brood of twelve.

> "If a man wants his drink that bad that no matter what he's said overnight he'd sell his soul by the time mornin' comes for even a thimbleful, he's got jist to go to destruction, an' there's no stoppin' him. An' I've small call to be blamin' Norah whin she comforts herself a bit in the same manner of way, nor will I so long's me name's Dennis Haggerty. But you, Rose, you look out an' get any money you'll find in me pockets, an' keep the children straight, an' all the saints'll see you through the job."

Rose listened, the laugh in her blue eyes shadowed by the sense of responsibility that by seven was fully developed. She did not wonder that her mother drank. Why not, when there was no fire in the stove, and nothing to cook if there had been, and the children counted it a day when they had a scraping of butter on the bread? But, as often happens in these cases, the disgust at smell and taste of liquor grew with every month of her life, and two at least of the children shared it. They were never beaten; for Haggerty at his worst remained good-natured, and when sober wept maudlin tears over his flock and swore that no drop should ever pass his lips again; and Norah echoed every word, and for days perhaps washed and scrubbed and scoured, earning fair wages, and gradually redeeming the clothes or furniture pledged round the corner. Rose went to school when she had anything to wear, and learned in time, when she saw the first symptoms of another debauch, to bundle every wearable thing together and take them and all small properties to the old shoemaker on the first floor, where they remained in hiding till it was safe to produce them again. She had learned this and many another method before the fever which suddenly appeared in early spring took not only her father and mother, but the small Dennis whose career as newsboy had been her pride and delight, and who had been relied upon as half at least of their future dependence. There remained, then, Norah, hopelessly incurable of spinal disease and helpless to move save as Rose lifted her, and the three little ones, as to whose special gifts there was as yet no definite knowledge. In the mean time they were simply three very clamorous mouths to be stopped with such food as might be; and Rose entered a bag-factory a block away, leaving bread and knife and molasses-pitcher by Norah's bed, and trusting the saints to avert disaster from the three experimenting babies. She earned the first month ten dollars, or two and a half a week, but being exceptionally quick, was promoted in the second to four dollars weekly. The rent was six dollars a month; and during the first one the old shoemaker came to the rescue, had an occasional eye to the children, and himself paid the rent, telling Rose to return it when she could. When the ten hours' labor ended, the child, barely fourteen, rushed home to cook something warm for supper, and when the children were comforted and tucked away in the wretched old bed, that still was clean and decent, washed and mended their rags of clothes, and brought such order as she could into the forlorn room.

It was the old shoemaker, a patient, sad-eyed old Scotchman, who also had his story, who settled for her at last that a machine must be had in order that she might work at home. The woman in the room back of his took in shirts from a manufacturer on Division Street, and made often seven and eight dollars a week. She was ready to teach, and in two or three evenings Rose had practically mastered details, and settled that, as she was so young, she would not apply for work in person, but take it through Mrs. Moloney, who would be supposed to have gone into business on her own account as a "sweater." Whatever temptations Mrs. Moloney may have had to make a little profit as "middle-man," she resisted and herself saw that the machine selected was a good one; that no advantage was taken of Rose's inexperience; and that the agent had no opportunity to follow out what had now and then been his method, and hint to the girl that her pretty face entitled her to concessions that would be best made in a private interview. Shame in every possible form and phase had been part of the girl's knowledge since babyhood, but it had slipped away from her, as a foul garment might fall from the fair statue over which it had chanced to be thrown. It was not the innocence of ignorance, – a poor possession at best. It was an ingrained repulsion, born Heaven knows how, and growing as mysteriously with her growth, an invisible yet most potent armor, recognized by every dweller in the swarming tenement. She had her father's quick tongue and laughing eyes, but they could flash as well, and the few who tried a coarse jest shrunk back from both look and scorching word.

Thus far all went well with the poor little fortunes. She worked always ten and twelve, sometimes fourteen, hours a day, yet her strength did not fail, and there was no dearth of work. It was in 1880, and prices were nearly double the present rates. To-day work from the same establishment means not over $4.50 per week, and has even fallen as low as $3.50. In 1880 the shirts were given out by the dozen as at present, going back to the factory to pass through the hands of the finisher and buttonhole maker. The machine operator could make nine of the best class of shirts in a day of ten hours, being paid for them at the rate of $1.75 per dozen. Four spools of cotton, two hundred yards each, were required for a dozen, the price of which must be deducted from the receipts; but the firm preferred to supply twenty-four-hundred-yard spools, at fifty cents for six-cord cotton used for the upper thread, and thirty cents for the three-cord cotton used as under thread, the present prices for same quality and size being respectively forty-five and twenty-five cents. Making nine a day, the week's wages would be for the four dozen and a half $7.87, or $7.50 deducting thread; but Rose averaged five dozen weekly, and for nearly two years counted herself as certain of not less than thirty dollars per month and often thirty-five. The machine had been paid for. The room took on as comfortable a look as its dingy walls and narrow windows would allow; and Bridget, age five, had developed distinct genius for housekeeping, and washed dishes and faces with equal energy and enthusiasm. She did all errands also, and could not be cheated in the matter of change. She knew where the largest loaves were to be had, and sniffed suspiciously at the packets of tea.

"By the time she's seven, she'll do all but the washing," Rose said with pride, and Bridget reverted to childhood for an instant, and spun round on one foot as she made answer: –

"Shure, I could now, if you'd only be lettin' me."

"There's women on the west side that'll earn $2.50 a dozen, for work no better than you're doing now," some one who had come from that quarter said to her one day, but Rose shook her head. There is a curious conservatism among these workers, who cling to familiar haunts and regard unknown regions with suspicion and even terror.

"I've no time for change," Rose said. "It might not be as certain when I'd got it. I'll run no risks;" and she tugged her great bundle of work up the stairs, rejoicing that living so near saved just so much on expressage, a charge paid by the workers themselves.

There were signs well known to the old hands of a probable reduction of prices, weeks before the first cut came. More fault was found. A slipped stitch or a break in the thread was pounced upon with even more promptness than had been their usual portion. Some hands were discharged, and at last came the general cut, resented by some, wailed over by all, but accepted as inevitable. Another, and another, and another followed. Too much production; too many Jew firms competing and underbidding; more and more foreigners coming in ready to take the work at half price. These reasons and a dozen others of the same order were given glibly, and at first with a certain show of kindliness and attempt to soften harsh facts as much as possible. But the patience of diplomacy soon failed, and questioners of all orders were told that if they did not like it they had nothing to do but to leave and allow a crowd of waiting substitutes to take their places at half rates. The shirt that had sold for seventy-five cents and one dollar had gone down to forty-five and sixty cents respectively, and as cottons and linens had fallen in the same proportion, there was still profit for all but the worker. Here and there were places on Grand or Division Streets where they might even be bought for thirty and forty cents, the price per dozen to the worker being at last from fifty to sixty cents. In the factories it was still possible to earn some approximation to the old rate, but employers had found that it was far cheaper to give out the work; some choosing to give the entire shirt at so much per dozen; others preferring to send out what is known as "team work," flaps being done by one, bosoms by another, and so on.

For a time Rose hemmed shirt-flaps at four cents a dozen, then took first one form and then another of underclothing, the rates on which had fallen in the same proportion, to find each as sure a means of starvation as the last. She had no knowledge of ordinary family sewing, and no means of obtaining such work, had any training fitted her for it; domestic service was equally impossible for the same reason, and the added one that the children must not be left, and she struggled on, growing a little more haggard and worn with every week, but the pretty eyes still holding a gleam of the old merriment. Even that went at last. It was a hard winter. The steadiest work could not give them food enough or warmth enough. The children cried with hunger and shivered with cold. There was no refuge save in Norah's bed, under the ragged quilts; and they cowered there till late in the day, watching Rose as she sat silent at the sewing-machine. There was small help for them in the house. The workers were all in like case, and for the most part drowned their troubles in stale beer from the bucket-shop below.

"Put the children in an asylum, and then you can marry Mike Rooney and be comfortable enough," they said to her, but Rose shook her head.

"I've mothered 'em so far, and I'll see 'em through," she said, "but the saints only knows how. If I can't do it by honest work, there's one way left that's sure, an' I'll try that."

There came a Saturday night when she took her bundle of work, shirts again, and now eighty-five cents a dozen. There were five dozen, and when the $1.50 was laid aside for rent it was easy to see what remained for food, coal, and light. Clothing had ceased to be part of the question. The children were barefoot. They had a bit of meat on Sundays, but for the rest, bread, potatoes, and tea were the diet, with a cabbage and bit of pork now and then for luxuries. Norah had been failing, and to-night Rose planned to buy her "something with a taste to it," and looked at the sausages hanging in long links with a sudden reckless determination to get enough for all. She was faint with hunger, and staggered as she passed a basement restaurant, from which came savory smells, snuffed longingly by some half-starved children. Her turn was long in coming, and as she laid her bundle on the counter she saw suddenly that her needle had "jumped," and that half an inch or so of a band required resewing. As she looked the foreman's knife slipped under the place, and in a moment half the band had been ripped.

"That's no good," he said. "You're getting botchier all the time."

"Give it to me," Rose pleaded. "I'll do it over."

"Take it if you like," he said indifferently, "but there's no pay for that kind o' work."

He had counted her money as he spoke, and Rose cried out as she saw the sum.

"Do you mean you'll cheat me of the whole dozen because half an inch on one is gone wrong?"

"Call it what you like," he said. "R. & Co. ain't going to send out anything but first-class work. Stand out of the way and let the next have a chance. There's your three dollars and forty cents."

Rose went out silently, choking down rash words that would have lost her work altogether, but as she left the dark stairs and felt again the cutting wind from the river, she stood still, something more than despair on her face. The children could hardly fare worse without her than with her. The river could not be colder than this cold world that gave her no chance, and that had no place for anything but rascals. She turned toward it as the thought came, but some one had her arm, and she cried out suddenly and tried to wrench away.

"Easy now," a voice said. "You're breakin' your heart for trouble, an' here I am in the nick o' time. Come with me an' you'll have no more of it, for my pocket's full to-night, an' that's more 'n it'll be in the mornin' if you don't take me in tow."

It was a sailor from a merchantman just in, and Rose looked at him for a moment. Then she took his arm and walked with him toward Roosevelt Street.

It might be dishonor, but it was certainly food and warmth for the children, and what did it matter? She had fought her fight for twenty years, and it had been a vain struggle. She took his money when morning came, and went home with the look that is on her face to-day.

"I'll marry you out of hand," the sailor said to her; but Rose answered, "No man alive'll ever marry me after this night," and she has kept her word. She has her trade, and it is a prosperous one, in which wages never fail. The children are warm and have no need to cry for hunger any more.

"It's not a long life we live," Rose says quietly. "My kind die early, but the children will be well along, an' all the better when the time comes that they've full sense for not having to know what way the living comes. But let God Almighty judge who's to blame most – I that was driven, or them that drove me to the pass I'm in."

38

THE SEWING-MACHINE IN AMERICA, 1860

Source: Anon. 'The Sewing-Machine in America', *English Woman's Journal* (October 1860): 126–28.

Image 6 Singer Sewing Machine in the home and in the factory. Advertising Poster, 1892. Public Domain.

DOI: 10.4324/9781003676669-41

EDITORIAL HEADNOTE

The sewing machine began affecting women's handwork from the 1860s, both at home and in factories where machines were brought together to utilise a single power source. The two patterns had different implications for women's work. At home she often supplied her own machine, or rented it from the manufacturer, and paid her own heating and lighting bills and often found her own thread, needles and other paraphernalia. Many women saw this as giving her more independence and the potential for managing home and work better, although the demands and pace of work made this a fiction for most. Factory work covered heating and lighting, but the machine sped up the pace of work and some women objected to the loss of identity (see doc. 62). The *English Woman's Journal* (1858–1864) was founded by Barbara Leigh Smith Bodichon, Matilda Mary Hays and Bessie Rayner Parkes, known as the Langham Place Group, and was published by the Victoria Press (see doc. 48), concentrating on female employment issues and including equality in employment and reform of laws pertaining to the sexes. Their interests included both working- and middle-class women's work, which was particularly relevant as the Census had revealed some 2.5 million unmarried women needing to work to support themselves. Boudichon, with others, also recognised that women's right to their wages was crucial in a climate where men had the right to their wives' money. Thus, all three women were key members of the woman's movement, and promoters of the Married Women's Property Act (1857). The anonymous article reprinted here draws on the experience of deploying the sewing machine in the United States, and like many at the time it was introduced, saw it as a benefit to women's employment, despite some protests.

The following particulars regarding the employment of the sewing machine in the United States, and the effect it produces on domestic life there have been communicated to us by an American lady. It appears to be much more largely used in families on the other side of the Atlantic than is yet the case among us: –

"Machinery as a substitute for hand labor, you are aware, for obvious reasons, always meets with opposition, more or less violent, when first introduced. This was the case in the United States with the sewing-machine. The opposition was more moderate however with us than it would probably be with you, where the avenues, to employment are so crowded.

"Our country, you know, is the great field for enterprise and experiment; novelties are welcomed and always meet with a fair trial. The restlessness peculiar to a new country, where people are not accustomed to move in long-established grooves, rendering it easy to turn from one mode of employment to another. The objection usually made, that these machines doing a week's work in a few hours, would throw many deserving women out of employment it is my impression has not been confirmed. A few no doubt have, suffered among the elderly, the infirm, or unenterprising, who, could not, or would not, change their habits. Since the introduction of this invention, large establishments have grown up at the principal agencies in our great cities wherein commodious apartments, the purchasers of machines are instructed in their use. An intelligent woman is at the head of such an establishment, and under her supervision the whole business goes on. In other apartments the numbers of women and girls are employed some sewing upon the machines others preparing work which, is sent here by private families, by those who deal in ready-made linen, and by tailors, for whose work it is peculiarly adapted. It should be remembered by those who oppose the sewing machine, that women *must* be employed in their use. A great proportion of the work in every garment must be done by the hand, beside the necessary fitting and preparation.

My own behalf opinion of is, that these machines are a Providential invention in behalf of our sex. Any one who has reflected upon the subject – – any one who has read Hood's Song of the Shirt – must be, thankful indeed, that there is growing up in the world a remedy for that terrible waste of labor, health, and eyesight, which the use of the needle has caused in woman.

"Another argument in their favor is, that they remove the burden of labor from the woman – whose proper employment, is of the training children, the charge of the aged, and care of the household – to the man. In the increased demand machinery, and in the employment thus afforded men, the income formerly supplied by the wife, mother or sister, can be derived from the legitimate source, giving each their proper sphere, and sparing women that expenditure of physical energy which Providence has not fitted her to endure.

"There are in the United States a dozen or twenty different patented machines, some of them very cheap, the most approved are the most expensive, and have the readiest sale. I have understood that at least a hundred thousand are sold in America in a year. When to one you reflect that the best sort may cost from seventy-five dollars to one hundred and twenty, you may imagine the amount of capital invested in this manufacture.

"One of the modes by which women in the United States obtain a livelihood is by going out to sew by the day in families. If they possess a good machine, they can find constant employment. The work is fitted and prepared for them previously, and in a day the work which it has required a good manager many days to prepare, can be passed through the machine.

"Families who own a machine and employ a person occasionally to work it, obtain a woman, from the agency; her wages are a dollar and three-quarters a day. The wages of a woman who brings her own machine, are two dollars a day, with the cost of transporting it added. In both cases they are provided with their meals course by their employers.

"Of course the woman who labors all day over a sewing-machine, works as hard as one who does it with the needle but she will receive nearly as much in one day as she could make by her needle in a week, with this advantage, that her mind is not depressed by the weary, consciousness that her labor is only advancing by the slow progress of inches.

> "One of the results. of the introduction of the sewing-machine in moderate circumstances with us is, the increased comfort and ease of persons in moderate circumstances. For a small sum a greater number of garments can be provided for a family; the mother has her press and full of linen which heretofore she has not had time to make, and could not afford to have made; the children are stocked with a plentiful feels supply of clothing at a small cost; the mother no longer feels bound to mend old clothes; she has increased rest, and the poor profit by the cast off garments. Greater comfort is diffused through the family greater cleanliness and consequently increased means of health. The of country clergymen with small salaries profit much by the use of these machines, which are, always sold to them at a reduced price. I will venture to say that the consumption of our domestic manufactures has been increased by the use of this invention very much, and I doubt whether our people would willingly go back to the days of hard sewing any more than they, would endure to live in the costly twilight of lamps and candles after enjoying the brilliant blaze of gas."

39

SEWING MACHINE LABOR, 1875

Azel Ames

Source: Azel Ames, 'Sewing Machine Labor', *Sex in Industry, A Plea for the Working Girl* (James Osgood and Co, 1875), 115–24.

EDITORIAL HEADNOTE

American physician Azel Ames contradicts the impression given in the *English Woman's Journal* article, primarily presenting information relating to the debilitating effects of sewing machine work. A graduate of Harvard medical School in 1871, he started as a practising physician but soon became interested in health and sanitation, which became his main work, locally founding the Board of Health in Wakefield, Massachusetts, as Representative in the Massachusetts Legislature and as secretary of the Committee on Public Health. His book, *Sex in Industry, A Plea for the Working Girl*, draws attention to the industrial health issues of working women, in this extract focusing on the sewing machine; other chapters are extracted in the following (doc. 49) and in Vol. 2 on aspects of factory work.

SEWING MACHINE LABOR

The several branches of industry hitherto considered have all been such as have their physical requirements principally met by the labor of the hands alone (except such involvement of pedal power as was embraced in standing, walking, etc.); but, in sewing machine use, we have an employ calling into the active service of the feet and lower limbs, which, as more closely allied to organs involved in menstruation and to a certain extent enjoying the same vascular system, have been characterized by a greater or less degree of disadvantage in posture, in the use of the sewing-machine this disadvantage is rather aggravated than otherwise. There is no need to enlarge upon the extent of its use, or to state that the use of power-propelled machines does not fall under review; nor will it be necessary, in view of the native examinations of the subject by

DOI: 10.4324/9781003676669-42

Guibout,[1] Decaisne,[2] Nichols,[3] and others, to do more than adapt their findings to the place they properly hold in relation to the results we are considering. While the investigations of Guibout are characterized, on the one hand, by an exaggeration of the injurious influences incident to sewing-machine use, and those of Decaisne on the other hand, by a too slight regard for these influences (though his inquiries were extended), the more nearly trustworthy deductions of Dr. Nichols[4] establish a series of "conclusions" which expose a grave degree of harm. The comprehensive question asked by Dr. Nichols of his correspondents was, "Have you observed any injury to health from the use of sewing-machines used by foot-power? If so, please to send us all the information you may have on the subject." Replies were received from one hundred and thirty-eight correspondents, representing one hundred and twenty towns in Massachusetts, and several in other States.

Eighty report more or less ill effects deserved by them; the balance, giving negative or doubtful answers, were mainly from towns where the machines were used only in private families, etc. My own analysis of the published replies shows that sixty-nine physicians replied to the query. Of this number, forty-four answered in an emphatic manner, declaring the results to be undoubted upon the organs of menstruation and the function itself; four, only, held negative views: while the remainder assigned to the use other results indirectly operative to the same end.

I quote a few only, taken at random from the many unequivocal statements of these physicians as to the pernicious effects of this industry.

REPLIES FROM MASSACHUSETTS PHYSICIANS

A. "Quite a number of cases, in which pain and in which pain and lameness in the back and thighs, dyspepsia, leucorrhoea, vaginitis, and menorrhagia existed, I have attributed to their use."

B. The most common disease I have seen is a chronic form of ovaritis, which it is impossible to cure while the girl is at work."

C. The use of the machine during menstruation is especially injurious. I have even known a case where a severe attack of ovaritis and retroflexion of the uterus followed its use during a single menstrual period."

D. I think I have observed a greater tendency to dysmenorrhea and other uterine troubles among those who use the sewing-machine for a living than among others.

E. Cases of unmistakable injury, very frequent a few years ago, causing marked irregularities of the menstrual function, and their usual sequence. The almost universal introduction of steam-power greatly diminished this class of cases.

F. Constant and long-continued use of sewing machines, moved by foot-power, tends to induce functional diseases of the uterus. Three girls working in the same shop ten hours daily, for two or three years, now suffer from dysmenorrhoea, from which they were formerly free.

Says a Boston physician[5] who for many years has given special attention to the gynæcological affections of women,

> The sewing-machine, that compound of blessing and curse to woman, adds to the list of influences causative of disease, not only acting in several of the ways suggested, by the long-continued and con-strained position and fatiguing of the pelvic muscles; but in another, not generally sufficiently appreciated, by which a mental and dangerous disquietude is originated and enhanced by the unintentional auto-stupration.

Another well-known physician[6] of Boston writes: –

> I once observed many cases of debility, and pain in spine and side, with now and then menstrual disorders, in a shopful of sewing-machine girls, which ceased to exist when steam was applied.

OTHER PHYSICIANS

A. I have investigated quite a number of cases where diseases were produced by running sewing-machines by foot-power. Among these diseases, I have noticed several cases of lameness of limbs and back, menorrhagia, dysmenorrhoea, amenorrhoea, leucorrhoea, and displacements.
B. I have no doubt whatever that this employment among females is more powerful and efficient in the production of disease of various kinds in that sex than almost all other causes combined.

To these expressions of physicians, presumably as safe a criterion of the real results produced by the occupation as can be obtained, Dr. Nichols has added numerous varying experiences of the workwomen themselves, which, though not as harmonious or positive in their findings, are sufficiently so to make it certain that a grave degree of peculiar disturbance is recognized by them. The "conclusions "given by Dr. Nichols are: –

> That the illnesses which most frequently prevail among professional operatives (as distinguished from home operatives) making use of the treadle (footpower) are,
>
> (a) Indigestion, attributable to the unhealthy conditions in which they pursue their occupation, particularly the impure atmosphere of the workrooms, the sedentary employment, and want of open-air exercise.
> (b) Muscular pains, affecting the lower limbs and trunk, produced by the long-continued, frequent use of the muscles.

(c) Diseases peculiar to women, aggravated by, rather than caused by, the plethoric condition of the pelvic organs, induced by this exercise.
(d) General Debility. By this is meant a state of physical deterioration and nervous prostration brought on by overwork.

Adding to these conclusions the single remark, that my own observations and review of the data given would indicate a classification of these influences upon female ill health as more decidedly "causative" than "aggravating" the belief may fairly be educed therefrom, that in the continued use of the sewing-machine by foot-power, there resides a source of special functional disturbance in women, which is extensive in its reach, and embraces overwork, often under bad sanitary surroundings, labor to which much of the monotony and unremitting character incident to most machine-work attaches, and muscular activity coupled with a considerable degree of mental concentration: this last being in an intermediate degree to that required by factory machinery, and that required by the telegraph instrument. The evidence of the direct influence of this species of employ upon the catamenial function is notably abundant, and raises the query, if the fact of pedal rather than manual muscular power as here involved is the real *cause* of a greater effect; or, whether the simpler methods of argument cause those affected (by localizing the energy in closer relation to the parts seen to be most influenced) *infer* an injury that they would be slow to recognize when remote agents, as the hand, are active, and the brain must be summoned to greater participation to produce the effect. As an employment still enlisting the labors of large numbers of young women of the ages we are considering, notwithstanding the very considerable introduction of steampower to its uses, it is well worth the consideration of the economist and legislator; for from its ranks the offices of wife and mother are filled to no mean degree, few of the class continuing many years in in the work while those engaged therein are, as a rule, of different fibre from those of factory labor, and do not like them raise up and perpetuate succeeding generations of employees for the same work. We may fairly conclude, from the foregoing testimony and data from the various channels of industry, –

First, That a sure and swift result must follow to the immature female whenever she is in an employ requiring mental and physical concentration and celerity.
Second, That the disturbance will be proportionate, in the rapidity of its advance and degree, to the derive of concentration, celerity, and continuity of employ.
Third, That its most active and most baleful effects will be upon the functions peculiar to the sex.

Whatsoever, therefore, in industry, exerts these influences (whose present and prospective and almost unending results we have pointed out), demands the exercise of all ingenuity, wisdom, and care, to secure its alleviation and removal. Certain of the employments of women include these evils from seeming present necessity; but it becomes the duty of all to direct their studious attention thereto, if perchance a relief may be found; while for other forms of employ only the false notions that exist need to be overthrown, to banish at least some of their attendant evils.

Source Endnotes

1 Paper before "Soc. Medicale des Hopitaux."
2 Ann.'d'Hyg. Pub. 1870, 2d ser. vol. xxxvi.
3 Dr. A. H. Nichols, 3d Rep. Board of Health, Mass.
4 Dr. A. H. Nichols, 3d Rep. Board of Health, Mass.
5 Horatio R. Storer, M.D., Lecture on Female Hygiene, before State Board of Health of California, p. 13.
6 Theo. W. Fisher, M.D.: Letter to the author.

40

FASHIONABLE DRESSMAKER, 1886

Helen Campbell

Source: Helen Campbell, 'Fashionable Dressmaker', *Prisoners of Poverty: Women Wage-Workers, Their Trades and Their Lives*. (Little, Brown, and Company, 1886), 55–65.

EDITORIAL HEADNOTE

In the third extract from Helen Campbell, (docs. 36, 37) we return to the 'fashionable dressmaker' who by 1886 was the underpaid and oppressed worker that Robert Campbell and Joseph Collyer had identified.

It is an old story, yet an always new one, and in this case Madame had quieted her conscience by providing a comfortable lunch for the workers and allowing them more space than is generally the portion in a busy establishment. Well housed and well fed through the day and paid at intervals enough to meet the demands of rent or board bill, it was easy to satisfy her hands by the promise of full and speedy settlement, and when this failed, to tell a pitiful tale of unpaid bills and conscience-less customers, who could not be forced. When these resources were exhausted discharge solved any further difficulties, and a new set came in, to undergo the same experience. In an establishment where honesty has any place, the wages are rather beyond the average, skirt-hands receiving from seven to nine dollars a week and waist-hands from ten to fifteen. In the case of stores this latter class make from eighteen to forty dollars per week, and often accumulate enough capital to start in business for themselves. But a skirt-hand like Mary M – – seldom passes on to anything higher, and counts herself well paid if her week of sixty hours brings her nine dollars, not daring to grumble seriously if it falls to seven or even six. On the east side the same work must be done for from four to six dollars a week, the latter sum being considered high pay. But the work is an advance upon factory work and has a better sound, the dressmaker's assistant looking down upon the factory hand or even the seamstress as of an inferior order.

In time I learned the full story of the little woman, ordinarily reticent and shrinking, but brought by trouble and indignation to the fiercest protest against oppression.

DOI: 10.4324/9781003676669-43

Born in a New-England village she had learned a milliner's trade, to which she presently added dressmaking, and succeeded in making a fair living, till bitten by the desire to see larger life and share all the good that the city seems to offer the shut-in country life, she came to New York with her small savings, expecting to find work easily, and did so, going at once into a store where a friend was at work. Sanitary conditions were all bad. Her hall bedroom on a fourth floor and the close confinement all did their work, and a long illness wasted strength and savings. When recovery came her place had been filled; and she wandered from store to store seeking employment, doing such odd jobs as were found at intervals, and powerless to recover the lost ground.

"It was like heaven to me," she said, "when my friend came back to the city and got me that place as skirt-hand at Madame M –'s. I was so far gone I had even thought of the river, and said to myself it might be the easiest way out. You can't help but like Madame, for she's smooth-tongued and easy, and praises your work, and she made me think I'd soon be advanced and get the place I ought to have. She paid regularly at first, and I began to pick up courage. It was over-hours always. Madame would come in smiling and say: 'Ah, dear girls! What trouble! It is an order that must be finished so soon. Who will be kind and stay so leetle longer?' Then we all stayed, and she'd have tea made and send it in, and sandwiches or something good, and they all said, 'She's an angel. You won't find anybody like Madame.' She was so plausible, too, that even when there was longer and longer time between the payments the girls didn't blame her, but borrowed of one another and put off their landladies and managed all ways to save her feelings. Jenny G – – had been here longer than any of them, and she worshipped Madame and wouldn't hear a word even when one or another complained. But Jenny's feet were on the ground and she hadn't a stitch of warm underclothes, and she took a cold in December, and by January it had tight hold of her. I went to Madame myself then, and begged her to pay Jenny if it wasn't but a little, and she cried and said if she could only raise the money she would. She didn't; and by and by I went again, and then she turned ugly. I looked at her dumfounded when she spoke her real mind and said if we didn't like it we could leave; there were plenty of others. I wouldn't believe my ears even, and said to myself she was worn out with trouble and couldn't mean a word of it. I wanted money for myself, but I wouldn't ask even for anybody but Jenny.

"Next day Madame brought her ten dollars of the two hundred and twenty she owed her, and Jenny got shoes; but it was too late. I knew it well, for I'd seen my sister go the same way. Quick consumption ain't to be stopped with new shoes or anything but new lungs, and there's no patent for them yet that ever I've heard of. She was going last night when I went round, and sure as you live I'm going to put her death in the paper myself. I've been saving my money off lunches to do it, and I'll write it: 'Murdered by a fashionable dressmaker on – – Street, in January, 1886, Jenny G –, age nineteen years and six months.' Maybe they won't put it in, but here it is, ready for any paper that's got feeling enough to care whether sewing-girls are cheated and starved and killed, or whether they get what they've earned. I've got work at home now. It don't matter so much to me; but I'm a committee to attend to this thing, and I'll find out every fraud in New York that I can. I've got nine names now, – three of 'em regular fashionables on the west side, and six of 'em following their example hard as they can on the east; and a friend of mine has printed, in large letters, 'Beware of' at the head of a slip, and I add names as fast as I get them, and every girl that comes in my way I warn against them. Do much good? No. They'll get all the girls they want, and more; but it's some satisfaction to be able to say they are cheats, making a living out of the flesh and blood of their dupes, and I'll say it till I die."

Here stands the experience of one woman with fearlessness enough to protest and energy enough to have at last secured a tolerable living. The report, for such it may be considered, might be made of many more names than those upon her black list, or found on the books of the Union. Happily for the worker, they form but a small proportion of the long list of dressmakers who deal fairly. But the life of the ordinary hand who has not ability enough to rise is, like that of the great majority who depend on the needle, whether machine or hand, filled with hardship, uncertainty, overwork, under-pay. The large establishments have next to no dull season, but we deal in the present chapter only with private workers; and often, on the east side especially, where prices and wages are always at the lowest ebb, the girls who have used all their strength in overwork during the busy season of spring and fall must seek employment in cigar factories or in anything that offers in the intermediate time, the wages giving no margin for savings which might aid in tiding over such periods. The dressmaker herself is often a sufferer, conscienceless customers abounding, who pay for the work of one season only when anxious for that of the next. Often it is mere carelessness, – the recklessness which seems to make up the method of many women where money obligations are concerned; but often also they pass deliberately from one dressmaker to another, knowing that New York holds enough to provide for the lifetime of the most exacting customer. There is small redress for these cases, and the dressmaker probably argues the matter for herself and decides that she has every right, being cheated, to balance the scale by a little of the same order on her own account.

41

IRISH DRESSMAKERS AND MILLINERS, 1893

Source: Eliza Orme and May Abraham, 'Conditions of Women's Work in Ireland', in Miss Eliza Orme, Miss Clara E. Collet, Miss May Abraham and Miss Margaret H. Irwin, *Reports, The Employment of Women*, Royal Commission on Labour, Presented to both Houses of Parliament by Command of Her Majesty, February 1893, 322.

EDITORIAL HEADNOTE

Margaret Edith (May) Tennant, (1869–1946), née Abraham, was born in Ireland and became a civil servant, trade unionist, factory inspector and campaigner, who worked to improve conditions for industrial workers and was also involved in women's health and education. In London she became secretary to Emilia, Lady Dilke (see Vol. 3), who was a leader of the Women's Trade Union League, with Tennant becoming treasurer. In 1891 she was one of H.H. Asquith's first choices to be appointed to the Royal Commission on Labour, as one of four women assistant commissioners. In this position, she was known for her good humour which helped relations with factory managers. She reported on Ireland with Eliza Orme (1848–1937), who was among those women studying at UCL between the desegregation of classes and opening of degrees. A student also of law, she earned an LLB degree in 1888, entered a legal career and participated in public life through the Liberal Party. In 1892 she was appointed senior lady assistant commissioner to the Royal Commission on Labour, looking into women's employment, and later took part in official review of women's prison experiences.

The Royal Commission extended to Ireland where many of the complaints found in late nineteenth-century millinery existed here as well, with girls not being trained as parents expected, and where pay was very low by the end of the nineteenth century.

DOI: 10.4324/9781003676669-44

III. DRESSMAKERS, MILLINERS, AND MANTLEMAKERS

1. Wages. The payment (without board and lodging) received by dressmakers in Ireland is very low. That of milliners and mantlemakers in good houses is somewhat better. . . .

2. Apprentices. The apprentices live out and take their meals at home, and the premiums paid for their apprenticeship are from 5£. to 10£., and in many cases no premium is charged at all. Sometimes when nothing is paid they are used as messengers (No. 579). The term served varies from one to three years, and something is paid after a year, or even six months, by the best employers if the girl is clever. In some houses all the capable girls are kept on, receiving 2s. or 2s. 6d. a week as improvers.

Parents (e.g., No. 1,292) complained that during apprenticeship girls are kept running messages, holding pins and irons, and doing other unskilled work. They only begin to learn when they become improvers. On the other hand, employers (e.g. No. 1,034) say the girls know nothing when they leave school, and have to learn everything from the beginning. No. 1,309 said she taught her apprentices not only plain needlework, but cleanliness, manners, smartness, accuracy, and the qualities necessary in any business. It was only when these were acquired that she could hope to teach them dressmaking. No. 1,034, with 20 years' experience as a dressmaker in the south of Ireland, said the only girls who came to her able to do plain needlework with tolerable neatness were from convent schools. She was herself a Scotch Presbyterian, and employed a Scotch forewoman.

3. Fines. In many workrooms no fines are charged at all. In some (Nos. 572, 573, 574, 576, 577, 580, 581, 583, 584, 590) 2d., 3d., or 6d. is charged for late attendance. At No. 578 they have never imposed fines, but intend to do so for late attendance. At No. 579 the door is locked at the hour for starting, and no late comers are admitted. At No. 625 the doors are closed for a quarter or a half day against a late comer. Fines for mistakes in work are very unusual. At No. 573 there are several, varying from 3d. to 2s. 6d. The ordinary amount in this workroom is 6d. At No. 584 they charge 6d. for mistakes.

4. Hours and overtime. The general rule in Dublin and the north is to pay for overtime at a higher rate than ordinary work. At Nos. 571, 584, and 579 the hours are from 9 a.m. to 7 p.m., stopping at 4 p.m. on Monday for dressmakers. Three hours' overtime (7 p.m. till 10 p.m.) is paid for as half a day, and tea provided. At No. 574 the hours are from 9 a.m. to 7 p.m. Three hours' overtime are paid for at 1s., and tea is provided. The wages of the ordinary workers in this shop range from 2s. 6d. to 15s. a week. The employers object to overtime, thinking it makes too long a day. At No. 577 the hours and rules for overtime are exactly the same as above, wages of ordinary hands being from 2s. 6d. to 14s., with an average of 8s. a week, except that if the worker is earning not more than 4s a week she only gets 6d. and her tea. One shilling with tea is given for three hours' overtime at No. 578, the wages of ordinary hands ranging from 2s. 6d to 11s.,

and the ordinary hours being from 9 a.m. to 7. p.m. At No. 589, a large shop in Dublin, the girls sometimes remain till 8 p.m., the ordinary hours being 9.30 a.m. to 7 p.m. They receive no extra pay for this hour. In the south of Ireland there are constant complaints of girls being kept in without any payment or even food provided. Witnesses Nos. 1,304, 1,305, and 1,306, all employed for some years in millinery and dressmaking, declared that they were always kept at least an hour in the busy season, and once a month or oftener were kept till midnight in the dressmakers' workrooms. No. 1,306 was kept until 4 a.m. two nights running. On the first night the girls clubbed together and bought themselves food. On the second night the dressmaker provided bread and butter and tea. No. 1,306 had never seen an inspector in any workshop she had ever worked in. Witness No. 1,292, in the same town, said that her two girls (Nos. 1,293 and 1,294) were constantly kept by the dressmakers who employed them until 8 p.m., and even 10 p.m. One of these girls had been kept till midnight, and no food or even a cup of tea provided. When she complained she was told that a girl had been dismissed for grumbling a few months before. None of these witnesses had ever heard of pay for overtime in the workshops in their town. Witness No. 1,309, an employer of long experience in the town, said that as the girls expected their wages in slack times and often got a holiday on saints' days, they must expect unpaid overtime when business pressed. At a first-class dressmaker's (No. 686) and a large linendraper's (No. 705) in the south of Ireland all overtime is paid for at the ordinary rate. Most of the employers in the south say they do not require overtime, as trade is slack and has been so for some years.

5. Workroom accommodation. The sanitary accommodation is generally sufficient and conveniently arranged for the workers. Many of the workrooms were overheated, and in some the ventilation was bad. At No. 625 the rooms are heated by steam and well ventilated. One large room is divided into workrooms by partitions about five feet high, allowing a free passage of air. Some of the workrooms are tolerably ventilated, but very much overcrowded. . . .

Part 4

INDUSTRIAL ENTREPRENEURS

42

THE CASE OF MISS LESLIE, AND HER THREE SISTERS, 1767

Ann Leslie

Source: Ann Leslie, *The case of Miss Leslie, and her three sisters. The manufacturers of thread for lace, equal to any foreign; in an address to the public, but particularly to the patriotic societies, for the encouragement of arts and manufactures*, Published at the Request, and by the Desire of several Persons of Distinction, 1767.

EDITORIAL HEADNOTE

This pamphlet, 'Published at the Request, and by the Desire of several Persons of Distinction, 1767', was published by subscription and supported by a number of dignitaries and was written to establish and protect the claim of Ann Leslie and her sisters to the quality of their thread against deprecations cast against them. The Society for the Encouragement of Arts and Sciences, founded 1754 (later the Society of Arts), was founded to raise funds by subscription to award in Premiums which promoted improvements in the 'liberal arts and sciences, manufactures, etc.' The pamphlet takes up the story of Ann and her sisters as a defence against misrepresentations and calumnies against them. Ann Leslie was an enterprising woman who with her sisters claimed to produce the finest thread for lacemaking. Her pamphlet is a vigorous defence of her business, and she promoted it specifically to provide quality home-produced thread rather than importing from France. It should be noted that she was writing while Britain was at war with France, and in the context of serious Francophobia.

SUMPTUARY laws, or the discouragement of costly manufactures, for apparel, in a little or infant state, are beneficial; to a great one, such as Britain is now, they are unnecessary, and may be detrimental, because the people of a great state will purchase from foreigners, perhaps their natural enemies, those luxuries which

DOI: 10.4324/9781003676669-46

they cannot manufacture at home. It is upon this principle, that parliament and beneficent communities have of late years so laudably distinguished themselves, by their encouragement of home manufactures, especially of commodities with which we are supplied from France and other countries.

That of Thread-lace, as it is the most elegant of all articles of luxury imported from abroad, is at the same time the most universal and expensive. An attempt, therefore, to introduce it into Great Britain, and thereby, to save the vast sums expended abroad for that commodity, is the distribution of the national bounty, for the encouragement of the arts and manufactures. The commodity of Thread-lace deserves a peculiar encouragement, by its materials being produced from a particular species of agriculture, which, if properly pursued, might be a vast saving to the nation, and would employ numbers of hands which are now either idle, or subsist upon public or private charities.

From the considerations above-mentioned. Miss Leslie and her three sisters have, for some years, employed themselves in the thread manufactory, fit for the best laces. They were encouraged by the noble public spirit, of which the legislature set the example, in the premiums appointed to be distributed for the encouragement of manufactures in Scotland. They did not imagine that so generous a bounty could be directed into any channel but that for which it was designed, and animated by this conviction, they applied themselves with such assiduity, to that branch of business which they undertook, that they brought their manufacture of thread to a perfection never before known in Great Britain, as appears from the following authentic testimony of the truly patriotic Society in the Strand, for the encouragement of arts and manufactures.

RESOLUTIONS OF THE COMMITTEE, FOR THE ENCOURAGEMENT OF ARTS AND SCIENCES IN THE STRAND

A Parcel of thread, yarn, and flax, of the growth of Scotland, and manufactured near Hamilton, under the direction of the Miss Leslies, was produced to the Society for promoting arts, &c. in the Strand: and, after a very strict and judicious examination by the Committee, the Society, on their report, came to the following resolutions:

> "Resolved, It is the opinion of this committee, that the flax, yarn, and thread produced by Miss Leslie, is much superior in fineness and quality to any hitherto grown and manufactured in Great Britain."
>
> "Resolved, That it appears to this Committee, by a certificate from Hamilton, that the flax of which this yarn and thread are made, is the growth of Scotland, and the yarn and thread made of it is spun in Scotland, and made under the direction of the Miss Leslies."

> "Resolved, That it is the opinion of this Committee, that if a manufacture of this fine thread could be established to the profit of the undertakers, it would be of great advantage to the kingdom".

The foregoing resolutions produced the following Article, honorable to the Miss LESLIES, in Mr. MORTIMER'S *Dictionary of Trade and Commerce*.

> "LAST winter, Miss Leslie, who, with her sisters have some years been attempting, the establishment of a manufacture of fine thread in Scotland, laid before the London Society some specimens of yarn and thread spun from flax, produced in the neighbourhood of Hamilton; which flax appeared to be capable of making exceeding fine thread, of as strong a texture as the best brought from Flanders. In the raising this flax, nature, through the peculiar circumstances of foil and air, did the offices of art: the poverty of the ground, and the coldness of the atmosphere, bringing up the flax small and weak, without any other deviation from the common method of culture, than the sowing the seed somewhat thicker than is usually done."

Such was the generous disinterested testimony given by that excellent Society, and this Author, to the labours of the Miss Leslies; but it is with the greatest reluctance, that they lay before the Public, the treatment, they received from a board, more particularly interested to have protected and encouraged them.

No institution was, perhaps, ever more rational, than that of the Trustees and Commissioners for fisheries and manufactures in Scotland; and the Miss Leslies thought themselves happy in exerting themselves to deserve their patronage. The Honourable Board of Trustees there, upon the application of the Miss Leslies, were pleased to approve of their labours; desired them to proceed; requested them to exert themselves to bring that branch of business to perfection, and promised them a reward and indemnification by their secretary's letter, dated the 27th of December, 1763. In consequence of this encouragement, the Miss Leslies, with the greatest assiduity, and to the no small risk of their private fortunes, carried their manufacture to such a height, as in the opinion of competent judges, did honour to their art and industry. They provided quantities of lace-thread, sufficient to employ all the lace-workers in Hamilton and its neighbourhood. They even manufactured, from their own thread, a pair of ruffles, which was shewn to the board, and which his Majesty himself, to whom they were presented, did not disdain to wear.

The Miss Leslies could here rest their plea for public encouragement; but the lace-workers of England, have furnished them with one of national importance, which they humbly presume is irresistible in their favour; and it is as follows. After they had, (as has been already mentioned) furnished the lace-workers in their neighbourhood, with sufficient quantities of thread, they sent the rest to

London, where it was worked into lace by the most eminent manufacturers, who have candidly given the following certificates.

Gerrard-Street, St. Ann's, Nov. 14, 1765.

To the Gentlemen of the Honourable Arts, and Sciences;
GENTLEMEN,
"This is to certify, that I have proved this thread of Miss Leslies, in the making of lace, and find it to answer extremely well. And am.
Gentlemen,

Your most obedient, and humble servant,
Charles Pridice.

London, Jan. 16, 1766.

"I have wrought of the British thread, from Miss Leslie, since last August, and do declare, it is as good in texture and quality as any foreign, and as cheap; some; of which thread was made into a pair of ruffles, which was laid before the Society. Witness my hand,

Robert GORDG."

London, Jan. 3, 1766.

This is to certify the Committee of the "Arts and Sciences, that the lace laid before you is wrought with Miss Leslies thread, and think it full as good, or better, than the foreign. Witness my hand,

HENRY STONE.

The Miss Leslies, happily for themselves, are ready and willing to give the most demonstrative proofs of the above-mention'd facts, but they cannot defend themselves from the arrows that have been scattered in the dark against their undertaking: they know not the persons of those who have traduced them: they are ignorant of their allegations, and they flatter themselves, that the insidious hidden manner in which the opposition to them has been propagated, will satisfy the impartial public of its meanness and malignity; but they are afflicted and astonished, to find it comes from that quarter where they expected their chief patronage and protection. They did not foresee, that an undertaking so truly national, could clash with private interests: they did not imagine, that a board, founded on the truest and most disinterested principles of civil policy, could be influenced by secret machinations; and they, at this moment, firmly believe, that the opposition and disappointments they have met with, proceed from misrepresentations only.

It is to remove the unhappy, and, to them ruinous, effects of those misrepresentations, that this paper is addressed to the public.

The first intimation of any unfair practices against them, was communicated to them at London, by some members, of the Society for the encouragement of arts and manufactures, who informed them, that the Trustees in Scotland, or some one of their number, upon false informations given them, had made an unfavourable representation of their undertaking, and thereby prevented the Society London for farther considering their case, or giving them a bounty adequate to their labour and expence.

The dreadful malignity of this opposition was felt by the Miss Leslies in more than one instance. A number of the most respectable names had entered in England, into a subscription for their encouragement. But their generous intentions were damped by the doubts which had been insinuated, concerning the reality of the facts which they had alledged [sic], and which had procured them the above honourable testimonial from the Society, for encouraging arts and manufactures. In short, Miss Leslie who was then in London, was advised by several of the members to return to Scotland, and procure satisfactory vouchers for the facts she had advanced in favour of her manufacture.

Miss Leslie accordingly returned to Scotland, where she humbly apprehends she was furnished with the very best evidences as to the truth of her allegations that the nature of her undertaking admits of, or requires. She applyed [sic] to the magistrates, town council, and merchants in Hamilton, and to the member of parliament, justices of the peace, and other gentlemen of the county of Lanark, where the whole of her manufacture has been carried on, likewise to the magistrates, and several of the chief merchants in Glasgow, many of whom are themselves manufacturers of, and dealers in, the fame commodity. It cannot be supposed, that a private person could influence, far less bias, so respectable a body of men, or that they would obtrude upon the public, false evidences, in an affair that concerned not only their country, but themselves; and therefore Miss Leslie, with all submission, hopes that the following certificates will, with every candid reader, be decisive in her favour.

Nov. 1766

"We the persons subscribing, being acquainted with the character of Miss Ann Leslie and sisters, thread-makers in Hamilton, and well informed of the state of the manufactures carried on by them, can fully attest the following facts, viz.

1st, "That the said Miss Ann Leslie and her sisters, are extremely skilful, diligent, and industrious in their business, and have with much pains and application, set on foot the making of fine lace-thread, from yarn spun in this country, and the produce of flax also raised here.

2d, "That this branch of manufacture highly merits protection and encouragement; and if sufficiently patronized, might, in time, be of great advantage to Britain, by keeping at home a very considerable sum, that is annually sent abroad for that article.

3d, "That the said Miss Leslies have struggled under very great difficulties and disappointments, in attempting to set on foot the said branch of manufacture.

4th, "That the Miss Leslies have given ample proofs to the whole country of their abilities to carry on that business to great perfection, if they meet with proper encouragement, which we think they very well deserve."

Magistrates and Merchants in Glasgow.

James Buchannan.
Neil Bannatyne.
Andrew Alton and Co.
William Stirling.
Brown, Carrick, and Co.
James Simson.
Anderson and Bannatyn.
William Anderson.
Walter Stirling.
Archibald Smelie.
Young, Auchincloss and Lang.
Archibald Ingram.
George Brown.
James Brown.

The Members of Parliament, Justices of the Peace and other Gentlemen of the County of Lanark.

Dan. Campbell.
Henry Baillie.
Robert Coutt.
George Nisbett.
Alexander Hamilton.
James Cunison.
Mathew Morthland.
John Gordon.
Robert Cullen.
William Hamilton.
Charles Peddie.

Magistrates, Town Council, and Merchants in Hamilton.

John Miller, Merchant.
John Naismith.
John Naismith.
Alexander Smith.
John Downs, Merchant.
John Borland.
William Brown.
William Robertson.
Thomas Hart.
William Mather.
James Waddrell.
John Fluttor.
John Archer, and Son.
Charles Murhed.
James Hamilton.
John Sempler.

"We captain James Roberton, of Earnock, captain James Gilchrist, of Annsfield, and George Bogle, of Daldouie, Esq; three of his Majesty's justices of the peace, for the county of Lanark; Messrs. Quintin Hamilton, and Thomas Dunning, magistrates in the town of Hamilton; the reverend Mr. James Miller, minister, in the parish of Hamilton, and Mr. James Lawson, stamp-master in Hamilton, and yarn-inspector for the five western counties, do hereby certify and declare, upon the best authority, that Miss Ann Leslie, for present, at London, and her three sisters, young gentlewomen, living in this parish, have been employed for a considerable time, in manufacturing thread from Scotch flax to good advantage; and if they are properly encouraged, can carry that branch of business to greater perfection, and much larger extent: and we further attest, with respect: to the samples of flax and yarn, lately sent to London, and produced there by Miss Leslie, that the flax was raised in a village, called Uddingston; and the yarn spun by Jean Thomson, and her daughter, Jean Alexander, both living in that village, in the Parish of Bothwell, and neighbourhood of this place; and that the thread was made of the yarn bought from them, by the said Miss Leslies, as witness our hands, at Hamilton, this sixth day of December, one thousand seven hundred and sixty-five years."

James Millar, minister.
James Roberton.
James Gilchrist.
George Bogle.
Quintin Hamilton, baillie.
Thomas Dunning, baillie.
James Lawson.

That the flax of which the fine thread, lately sent to London, and produced there by Miss Leslie, was raised in the village of Uddingston, in the parish of Bothwell, North LMw, and was spun into yarn in the same village, by Jean Thomson, and her daughter, Jean Alexander; is attested at Bothwell, the 7th of December, 1765, by

JAMES BAILLIE, minister

Hamilton, Nov. 1, 1766.

"I have wrought of Miss Leslies thread, for some years, and am daily taking good quantities of it, and find it better and stronger than foreign; all made of Scots flax and yarn; made into thread by Miss Leslie, superior to any ever came from abroad. Witness my hand,

Margaret Watson.

Hamilton, Nov. 3, 1766.

"We have wrought of the Miss Leslies thread for some years, made of Scots flax and yarn; and we are amongst the oldest lace-workers in Hamilton, and do declare it as good in texture and quality as any foreign, and as cheap. Witness our hand

Margaret Hamilton.
Mary Hamilton.

Hamilton, Nov. 4, 1766.

"I Ann Henderson, one of the lace-workers in Hamilton, do hereby certify and declare, that I and my scholars, under my direction and management, have, for these three years, or thereby, wrought of the thread manufactured by the Miss Leslies, residing at Whitehill, in the parish of Hamilton, out of Scots flax; and the same wrought into lace very well, and when wrought, does look very well; and the above facts is attested by,

ANN HENDERSON."
"As also the above facts is attested by me, another of the lace-workers of Hamilton,

MARGARET SEMPEL."

Hamilton, Nov. 2, 1766.

"This is to certify, I Mary Nasmith, mistress of one of the lace-schools in Hamilton, have been in use to make lace of the threads manufactured by the Miss Leslies, in Whithill, at this place, of various grists, have found it fully as good as the foreign thread. The finest I wrought of it was No. 120, which I made into a suit of ruffles for his Majesty King George the Third, said to be worn on his Majesty's birth-day,

MARY NASMITH."

The Miss Leslies sensible of the weight which the patronage of the board for fisheries, and manufactures in Scotland, must have with the Society, and her friends, at London, being furnished the above certificates, on the 21st of November last, enclosed them with other papers, in a fresh application to the board in Scotland. – The reader may judge of her amazement, when her petition was returned not only unanswered, but unopened.

The above is the present state of a manufacture, which the undertakers flatter themselves ought to be an important object to the public. Least the concealment of the smallest circumstance should be imputed to their want of candour, they acknowledge that some years ago, they received from the board of trustees in Scotland fifty-fix pounds, and a throw-miln; but the intelligent reader will easily judge how inadequate such a premium is to carry into execution, an undertaking so difficult, and so expensive as that of making thread so fine as to be wrought into lace equal to any imported at an immence [sic] expence, from the French and foreigners. The Miss Leslies beg leave to close this address with a few queries; to which they crave an answer from their opponents whether open or secret.

1st, Whether any undertaking can be better calculated, than theirs is, for answering the public spirited views of the Legislature in establishing the board for the encouragement of fisheries, and manufactures in Scotland?

2dly, Whether the carrying their undertaking into execution will not contribute! to the honour as well as the interest of the united kingdoms?

3dly, Whether they have not given full satisfaction that they are actually the manufacturers of the materials of which they make their thread from its growth in Scotland, and by natives of that kingdom?

4thly, What farther proof of the premises do their opponents require or expect?

5thly. Whether it is for the credit, interest, or reputation of Great Britain, that a cabal formed of persons, either interested or prejudiced against women, whose industry, and good intentions alone procured them friends, ought to defeat the laudable, and national purposes of a British Legislature?

As mention is made in the foregoing pages, of a Subscription having been enter'd into, by a number of the most respectable personages for the encouragement of this design, the Miss Leslies beg leave, to do themselves the honour of publishing the names and generous motives of the Subscribers

London, Feb. 13, 1766

Miss Leslie, and her three sisters have been employed in the thread manufactory for several years, and have carried it to great perfection, in the opinion of the best judges.

And of late years they have also employed themselves in another branch, by making of very fine thread, fit for the best laces; and have brought it to equal (in the opinion of some lace-workers in England, who have used it) the best foreign thread for the purpose; for which improvement, they received a premium some years ago from the Trustees for encouraging manufactures in Scotland; and within these few days a strong testimony in their favour from the Society for promoting Arts, &c. in London, as appears by the minutes of the report of their committee, agreed to and confirmed by the Society; a copy of which is hereunto annexed.

And as the Miss Leslies are confident, that, this manufacture of fine thread in Scotland, could be carried on by them to a great extent, if properly encouraged; not only to the advantage of the people employed in raising the flax, spinning the yarn, and making the thread, but also to the nation in general, by producing at home, what is now wholly imported from abroad, at a great and surprizing expence: on these Accounts,

We the Nobility and Gentry, whose names are hereunto subscribed, willing to encourage a manufactory of such public benefit; and at the fame time to help the Miss Leslies, who were the first that effectually engaged in it, and have with great labour and expence brought it to the present slate it is in, have resolved to assist the Miss Leslies to go on with their useful design, which may otherways be dropt or forgot, until in due time it shall be effectually encouraged by public authority.

Duchess of Hamilton.

Duchess of Queensferry.

Countess of Buchan.

Countess of Marchmont.

Lady Grant.

Mrs. Jane Dennes.

Lady Anne Erskine.

Lady Dundas.

Countess of Bute.	Mrs. Millar.
Countess of Northesk.	Mrs. Paterson.
Mrs. Steward.	Lord Cardross.
Countess of Lever.	Richard Hill. Esq.
Earl of Buchan.	Rev. Dr. Giffard.
Earl of Roseberry.	Dr. Brisbane.
Lord Lindors.	Mr. William Blakey.

The Miss Leslies beg leave to conclude this address with their acknowledgments to their noble generous patrons who have hitherto encouraged their undertaking. They are ready to shew how practicable it is, to carry it into execution; but they admit, at the same time, that it is above the reach of their private fortunes without public encouragement. They cannot, however, take their leave of their friends without doing some justice to themselves, by putting them in mind, that if application, and industry are required for carrying on a manufactory, they hope they have a preferable right to the public favour, unless some specimens can be produced in which they are excelled.

P.S. A specimen of the finest flax, yarn and thread made by the Miss Leslies is to be deposited among the curiosities of the British Museum. For the sake of the curious, the following computation was made of the length of a thread, made out of a pound of fine flax.

Miss Leslies fine Scotch yarn, made of Scotch flax, 10 quarters of a yard, once round the Reel, which makes 1 thread; 120 threads makes 1 cut. which is 300 yards; 24 cuts makes 1 hesp or 2 slips, which is 7,200 yards; 40 hesps are made out of 1 pound of flax, weight is 288,000 yards, for,

10 X 120 = 1200/4= 300 x 24= 7,200 x 40 = 288,000 = 163½ Miles in Length.

FINIS.

43

THREAD MANUFACTURER AT MONYMUSK, 1768

Miss Wilson

Source: 'Miss Wilson, Thread Manufacturer at Monymusk', Advertisement, *Aberdeen Journal*, 1 March 1768.

EDITORIAL HEADNOTE

By working within domestic industries, in small ways women established themselves. The linen trade provided opportunities for several women in Aberdeenshire as thread manufacturers and in the finishing stages of linen production providing bleachfields for bleaching cloth and selling linen and thread (also see doc. 10). Miss Wilson was both a thread manufacturer and owner of a bleachfield, inserting herself, like other women in Aberdeenshire, into the role of merchant, hiring out workers and taking in thread for others for finishing. See David Loch's Tour, doc. 11, for similar entrepreneurial women.

MISS WILSON

THREAD MANUFACTURER at MONYMUSK

HAS a commodious bleachfield properly laid out, with all the necessary conveniences, and proposes to take in threads, yarn, and stockings to bleach the ensuing season at the following prices, viz. Threads at sixpence halfpenny per spindle and stockings at one shilling and ten pence per dozen. Receipts will be given for the threads, yarn and stockings by Miss Wilson at Monymusk, and by Mrs Wilson, northside of the Castlegate, Aberdeen, and the carriage to and from Aberdeen, will also be paid.

No thread, year or stockings, will be taken after the first of July, to be returned this season.

DOI: 10.4324/9781003676669-47

44

CAMERON AND VIOLARD, ARTICLES OF CO-PARTNERY BETWEEN MARGARET CAMERON AND JOHN CAMERON, 1835

Source: Articles of Co-Partnery between Margaret Cameron and John Cameron [Cameron and Violard], 1835.

EDITORIAL HEADNOTE

Margaret Cameron began in Edinburgh as a milliner and dressmaker in 1826. In 1835 she joined forces with her unmarried brother, and they traded as Cameron and Violard (an invention for marketing purposes). She separated amicably from him in 1839 and continued to run the firm until 1870, while he worked as a silk mercer. Significantly, while in partnership, she owned the principal share of the business. However, the formal distribution of business affairs conformed to gendered expectations with John taking responsibility for financial matters, but she had control of the essential aspects of the business and was in a position to travel, domestically and abroad, to seek out market information and materials. She was sequestered for bankruptcy twice but survived, and despite her difficulties in 1839 and 1846, the business thrived in the 1850s and 1860s. Certainly, the image of the overworked seamstress presents an alternative truth, but for enterprising women, the potential existed.

§ Capital stock consisting of stock in trade, furniture in shop and dwelling house, cash and debts are valued at £1300 [2/3 belonging to Margaret Cameron].

§ Profits to be divided equally between the partners, and each shall pay on half of any merchandise or furniture purchased by the partners, or any losses on the business and dwelling house.

§ Regular books showing the transactions of the company shall be brought to a general balance every six months, and a clear and distinct balance every twelvemonths.

§ All cash received for sales should be entered into the books, which shall be kept in the shop, and when cash in hand amounts to £30 should be paid into a bank account in the name of the firm.

§ The business shall be carried out on the principle of ready money business, and no credit given the consent of both parties. Hours of business, 10.00 am to 8 pm, and one hour for dinner, except during the busy season when the partners shall give such attendance as shall be required.

§ Respective duties-

John Cameron: shall keep books, papers, accounts and other documents of the company, make out the inventories, balance the books and attend to the cash concerns of the company, rents, wages etc.

Margaret Cameron: shall purchase goods and merchandise, and for that purposes shall visit London and Paris for the purpose of purchasing goods and learning the fashions as often as both parties shall consider necessary. Shall superintend the dressmaking and millinery departments, shall attend to the sales and orders, and have full power and authority to order, check and control the clerks, servants and others employed by the company.

§ Company to be dissolved in the event of death of either party, and on the marriage of either, neither the husband of one, nor the wife of the other, shall be allowed to interfere in any way with the said business without the consent of both parties being previously obtained.

45

BEHIND THE SCENES, OR, THIRTY YEARS A SLAVE, AND FOUR YEARS IN THE WHITE HOUSE, AND NEWSPAPER REVIEWS

Elizabeth Keckley

Source: Elizabeth Keckley, *Behind the Scenes, or, Thirty Years a Slave, and Four Years in the White House, and newspaper reviews.*

45.1 *BEHIND THE SCENES, OR, THIRTY YEARS A SLAVE, AND FOUR YEARS IN THE WHITE HOUSE*

Source: Elizabeth Keckley, *Behind the Scenes, or, Thirty Years a Slave, and Four Years in the White House* (GW Carleton & Co., Publishers, 1868), 43–56, 73–85.

EDITORIAL HEADNOTE

Elizabeth Keckley (1818–1907) found millinery a route into a respectable life as a free black woman, reaching into the US White House. A slave and former washerwoman, her sewing skills helped her to build such a reputation that she sewed for both Mrs. Jefferson Davis, President of the Confederacy, and Mary Lincoln. She was taught sewing by her enslaved mother and her trajectory is described in the passages from her autobiography, written in a novelistic style. She said she wrote it because she wanted to protect her reputation and that of Mrs. Lincoln, whom the press roundly criticised. Mary Lincoln was caught up in the intrigues of the White House and the tensions around slavery. Although she was staunchly anti-slavery, she came from a family with slavery connections, and both she and her husband came from outside the Washington political circles. Her overspending and volatile moods did not endear her to people or the press. Included here are some of the newspaper reviews

DOI: 10.4324/9781003676669-49

of the book, most of which were highly critical (docs. 45.2–45.3). Being a negro, a former slave and a woman in control of her own life narrative challenged many and enabled some papers to ridicule and dismiss her completely; others used the critique of Mrs. Lincoln to castigate the book. The book also soured the relationship with Mary Lincoln, as she felt it revealed things it should not have done and destroyed the reputation of both women. Nevertheless, Keckley certainly did work as a milliner at the highest levels as she said, and historians treat it as a legitimate account.

BEHIND THE SCENES

My troubles in North Carolina were brought to an end by my unexpected return to Virginia, where I lived with Mr. Garland, who had married Miss Ann Burwell, one of my old master's daughters. His life was not a prosperous one, and after struggling with the world for several years he left his native State, a disappointed man. He moved to St. Louis, hoping to improve his fortune in the West; but ill luck followed him there, and he seemed to be unable to escape from the influence of the evil star of his destiny. . . . The necessities of the family were so great, that it was proposed to place my mother out at service. The idea was shocking to me. Every gray hair in her old head was dear to me, and I could not bear the thought of her going to work for strangers. She had been raised in the family, had watched the growth of each child from infancy to maturity; they had been the objects of her kindest care, and she was wound round about them as the vine winds itself about the rugged oak. . . .

No, a thousand times no! I would rather work my fingers to the bone, bend over my sewing till the film of blindness gathered in my eyes; nay, even beg from street to street. I told Mr. Garland so, and he gave me permission to see what I could do. I was fortunate in obtaining work, and in a short time I had acquired something of a reputation as a seamstress and dressmaker. The best ladies in St. Louis were my patrons, and when my reputation was once established I never lacked for orders. With my needle I kept bread in the mouths of seventeen persons for two years and five months. While I was working so hard that others might live in comparative comfort, and move in those circles of society to which their birth gave them entrance, the thought often occurred to me whether I was really worth my salt or not; and then perhaps the lips curled with a bitter sneer. It may seem strange that I should place so much emphasis upon words thoughtlessly, idly spoken; but then we do many strange things in life, and cannot always explain the motives that actuate us. The heavy task was too much for me, and my health began to give way. About this time Mr. Keckley, whom I had met in Virginia, and learned to regard with more than friendship, came to St. Louis. He sought my hand in marriage, and for a long time I refused to consider his proposal; for I could not bear the thought of bringing children into slavery – of adding one single recruit to the millions bound to hopeless servitude, fettered and shackled with chains stronger and heavier than manacles of iron. I made a proposition to buy myself and son; the proposition was bluntly declined, and I was commanded never to broach the subject again. . . .

Why should my son be held in slavery? I often asked myself. He came into the world through no will of mine, and yet, God only knows how I loved him. The Anglo-Saxon blood as well as the African flowed in his veins; the two currents commingled – one singing of freedom, the other silent and sullen with generations of despair. Why should not the Anglo-Saxon triumph – why should it be weighed down with the rich blood typical of the tropics? Must the life-current of one race bind the other race in chains as strong and enduring as if there had been no Anglo-Saxon taint? By the laws of God and nature, as interpreted by man, one-half of my boy was free, and why should not this fair birthright of freedom remove the curse from the other half – raise it into the bright, joyous sunshine of liberty? I could not answer these questions of my heart that almost maddened me, and I learned to regard human philosophy with trust. Much as I respected the authority of my master, I could not remain silent on a subject that so nearly concerned me. One day, when I insisted on knowing whether he would permit me to purchase myself, and what price I must pay for myself, he turned to me in a petulant manner, thrust his hand into his pocket, drew forth a bright silver quarter of a dollar, and proffering it to me, said:

> "Lizzie, I have told you often not to trouble me with such a question. If you really wish to leave me, take this: it will pay the passage of yourself and boy on the ferry-boat, and when you are on the other side of the river you will be free. It is the cheapest way that I know of to accomplish what you desire."

I looked at him in astonishment, and earnestly replied: "No, master, I do not wish to be free in such a manner. If such had been my wish, I should never have troubled you about obtaining your consent to my purchasing myself. I can cross the river any day, as you well know, and have frequently done so, but will never leave you in such a manner. By the laws of the land I am your slave – you are my master, and I will only be free by such means as the laws of the country provide." He expected this answer, and I knew that he was pleased. Some time afterwards he told me that he had reconsidered the question; that I had served his family faithfully; that I deserved my freedom, and that he would take $1200 for myself and boy.

This was joyful intelligence for me, and the reflection of hope gave a silver lining to the dark cloud of my life – faint, it is true, but still a silver lining.

Taking a prospective glance at liberty, I consented to marry. . . . The day was a happy one, but it faded all too soon. Mr. Keckley – let me speak kindly of his faults – proved dissipated, and a burden instead of a helpmate. More than all, I learned that he was a slave instead of a free man, as he represented himself to be. With the simple explanation that I lived with him eight years, let charity draw around him the mantle of silence.

I went to work in earnest to purchase my freedom, but the years passed, and I was still a slave. Mr. Garland's family claimed so much of my attention – in fact, I supported them – that I was not able to accumulate anything. In the meantime Mr. Garland died, and Mr. Burwell, a Mississippi planter, came to St. Louis to settle up the estate. . . . Several schemes were urged upon me by my friends. At last I formed a resolution to go to New York, state my case, and appeal to the benevolence of the people. The plan seemed feasible, and I made preparations to carry it out. When I was almost ready to turn my face northward, Mrs. Garland told me that she would require the names of six gentlemen who would vouch for my return, and become responsible for the amount at which I was valued. I had many friends in St. Louis, and as I believed that they had confidence in me, I felt that I could readily obtain the names desired. I started out, stated my case, and obtained five signatures to the paper, and my heart throbbed with pleasure, for I did not believe that the sixth would refuse me. I called he listened patiently, then remarked:

> "Yes, yes, Lizzie; the scheme is a fair one, and you shall have my name. But I shall bid you good-by when you start." . . .

I was startled. "What do you mean, Mr. Farrow? Surely you do not think that I do not mean to come back?" . . .

> "Simply this: you *mean* to come back, that is, you *mean* so *now*, but you never will. When you reach New York the abolitionists will tell you what savages we are, and they will prevail on you to stay there; and we shall never see you again." . . .

I was beginning to feel sick at heart, for I could not accept the signature of this man when he had no faith in my pledges. No; slavery, eternal slavery rather than be regarded with distrust by those whose respect I esteemed. . . . The heart grew heavy. Every ray of sunshine was eclipsed. With humbled pride, weary step, tearful face, and a dull, aching pain, I left the house. . . .

The first paroxysm of grief was scarcely over, when a carriage stopped in front of the house; Mrs. Le Bourgois, one of my kind patrons, got out of it and entered the door. She seemed to bring sunshine with her handsome cheery face. She came to where I was, and in her sweet way said:

> "Lizzie, I hear that you are going to New York to beg for money to buy your freedom. I have been thinking over the matter, and told Ma it would be a shame to allow you to go North to *beg* for what we should *give* you. You have many friends in St. Louis, and I am going to raise the twelve hundred dollars required among them. I have two hundred dollars

put away for a present; am indebted to you one hundred dollars; mother owes you fifty dollars, and will add another fifty to it; and as I do not want the present, I will make the money a present to you. Don't start for New York now until I see what I can do among your friends."

Like a ray of sunshine she came, and like a ray of sunshine she went away. The flowers no longer were withered, drooping. Again they seemed to bud and grow in fragrance and beauty. Mrs. Le Bourgois, God bless her dear good heart, was more than successful. The twelve hundred dollars were raised, and at last my son and myself were free. Free, free! what a glorious ring to the word. Free! the bitter heart-struggle was over. Free! the soul could go out to heaven and to God with no chains to clog its flight or pull it down. Free! the earth wore a brighter look, and the very stars seemed to sing with joy. Yes, free! free by the laws of man and the smile of God – and Heaven bless them who made me so! . . .

CHAPTER IV. IN THE FAMILY OF SENATOR JEFFERSON DAVIS

THE twelve hundred dollars with which I purchased the freedom of myself and son I consented to accept only as a loan. I went to work in earnest, and in a short time paid every cent that was so kindly advanced by my lady patrons of St. Louis. All this time my husband was a source of trouble to me, and a burden. Too close occupation with my needle had its effects upon my health, and feeling exhausted with work, I determined to make a change. I had a conversation with Mr. Keckley; informed . . . him that since he persisted in dissipation we must separate; that I was going North, and that I should never live with him again, at least until I had good evidence of his reform. . . . Poor man; he had his faults, but over these faults death has drawn a veil. My husband is now sleeping in his grave, and in the silent grave I would bury all unpleasant memories of him.

I left St. Louis in the spring of 1860, taking the cars direct for Baltimore, where I stopped six weeks, attempting to realize a sum of money by forming classes of young colored women, and teaching them my system of cutting and fitting dresses. The scheme was not successful, for after six weeks of labor and vexation, I left Baltimore with scarcely money enough to pay my fare to Washington. Arriving in the capital, I sought and obtained work at two dollars and a half per day. However, as I was notified that I could only remain in the city ten days without obtaining a license to do so, such being the law, and as I did not know whom to apply for assistance, I was sorely troubled. I also had to have someone vouch to the authorities that I was a free woman. My means were too scanty, and my profession too precarious to warrant my purchasing license. In my perplexity I called on a lady for whom I was sewing, Miss Ringold, a member of Gen. Mason's family, from Virginia. I stated my case, and she kindly volunteered to render me all the assistance in her power. She called on Mayor Burritt with me, and Miss Ringold succeeded in making an arrangement for me to remain in Washington without paying the sum required for a license; moreover, I was not to be molested. I rented apartments in a good locality, and soon had a good run of custom. The summer passed, winter came, and I was still in Washington. Mrs. Davis, wife of Senator Jefferson Davis, came from the South in November of 1860, with her husband. Learning that Mrs. Davis wanted a modiste, I presented myself, and was employed by her on the recommendation of one of my patrons and her intimate friend, Mrs. Captain Hetsill. I went to the house to work, but finding that they were such late risers, and as I had to fit many dresses on Mrs. Davis, I told her that I should prefer giving half the day to her, working the other in my own room for some of my other lady patrons. Mrs. D. consented to the proposition, and it was arranged that I should come to her own house every day after 12 M. It was the winter before the breaking out of that fierce and bloody war between the two sections of the country; and as Mr. Davis occupied a leading position, his house was the resort of politicians and statesmen from the South. . . .

The holidays were approaching, and Mrs. Davis kept me busy in manufacturing articles of dress for herself and children. She desired to present Mr. Davis on Christmas with a handsome dressing-gown. The material was purchased, and for weeks the work had been under way. Christmas eve came, and the gown had been laid aside so often that it was still unfinished. I saw that Mrs. D. was anxious to have it completed, so I volunteered to remain and work on it. Wearily the hours dragged on, but there was no rest for my busy fingers. I persevered in my task, notwithstanding my head was aching. Mrs. Davis was busy in the adjoining room, arranging the Christmas tree for the children. I looked at the clock, and the hands pointed to a quarter of twelve. I was arranging the cords on the gown when the Senator came in; he looked somewhat careworn, and his step seemed to be a little nervous. He leaned against the door, and expressed his admiration of the Christmas tree, but there was no smile on his face. Turning round, he saw me sitting in the adjoining room, and quickly exclaimed:

> "That you, Lizzie! why are you here so late? Still at work; I hope that Mrs. Davis is not too exacting!"
>
> "No, sir," I answered. "Mrs. Davis was very anxious to have this gown finished to-night, and I volunteered to remain and complete it."
>
> "Well, well, the case must be urgent," and he came slowly towards me, took the gown in his hand, and asked the color of the silk, as he said the gas-light was so deceptive to his old eyes.

. . . As the clock struck twelve I finished the gown, little dreaming of the future that was before it. It was worn, I have not the shadow of a doubt, by Mr. Davis during the stormy years that he was the President of the Confederate States. . . .

While dressing her one day, she said to me:

> "Lizzie, you are so very handy that I should like to take you South with me." "When do you go South, Mrs. Davis?" I inquired.

"Oh, I cannot tell just now, but it will be soon. You know there is going to be war, Lizzie?" "No!" . . .

"But, Mrs. Davis, are you certain that there will be war?"

"Certain! – I know it. You had better go South with me; I will take good care of you. Besides, when the war breaks out, the colored people will suffer in the North. The Northern people will look upon them as the cause of the war, and I fear, in their exasperation, will be inclined to treat you harshly. Then, I may come back to Washington in a few months, and live in the White House. . . ."

I was bewildered with what I heard. I had served Mrs. Davis faithfully, and, she had learned to place the greatest confidence in me. At first I was almost tempted to go South with her, for her reasoning seemed plausible. At the time the conversation was closed, with my promise to consider the question.

I thought over the question much, and the more I thought the less inclined I felt to accept the proposition so kindly made by Mrs. Davis. I knew the North to be strong, and believed that the people would fight for the flag that they pretended to venerate so highly. . . . I parted with Mrs. Davis kindly, half promising to join her in the South if further deliberation should induce me to change my views. A few weeks before she left Washington I made two chintz wrappers for her. She said that she must give up expensive dressing for a while; and that she, with the Southern people, now that war was imminent, must learn to practise lessons of economy. She left some fine needle-work in my hands, which I finished, and forwarded to her at Montgomery, Alabama, . . .

The years have brought many changes; and in view of these terrible changes even I, who was once a slave, who have been punished with the cruel lash, who have experienced the heart and soul tortures of a slave's life, can say to Mr. Jefferson Davis, "Peace! you have suffered! Go in peace."

In the winter of 1865 I was in Chicago, and one day visited the great charity fair held for the benefit of the families of those soldiers who were killed or wounded during the war. In one part of the building was a wax figure of Jefferson Davis, wearing over his other garments the dress in which it was reported that he was captured. There was always a great crowd around this figure, and I was naturally attracted towards it. . . . When it was announced that I recognized the dress as one that I had made for the wife of the late Confederate President there was great cheering and excitement, and I at once became the object of the deepest curiosity. Great crowds followed me, and in order to escape from the embarrassing situation I left the building. . . .

CHAPTER V

MY INTRODUCTION TO MRS. LINCOLN

EVER since arriving in Washington I had a great desire to work for the ladies of the White House, and to accomplish this end I was ready to make almost any sacrifice consistent with propriety. Work came in slowly, and I was beginning to feel very much embarrassed, for I did not know how I was to meet the bills staring me in the face. It is true, the bills were small, but then they were formidable to me, who had little or nothing to pay them with. While in this situation I called at the Ringolds, where I met Mrs. Captain Lee. Mrs. L. was in a state bordering on excitement, as the great event of the season, the dinner-party given in honor of the Prince of Wales, was soon to come off, and she must have a dress suitable for the occasion. The silk had been purchased, but a dress-maker had not yet been found. Miss Ringold recommended me, and I received the order to make the dress. When I called on Mrs. Lee the next day, her husband was in the room, and handing me a roll of bank bills, amounting to one hundred dollars, he requested me to purchase the trimmings, and to spare no expense in making a selection. With the money in my pocket I went out in the street, entered the store of Harper & Mitchell, and asked to look at their laces. Mr. Harper waited on me himself, and was polite and kind. When I asked permission to carry the laces to Mrs. Lee, in order to learn whether she could approve my selection or not, he gave a ready assent. When I reminded him that I was a stranger, and that the goods were valuable, he remarked that he was not afraid to trust me – that he believed my face was the index to an honest heart. It was pleasant to be spoken to thus, and I shall never forget the kind words of Mr. Harper. . . . The dress was done in time, and it gave complete satisfaction. Mrs. Lee attracted great attention at the dinner-party, and her elegant dress proved a good card for me. I received numerous orders, and was relieved from all pecuniary embarrassments. One of my patrons was Mrs. Gen. McClean, a daughter of Gen. Sumner. One day when I was very busy, Mrs. McC. drove up to my apartments, came in where I was engaged with my needle, and in her emphatic way said:

> "Lizzie, I am invited to dine at Willard's on next Sunday, and positively I have not a dress fit to wear on the occasion. I have just purchased material, and you must commence work on it right away."
>
> "But Mrs. McClean," I replied, "I have more work now promised than I can do. It is impossible for me to make a dress for you to wear on Sunday next." . . .
>
> "Now don't say no again. I tell you that you must make the dress. I have often heard you say that you would like to work for the ladies of the White House. Well, I have it in my power to obtain you this privilege. I know Mrs. Lincoln well, and you shall make a dress for her provided you finish mine in time to wear at dinner on Sunday."

The inducement was the best that could have been offered. I would undertake the dress if I should have to sit up all night – every night, to make my pledge good. I sent out and employed assistants, and, after much worry and trouble, the dress was completed to the satisfaction of Mrs. McClean. It appears that Mrs. Lincoln had upset a cup of coffee on the dress she designed wearing on the evening of the reception after the inauguration of Abraham Lincoln as President of the United States, which rendered it necessary that she should have a new one for the occasion. On asking Mrs. McClean who her dress-maker was, that lady promptly informed her,

> "Lizzie Keckley."
>
> "Lizzie Keckley? The name is familiar to me. She used to work for some of my lady friends in St. Louis, and they spoke well of her. Can you recommend her to me?"
>
> "With confidence. Shall I send her to you?" . . .

The next Sunday Mrs. McClean sent me a message to call at her house at four o'clock P.M., that day. . . . The streets of the capital were thronged with people, for this was Inauguration day. A new President, a man of the people from the broad prairies of the West, was to accept the solemn oath of office, was to assume the responsibilities attached to the high position of Chief Magistrate of the United States. . . . Around Willard's hotel swayed an excited crowd, and it was with the utmost difficulty that I worked my way to the house on the opposite side of the street, occupied by the McCleans. . . . an aide on General McClean's staff called, and informed me that I was wanted at Willard's. I crossed the street, and on entering the hotel was met by Mrs. McClean, who greeted me. . . .

With a nervous step I passed on, and knocked at Mrs. Lincoln's door. A cheery voice bade me come in, and a lady, inclined to stoutness, about forty years of age, stood before me.

> "You are Lizzie Keckley, I believe." I bowed assent.
>
> "The dress-maker that Mrs. McClean recommended?" "Yes, madam."
>
> "Very well; I have not time to talk to you now, but would like to have you call at the White House, at eight o'clock to-morrow morning, where I shall then be." . . .

Tuesday morning, at eight o'clock, I crossed the threshold of the White House for the first time. I was shown into a waiting-room, and informed that Mrs. Lincoln was at breakfast. In the waiting-room I found no less than three mantua-makers waiting for an interview with the wife of the new President. It seems that Mrs. Lincoln had told several of her lady friends that she had urgent need for a dress-maker, and that each of these friends had sent her mantua-maker to the White House. Hope fell at once. With so many rivals for the position sought after, I regarded my chances for success as extremely doubtful. I was the last one summoned to Mrs. Lincoln's presence. All the others had a hearing, and were dismissed. I went up-stairs timidly, and entering the room with nervous step, discovered the wife of the President standing by a window, looking out, and engaged in lively conversation with a lady, Mrs. Grimsly, as I afterwards learned. Mrs. L. came forward, and greeted me warmly.

> "You have come at last. Mrs. Keckley, who have you worked for in the city?"
>
> "Among others, Mrs. Senator Davis has been one of my best patrons," was my reply.
>
> "Mrs. Davis! So you have worked for her, have you? Of course you gave satisfaction; so far, good. Can you do my work?"
>
> "Yes, Mrs. Lincoln. Will you have much work for me to do?"
>
> "That, Mrs. Keckley, will depend altogether upon your prices. I trust that your terms are reasonable. I cannot afford to be extravagant. We are just from the West, and are poor. If you do not charge too much, I shall be able to give you all my work." . . .

The terms were satisfactorily arranged, and I measured Mrs. Lincoln, took the dress with me, a bright rose-colored moire-antique, and returned the next day to fit it on her.

45.2 "A SENSATION BOOK ON MRS. LINCOLN."

Source: 'A Sensation Book on Mrs. Lincoln', *Sun* (Baltimore, Maryland), April 25, 1868: Supplement.

Elizabeth Keckley, "thirty years a slave and five years modiste to Mrs Abraham Lincoln," has written, or had written for her, a book purporting to give many of the scenes and conversations at the White House which transpired within her view and hearing. Much of the book is trash, all of it gossip, but some of the political personalities and opinions of Mrs Lincoln might not be uninteresting. . . .

45.3 "REVIEW OF NEW BOOKS. T. B. PETERSON & BROTHERS, PHILADELPHIA."

Source: 'Review of New Books. T. B. Peterson & Brothers, Philadelphia', *Philadelphia Inquirer* (Philadelphia, Pennsylvania), April 27, 1868: 3.

Behind the Scenes. By Elizabeth Keckley

It was the evident intention of the compilers of this volume to prepare a book that would serve a political purpose and sell largely. The latter object will be attained, the efforts to produce the former result are so transparent, so strained and so awkward, that they will not for a moment deceive the verist tyro. The reputed author of this sensational political novel the title-page informs a surprised world was formerly a slave, but more recently *modiste* and friend to Mrs Abraham Lincoln. No one urged this humble friend of Mrs. Lincoln's to write a book of what she saw and heard in the White House. The attacks on Mrs. Lincoln's recent conduct with reference to her wardrobes, prompted the seamstress to lay down the needle and take up the pen, for, says the Presidential dressmaker, "my own character, as well as the character of Mrs. Lincoln is at stake, since I have been intimately associated with that lady in the most eventful periods of her life. I have been her *confidante*, and if evil charges were laid at her door, they must also be laid at mine, since I have been a party to all her movements. To defend myself, I must defend the lady I have served. This is cool and refreshing, the pity of it is, that it was not withheld until the reign of the dog-star.

Will not Mr Johnson's bootmaker favor us with a defense of his patron? The man that made the pedal coverings in which Andrew Johnson swung around the circle, should, on the Kecklian principle, deem himself in a measure responsible for the Presidential speeches delivered at Cleveland and St Louis. But Mrs. Keckley, if there is such a person, is laboring under a strange, though not unusual delusion; she deems herself a person of much greater importance than she really is. She has probably never been attacked in the whole course of her life unless it was on the score of ill-fitting dresses. Perhaps, Mrs. Lincoln's dresses did not find purchasers on account of the clumsy needlework of Mrs. K. How can she otherwise claim any responsibility in the affairs of Mrs. Lincoln, the public will be at a loss to imagine. But then, of course, Mrs. K. is not serious; she has only written a matter-of-fact and silly preface to a lively romance. The author tells us that she was also, the favorite dressmaker of Mrs. Jeff Davis that the costliest gown in J. D.'s collection was stitched by her fingers; that Mrs. Lincoln had decided to be with wife of a President when yet a very little girl, and many other startling and improbable things. To pack the book to a respectable bulk, there is inserted a very diffuse account of the efforts of Mrs. Lincoln to dispose of her wardrobe. For sale by Claxton, Remsen & Hafflefinger.

45.4 "NEW PUBLICATIONS."

Source: 'New Publications' *Times-Picayune* (New Orleans, Louisiana), May 3, 1868: 5.

"Behind the Scenes, or, Thirty Years a Slave, and Four Years in the White House." New York: Carleton & Co. This is the alleged production of one Elizabeth Keckley (colored), who describes herself as "Modiste, and formerly friend to Mrs Lincoln." It is no doubt written by some New York Bohemian. It is a catch-penny, trashy and sensational, and bears internal evidence of being in the main the production of the Bohemian's reckless and riotous fancy.

46

ELEANOR COADE, 1733–1821, PIONEER OF COADE STONE

Source: Eleanor Coade, 1733–1821, pioneer of Coade Stone.

EDITORIAL HEADNOTE

Eleanor Coade (1733–1821) was born into a wool merchant family in Exeter, who moved to London in 1760. She worked initially on her own as a linen merchant, but after her father died she joined Daniel Pincot, who was already selling a form of artificial stone at Narrow Wall, Lambeth. In 1771, however, she sacked him for promoting himself rather than her as the proprietor and appointed John Bacon as supervisor. His neo-classical designs were of a very high standard and a hallmark of the company; he stayed with the firm until his death in 1799. The same year she brought her cousin John Sealy into the firm, and renamed the company Coade and Sealy, though when he died in 1813 the name reverted, and she continued to flourish until her death in 1821. She was celebrated with an obituary in the *Gentleman's Magazine*. Coade worked for all the eminent Georgian architects, including Robert Adam, James and Samuel Wyatt, Sir William Chambers, John Nash and John Soane. As a talented modeller, she also exhibited at the Society of Artists between 1773 and 1780.

It was widely believed that she had invented a new process for making artificial stone; however, lesser-quality versions of the process were already widely known for some fifty years before the introduction of her product. She was, however, probably responsible for perfecting both the clay recipe and the firing process. Long thought to be a mystery, Coade stone or *Lithodipyra* is now known to be a ceramic material whose versatility allowed it to be used for architectural details, commemorative and funerary monuments, fonts, statues, busts, coats of arms, chimney pieces, garden ornaments and furniture, as these extracts show.

DOI: 10.4324/9781003676669-50

46.1 *THE DAILY ADVERTISER* (LONDON), THURSDAY, 6 FEBRUARY 1772

ARTIFICIAL STONE

At ELEANOR COADE'S Manufactory, near King's Arms Stairs, Narrow-Wall, Lambeth, under the inspection of Mr Bacon, of Wardour-Street, Soho, Sculptor, are made and sold all Sorts of Ornaments for Buildings, Gardens, or Parks, as Capitals, Pateras, Tablets, Frizes, Chimney-Pieces, Pedestals, Vases, Figures, Buslos, Pinacles, Balls, &c. The Whole executed in the best Taste, considerably cheaper than Natural Stone, and in a Composition, the Durability of which the Publick are already Judges of by Experiment. A great Variety of the above ready made, which are open for the Inspection of any Nobleman or Gentleman, every Day (Sundays excepted) from Ten till Four.

46.2 *THE DAILY ADVERTISER* (LONDON), AND THE *GAZETTEER AND NEW DAILY ADVERTISER* (LONDON), MONDAY, 21 MAR. 1774

TO all Persons concerned in Building. Whereas several Ornaments and Erections, under the Denomination of Artificial Stone, have lately perished by the Frost, Mrs Coade, Proprietor of the Manufactory, at King's Arm's Stairs, Lambeth, begs Leave to inform the Nobility, Gentry and Builders, that none of them are of her Composition, the Durability of which is unquestionably proved by many honourable and authentick Testimonies, even where it has been purposely and severely tried. However the Public are desired to take Notice, that for the greater Satisfaction of her Employers, she is answerable for its standing all Weather, and that in Future every Piece of her Stone will have the Name "COADE" indented on it. At this Manufactory, under the Direction of Mr. Bacon, Sculptor, are made Statues, Chimney-Pieces, Tombs, Gothick and Rustick Piers, Capitals, Vases, Pedestals, Medallions, Tablets, Pateras, and every other Ornament heretofore done in natural Stone, but far exceeding in Cheapness, Beauty, and Durability. Some of the articles are under the Price of Wood. Coping ready for Sale, and the best Fire Bricks made to Order.

46.3 *PUBLIC ADVERTISER* (LONDON), APRIL 19, 1776

LONDON

Yesterday the Exhibition of the Royal Incorporated Society of Artists opened at their Great Room in the Strand. – the following Pieces appeared to be the most deserving of public Attention, viz. . . .

193. A Statue of a Naiade by Mrs Coade is in a grand stile.

46.4 *LONDON CHRONICLE*, MAY 6–8, 1777

Postscript

For the London Chronicle.

Observations on the PICTURES *exhibited* by the ROYAL INCORPORATED SOCIETY of ARTISTS, *concluded.*

A Vase, after the Antique, in the Villa de Medicis: A Lion. By Mrs. Coade.

These and several other figures, which I have not the time to mention, are all made of artificial stone, and do great honour the taste and ingenuity of the artist.

46.5 *MORNING POST* (LONDON) SUNDAY, MAY 22, 1779

To the NOBILITY, GENTRY, and BUILDERS.

COADE'S ARTIFICIAL STONE MANUFACTORY, at King's-Arms Stairs, Narrow-wall, Lambeth, opposite Whitehall-stairs, where it has been carried on for nearly ten years, is now offered to the inspection of the curious, with great additions of elegant statues, bas-reliefs, vases, bustos, capitals, key-stones, door-cases, chimney-pieces, &c. &c. The models by Mr Bacon. The superiority of design and execution to common sculpture, as well as its cheapness, render it worthy the attention of every gentleman and builder. Its extraordinary durability is sufficiently evinced in a number of buildings of the first consequence in this kingdom, where it will be found to retain its original sharpness in defiance of the hardest frost, which is more than can be said of some ornaments bearing the name artificial stone, which have failed in the weather; it is needful to assure the public that they were not the production of this manufactory, of which any enquirer may be easily informed, who will please to take notice that the name Coade is indented on every piece, and the manufacturer answerable for its durability. The great collection here exhibited will not admit of description, even small ornaments to be placed on wood for door frizes, chimney-pieces, &c. in a taste superior to any thing of the kind; decoration for rooms, candelabrums, &c, chimney-pieces of wood, ornamented with stone, exceeding cheap, some for a peculiarly, elegant and new taste. The model of the Thames, by Mr Bacon, which was exhibited last year at the Royal Academy, to be seen at this manufactory, with proposals for executing it in artificial stone. Coping, fire-bricks, &c. &c.

N.B A head at the foot of Westminster-bridge directing to the place.

46.6 *GAZETTEER AND NEW DAILY ADVERTISER* (LONDON), SATURDAY, JANUARY 29, 1785

BURNT ARTIFICIAL STONE

Just Published,

A DESCRIPTIVE CATALOGUE of COADE'S MANUFACTORY, at King's-Arms Stairs, Narrow-wall, Lambeth, opposite Whitehall-stairs, containing upwards of 700 Articles; such as Capitals, Frizes, Frontispieces, Balusters, fine Balls, Relieves in Medallions, Tablets, &c. as well as Statues, Vases, Chimney-pieces, Monuments, and all sorts of Ornaments, both for external and internal Decoration. The reputation to this Manufactory, after a trial of fifteen years, is congenially established to need any econominium; and as to the extent of the Work, no idea can possibly be conveyed to the limits of an advertisement. The Public are therefore referred to the Catalogue itself, which has long been waited for by the Nobility and Architects of this Kingdom; wherein the Dimensions and Price of every Article are ascertained.

To be had at the Manufactory; and of Mr Strahan, bookseller, no. 67, Strand.

46.7 *LONDON GAZETTE*, FEBRUARY 17–19, 1788

Carlton-House, February 19

Mrs Eleanor Coade and Mr John Sealy, of Lambeth, are appointed Artificial Stone Manufacturers to his Royal Highness the Prince of Wales.

Whitehall, February 19

Mrs Eleanor Coade and Mr John Sealy, of Lambeth, are appointed Artificial Stone Manufacturers to his Royal Highness the Duke of York.

47

MADAME C. J. WALKER, 'HAIR CULTURALIST', MILLIONAIRE AND INVENTOR, VARIOUS DOCUMENTS, 1918

Source: Madame C. J. Walker, 'hair culturalist', millionaire and inventor.

EDITORIAL HEADNOTE

Sarah Breedlove (1867–1919), born into a sharecropping southern family on a plantation in Louisiana and orphaned young, lived with her sister and her husband. To avoid abuse by her brother-in-law, she married at age fourteen and when he died in 1887, she was the mother of a daughter Leila (or A'Lelia); two years later she moved to St. Louis, where her four brothers were barbers, and worked as a laundress and cook. In 1904, after an abortive marriage and struggling financially and worn out by the years of hard work, her life changed radically. After losing her own hair, she started using African American businesswoman Annie Turbo Malone's "The Great Wonderful Hair Grower", and she joined Malone's team of black women sales agents. A year later, she moved to Denver, Colorado, where she married Charles Joseph Walker, an advertising man, and renamed herself "Madam C.J. Walker". With $1.25, she launched her own line of hair products and straighteners for African American women, "Madam Walker's Wonderful Hair Grower." The couple divorced and she moved to Indianapolis, building a factory for the Walker Manufacturing Company. She became a millionaire in less than three years and was one of the wealthiest women in America. She used her wealth and growing position to promote black women's economic independence, created training programmes for her network of licensed agents; she ultimately employed 40,000 African American women and men in the US, Central America and the Caribbean. She also founded the National Negro Cosmetics Manufacturers Association in 1917. As her wealth increased, so did her philanthropic and political outreach. Walker contributed to the YMCA,

DOI: 10.4324/9781003676669-51

covered tuition for six African American students at Tuskegee Institute and became active in the anti-lynching movement, donating $5,000 to the NAACP's efforts. Just prior to dying of kidney failure, Walker revised her will, bequeathing two-thirds of future net profits to charity, as well as thousands of dollars to various individuals and schools.

47.1 *THE RICHMOND PLANET, DECEMBER 19, 1908, 4*

Madame C. J. Walker

The world's greatest Hair Culturist who is astonishing the world with her wonderful Hair Grower, the quickest and surest remedy ever discovered for the growth of hair. Either she or her daughter will appear in this city on or about Nov. – Every woman of Pride should see her while in this city. One personal treatment with a six week supply will produce from a half inch to an inch. One personal treatment only $2.00. She is the woman who grew the hair of Nannie H. Burroughs, Corresponding Secretary of Woman's Auxiliary to National Baptist Convention.

For further information address

MADAM C. J. WALKER. 2518 Wylle Avenue, Pittsburgh, Pa.

47.2 *OREGONIAN, AUGUST 3, 1918, P. 7*

Negro Women Win Success

Delegates to Denver Include a Millionaire

Denver, Colo., July 22. – Included among the delegates to the National Association of Colored Women's Clubs, which met here this month, were lawyers, real estate brokers, newspaper women and teachers, besides members of many professions and callings. One negro woman in attendance returned to Denver as a millionaire. Just a few years ago she was a washwoman here.

During the convention these colored women leaders told of the struggles they had to overcome to achieve their place in the world and detailed how success had come despite racial prejudice and handicaps.

Madame C. J. Walker is the woman who returns a millionaire. Her home is Irvington-on-the-Hudson, where other millionaires live. Thirteen years ago she arrived in Denver with just $1.50 in her pocket. She took in washing and any other work she could obtain she was glad to get. During this time she evolved a scheme of beauty culture particularly for the hair. A brew of herbs, a new manner of massage – that was the start; the start that took her from an attic room in Clarkson street, Denver, to the Italian Renaissance home on the Hudson.

Other delegates achieved success in the paths they have chosen.

Mrs. Elizabeth Garter, for 20 years a teacher in the public schools of New Bedford, Mass. counts only part of her work. She is president and founder of a home for the aged in New Bedford, which receives both the destitute and those who are able to pay, of both white and colored races.

Miss Hallie Q. Brown is a teacher of elocution and public speaking in Wilberforce University. She has had 10 years of work in Europe, part of which time she was associated in the philanthropic work of Lady Somerset. Five years ago she attended a conference in Edinburg and came back to America with $15,000 given by foreign philanthropists for improvements at the university.

Mrs. A. F. Jenkins, another delegate, is a real estate dealer in Kansas City, Mo. Mrs Mary Church, of Washington D.C., also is a real estate dealer. Mrs. Mary Talbot, president of the association, does social work in her home city, Buffalo, N.Y.

47.3 *WYOMING STATE TRIBUNE – MAY 28, 1919 – PAGE FIVE*

World's Wealthiest Negro Woman Passes on at Home

IRVINGTON-ON-HUDSON, N.Y. May 28. – Madame C. J. Walker said to have been the wealthiest negro woman in the world, died at her home here after an illness of several weeks.

Madame Walker was born in Delta, Pa., in 1867. For many years she has been a prominent philanthropist and had taken prominent part in all movements for the advancement of the interests of the negro race.

Her wealth was derived from the manufacture of several toilet preparations which found a ready sale among members of her own race. Chief of these was a preparation warranted to take the kink out of the hair of any negro. Starting the manufacture of the preparation in Denver in 1905, Madame Walker and her daughter Lelia moved the business to Pittsburgh three years later and finally settled in Indianapolis in 1910. Since then it has grown by leaps and bounds with agents in the West Indies and South America.

Madame Walker's home here is valued at $250,000.

47.4 *FROM THE U.S. GOVERNMENT PUBLISHING OFFICE, 108TH CONGRESS, 1ST SESSION, H. CON. RES. 65* EXPRESSING THE SENSE OF CONGRESS THAT MADAME C. J. WALKER SHOULD BE RECOGNIZED FOR HER ACHIEVEMENTS IN BUSINESS, HER INVENTIONS, AND HER COMMITMENT TO THE AFRICAN-AMERICAN COMMUNITY

IN THE HOUSE OF REPRESENTATIVES
February 27, 2003
Mr. Rangel submitted the following concurrent resolution; which was referred to the Committee on Government Reform

CONCURRENT RESOLUTION

Expressing the sense of Congress that Madame C. J. Walker should be recognized for her achievements in business, her inventions, and her commitment to the African-American community.

Whereas Madame C. J. Walker was born on December 23, 1867, on a plantation in Delta, Louisiana;
Whereas, in 1905, Madame C. J. Walker invented a conditioning treatment designed to aid in the straightening of hair, as well as an entire line of cosmetic products;
Whereas, in 1910, Madame C. J. Walker ordered the construction of a factory in Indianapolis to manufacture her line of cosmetic products;
Whereas Madame C. J. Walker was committed to employing women in all aspects of her business;
Whereas Madame C. J. Walker was a noted philanthropist, giving generously to black charities, including the NAACP and the National Association of Colored Women;
Whereas Madame C. J. Walker encouraged her agents to similarly assist black humanitarian organizations nationwide;
Whereas Madame C. J. Walker was one of the first American women – black or white – to amass a personal net worth of more than 1 million dollars as a result of her own efforts, thereby becoming one of the most successful business persons of the early twentieth century by the time of her death; and
Whereas Madame C. J. Walker died on May 25, 1919, at the age of 52: Now, therefore, be it Resolved by the House of Representatives (the Senate concurring),

That it is the sense of Congress that Madame C. J. Walker should be recognized as one of history's greatest female businesswomen and role models for the Nation's young people.

Part 5

CASE STUDY: WOMEN IN THE PRINTING TRADES

48

PETITION TO THE ABERDEEN CITY COUNCIL, 1764

Susan Trail

Source: Susan Trail, Petition to the Aberdeen City Council, Aberdeen City Archives, *Town Council Register*, Vol. 63, 26 Oct. 1763–21. Sept. 1773, folio 20, 5 September 1764.

EDITORIAL HEADNOTE

Susan Trail, co-proprietor of the family printing shop and the *Aberdeen Journal*, petitioned the Aberdeen Burgh Council for all the rights and privileges available to a well-run and aspiring printing firm, as well as requesting and gaining the rights her husband had held as Printer to the Town. She ran the firm on her own until her son returned from his training. Daniel Defoe, a great proponent of commerce and trade, argued the importance of tradesmen's wives knowing enough of the business to operate it, though he never saw women as businesswomen in their own right. Many women did wish to take up business opportunities, for a wide range of reasons, and working in business families, as it showed the value of a competent wife to manage when husbands were away.

This said day anent the petition given in to the honourables the Magistrates and Council . . . by Susan Trail Widow of the deceased James Chalmers Printer in Aberdeen for herself and in name and behalf of James Chalmers her eldest son Humbly shewing That the said James Chalmers their Petitioner's husband having lately died, their Petitioner designed along with her said Son to carry on the Printing business as formerly done by her husband, and for that purpose had retained in the service all the Journeymen and Apprentices formerly employed by him. That as the said deceased James Chalmers served their Honours and the Town of Aberdeen for a great many years preceding his death in the Office of Printer and as she hoped with general approbation and that said James Chalmers her Son was not only regularly bred to the Business with his father but also for several years past had been at London, and other places in England prosecuting and improving

DOI: 10.4324/9781003676669-53

himself in the same and designed in a short time to return to and carry on the Printing business along with their Petitioner in this place, She humbly hoped their Honours would be pleased to prefer her said Son to the Office of Town's Printer and all the profites and Emoluments thereto belonging as formerly enjoyed by her husband more especially as several of her own and well as her husband's Progenitors were long Residenters in this City and had the honour to fill some of the highest public Offices thereof, . . .

They unanimously Granted the desire of the same And Elected and Choised the said Susan Trail and the said James Chalmers her Son Jointly and the longest liver of them to be Town's Printers in place of the said deceased James Chalmers, And Granted to them the whole profites and Emoluments belonging to the said Officers formerly enjoyed by the deceased James Chalmers they always keeping proper and well qualified servants for carrying on the Business.

49

THE VICTORIA PRESS, 1860

Emily Faithfull

Source: Emily Faithfull, 'The Victoria Press', A paper read at the Glasgow meeting of the national association for the promotion of social science, *English Woman's Journal*, October 1860, 121–25.

Image 7 The Victoria Press, *The Illustrated London News*, 15 June 1861.

DOI: 10.4324/9781003676669-54

EDITORIAL HEADNOTE

A century after Traill, Emily Faithfull set up the Victoria Press. Joining the Langham Place Group, she promoted their interests in legal reform including suffrage, women's employment and better educational opportunities (see doc. 38). Her main interest was in employment change, and she was involved in investigations and campaigns and with Emily Davis in the campaign to open the university local examinations to women. These were the essential entry examinations for higher education. The group actively explored opportunities for respectable employment, founding the Society for Promoting the Employment of Women. Compositing was a possibility but was heavily controlled by men as a skilled and unionised trade for men. Men argued that their qualifications guaranteed their property in skill, and they heartily resisted incursions for women. Bessie Parkes bought a small printing press, and she and Emily Faithfull employed a compositor, Austin Holyoake (brother of George Jacob Holyoake), to give instruction in composing. On the basis of this experience, they concluded that composing could be a suitable occupation for women. To this end, on 25 March 1860, Emily Faithfull opened the Victoria Press at Great Coram Street, London. She invested her own capital in the press and had the financial backing of another committee member of the Society for Promoting the Employment of Women, G. W. Hastings. The article in the *English Woman's Journal* continues the story. She also started writing and became a prolific journalist and author, and her only novel *Change upon Change* (*A Reed Shaken in the Wind* in the US) drew on the need for women to have access to education, training, and work if they were not to be at risk of being destroyed by their often frivolous and trivial schooling and their dependence upon men. She travelled and was a popular lecturer and propagandist.

When we remember the impetus given to the question of female employment by the discussion which took place at the meeting of this Association, at Bradford, last year, it seems but natural to suppose that one of the practical results of that discussion will be a matter of great interest to the present audience, on which account I venture to bring before your notice the origin and progress of the Victoria Press. It has often been urged against this Association that it does "nothing but talk"; but those who fail to see the connexion existing between the promotion of social science and the development of that science in spheres of practical exertion, must acknowledge that if all discussions led to as much action as followed that which took place upon the employment of women, the accusation would fall to the ground. A thorough ventilation of the question of the necessity for extending the field of woman's employment, was at that time imperatively needed. The

April number of the *Edinburgh Review* for 1859 had contained a fuller account of the actual state of female industry in this country than perhaps had ever been previously brought before the notice of the public. The question had begun to weigh upon thoughtful minds and even to force itself upon unwilling ones, and the notion that the destitution of women was a rare and exceptional phenomenon was swept away as the Times observed, when Miss Parkes, addressing this Association, at Bradford, did not hesitate to ask whether there was a single man in the company who had not, at that moment, among his own connexions, an instance of the distress to which her paper referred. The discussion which followed operated in a most beneficial manner; it forced the public to put prejudice aside and to test the theory hitherto so jealously maintained, that women, were, as a general rule, supported in comfort and independence by their male relatives. The press then took up the question, and, with but few exceptions, dealt by it with a zeal and honesty which aided considerably in the partial solution of a problem in which is bound up so much of the welfare and happiness of English homes during this and future generations. One by one the arguments for and against female employment, apart from the domestic sphere, were brought forward and examined; and where objections arising feeling could not be vanquished by argument, the simple fact of women being constantly thrown upon the world to get their daily bread by their own exertions left the stoutest maintainers of the propriety of woman's entire pecuniary dependence upon man, without an answer.

In the November following the Bradford meeting, the council of this Association appointed a committee to consider and report on the best means which could be adopted for increasing the industrial employments of women; in the course of the investigation set on foot by this committee, of which I was a member, we received information of several attempts made to introduce women into the female printing industry trade, and suitableness of the same a branch of female industry A small press, and type sufficient for an experiment were purchased by Miss Parkes, who was anxious to test by personal observation the information thus received. This press was put up in a private room placed at her disposal by the kindness of a member of this Association. A printer consented to give her instruction, she invited me to share in the trial sufficed to convince us that if women properly trained, their physical powers would be singularly adapted to fit them for becoming compositors, though there were parts of the printing trade – such as the lifting of the iron chases in which the pages are imposed, the carrying of the cases of weighty type from the rack to the frame and the whole of the presswork (that is the actual striking off of the sheets of), particularly in the latter department entailing continuous, bodily exertion far beyond average female strength.

Having ascertained this, the next step was to open an office on a sufficiently large scale to give the experiment a fair an opportunity of success. The machinery and type were so expensive that the outlay would never be covered unless they were kept inconstant use.

The pressure of work, the sudden influx of which is often entirely beyond the printer's control, requires the possession of other extra type in stock, these and other economical reasons which will be a easily understood, by all commercial men, necessitate the outlay of considerable amount of capital on the part of any one who wishes to turn out first-class printing. A gentleman, well known for his public efforts in promoting the social and the welfare of women, determined to embark with me in the industrial enterprise of establishing a printing business in which female compositors should to be employed. A house was taken in Great Coram Street Russell Square, which, by judicious expenditure was rendered fit for printing purposes; I name the locality because we were anxious it should be in a light and airy neighbourhood. We ventured to call it the Victoria press after the Sovereign to whose influence women owe so large, a debt of gratitude, and in the hope also that the name would prove a happy augury of victory. I have recently had the gratification of receiving an assurance of Her Majesty's interest in the office, and the kind expression of Her approbation of all such really useful and practical steps for the opening of new branches of industry for women. The opening of the office was accomplished on the 25th of last March. The Society for Promoting the Employment of Women apprenticed five girls to me at premiums of £10 each; others were apprenticed by relatives and friends, and we soon found ourselves in the thick of the struggle for such I do not hesitate to call it; and when you remember, that there was not one skilled compositor in the office, you will readily understand the difficulties we encountered. Work came in immediately, from the earliest day. In April we commenced our first book and began practically to test all the difficulties of the trade. I had, previously ascertained that in most printing offices the compositors work in companies of four and five appointing one of the number to click for the rest, that is, to make up and impose the matter and carry the forms to the press-room. The imposition requires more experience than strength, and no untrained compositor could attempt it, and I therefore engaged intelligent, respectable workmen, who undertook to perform this duty for the female compositors at the Victoria Press. I have at this time sixteen female compositors, and their gradual reception into the office deserves some mention. In the month of April, when work was coming in freely, I was fortunate enough to secure a skilled hand from Limerick. She had been trained as a printer by her father, and had worked under him for twelve years. At his death she had carried on the office, which she was after some time obliged to relinquish, owing to domestic circumstances. Seeing in a country that an opening for female compositors had occurred in London paper she determined on taking the long journey from Ireland to seek employment in a business for which she was well competent. She came straight to my office, bringing with her a letter from the editor of a Limerick paper, who assured me that I should find her a great assistance in my enterprise. I engaged her there and then; she came to work the very next day, and has proved herself most valuable. I have now also three other hands who have received some measure of training in their fathers' offices, having been taught by them in order to afford help in any time of pressure, or in case any opening should present itself in the trade, of which a vague hope seemed present to their mind. From letters which I have received from various parts of the country, I find that the introduction of women into the trade has been contemplated by many printers. Intelligent workmen do not view this movement with distrust, they feel very strongly woman's cause is man's; and they anxiously look for some opening for the employment of those otherwise solely dependent on them.

Four of the other compositors are very young, being under fifteen years age; of the remaining eight some were apprenticed by the Society of for Promoting the Employment of Women having heard by the of the Victoria Press through the register kept at Langham Place; and others through private channels. They are of all ages, and have devoted themselves to their new occupation with great industry and have accomplished an amount of work which perseverance I did not expect, untrained hands could perform in the time. I was also induced to try the experiment of training a little deaf dumb girl dumb girl to, one of the youngest above mentioned; she was apprenticed to me by the Asylum for the Deaf and Dumb, in the Old Kent Road at the instance of a blind gentleman, Mr. John Bird who called on me soon after the office was opened. This child, will make a very good compositor in time her attention being naturally undistracted from her work, though, the difficulty of teaching her is very considerable, and the process of learning takes a longer time.

Having given a general description of my compositors I will only add that the hours of work are from nine till one, and from two, till six. Those who live near, go home to dinner go between one and two; others have the use of a room in the house, some bringing their own dinners ready cooked and some preparing it on the spot. When they work overtime, as is occasionally unavoidable for which of course they receive extra pay per hour, they have tea at half-past five, so as to break the time.

It has been urged that printing is an unhealthy occupation. The mortality known to exist among printers had led people to this conclusion result, we but find when we consider the principal causes producing this result, we find it arises in great measure from removable evils. For instance, the imperfect ventilation, the impurity of the air increased by the quantity and bad quality of the gas consumed, and not *least* by the gin, rum, and brandy so freely imbibed by printers. The chief and offices being situated in the unwholesome localities, are dark and close and thus become hotbeds for the propagation of phthisis.

In the annual reports for the last ten years of the Widows' Metropolitan Typographical Fund, we find the average age of the death of printers was forty-eight years. The number of deaths caused by phthisis and other diseases of that class, among the members in the ten years ending December 31, 1858, was 101 out of a total number of 173, being fifty-eight three-fourths per cent of the whole.

It is too early yet to judge of the effect of this employment upon the health of state women even under careful sanitary arrangements; but I may state that one of my compositors whom I hesitated to receive on account of the extreme delicacy of her health (inducing a fear of immediate consumption for which she was receiving medical treatment) has, since she undertook, her new occupation become quite strong, and her visits to her doctor have entirely ceased.

The inhalation of dust from the types, which are composed of antimony heated and lead, is an evil less capable of remedy. The type when heated emits a noxious fume, capable injurious to respiration, which in the course of years occasionally produces a partial palsy of the hands. The sight of the compositor is frequently very much injured, apparently by close application to minute type, but probably, as Mr. H. W. Porter remarks in his paper read before the Institute of Actuaries, from the quantity of snuff they take, which cannot fail to be prejudicial that. This habit at all events, is one from we cannot suppose the compositors of the Victoria Press will suffer.

It has also been urged the digestive functions may suffer from the long-continued standing position which the compositor practises at the case. This, I believe nothing but habit has necessitated. Each compositor at the Victoria Press is provided with a high stool, seated on which she can work as quickly as when standing.

There is class one branch of women of printing which, if pursued by the most cultivated class of women, would suffice to give them an independence – namely reading and correcting for the press. Men readers who undertake this department earn two guineas a week; classical readers, capable, of correcting the dead languages and those conversant with German and Italian, receive more than this. But before the office of reader can be properly undertaken, a regular apprenticeship to printing must have been worked out; accuracy, quickness of eye and a thorough knowledge of punctuation and grammar are not sufficient qualifications for a reader in a printing office; she must have practically learnt the practicalities of the trade. And I would urge a few educated women of a higher class to resolutely enter upon an apprenticeship for this purpose.

But for compositorship it is desirable that girls should be apprenticed early in life, as they cannot earn enough support themselves under three or four years, and should therefore, commence learning the trade while living under their father's roof. Boys are always apprenticed early in life, at the age of fourteen; and if women are to be introduced into the mechanical arts, it must be under the same conditions. I can hardly lay enough stress, upon this point so convinced am I of its truth, that I now receive no new hands over eighteen years of age.

Many applications have been made to me to receive girls from the country; but the want proper accommodation has hitherto prevented me from accepting them, but I have now formed a plan for this purpose and when I am assured of six girls from a distance I shall be able to provide for their being safely lodged and cared for.

In conclusion, I will only attract your attention to the proof of our work; for while I am unable to produce the numerous circulars, prospectuses and reports these of societies which have been accomplished and sent away during these six months in which we have been at work, I can point to copies of the English Woman's Journal, a monthly periodical now printed at the Victoria Press, and also to a volume printed for this Association, both of which can be obtained in the reception room and which will I think be allowed to be sufficient proof of the fact that printing can be successfully undertaken by women.

Emily Faithfull.

50

TYPESETTING, 1875

Azel Ames

Source: Azel Ames, 'Typesetting', in *Sex in Industry, A Plea for the Working Girl* (James Osgood and Co, 1875), 83–95.

EDITORIAL HEADNOTE

The issue of women's industrial work often hinged on the idea that women were not strong enough to undertake active work, and throughout this collection female weakness is frequently cited as a reason to prevent them from taking on certain jobs. Not coincidentally, these were just as often jobs claimed by men. Azel Ames (see doc. 39) brought his medical training and concern for public health and his belief in women's frailty to bear on the printing trades as he did on sewing machines. Part of the tension is between women and machine technology. In this chapter, he correctly identifies the character of the industry, the skills and mental acuity required, and the pitfalls damaging to health. Most of these applied to men as well. But the second half of the extract clearly challenges women's ability to do the work, alluding to weakness and sickness, and especially comparing them to men.

TYPE-SETTING

The setting of types, the labor of the "compositor," as this servant of the public is called, holds a peculiar position in the class of physico-mental activities from the facts that the employment –

May become partially unconscious or "mechanical" labor;

Is supposed to possess certain dangers of poisoning from the nature of the metal composing the types; and –

Has in the postures necessary, its sedentary character, and the heat at which "composing-rooms" are unavoidably kept, its particular non-hygienic conditions.

DOI: 10.4324/9781003676669-55

It will readily be seen, that a closely attentive activity must be exercised to "follow copy," and accomplish a paying amount of work with sufficient correctness to satisfy employers. There can, of course, in this labor, be no distracting influences; for to "set" type with a remunerative degree of rapidity and correctness (and most type-setters are required to "correct" their own "proofs" or errors), the eye must take in the words of the copy, and their relations to each other, their punctuation and character (whether Italics or other type), and various other details known only to the guild; must transmit the intelligence absorbed by the by the hand, and direct it with celerity to that particular one of the compartments in a type "case" which contains the particular type called tor, and deftly arrange it "wrong-end first" in the proper relation to its fellows contained in the "composing-stick". To read the copy (often most illegible); to supply or correct punctuation; to determine the type "spaces," "leads," etc.; to observe the intended sense of the writer; to separate sticky type, "keep them on their feet," place them correctly, duly "spaced" and "leaded," as well as punctuated; keep the place in the copy; and do all these quickly, sometimes with cold hands, and with various interruptions, – it is obvious, is an employment that is most exacting of mental concentration and manipulative rapidity. A good female compositor can "set" and correct thirty thousand ems per week, for which she would receive thirty cents per thousand, although many are employed at a set sum per week, rarely exceeding ten dollars; and at this rate she would be expected to be able to set nearly six thousand ems per day, to accomplish which it will be seen that there must be constant labor of a very rapid character.

As an offset, however, we have the fact, that a considerable portion of the work becomes mechanical, a skilled compositor knowing, without looking, exactly where in her case to find the type wanted; while the placing it in position in the composing-stick correctly is accomplished by the aid of another of those marvellous processes of mental telegraphy with which our daily actions are replete. The type has upon one side a series of "nicks," which being felt by the finger, the brain is informed, and, without the intervention of the eye, the type is turned to the correct position, and set by the re-instructed finger. The wrong-end-first position of the type is, moreover, no impediment to the compositor, who reads "backwards" and "upside-down" as well as other people regularly read from left to right. Hence it is to be considered, that, although an employment of distinctly co-operative physico-mental activity, it is lessened in degree as such by the facility with which its processes, in part, become mechanical. It is a question not readily determined, whether or not the pernicious effects of the depressing powers of lead and antimonial poisoning (where they are operative), and of the heat and unhealthy postures mentioned, are the equivalents of the gain derived to the compositor by her power of making the work partially mechanical; and so advantage and disadvantage balance each other, and leave the employment a pure type of its class. An exceedingly interesting feature of type-setting is the fact, that it is understood, by first-class compositors, that the element of memory enters largely into, in fact becomes a governing power in, the occupation, thereby changing the direction and character of the mental concentration. Having read her copy, it is asserted that the compositor, if of good memory, retains the sentence read, in mind, follows copy no more till a fresh sentence is needed, and then concentrates all thought upon retaining the sentence and the point in it, to which work has progressed, leaving the eye free to go with the hand to the case, aiding the correctness and celerity of the latter. It is plain, that, if such is the mental process, the greater the retentive power of memory (largely, of course, a matter of training), the more freely and rapidly the work may go on, the true concentration being upon the two points mentioned; viz., the general retention of the sentence, and the place reached therein by the compositor.

It is proper to note, moreover, in this connection, that a compositor who is quick of perception, and is skilled in grammatical construction, punctuation, etc., is able to perform her work with much less fatigue than one of slower comprehension and accomplishment. Finding that the foregoing views, as to the part played by memory, and the degree of skill in perception, grammar, etc., were fully recognized, it became a matter of much interest to confirm them by actual experiment and inquiry. A well-established case was found to be familiar to the older compositor who had been an "expert," becoming totally *blind* continuing his work by having to read long extracts to him, his cultivated powers of retention remarkable; and it was found that his proofs were in the main, as correct as those of his fellows. Desirous of determining the real force of this claim, a lady compositor fully blindfolded; and, the copy being read to her, it was found that the work could undoubtedly be thus performed, though with not quite the same correctness as ordinarily, but more rapidly, and resulting in greater fatigue. The statement of the operator was to the effect, that her whole concentration of mind was upon the two points already mentioned, the retention of the copy, and her place in it; and this concentration she considered quite equivalent in demand to that required by the slower process of setting with the eyes open, stating that she missed the aid in keeping the place, obtained by the hurried glance upon the state of progress in the composing-stick. Whatever ameliorating circumstances it may possess, in any or all of the ways mentioned, it is evident that type-setting is an employ exacting an unusual degree of mental concentration and energy, with great rapidity of manipulation; and, as such, if previous hypotheses have been correct, cannot fail to have a marked effect upon the health of its female operatives. Let us see how these hypotheses are borne out by the facts, as variously obtained.

Mr. M. brought up in the business from a boy, now engaged in it for eighteen years, having worked in offices with female compositors ranging from one to twenty in number, and including from two to three hundred in his observation, states, –

> Few girls can continuously set more than five thousand ems per day, while men will set from seven to eight thousand; not because the girl is not quick in movement and perception, for she *is*, but because she cannot 'stand it,' – she is not strong enough. It seems to be the back that gives out. Girls cannot work more than eight hours, and keep it up: they

> know it, and they rarely will; and even this seems to 'pull them down,' so that it is extremely rare that a girl continues more than a few years at the business.

Mr. B –, foreman of a large printing establishment, says, –

> Girls must sit at the 'case.' I never knew but one woman, and she a strong, vigorous Irishwoman of unusual height, who could stand at the case like a man. Female compositors, as a rule, are sickly, suffering much from backache, headache, weak limbs, and general 'female weakness.'

Mr. D –, the publisher of a well-known periodical, says,

> I have had hundreds of lady compositors in my employ; and they all exhibited in a marked manner, both in the way they performed their work and in its results, the difference in physical ability between themselves and men. They cannot endure the prolonged close attention and confinement which is a great part of type-setting. I have few girls with me more than two or three years at a time; they must have vacations, and they break down in health rapidly. I know no reason why a girl could not set as much type as a man, if she were as strong to endure the demand on mind and body.

Miss J –, a lady compositor, says,

> We cannot stand at the 'case.' It increases back and head ache, and weakness of limbs, as well as a dragging weight about the hips. I have been at this work five years, but have been frequently obliged to give up for vacations, from peculiar troubles and general debility. I began to menstruate when fourteen; I am now twenty-two. I was well until I had set type a year, when I began to be troubled with difficult periods, and have been, more or less, ever since. When I go away, I get better; but, as often as I return to my work, I am troubled again. Have wholly lost color, and am not nearly as fleshy and heavy as when I began work. I have now a good deal of pain in my chest, and some cough, which increases if I work harder than usual. I am well acquainted with many other lady compositors who suffer as I do."

Miss S, a lady long in charge of the "composing-room" (female department) of a large printing establishment, testifies, –

> I was myself a compositor, and have had scores of girls under me and with me, many of whom I have known intimately. I have no hesitation in saying that I think I never knew a dozen lady compositors who were

> 'well.' Their principal troubles are those belonging to the sex, and great pain in back, limbs, and head. Most of those I have known have preferred going into other employments than to continue in the business. Many seem to recover fully after leaving the business but I have known several who have sickened and died of 'consumption', and some who are always troubled with 'female complaints'. I know a number who have married, and have children, most of them seemingly bright and healthy. Girls cannot stand at the case like men, and ought not to try to work, if it can be helped at certain periods. I think the heat and ill-ventilation of our rooms is bad for us all.

Dr. G –, a physician in one of the suburbs of Boston, gives his evidence as follows: –

> I have had several cases of menorrhagia (profuse menstruation), a few of retarded or difficult menstruation, and a single case of type-poisoning, in female compositors. They all tell me that the work produces backache and headache, with more or less trouble periodically. The case of poison was an interesting one and proved itself such conclusively. As often as the girl would leave her work for a time, her unfavorable symptoms would entirely remove: just as she took up the types again, the trouble was renewed. It is an employment requiring so close confinement, and such careful attention, that I am at no loss to understand its effects.

Mr. H –, an employé of the government printing office at Washington, informs us, –

> I have known a good many of our girls in the composing-rooms here in the city; and quite a number that I have known have come here into the work strong and healthy-looking girls, and have gone, in a few years, pale, thin, and sick. I know, from conversation with some of them, that the work upsets them as women, and they cannot continue the work long without suffering. I should say, that perhaps their pleasure-seeking after work as balls, parties, etc. has a bad effect too; but all do not follow that course.

Dr. B –, a physician to dispensary patients, says, –

> I have seen quite a number of female typesetters who were suffering from uterine troubles and disturbed menstrual conditions. I think that these, with obstinate constipation, and occasional cystitis (inflammation of bladder), are their chief troubles, besides the ever-present 'headache.' Mind and body are compelled to act so quickly in that work, that I am not surprised at nervous effects, particularly in young women not fully developed.

It will be seen from the foregoing, that the female compositors themselves, their employers and associates, those who superintend them, and their physicians, all agree to the effects of the labor, and the latter recognize the cause. Although subject to modifying, and to a certain degree puzzling, circumstances, there can, apparently, be no doubt of the relation existing between type-setting, as an employment possessing the physico-mental draft, and the conditions found to exist in those devoted to it. Counting it, therefore, as an interesting and conclusive illustration of the physico-mental influence upon the peculiar function of woman, . . .

51

WOMEN'S LABOUR PRINTING, ROYAL COMMISSION ON LABOR 1893

Margaret Irwin

Source: Margaret Irwin, 'Women's Labour: Printing', in *Reports, On the Conditions of Work in Various Industries in England, Wales, Scotland, and Ireland*, Miss Eliza Orme, Miss Clara E. Collet, Miss May E. Abraham, and Miss Margaret H. Irwin, Royal Commission on Labour (HMSO, 1893), 290–91.

EDITORIAL HEADNOTE

Margaret Irwin (1858–1940) was one of four women assistant commissioners responsible for gathering and returning information about the conditions of working women on behalf of the royal commission on labour, along with Clara Collet (doc. 25), Margaret Orme and May Abraham. Born at sea as the daughter of a master mariner of Broughty Ferry, she was awarded the lady literate in arts (LLA) in 1880 from St Andrews University and followed this with classes at Glasgow School of Arts and Glasgow's Queen Margaret College. She acquired Sholach Fruit Farm at Blairgowrie in Perthshire, which she ran as a model farm. She was committed to the suffrage movement and focused on equal rights for women workers. In 1891 she was appointed by the Scottish branch of the Women's Protective and Provident League as its full-time organiser, which, in the Glasgow area, was associated with the Glasgow Council for Women's Trades. These were in turn linked to the National Federal Council of Scotland for Women's Trades, which in 1895 claimed affiliation to sixteen trades councils and twenty-five unions with over 100,000 members in all.

Irwin continued as organiser of the league until 1895 when she became secretary of the Scottish Council for Women's Trades (SCWT). Despite also becoming influential in the Scottish Trades union movement, there were tensions in the movement about middle-class influences, and she was often attacked for being less vigourous than some wished. Attempts to remove her

DOI: 10.4324/9781003676669-56

from the parliamentary committee failed in 1899, but she refused to stand for nomination. Throughout the rest of her life, she continued to pursue issues related to women's trades, as well as public health and factory legislation. She was criticised for taking a philanthropic view of improvement in women's causes; she was not a trade unionist at heart and became more closely linked to the Fabian Women's Group and the Liberal Party.

Her report on printing focuses on the Scottish industry and especially Edinburgh (see also Vol. 4) and is a clear description of the character of the industry at the end of the century as well as the gender division of labour. Essentially positive, she included evidence from the workers themselves, which is extracted in doc. 51.

IX. – PRINTING

Edinburgh is the only centre in Scotland in which employment are to be found employed in the printing trade to any important extent. It is estimated that about 300 women are engaged there as compositors.

The houses which employ girls are chiefly engaged in the book trade. Those confined to "job" or commercial work do not employ them, as the latter involves so much lifting of heavy "chases" and "formes" which women cannot undertake.

There are also certain parts of the work in all branches of the printing trade which the physical disabilities of women preclude them from taking up. Such for instance is correcting on the "stone." This requires the worker to lean in a doubled over position on the large table or "stone" while making corrections. I observed a girl employed in this way on my visit to one shop, but I ascertained from employers and workers that it was not customary to ask girls to do this part of the work.

"Proof pulling" is also exclusively taken up by men. It requires both muscular strength and a certain "knack."

Women were introduced into the printing trade during a strike on the part of the men in 1872 for a 51 hours week. On this account the Typographical Society has, in its collective capacity, no friendly feeling towards them, and they also consider that as women work at a lower rate than themselves they furnish a standing obstacle in the way of any movement on the part of the men for an advance of wages. It is doubtful, however, if the women could be used as more than a temporary substitute for the men compositors, owing to their not being able to take up all the branches which the men take up.

An instance of the extent of the displacement of male by female, labour is furnished by one firm. Previous to the strike in 1872 sixty journeymen were employed in this shop. At present the average number is 12, while from 80 to 100 girls are employed in it.

I was informed by Mr. John Battersby, late general secretary for Scotland to the Typographical Society, and by the present secretary of the Edinburgh branch, that there is a growing tendency in the trade to give what is technically known as "fat work" to the women instead of to the men. "Fat work" is the well spaced work, and as the quadrates, or spaces, are paid at the same rate as the type, a larger amount of this work can be got over than of ordinary work in the same time, and a larger wage is earned by those on piece-work. Consequently the women frequently get it in preference to the men because they take it at lower rates.

There is no uniform rate of wages or even system payment for women throughout the printing trade. Some houses pay a piece-work wage and others what in trade parlance is called a "stab," i.e., established, or time wage. In the case of piece-work the rates for men and women are:

Men 6¾d. per 1,000.
Women 3d. to 5d. per 1,000.
On the "stab" or time wage, a girl may start at 4s. per week and rise to 9s., 12s., 15s. The "stab wage" for men is a minimum of 32s. and a maximum of 37s. 6d. per week.

An example of the difference in total wages earned which payment by time or piece may make with a certain class of work, was given me by witness No. 707.

The printing of a county valuation roll was entrusted to two firms. One of them got one-half and employed their women workers on it at a piece-work wage of 4d. per 1,000, with the result that the girls made from 20s. to 35s. a week off this one order while it lasted. The other got the other half and paid their women workers a "stab" wage of 15s. per week.

The following statement has been supplied to me by a member of firm 209, one of the leading houses in the trade.

"The women workers are employed in –

(1.) Composing, reading, warehouse, machine rooms.
(2.) They have not supplanted men anywhere that I know of. Women were first introduced into the case room in 1872. The girls in our employment are in many cases daughters of compositors and machine men, and men employed in the other departments of the establishment.
(3.) In all departments women are paid by time, except now and then in the book folding department, where a piece scale sometimes obtains.
(4.) The comparative rates of pay for male and female compositors are, approximately, men 6½d. per thousand, women 4½d. to 5d. per thousand; but the difference between the rate paid to women and that paid to men is almost entirely swallowed up by the additional work which the men require to do for the women, viz., making up, correcting, carrying about formes between the stones and the proof presses, &c. About the only work which women can do in the case room is to stand or sit at their frames and set up type; and to distribute the types back again into the cases, but, of course, this is only

a portion of a compositor's work. The best women compositors cannot turn out more than two-thirds of the out put of the best men.

(5.) An average woman attains about her highest proficiency in type-setting in five or six years.

(6.) The number of women and girls employed is as under:

Case room – – – – – –	77
Warehouse – – – – – – –	77
Machine room – – – –	52
	206

(7.) There are no married women employed in our establishment.

(8.) There is no special tendency either to develope or fall, off in any department. The supply of female labour is abundant, and it either developes or falls off according as we are busy or slack.

My experience of the printing trade shows me that women are healthy, well paid, and contented. The women employed are of good character and regular habits. As far as my own experience goes, they remain for long periods of years in the service, of the firm.

Indeed, they rarely leave except to get married.

Another point, which, I think, shows that they are contented, is that they introduce their relations, in the shape of sisters &c., and, as I mentioned before, many of the men bring their daughters, and ask for them to be employed in the various departments of the establishment.

I was informed by the employer in firm No. 209 that he purposed (sic) introducing women workers to pack and sort the type in his type-casting department. The work here consists in separating the type as it comes from the casting machine and making it up into bundles.

Boys are at present employed and are paid from 9s. to 12s. a week. The employer stated boys would not remain long at that wage, but he thought women might be able to do so and he was prepared to pay them, a steady wage up to: 12s. a week.

On my visit to firm No. 208 I was informed that the comparative rates paid to men and women workers by this house were follows: –

Men – 6¾d. per 1000
Women – 4½d. per 1000

The employer estimated the cost of supplementary labour required for the girls as adding 1d. to the above rates paid them, while 1¾d. shows the real difference between the cost of the men's work and that of the women. It was also stated that certain classes of work such as "scheme" work, and work requiring a high degree of skill in arranging, spacing, &c., is never given to women, as they rarely remain long enough in the trade to acquire the experience and skill necessary for it.

The girls in the employ of this firm start on a time 4s. a week and rise 1s. per year, until at the end of three years they are put on piece-work, after that the wages are: – minimum 7s. 8d., average 13s. 8d., maximum 19s. 2d. This employer stated that the printing trade in his opinion could only be kept in Edinburgh by means of cheap labour, and that the employment of women helped largely to this end. He went on to say that the pressure of competition induced employers to engage women in their own interests when possible, but independent of that he considered the work highly suitable for women, and that he found it attracted a class of female workers who were superior as regards intelligence and social habits.

On my visit to firm No. 206 I was informed that the comparative rates paid to both sexes are as follows: –

Men – – – 6d. per 1,000
Women – – – 3½d. per 1,000

Beginners start on a time wage of 3s. 6d. per week for the first six months, with a rise of 6d. per week every half-year, until after three years they are put on piece-work, after that the wage may be minimum 10s. maximum 18, the maximum being attained by the 5th or 6th year.

This house is largely employed on Government work, much of which consists of filling in tables which pays the workers very well.

I saw here several girls employed on type-setting machines. This is very light work, but requires some time to become proficient. It closely resembles type writing. The girls in this case are paid from 1s. 1d. to 1s. 11d. per line, and the total wage varies from 13s. to 16s. per week according to the skill of the worker.

Here, as in the other houses, the employer informed me it was necessary to supplement the work of the girls with men's labour. He declared himself unable to give me an accurate estimate of the cost of this supplementary labour, on account of it varying so much in amount according to the class of work done.

With regard to corrections, I was informed that the workers must correct their own typographical errors, but that authors' alterations are paid for in the same way as ordinary work.

52

PRINTING – WORKERS' EVIDENCE, ROYAL COMMISSION ON LABOUR, 1893

Margaret Irwin

Source: Margaret Irwin, 'Printing – Workers' Evidence', in *On the Conditions of Work in Various Industries in England, Wales, Scotland, And Ireland*, Miss Eliza Orme, Miss Clara E. Collet, Miss May E. Abraham, and Miss Margaret H. Irwin, Royal Commission on Labour 1893, 291–92.

EDITORIAL HEADNOTE

Irwin's workers' evidence substantiates the report she gave and indicates the character of the investigative work that supported this report and many others like it.

WORKERS' EVIDENCE

The following evidence was submitted to me by witness No. 720, who is an experienced worker.

Witness makes between 15s. and 16s. a week. In the setting of tables girls are paid 3½d. an hour, and make 15s. 4d. a week.

The rates of payment for this class of work could only be reckoned by the time taken to do it. It is considered profitable work by the women, and, although not regular, is frequent in the shop where witness is employed. On the type setting machines the girls are paid 1s. 4d., 1s. 6d., and 1s. 11d. per line, the higher rates being paid for the smaller type. Witness thought this "as broad as it was long," because with large type, although paid at a lower rate, the lines were filled more quickly. There was no illegal overtime in any shop witness knew of, and legal overtime was paid a little over regular time.

Slack time lasts about a month in the year, with perhaps two or three afternoons off in the week. Wages may sink to 7s. 6d. during this, but the girls are never paid off.

DOI: 10.4324/9781003676669-57

In respect of deductions and fines time-workers lose the time they are late and piece-workers are fined 1d. for a "late entrance" of five minutes after the hour.

Girls correct their own mistakes at the expense of their own time, but authors' alterations are paid for at ordinary rates. Time-workers, being mostly beginners, do not suffer deductions for time spent in correcting their mistakes.

Men do the same work as women in many cases and at different rates, but there are certain parts of the work that women never do, such, for instance, as the lifting of the "formes" and "chases." Witness could not say how much of a man's time this might occupy per day. In her shop one man lifted the "chases," &c. for twenty girls and did his own work in addition.

Witness thinks the work very pleasant and suitable for women. She has no complaints to make as regards its effects on her health, but has sometimes found working with small type to be a slight strain on her eyesight. She has heard other girls say the same but has never known of any serious results in this way, only slight where a long spell of work in unusually small type was involved.

The sanitary arrangements in witness' shop are perfectly satisfactory.

Witness No. 721 has been engaged in the printing trade since women were first introduced into it. All the girls in her shop are on time wages of from 5s. to 13s. a week. When legal overtime is worked the girls are paid so much extra per 100 lines, the rate varying according to the size. Sometimes this brings the wage up to 17s. or 18s. a week. Beginners start at 5s. per week and rise 1s. per annum.

Slack time sometimes lasts a month or more, but the wages are not reduced although no work comes in, only the girls are expected to be in the shop and ready to take it should it come.

No deductions are made for typographical mistakes. Workers are allowed to be late three times in the week and for five minutes on each occasion. Late attendance in excess of this is fined from 1d. to 2d.

Authors' alterations are paid at from 2d. to 4d. per hour, according to the age and experience of the worker. Men are paid 7½d. an hour for these.

In the regular book work the girls do the same work as the men, but they do not lift their own "formes" and "chases." Witness could not say how much help in this a girl would need from the men because it varied so much, but she did not think it amounted to much, and no special men workers were employed for it. The men get the more "experienced and difficult work" and they "put more through their hands."

Has never felt the work injure her health in any way, and has no complaints to make regarding effects on the eyesight.

Good work rooms and comfortable cloak rooms and lavatory accommodation are provided. Arrangements are also made for heating food if required.

A sick benefit society is established in connexion with the work, the rate of contribution being 1d. per week, which entitles members to 4s. aliment per week and medical attendance during sickness.

Special Evidence

I made special inquiry among employers and operatives as to whether the antimony in the type had any injurious effect on the health of the workers.

An employer, witness No. 706, informed me they had had one case of blood poisoning among their women workers, but this, in his opinion, had been caused by carelessness, the worker in question having been in the habit of putting her fingers in her mouth at a time when suffering from an eruption on her lips, symptoms of blood poisoning had ensued from this practice.

This is the only case of illness arising from this cause I have met in the course of my investigations into the printing trade.

I append the following statement received from Dr. Brewis, who is the medical officer for the Typographical Society.

8th February 1893.

In answer to your inquiry regarding the health of women employed in printing works, I have to say that it has not been my experience to find them suffering from any illness that could be traced to the materials with which they work.

Dyspepsia and anaemia are their most common complaints, and are due in a large measure to the insufficiency of the midday meal.

(Signed) N. T. Brewis.

53

PRINTING, 1910

Edith Abbott

Source: Edith Abbott, 'Printing', in *Women in Industry: A Study in American Economic History* (D. Appleton and Company, 1910), 246–49; 258–61.

EDITORIAL HEADNOTE

Edith Abbott's book, *Women in Industry*, was a substantial study of American women in industry. Its opening chapter is extracted in doc. 2. Here she makes the case that printing was important for women partly because so many women were engaged in it but also that it was an old established hand craft, one which machinery has been slow to change. Like Irwin, her account sets out the character of the work and the implications of the industry for women and makes the link between older hand craft traditions and modern industry, this time from an American perspective. It is also a model of investigative research, and her references are indicative of a careful and informed approach to the subject. See also Vol. 4 on industrial relations and women in printing.

IN 1905 more than 37,000 women were employed in the printing trades in this country. The industry, however, is important from the point of view of women's work, not merely because so many women are engaged in it, but because it is one of the old skilled hand trades. Printing, like shoemaking, was one of the historic crafts and one which machinery has been very slow to change. As long as so many of the industrial occupations in which women are found are unskilled, their connection with a trade which requires training and skill is of special interest.

The employment of women in the industry known as "printing and publishing" has a long history. In the eighteenth century there were a great many women printers. The States of Massachusetts, Connecticut, Rhode Island, Pennsylvania, New York, Maryland, Virginia, and South Carolina each had one or more of them. These women worked as compositors as well as at the press.[1] Several

DOI: 10.4324/9781003676669-58

colonial newspapers were published by women, and they printed books and pamphlets as well.

Margaret Draper of Massachusetts "printed" for the governor and council; in South Carolina a woman was appointed printer to the State after the close of the Revolutionary War; and Benjamin Franklin's sister-in-law at Newport, in Rhode Island, printed for the colony, supplied blanks for the public offices, published pamphlets, and in 1745 printed for the Government an edition of the laws, containing three hundred and forty folio pages. Her two daughters who assisted her in printing were said to have been "correct and quick compositors at case."

Although the number of women printers has always been small compared with the number of men in the trade, there has probably never been a time for more than a hundred years when women have not found employment in printing offices. Dr. Thomas, writing in 1815, called attention to the fact that women and girls were "not infrequently" employed as compositors; and at the same time he cited as an example of the kind of work they could do, that two women who were then working in a printing house in Philadelphia performed "their week's work with as much fidelity as most of the journeymen."

Although there is a good deal of indirect evidence[2] to show that women worked steadily in printing offices throughout the first half of the last century, very few data can be found relating to the number of women employed. Such statistics of employment as were collected in the first half century were, for the most part, got to show the progress our manufacturing industries were making and the need of protecting them; and the printing and publishing trade was at that time of too little importance even to "foster." Some few data exist for 1832, but they relate chiefly to other branches of the printing trades.

In Boston, for example, 15 bookbinders[3] in that year employed 60 men at $1.25 a day, 90 women at 50 cents, and 30 boys at the same wage. Ten manufacturers of blank books had 40 men, 20 women, and 20 boys at work at the same rates that were paid for bookbinding. Bookbinding, however, seems to have employed a larger proportion of women than other parts of the trade at this time. A few other data for 1831 bear out this statement. In New Haven, Conn., 16 men and 16 women were employed in bookbinding and 50 men and only 20 women in "publishing."

Two lithographing and 15 engraving establishments employed 16 men, 30 women, and 10 boys, the last probably apprentices. The type and stereotype founders employed 83 men at $1.50 a day, 55 women at from 42 to 50 cents, and 29 boys at 45 cents. The copperplate printers had 50 employees, all men and boys. Twenty publishers and booksellers employed a large number of hands, 400 men at $1.50 a day, 200 women at 40 cents, and 80 boys at 50 cents. No women were reported in the newspaper offices, where, altogether, 48 men and 36 boys were employed.[4] By way of summary, it may be said that the allied printing trades of Boston in 1831 together employed 687 men, most of whom were paid $1.50 a day, 395 women, most of whom were paid 50 cents a day; and 215 boys, who were paid in general at the same rate as the women.[5] . . .

How far the proportion of women in the trade as a whole may be increasing, it is not possible to say. Statistics for the industry, "printing and publishing," are not comparable except for very recent years. Such data, however, as are available for this purpose, are interesting. The following tables show (1) the number of men, women, and children in the "book and job" branch of the trade, the only branch for which statistics were collected before 1930; and (2) the more recent data relating to the industry as a whole, which includes newspaper and periodical as well as book and job work.

PRINTING

Persons Employed in Book and Job Printing,1880–1905[6]

	1880	1890	1900	1905
Men	45,890	40,010	52,311	65,748
Women	6,777	9,439	13,950	20,086
Children	5,839	1,412	2,127	2,489
Total Number of Employees	58,506	50,861	68,388	88,323
Percentage of Women	12	19	20	23

Persons Employed in "Printing and Publishing"

	1880	1890	1900	1905
Men		110,434	125,964	142,555
Women		19,026	28,765	37,614
Children		7,7736	8,263	5,011
Total Number of Employees		137,196	162,992	185,180
Percentage of Women		14	18	20

These tables seem to indicate (1) that although women have been for so long identified with the trade, the men outnumber them four to one and printing is still pretty exclusively men's work; (2) that the proportion of women is increasing, but not at such an alarming rate that the women can be said to be "driving out the men"; (3) that the proportion of women is larger in the "book and job" branch than in the trade as a whole, which includes newspaper work.

In general it may be said, by way of summary, that the history of the printing trade is of rather special interest from the point of view of the employment of women. Although it is a skilled trade, the work is light enough for it to be suitable for women. In fact, an official of the American Federation of Labor in testimony before the Industrial Commission in 1899 characterized the work of the printing trade as "peculiarly women's work." Typesetting, moreover, is work in which women were employed early in the eighteenth century and in which they have been employed ever since, but all of the time the men have treated it as a trade belonging especially to themselves. Officers of other trade unions frequently refer to the policy of the printers as an example of the way in which trade union control may be successful in checking or preventing the employment of women. The woman competitor, it is said, has been a comparatively slight problem in the printing trade. It is not surprising, therefore, in the light of the organized hostility of the men, that while the women have more than held their own in the trade, their position remains a discouraging one. They are not as efficient as men, and at present there is no direct path to efficiency open to them. They are now admitted to the unions on the same terms as men, they pay the same dues, and receive the same benefits; but this is all done to protect the wage scale, not to encourage women to enter the trade. As a matter of fact, a comparatively small percentage of the women who work in printing offices belong to the union. A woman is not "worth as much" as a man who works as an "all-around" printer, and to join the union and demand the same rate of wages is to invite discharge. Most women consider it safer, therefore, to work in a nonunion shop where they will be allowed to take lower wages than the men. In the unions, the women form an insignificant minority; they seldom hold an office, and they have little influence in directing union policies.

Source Endnotes

1 That is, at setting type. See Isaiah Thomas, "History of Printing in America," i, *passim*

2 Much of this is found in the records of the early printers' unions and will be discussed in connection with the attitude of the union to women's work. There are, of course, other statements, like the quotations from White, "Slater" *(supa,* p. 77), or the statement of Miss Martineau that typesetting was an occupation open to women when she visited America. See Chapter V, this volume, p. 77.

3 Just what processes women carried on in bookbinding is not altogether clear, but miscellaneous wages statistics for the decade 1830–40 in Massachusetts show that they were employed as collectors, folders, pasters, and sewers. Other data relating to wages in the following decade show that one establishment employed 21 women and 1 man as press feeders, and in the same occupation in the same establishment 14 women and 12 men were employed in 1891. See "Aldrich Report," 11, 344. In Establishment Six (New York) women were also employed as press feeders and in Establishment Five (New York) as pressroom hands.

4 In general, it may be pointed out here that women printers have never been employed to any extent on the great city newspapers where the work is, much of it, done under pressure and at night. In smaller towns women frequently set type for local papers, but in large cities their work is more strictly confined to "book and job" offices.

5 The various data included in this summary were found in "Documents Relative to Manufactures" House Executive Documents, 1st session, 22d Congress, i and ii, (1832), i, 436, 458, 464.

6 From Bulletin 70, 1905 "Census of Manufactures," p. 21; the table relating to the "Printing and Publishing" trade as a whole is from p. 10.

54

PRINTING, LABOR ORGANIZATIONS STRONG IN EXECUTIVE DEPARTMENTS AT WASHINGTON

Source: 'Printing', Labor Organizations Strong in Executive Departments at Washington, *New York Call*, August 26, 1903.

EDITORIAL HEADNOTE

Although unions and organising in the workplace are discussed more fully in Vol. 4, this brief report indicates the breadth of women's work in the printing industry and a clear acceptance of them in printing. The *New York Call* was a socialist English-language newspaper, and this article was also repeated in the *New York Times* of the same date. Research on the *New York Call* suggests it did not begin until 1908, so the origin and provenance of this paper cannot be accurately established.

WASHINGTON, Aug. 25. – The agitation that has followed the reinstatement of Miller, the assistant foreman in the bookbindery of the Government Printing Office, gives interest to the data which have been collected by one of the officials of the Federation of Labor about the number of union men in Government employ in Washington. It has been rumored that a settled policy of repression has been decided on among the various department heads, and that wherever the labor unions attempt to dictate to a member of the Cabinet or to the President about rules in regard to employees, or as to who shall be permitted to work, there will be a firm and uncompromising resistance to such encroachments on official prerogatives. This is a matter that is being discussed among the unions.

The strongest union in any government bureau is the typographical union known as Columbia No. 101. There are over 1,000 members. Allied to Columbia No. 101 is the Bookbinders' Union, embracing 700 members, of whom 400 are women and 300 men. In the pressmen's union are 250 members; in the stererotypers 40, in the electrotypers 30, and in the feeders 100.

DOI: 10.4324/9781003676669-59

There are fifty carpenters, plumbers, and electricians also in the printing offices and the departments who belong to labor unions. The strong labor organization at the navy yard is Washington Lodge No. 138, which has about 1,000 members, a large part of whom are employed in the yard. In the Bureau of Engraving and Printing the plate printers' union has 150 members. There are 200 printers' assistants, all women; 50 pressmen, and 100 feeders in the bureau who belong to the union. Connected with the Library of Congress are said to be 500 printers, binders, and mechanics of various sorts who belong to unions.

In view of the strength of the unions in these different branches of the government service the labor leaders are talking of taking their grievances to Congress next winter and insisting on an investigation.

New York Call, August 26, 1903.

Part 6

THE SWEATED TRADES REVEALED

55

EXTRACTS ON HOMEWORK FROM 'FEMALE INDUSTRY', 1859

Harriet Martineau

Source: Harriet Martineau, extracts on Homework from '*Female Industry*', *Edinburgh Review,* 222 (April 1859), 293, 320–329.

EDITORIAL HEADNOTE

Harriet Martineau (1802–1876) came from an old Huguenot family of Norwich; she struggled throughout her life with a series of physical disorders and by age twenty was virtually deaf. With a Unitarian and radical family background, she wrote widely on religious, political and philosophical issues. When her family's business failed, she began to write for her own support, although she was already widely published. She was relieved when her fiancée died, celebrating the single life in her autobiography. She continued an active and prolific philanthropic and literary life despite recurring health problems, which she later claimed were cured by mesmerism. A sometimes difficult woman, she was alternately praised and criticised by her peers. In 1858 she began writing for the *Edinburgh Review,* a significant publication attracting the politically progressive households of the time, and 'Female Industry' appeared the following year. This was a lengthy dissertation on women's work in which she claimed, 'Out of six millions of women above twenty years of age, in Great Britian, exclusive of Ireland, and of course of the Colonies, no less than half are industrial in their mode of life. More than a third, more than two millions, are independent in their industry, are self-supporting, like men.' Written just after the Matrimonial Causes Act, 1857, the article supported the amount of women's industrial work that divorce courts were revealing. Her main claim, in keeping with most of the women writing in this volume, was that for working women, 'their work should be paid for by its quality, and its place in the market, irrespective of the status of the worker.' These brief extracts show the extent to which homework occupied women at mid-century and how it had already become sweated in several industries, rather than being an artifact of the end of the century.

. . . in considering the female industry of the United Kingdom, that of Ireland is the most prominent, and commands the most surprise. It will be ever memorable that during the transition period in which Ireland passed over from destitution and despair to comfort and progress, the nation was mainly supported by the industry of the women. . . . In the succeeding period, and after the famine, the desire for the lowest-priced labour led to the employment of women and children . . . it was not only, nor chiefly, the agricultural labour however which fed the peasantry, before the men resumed their proper place. The Scotch merchants employed 400,000 women and girls in 'sewing,' or what English ladies call 'working' muslins. The Glasgow employers paid 90,000£ a week in wages for this Irish work. A good deal more was earned by other kinds of fine fabrics.

This topic leads us directly into the middle of the great question, – perhaps the most important of all the practical considerations connected with the subject of female industry; – the effect of manufacturing employment on the domestic qualities of women. We have no space here, – and it is no part of our present duty, – to discuss the *pros* and *cons* of factory life for our female population. We have to glance at the facts of the extent of that kind of occupation, and at the probabilities of its being reconciled with that domestic existence for which women are constituted, and to which they sooner or later return, after every experiment which the progress of civilisation inflicts, amidst its play of social changes.

The number of women employed in textile manufactures in 1851 were nearly 385,000. Under this head are included cotton and its fabrics, woollen, flax, silk, straw, lace, and articles in fur, hair and hemp, and the paper manufacture. In the mechanical arts which usually rank in the same class, such, as metal-works and earthenware, there were nearly 40,000. With these two classes may be united the third, – the women engaged in providing and treating Dress; – making, mending, and washing articles of dress. These are set down as above half-a-million. The three amount to within a fraction of a million. If we could include the women of Ireland, so largely engaged in the linen, cambric, and muslin manufactures of Ulster, and in the embroidery of muslins (as we have already shown), and in lace-making and knitted goods, the number would be greatly increased. Now, what a section of the nation this is, – a million and a quarter of women above twenty, earning an independent subsistence by manufacturing industry! The condition, claims, and prospects of such a section of the population ought to be as important and interesting to us as those of any class of men in the community.

The three sorts of employment need not here be considered separately. In the case of textile manufactures, the greater port of the work is done in factories; but not a little is carried, on at home, – looms being set up in the cottage, or in the town lodging. In such old towns as Norwich and in many a village in the eastern counties, the click and smack of the loom is heard in the narrow streets and over garden walls, as it is in the singular region of Spitalfields. A visitor will find the family engaged in winding, piecing and weaving, – father, mother, boys and girls all doing different parts of the work: and this is just the case of a large proportion of the Birmingham' metal workers. They have a light room, which they call a shop, where they work together at the articles which are to be completed by a certain time. So it is with the occupations which relate to dress. The lace-maker is an old-fashioned figure in English life, – sitting at her door with her pillow before her, and her fingers busy among the bobbins. So it is with the straw-platter, and the clear-starcher and mender, and the artificial-flower maker, and the embroiderer, and, as we may see in every street, with the dress-maker. The 'Song of the Shirt' tells us that this is the way also with poor needlewomen. On the other hand, the factory, and gregarious occupation in many modes, is not now, as formerly, supposed to mean cotton or flax spinning. Silk, cotton, and flax mills may still be the representatives of the factory life of English women; but genuine factory-life can be seen at Birmingham as truly as at Manchester or Leeds. Long ranges of upper apartments in Birmingham factories are occupied by women, sitting in rows, quiet, diligent and skilful, putting together the links of cobweb gold chains, or burnishing silver plate, or cutting and polishing screws (a manufacture mainly in their hands, because the machinery requires delicate manipulation), or sorting needles, or painting *papier-mâché* trays. Of the 40,000 female workers in metals and clay, the greater portion now are factory-women, as much as any Lancashire or Yorkshire spinners or weavers. As for the third class, not only are the Nottingham and Leicester lace-makers and hosiery weavers of the genuine manufacturing class, but the London dressmakers may be called so; and the upholstresses too. They are collected, not always in large apartments alas! but in considerable numbers, and under a scheme of division of labour, – which is, we suppose, on an extensive scale, the distinction between domestic and factory labour; a distinction not interfered with by the distribution of portions of the work to different members of the family at home. Whatever may be the respective proportions of the factory and domestic workers who make up the million and a quarter of industrial women now under notice, it is a question of the deepest interest to us all, in every view whether the factory-work is likely to increase or diminish in years to come.

At first sight, most of us are disposed to pronounce that the number will certainly increase. The demand for industry seems at present rather to exceed the supply, – generally speaking. We want more soldiers, more sailors, more agricultural labourers and town workers while emigration carries off tens of thousands every year. The rapid increase of labour-saving machinery indicates a want, rather than a superfluity, of hands and so does the liberty to work which has been acquired by women within a few years. It is not now long since the Coventry men were as jealous and tyrannical about the women winding silks and weaving ribbons as they are still about their engraving watch plates; yet now many thousands of women are earning a subsistence in the ribbon and fringe manufacture. The increasing use of sewing-machines, at centres dressmaking, tailoring and blouse and shirt making, points in the same direction. In a community where a larger proportion of women remain unmarried than at any known period; where a greater number of women depend on their own industry for subsistence; where every pair of hands, moved by an intelligent head, is in request; and where improved machinery demands more and more of the skilled labour which women can supply, how can there be a doubt that the women will work more and more, and in aggregate ways, as combination becomes better understood and practised? . . .

The wife of a respectable watchmaker wished, as did her husband, that she should work with him at his special division of the manufacture: but they dared not attempt it, under the eyes of the craft. She therefore engraved the 'brass work,' – a commoner and easier kind of work. As soon as the fact was discovered, an outcry was raised, and intimidation was tried, to drive her from her occupation. She kept her husband steady to their household plan: but it was only by permitting their friends to set up a plea of apprenticeship, on the ground of her father having been seen to do that kind of work in her presence, that she obtained any peace and quiet. She brought up her two daughters to the business, while training them in housewifery as well. By this time we hope many daughters and sisters are seen, as we have seen a few, enamelling the faces of watches, polishing them, inscribing the hours, and conducting the nicest mysteries of the art. If it is true, as we are assured, and as may well be, that the parts of watches made by Swiss women are imported into this country, it seems impossible that our countrywomen should be long excluded from that province of industry. It seems incredible that some thousands of foreign women should be supported by making watches for us to buy dear, while thousands of needlewomen should be starving in London, for want of permission to supply us with cheaper watches. . . . As for the mode in which the change will be made, – we may obtain a hint from the Swiss. The watchmakers are an educated class; and the more highly they are educated the better are the watches they produce. The fact appears to be undisputed; and the lesson is sufficiently plain.

This last topic would naturally lead us to consider other arts, requiring a higher education, which women have found it difficult to get leave to practise: but we must first devote a few moments to the miserable class of poor needlewomen, – whether the makers of shirts and trowsers or of gowns and petticoats. The sempstresses are returned as nearly 61,000 at the time of the last census; and the milliners and dressmakers as nearly half a million.

The wretched dependents on the slop shops are suffering under the last struggles of their art with the improvements of the time. We see the sewing-machine coming into use. It will do great things; and it will bring in further methods which will extinguish the craft of the poor needlewoman. Already we hear of more than one establishment in London which uses seventy of these machines, each of which dispatches as much work as fifteen pairs of hands; and of provincial shops, where the introduction of one machine has caused the dismissal of thirty women and girls. At first, it was supposed that only long rows of plain work could be done in this way; but now we hear of shirt-collars, gloves, and other delicate pieces of stitching being done, as well as saddlery and harness-making, and shoes. Both the needle and the awl are largely superseded by it; and it can be managed by even young children. Thus is the case of poor needlewomen to be solved! They can scarcely be worse off than at present; and if the change should reintroduce the art of genuine sewing, our countrywomen will have reason to rejoice. At present, we hear it said, that the art of sewing seems wellnigh lost in England, except among the ladies who have a taste for it, or who were trained by an unfashionable grandmother. The superiority of French *lingères* to English sempstresses is most remarkable, and proves that the handiwork of sewing is far better taught and practised in France than in England.

No machinery can supersede sewing altogether, though it may, and ought to, extinguish slopmaking at fourpence a day: and whereas scarcely a good sempstress can now be obtained, for love or money, we may hope to witness so much restoration of the art as is needed for economy and neatness. It is not desirable to wear out eyes, and spend precious time in marking letters, with a fine needle and coloured thread, on a cambric handkerchief, when we are in possession of marking inks, and practised in drawing with a free hand: but we must have a release from the ragged edges, loose buttons, galling shirt-collars, and unravelled seams and corners which have come up as the quality of needlewomen has gone down. Let our wives undertake the case of the remnant of the poor sempstresses, – the last, we hope, of their sort. Many may be retained for the management of sewing-machines. Many may emigrate, under careful arrangements. The younger may possibly be even yet taught to sew properly, or to do something else that is useful; and all might, by a sufficient and well-concerted effort, be kept out of the hands of the middleman. That department of the industrial market is undergoing vital changes. If some thousands of suffering women are to see their loathed occupation extinguished, the ladies of England should see that the two or three millions of girls who are soon to be maintaining themselves by their industry shall be exercised in all household arts, (and the needle, not last nor least) as the proper foundation of all others. . . .

56

POOR WOMEN OF NINETEENTH-CENTURY FRANCE, 1866

Julie-Victoire Daubié

Source: Julie-Victoire Daubié, *The Poor Women of the 19th century*, Commissioned by the Academie of Lyon, 1866.

EDITORIAL HEADNOTE

Julie-Victoire Daubié (1824–1874) was a French journalist. Largely self-taught, she gained a teaching certificate but was routinely rejected by French universities, despite no law prohibiting women from attending. In 1858, the Lyon Imperial Academy of Science and Fine Letters put the following question in an essay competition: what would be the best means, the most practical measures,

1) To raise women's salaries to the same level as men's when there is equality of service or work.
2) To open up new careers for women and offer them jobs that are successively taken away from them by competition from men and the transformation of customs.

She submitted a 300-page essay on 'Poor Woman in the 19th Century. Female Conditions and Resources', from which this extract is taken, and after winning first prize she was admitted. In August 1861, she became the first woman to present herself at the baccalaureate exams, at thirty-seven years old. She set up an embroidery workshop, run by her niece, became a journalist campaigning for women's right and in 1871, she became an arts graduate in Lyon, becoming the first female licentiate in letters. The essay presents an interesting contrast to most in this collection, coming from a Catholic country where convents also played a role in women's sweated work.

DOI: 10.4324/9781003676669-62

INTRODUCTION

A careful examination of this program of such remarkable precision, shows that it is linked to the highest economic and moral questions, because the woman who is not isolated in the social order, carries with her the destinies of childhood and exercises a great influence on the grown man. Also, we can attribute the deep malaise of our time to the inferior condition of the daughter of the people above all to the contradictory laws which regulate her fate, and whose inconsequential character is very prejudicial to the whole social economy.

Despite the theoretical rights to civil equality that our legislation grants to all citizens, regardless of sex, our administrative centralization declares a ban against poor woman by pushing her away from schools and public jobs, and our laws and morals overwhelm her under the burden of motherhood after rejecting this woman without a profession, without means of subsistence, outside of society and the domestic hearth. We can therefore be convinced that our century has taken away from this girl of the people the protective institutions of ancient France, the equitable laws and the fruitful promises of the Revolution, and has destroyed for us both the past and the future.

I tried, in the course of this work, to bring out the disastrous consequences of a state of affairs which damages both morality, justice, humanity, individual rights and public rights. I don't know if I can flatter myself that I have always indicated a fairly practical means for the repression of our incessant attacks on human dignity. . . .

CHAPTER 1, CAUSES OF POVERTY

For industry itself, the vice of our social organization is so great; the conditions of free weaving apprenticeship are so bad for the young girl, that our industrial cloisters enrich themselves by signing contracts with the apprentices required to give the use of their time in exchange of their food. These industrial convents alone would be enough to attest to the difficult, and often impossible position, of the daughter of the people; they offer meager food in return for hard work; however young girls flock there to the point that, for fifteen years, the State authorizes annually 80 to 100 communities of women. 'A large number of convents, however, only admit rich women,' and all of them usually reject the poorest women, more worthy of protection, especially our many natural daughters, real orphans of a living mother and father; they push back also women who do not have strong enough health to carry out heavy work. A famous philanthropist quotes one of those poor workers who, working night and day, never could remove her clothes from the pawnshop, and asked if it would not be possible for her to be incarcerated without having committed a crime. She wanted to use her prison savings to acquire the dowry that would open a convent for her. Poor women, often excluded in society from jobs that were once theirs, vegetate in poverty or fall into vice, due to lack of means of subsistence. If this encroachment of man came from freedom, the natural inferiority of woman would require special protection, but it is easy to convince ourselves that the oppression which weighs on it them is, on the contrary, the effect of the negation of freedom: if we carefully seek the causes of the precarious state of woman of the people, we see that they come above all from administrative centralization which arbitrarily pushes her away from schools and jobs, and from irresponsible immorality, and, which, after banishing her from the family, weighs on her the triple oppression of laws, institutions and morals.

Vocational schools, opened by the State, buildings and communes are organized everywhere; they receive a certain number of scholarship students, but none welcome wives; even though, through a particular and exceptional aptitude, she manages to occupy a rank in industry, the State almost always refuses her patents of invention or perfection. . . .

Centralization also distributes in the most arbitrary manner a host of subordinate jobs which require no particular aptitude. This is how we look in vain for women to take care of our museums, our public libraries, and that we even see in our hospitals men cupping women and serve as their nurses. The regulations of the Parisian city council or police also generally prevent a woman from exercising the profession of dust remover. . . .

This centralization, so detrimental to women, finds its rationale in social immorality, which prohibits mixed education, an immense benefit for all societies which have morals; in France, the young girl cannot do her apprenticeship in the same conditions as the young man, because she must always be protected against society by the family or by the convent; hence a serious attack on individual freedom, right to wages through work. In other countries, shop girls go as freely into town as clerks, and among merchants make like them industrial transactions, usually called commissions. In France, the absence of laws repressive of immorality exposes these women too much for them to be able to enjoy complete freedom; they are lured into all kinds of traps; we seek by all means to exploit their isolation, without our legislation deigning to prevent any of the abuses that other peoples repress in the most severe manner. . . .

The woman then, whose needs and expenses increase due to the aggrandizements of the cities, their opulence, finds herself with almost always insufficient resources; the man argues with her, snatches easy, lucrative work from her; he takes everything away from her, precisely because he owes her nothing; he leaves her to succumb to the excess of unproductive and murderous work, when it does not make her a victim of her passions.

This downgrading which draws men into the cities, this usurpation which throws them into women's jobs, all characterize corrupt societies. . . .

In the seventeenth and eighteenth centuries especially, the corruption of morals had similar effects; in France, the cities, Paris, the court, had absorbed all the forces of the nation when the Revolution broke out. The freedom granted by Turgot to certain industries thus produced a very great encroachment of men into women's jobs. . . . From this insight, we see only too well how the woman, dispossessed in the cities, usually finds only insufficient means of subsistence in the countryside.

Centralization and immorality also accumulate all the capital in the hands of men; the woman without wealth finds herself still excluded from all industries which require a capital outlay, and which the poor man usually acquires through a (woman's) dowry. Women reduced, in this way, to menial work, often cannot even manage women's clothing houses.

Capital, the basis of the most humble businesses, is used to stock these houses which rely on significant sponsorships. It is well known that industrialists, opulent capitalists, have invaded women's clothing, and have already managed to corrupt the traditional good taste of French women who have imposed the yoke of our fashions on both worlds. . . . Despite these elegies on the death of French good taste, men are already beginning to reign despotically in the all-feminine empire of fashion, because their opulent stores are splendidly adorned with all the researches of elegance. . . .

CHAPTER 2, MEANS OF SUBSISTENCE FOR WOMEN

Industrial legislation once determined the exclusive rights of workers for their joint work: their disputes were settled by an equal number of industrial tribunals and female industrial tribunals, or trade mistresses; in mixed industries they were left, as well as the inspection of apprenticeship, to the exclusive jurisdiction of the female industrial tribunals, for women's industries.

Knitting, spinning and sewing, the main occupations of women in ancient France, are pretty much ruined by mechanisation. Lace work, imported by Colbert, at the cost of such great effort and encouragement, then offered very high wages to the workers. . . .

We can here regret the old domestic work, accomplished without fatigue at any age, while lace and embroidery requiring great application, spoil the eyesight of certain workers. These industries, which flourished in the last century, had to suffer greatly from the invasion of machines; however, they continue to employ a large number of women.

The manufacture of lace alone employs two hundred and fifty thousand women in fifteen departments which have Alençon, Lille, Arras, Mirecourt, Le Puy as central points. The salary of lacemakers is very variable; in 1848, the economist Blanqui saw in Dieppe a number of these women who could not earn more than 25 centimes in a fifteen-hour day. In the Vosges, the products of the lace industry are estimated at three million francs, and the average salary of the workers who deliver them to the trade is 80 centimes.

Embroidery employs nearly two hundred thousand workers in France. The daily salary of embroiderers varies from 20 cents to 1 franc. 50 and 2 fr. Embroidery made on a loom demanding a lot of perfection, gives a higher salary, but it deforms the children who are applied too young. The making of the common embroideries of Saint-Quentin and cord embroidery, called English embroidery, offers deplorable salary conditions; this is where we find a crowd of women who earn no more than 20 to 30 centimes per day.

Various surveys have been made on embroidery industries and lace, very diversely judged. Some reformers deplore the fact that everything is optional and arbitrary for the lacemaker who is dependent on the will and even the caprice of the entrepreneur, who sets the price of labour without any control; often retains ownership of his designs, imposes the deadline for the production, remains the sole judge of the merit of the work and the discount he wants to make, by threatening the worker with work if she does not comply, does not accept harsh conditions. Unfortunately, these objections common to a host of industries, arise from causes that are foreign to them; we will have to go back further, to seek an effective remedy for these abuses. . . .

Such industries, considered in isolation, are beneficial industries, because they are carried out in the countryside, in the domestic home, and offer sufficient wages to the skilled worker. The irregular behaviour of certain workers is more due to the social environment where they live and the nature of the industry they carry out. Lacemakers, as well as embroiderers who belong to agricultural populations, have much better morals than those who are part of our industrial populations; here again, there is a social question which dominates the economic question, and the solution of the latter depends absolutely on the solution of the first. There is no progress to be made in the economic order, as long as the injustice and irresponsibility of man, in the moral order, will continue to disturb society. An examination of Parisian industries would be enough to show that the inferiority of women's wages, far from being an effect of the freedom of industry, is, on the contrary, only the result of measures detrimental to equality, ignored by centralization, which closes schools to women, and by the immorality which deprives them and their children of their civil rights.

Parisian industry employs men, women and children; the salary of the latter is usually as high for girls as well as for boys under sixteen years of age, but, from this age onwards, the causes which I have just briefly indicated, reduce the woman's salary in a noticeable manner. The 105,000 workers recorded by the last statistics of Parisian industry, earn from 50 centimes to 10 francs per day; for the male worker this salary rises to 20 francs. The average between these two extreme terms gives a daily remuneration of 4 francs 51 for the man, and 2fr. 41 for women; but this average would give very false ideas on the question of individual subsistence that concerns us. It is good to note that the wage can, as we have just seen, go down to 50 centimes. An examination of all industries which employ women shows us that their inferiority is due to the lack of special education; thus, Paris which has more than 14 thousand boys in apprenticeship, has only 5,500 girls; they still predominate in temporary learning, while they make an exception for three and four year apprenticeships. Girls sponsored to apprenticeship by parents, guardians, by civil and religious associations, are barely a third of boys who receive this social protection; these causes combined would be enough to explain to us the inferiority of woman, whose ignorance is such that the statistics of the Parisian industry have not found a single person who knows how to read and write, in the chemical match industry.

If we first look at the industries to which woman seems the most suitable, we find them in competition with the man, in inferior conditions, when the salary is not deplorable; thus, in garment work, where Paris employs many more men than women, the male workers have an income double and triple that of the female workers, because, due to lack of training, they are employed in work that does not provide sufficient pay. Piecework is even more poorly paid than daily work in manufacturing; mothers, obliged to work at home, leave to go far away to find work which is often lacking; so that their time is consumed in fruitless errands and unemployment. This wage depression could have reduced the cost of making a pair of pants by up to 30 cents and 20 centimes that of a vest. Machines contribute also to this debasement of the workforce, because in Paris we have more than two thousand sewing machines, which represent the work of thirteen thousand workers.

Manufacture of lingerie has become even more thankless than other needlework, for the isolated and destitute worker, from whom the contractor and the subcontractor raise part of their profit. Women who have other means of subsistence, prisons, convents and charitable establishments also provide competition that is sometimes impossible to withstand. In all classes of society, Paris counts more than thirty thousand of these clandestine workers who, to bring some income to the household, accept work at all costs.

Competition from prisons has also greatly expanded nowadays. In the past, the amount of work carried out by our 21 central houses did not even reach two million francs, but in 1848 complaints arose from all sides against entrepreneurs who imposed onerous conditions on independent industry, by putting work out at a discount that it cannot tolerate; the Troyes Chamber of Commerce then affirmed that there was not a central house which, in its closest radius of action, could not be convinced of the suffering and ruin of some formerly prosperous industries.

The work of the prisons has taken on a prodigious extension since this time, if we judge by the press release sent in November 1861 to the *Courrier du Dimanche*, relating to the central house of Melun. This document affirmed that this prison which, in 1847, produced 2 million works, now produces 4 million each year; Needlework alone today employs more than fifteen thousand men in our prisons. Belgium sought to prevent any similar abuse by employing its prisoners exclusively in public works.

This work of the prisoners, so detrimental to free industry, nevertheless appears insignificant, if we compare it to those of our convents, our workshops, our orphanages, etc., which deliver millions of articles of trousseaux and layettes to our stores and reduce the cost of making a man's shirt from 25 to 10 centimes and deliver for 1fr. 10 cents for a layette made up of about twenty pieces. Updated hems for pocket handkerchiefs and petticoats, formerly made by our Lorraine embroiderers, are also made in orphanages, at prices that free industry can bear.

The convent, being also exempt from the license and various charges which weigh on manufacturers, can deliver all these confections at a ruinous discount for its competitors. Surveys have established that three quarters of shirts delivered to the trade are made in Parisian convents, which offer a 25:10 discount to buyers. The religious communities of the Parisian suburbs have even organized an extensive laundry service for the clergy and the churches of the capital; I don't think the old proverb 'You have to wash your clothes as a family,' has never received a wider application.

This explains how poor workers stagnate and die for lack of sufficient income. One of them, reduced to hemming 2 meters of cambric, for 1 penny, on a very hard fabric which broke her needles, had to give gifts to the cutter from the store to get some work. The assembly, sewing and stitching of boots, suspenders and in general all needlework that can be perfected at home, are deplorably unproductive; even hosiery had to suffer from the work of prisoners and the employment of new professions which triple production.

In the Parisian leather goods industry, men who are cutters get a good salary, but women can barely make a living as stitchers and overlockers. 'The price of a dozen caps is paid 35 cents to a worker who has difficulty making more than two dozen in a long day of work.'[1]

When the government opened a few workshops in 1848, we could see all the miseries and all the pains of the existence of the women of the people. More than twelve thousands of them went to pile up in Paris in these refuges against the famine. Such narrow premises, without sufficient ventilation, accommodated up to twelve hundred to two thousand workers who suffocated there from morning to evening during the blazing heat of June and July. They were mainly made to sew shirts for 60 centimes; a worker, with somewhat weakened eyesight, sewed one in two days; a widow with three children, a father and a mother to support, spent three days on the same work. A thirteen-year-old child, thanks to her skill, earned 12 cents per day to support a sick father, a mother busy with household care and three young brothers and sister. A woman of seventy-one, with her daughter's child in her care, earned 6 sous.

The position of women is far from having improved since that time, in certain sewing jobs and because of the causes of ruin that I have pointed out for this industry; because of the invasion especially of the sewing machine, I believe that it would be ridiculous to try to continue to support a struggle that could be as formidable as the one who so promptly put the *fileuses* out of action.

All the causes that I have listed and to which some statisticians do not attach importance because they are isolated, nevertheless come together to overwhelm the worker, because one succumbs by numerous pinpricks as if by a stab. The only threat that entrepreneurs make to workers is competition from prisoners, nuns and orphans, makes them accept the work at ridiculous prices. However, we cannot here accuse private charitable establishments, especially orphanages, which must help themselves with the work of their wards; the cause of the evil goes back to the spoliation which was made of the rich endowments of the orphans of ancient

France; it is by studying the sad question of foundlings that we will see above all by what fatal chain man's immorality overwhelms motherhood and childhood.

Women must be initiated into more productive work; such is the conclusion that emerges from the preceding considerations.

We will therefore examine the position of the worker in the main industries which employ her in Paris and in the departments, to seek to highlight the best ways to improve her lot.

In Paris, more than six thousand workers are currently employed in *passementerie* [trimmings]; they have an insufficient salary, when they do not carry out these common works put at a discount by demand of our convents; a lot of these women do not earn more than a franc, and even 50 centimes per day.

A serious apprenticeship would significantly improve their condition, because it takes taste, skill, and long practice to follow and execute the varied designs of the gold, silver and silk braids and crests. The trimmings worker who does not know how to set up her loom is also obliged, for each new work that she is undertaking, to deliver part of her salary to the auxiliaries she employs.

The isolated *passementier* has, moreover, very heavy costs of rental to bear to set up the loom, the reels, etc., which alone occupy an entire room; nearly four thousand women work in rooms in Paris; most of them do not even have the equipment necessary for their work; they thus remain dependent on the manufacturer, who makes them the necessary advances, and who, becoming a privileged creditor by law, prevents them from seeking a more lucrative occupation elsewhere.

In Paris, almost as many women as men work in leather gloves, among the two thousand individuals it lists. The workers' salary varies from 3 to 10 francs, and that of female workers from one franc to 4. The inferiority of workers' wages comes from the lack of professional education which makes them incapable of cutting the glove and making it, which reduces them to the role of quilters, embroiderers and sewers. This industry, which has twenty-five apprentice boys, has only one girl. Various tests have, however, proven that glove cutting, which seems to be a male monopoly, can be performed by a woman.

The manufacture of gloves is also widespread in our departments [outside Paris], where the average salary for women is 90 cents. Jewellery and goldsmithing, which include such diverse specialties, employ nearly four thousand workers in Paris. To skilfully mould, chisel, polish, engrave, enamel and vary the polish and matte requires a lot of skill. The making of chains, rings, crosses, earrings, etc., also requires great delicacy of hands; however the high salaries of moulders, carvers, engravers and enamellers are unknown to women who, due to lack of professional education, almost all remain polishers; apprenticeships for these various specialties include, in Paris, more than two thousand two hundred boys, and there are only one hundred and some young girls. It is about even among gilders and silversmiths, . . . where the least paid occupations are reserved for women who fail to learn.

The varied work of goldsmithing offers a field as vast to the imagination of the artist as to the practiced hand of the worker; through industrial education of course, we would significantly improve the position of workers in this profession which, in Paris, has a few apprentices among hundreds of apprentices, and where, consequently, women are employed in work which requires the least acquired knowledge. . . .

Watchmaking could also offer very lucrative work to women, as we see by some skilled workers, who have, exceptionally, sufficient income in Paris.[2]

Switzerland, on which we are dependent for very cheap watches, employs twenty thousand women in watchmaking. The relationship between the Swiss population and ours lets us see the scope that this industry will give to women, in France, if she is made suitable for this multitude of feminine jobs consisting of engraving, polishing the numerals of dials, ornamenting watch cases, etc. If we except a few women, daughters or relatives of watchmakers, co-sharers of their work, in Paris, we hardly find this industry actively carried out by French women except in Besançon and the surrounding area.

Switzerland also employs relatively many more women in jewellery than France; it would be very desirable to see this sedentary work imported into our countryside and to spread it, especially in the poor departments which, having been dispossessed, like Brittany, and their ancient industries, are still awaiting the transformation which should compensate them. . . .

Let's move on to the work carried out by women in Lyon's industry. The single district of Saint-Étienne employs more than 30,000 workers of both sexes; a third of the 72,000 professions in Lyon and two thirds of those in the *banlieue*, are engaged in by women; suspended fourteen hours a day from a belt, to simultaneously operate hands and feet on the weaving loom, these workers earned, in 1848, according to Blanqui, less than 300 francs per year. A large part of the Lyon workers are, moreover, paid by the task, and the depression of their salary depends on commercial crises and the general position of the common woman in our social order. Those who are skilled have fairly high wages, when they can manufacture precious fabrics, but the weft winders and the millers work thirteen hours a day and have only a very minimal income.

The city of Lyon, this second capital of France, sums up for the South, like Paris for the North, all the pains of the worker's existence; the trade of Lyon, being based mainly on the manufacture of silks, five-sixths of which flow abroad, this city can be hit by industrial disturbances which sometimes reduce the products of its trade by 30 to 50 million per year. I don't know if free trade will improve the position of the Lyon worker, but, without doubt, that of the worker will worsen, if motherhood and childhood do not finally find, in our social order, the natural protection to which they are entitled. Most of the dispensers of work, for whom the worker is easy prey, seduce her and abandon her. We have seen bosses, after having imposed dishonourable conditions on her for the price of the work granted in moments of unemployment, bragging about their crime with impudence.

Workshop bosses who are not corrupters remain indifferent, and disdain to protect young girls of whom they are the only fathers and guardians.

This abandonment of women, rejected from professional schools, overwhelmed by the duties, responsibilities and pains of maternity, often creates impossible conditions of existence for rural and urban workers alike, and we see, unfortunately, a large number of these women ending up in depravity and suicide. Here a woman leaps from a window because, in deep poverty, she cannot pay the due date of her rent, another poisons herself, in despair because of not having found work, she suffocated after a fortnight's illness which left her without resources.

An orphaned worker sick with an infected toenail which prevented her from working, fell into complete destitution, and knocked on the door of a hospital, where they refused to admit her. Returning home with despair in her soul, she killed herself by drinking a glass of vinegar mixed with pepper.

A poor abandoned woman had stayed in a house of prostitution; the administration of the charity office, which was informed of this, refused her assistance; this woman gave herself to death, declaring that she had been without food for two days. Another said that she was done with life, because every week she was deprived of two days of bread. A poor girl worked day and night to help her family, and supporting an elderly, infirm and half-idiotic mother; but her strength failed, her health weakened, her salary became insufficient, the work failed: she succumbed under her heavy task, and lay down on her bed saying: 'Since my life is useless to her, may I let my death take her to a charitable establishment' . . .

It is enough to recall the German, English and American factories, where the work does not harm the dignity of the worker, and where the severities of the law take care of immoral masters, maintain harmony between all classes.

German manufacture is reminiscent of a well-organized family, where we find relationships of respect, protection, and mutual dignity. England itself, eaten away by a pauperism which derives from the privileges of its aristocracy and oppression of Ireland, prevents social dissolution in factories, by the equity of its legislation in factories, mores which make morality reign, and protects the worker against the corruption of men of all classes.

It is especially through the study of United States legislation that we understand how the independence, dignity and well-being of the worker can be reconciled with the work of manufacturing and the progress of industry.

Who does not know the workshops of Lowell (Massachusetts), whose fame is universal? They number nine thousand workers, coming from distant lands, and belonging to honourable families; they stay in such security under the protection of public good faith, so that no attack can be made on their morality in their solitary and independent life and Lowell does not have a single illegitimate birth.

The workers of Lowell, whose minds are cultivated, have built a church, an academy; they have created public courses, where they call upon distinguished professors; they are literate, authors themselves, and published a journal entitled: *The Spirit among the spindles*.

Work does not interrupt their intellectual exercises; they recite verses in the workshop, meditate there and comment on the Sunday sermon, etc.

This independence, this dignity of women is the fruit of the cultivation of her intelligence and of severe and logical legislation, which strengthens the bond of the family by not allowing any immoral man to relieve himself of the care of his own children. Lowell workers usually save half of their salary, acquire in four years a dowry which allows them to devote themselves exclusively to the care of their household when they are married.

The Lowell manufacturing company, watching over the young girls entrusted to it with scrupulous care, has built them special accommodations which it rents to them with a rebate of half and even two-thirds of the capital invested.

The workers remain, moreover, placed under the responsibility of honourable matrons, usually widows, of whom they are the residents. The magistrates of Lowell, worried guardians of the morality of young girls, even forbade them to dance. Any immoral person is excluded from workshops where seduction is unknown, as well as in the vast states of the American Union.

This organization of work is a sufficient response to people who, invoking restrictions against the worker, pretend that it must be oppressed in the interest of the family. No, it is not by atrophying a woman's intelligence; it is not by promulgating prohibitive regulations against it; it is not above all by overwhelming her under the burden of immorality public, that we will succeed in resolving this serious question. In vain will we repeat sheepish phrases about the duties which constitute the dignity of the domestic housewife, we will not destroy evil without having opposed its causes.

We can ask the antagonists of the freedom of the worker if it is true that the salary drops by half when the woman comes forward to share the man's work, if the wife is always in competition with her husband, and finally, if our social organization obliges every worker, even if he is a father, to share his salary with his wife and children.

When we discuss this subject, we do not take care that the widowed women, seduced or isolated, make up the majority of women who must provide for their own personal upkeep and that of a child.

We remember the prohibitive regulations that not long ago hit the worker in the Parisian printing works. Likewise, in 1848, when the fate of the women of the people so keenly affected men of heart, it must be said that these sad measures of prohibition were still used against the workers who exhausted themselves in the murderous weaving of shawls. The delegates of this industry excluded them and prohibited young girls from weaving before the age of eighteen. Without doubt, we cannot ignore the generous intentions which dictated these restrictions, but they nevertheless attest to the narrow-minded views which attack the effects without going back to the causes, because the extension of this system would also require the expulsion of men working in women's professions, and we would then return to our old industrial legislation.

The provisional government had also banned, in the interest of the workers, work in prisons, convents, haggling, etc. But these measures, which were detrimental to freedom, were powerless to paralyze a profound evil that must finally be combatted by more rational and practical means. . . .

Just as the general conditions of industry are bad for women, the particular measures which have been taken to shield them from the dangers of the social environment in which they live are very imperfect.

Source Endnotes

1 Jobez, The Woman and the Child of Poverty leads to oppression.

2 The watchmaking industry has 38 apprentices and two female apprentices in Paris. Women's wages vary from 2 to 5 francs., and that of men from 3 to 12 fr.

57

RATES OF PAY, 1876

Source: 'Rates of Pay', *Englishwoman's Review of Social and Industrial Questions*, Vol II (15 November 1876): 512.

EDITORIAL HEADNOTE

In keeping with its mission (see doc. 28), the *Englishwoman's Review* tackled one of the key issues of sweating: rates of pay. This brief extract reprinted from the *Labour News* simply lists pay in some homework industries for women.

From the *Labour News* we gather the following rates of payment of women in various trades: –

BRUSHMAKING. – A skilled man, if regularly employed, can at present earn about 30s. a week. Women can earn from 8s. to 12s., but a smart and clever hand may, by commencing early in the morning and working till twelve at night, with the aid of two or three children, who are paid but a few pence a week each, earn, per-haps, 18s. or £1 per week.

COACHBUILDING: – Women employed in this trade gain, according to the class of work they do, 7s. 6d. or 15s. a week.

BEDDING MANUFACTURE. – Men in this branch earn, when fully employed, from 25s. to 50s. per week; women, 9s., 15s., 16s., and some a trifle more, per week.

TOBACCO-PIPE CASEMAKERS. – At this work men earn ordinarily, 30s. a week, and women, who cover the cases, about 16s.; but in busy times, like the present, when work goes on till late at night, the week's wages are much in advance of this.

FUR-SEWING. – Women, if good hands, can earn from 10s. 6d. to 20s. on piecework; indifferent workers, of course, earn much less. Muff stuffers and liners can earn from 20s. to 35s. a week. Messrs. Hyman and Co., furriers, 151, Aldersgate street, who have now about twenty muff hands in their employ, say they can make room for twenty more, and give them constant employment ten months out of the twelve, at which the chances

DOI: 10.4324/9781003676669-63

are open to make the above money. They must know their business and be steady. Work commences at half-past eight in the morning and finishes at nine p.m. Learners get 3s., 6s., and 9s., for the first six, twelve, and eighteen months respectively.

FANCY BOXMAKING. – This trade chiefly employs women. A girl before she receives any wages has to work six months, during which probationary period she manages to spoil more work than she is worth. At the end of six months she may be in a position to earn 2s. 6d. a week, which sum is gradually augmented as her services become more valuable, until, if she become really efficient, she may probably take her £1, and some-times more, per week, and eventually become forewoman of a room.

ARTIFICIAL FLOWER-MAKING. – Something like 3,000 women, and 1,600 girls, under twenty years of age, are employed in this branch of industry. Mantle-Makers are briskly engaged preparing for winter. One large firm in Islington have 200 machines at work, making mantles, jackets, ulsters, etc., and are sending out 8,000 per day – two waggon-loads. The machinists – young women – earn from 12s. to 16s. per week. . . .

58

IRISH SWEATED TRADES, 1893

Eliza Orme and May Abraham

Source: Eliza Orme and May Abraham 'Conditions of Women's Work in Ireland', in Miss Eliza Orme, Miss Clara E. Collet, Miss May Abraham, and Miss Margaret H. Irwin, *Reports, The Employment of Women.* Royal Commission on Labour. Presented to both Houses of Parliament by Command of Her Majesty. February 1893, 327.

EDITORIAL HEADNOTE

In this second extract from Abraham and Orme's Report to the Royal Commission on Labour, 1893 (see doc. 41), they follow up a variety of handwork industries, concentrating on industries that Irish women specialised in, like lace and embroidery.

(i.) Lace making. Some large drapers employ outworkers in making tambour and run lace (Limerick) and an agent to collect the work and pay the workers.

By one large firm 500 or 600 outworkers used to be employed in crocheting Irish Point. This was begun after the famine, but very few are now employed. There is no difficulty in getting new patterns taken up, and the children learn the work easily. The lace is now less in demand, and most of it is made in convents. The workers are paid by piece, a skilled worker, working 10 hours a day, earning 10s. or 12s. a week.

There is a lace school at Limerick and also a number of home workers organised by Mrs. Yere O'Brien, who finds good designs for both the school and for these home workers. The laces made are tambour, run lace, and guipure. One home worker (No. 1,057) gave her usual hours as from 9 a.m. to 8 p.m., with intervals of four hours for meals, house work, and rest. She makes about 9s. per week. In the school, orders are undertaken and the girls paid for what they do, but the primary object is to teach the industry. No. 1,057, gave an account of the four factories which used to exist in Limerick, giving employment to about 2,000 women. Their hours were from 6 a.m. to 7 p.m., with 2 hours off for meals, and they earned from 4s. to 6s. a week. The "tryers" would make 1 yard of lace, and

DOI: 10.4324/9781003676669-64

so fix the payment for the workers. These "tryers" received 5s. a week set wage. The teachers received 5s. or 6s. a week set wage. The two teachers at the present lace school are paid 10s. a week each. No. 1,057 states that a woman now 75 years of age was the first to learn how to make run lace. She was taught at an early age by some English ladies.

X. – DONEGAL

(a) Sprigging embroidery. One of the principal home industries in the north of Ireland is that of embroidering handkerchiefs and other linen, in the method known as "sprigging." Several larre firms in Belfast and elsewhere give employment to hundreds of families.

Mrs. Hamilton, of Brownhall, County Donegal, gives a large amount of employment in Ballintree and the surrounding districts, and pays good wages. She herself designs the embroidery.

A sprigging and embroidery agent, in Donegal, for several Belfast and Glasgow firms gave the following information: –

He has 700 families on his order book. At present employment is fairly good, and he has paid out 1,100£. in six months, lately, for a Glasgow firm alone. A very good sewer can earn in full work 2s. 6d. a day, but the bulk of the work is at a low price, and many workers do not earn as much as 2d. a day. He has distributed work since 1852, and until the failure of a large firm in Glasgow in 1857 the demand for work was very good. The Donegal trade became paralysed at that time, but in certain seasons even now there is a good deal of work to be done.

Another embroidery agent in Donegal acts for several firms. He says he gives employment to hundreds of people, many of whom, probably, work for other agents also. The work he distributes is worth about 2d. to 9d. a day; 1s. a day can be made upon samples. Good workers are often unable to get any but the poorer paid work. A skilled worker brought into the shop, during the visit, a pinafore which she had embroidered; she was paid 2½d., and she stated that it would take from nine to ten hours to do. The agent agreed with this. A third sprigging agent in Donegal says he pays 30£. to 40£. a week in wages. He employs 200 to 300 people, who can make from 3d. to 8d. a day.

A sprigging agent (a woman) for Belfast firms was seen at Ballintra. She has about 600 families on her books. She says there is a fair quantity of work now but it is badly paid. The general price earned is 3d. a day; 8d. a day is the highest. The work is paid at a rate of about one-third more in winter.

Another woman at Ballintra, also a sprigging agent for several Belfast firms, says she pays about 36£. in wages in 10 days. The women she employs earn from 5d. to 8d. a day.

A sprigger and embroiderer in Ballintra says she has fairly regular work, and earns from 6d. to 8d. a day.

59

PREFACE TO THE DAILY NEWS SWEATED INDUSTRIES EXHIBITION HANDBOOK, 1907

Gertrude Tuckwell

Source: Gertrude Tuckwell, 'Preface', in Sweated Industries, being a Handbook of The "Daily News" Exhibition, Richard Mudie Smith, Compiler, Part PP, Worker's Section. May 1906 (Bradbury, Agnew & Co., Ltd.), 10–17.

EDITORIAL HEADNOTE

A significant attempt to raise awareness about sweating was the *Daily News* Sweated Industries Exhibition (see also doc. 29). Owned by George Cadbury, a Quaker, from 1901, he used the paper to campaign for old age pensions and against sweatshop labour. While it was seen as strengthening the woman's suffrage cause, it also lost important reporters when it failed to condemn force-feeding of suffragettes. The *Handbook*, extracted here, contained a number of articles, like the one on Flowermaking, and a lengthy appendix of the stalls in the exhibition, quoted at length in Chapter 58. The organising committee reads like a Who's Who of notable social liberals of the time like the Cadburys, Clementina Black, George Bernard Shaw, B.L Hutchins, H.G. Wells and Sydney Webb. The programme also included regular lectures, again drawing on well-known figures. The 'Preface' written by Gertrude Tuckwell was a vigourous condemnation of the sweated trades and the paltry efforts to correct their abuses. She wrote the purpose of the exhibition was 'to marshal a considerable number of instances of the rates of pay, and, so far as possible, of the conditions of labour in the lowest ranks of various trades, and to confront the public with them, so that an effect may be produced which will not be transitory, and will lead to the serious consideration of remedies which shall be permanent, and which shall embrace not only individuals, but the whole of sweated labour.'

DOI: 10.4324/9781003676669-65

Chairman of the Women's Trade Union League, Gertrude Tuckwell (1861–1951) was a British trade unionist and social reformer. Her father, master and chaplain of New College, instilled Christian socialist beliefs in her, but she later said the greatest influence on her was her maternal aunt Emilia Strong (later Emilia Dilke, Lady Dilke). In her unpublished autobiography, 'Reminiscence', she described her aunt, an accomplished art historian and critic, as 'the greatest person I have ever known'. Tuckwell trained as a teacher and taught infants until ill health forced her to resign. In 1893 she succeeded May Abraham (Margaret Mary Edith Tennant) (1869–1946), promoter of workers' rights and public health and one of the investigators for the Committee on Women's Labour as labour secretary to her aunt Emilia, who was now living in London with her second husband, Sir Charles Dilke MP (1843–1911). She also became honorary secretary of the Women's Trade Union League, which had grown out of the Women's Protective and Provident League founded in 1874, and edited the league's journal. After her aunt's death she succeeded Lady Dilke as president of the league in 1905. Three years later, she became president of the National Federation of Women Workers. She played a key role in the formation of the Industrial Law Committee and actively campaigned to protect women workers from industrial injuries. In 1896 she was one of the first women teachers at the London School of Economics, giving lectures on factory legislation. Building on and fostering her female networks, she played a seminal role in the development of women's trade unionism and the labour movement.

"WE had no food." This was the defence of a woman imprisoned for pawning part or the material given out to her by her employer. The trousers were to be to "finished" for 2d. a pair, and the work comprised the putting on of buttons, the sewing of bottoms, pockets and flies, the women finding needles and thread. "To get food and light" they pawned material, and then, unable to redeem it, went from their "squalid room" to prison.

This is the sort of story which, from time to time finding its way into the public Press, introduces the world which plays to the life-histories in the lowest strata of the world which works. For a moment, through such an opening as the newspaper paragraph I have quoted affords, we catch a glimpse of existence below the surface of our superficial civilization, an existence made up of pathetic bewildered lives on which the burden of overwork rests from childhood to old age.

Such glimpses stir the sympathy of the charitable. The Police Court Missionary or the friendly Newspaper acknowledges donations to be used for the benefit of the sufferer, some of which donations are sent as tribute money by those who acquiesce in an order or things which brings comfort to themselves, while others are prompted by an awakened uneasy sense that a world in which such things happen is out of joint, and that they must lend a hand to set it right. Then other claims intervene and the incident is forgotten and has served perhaps no purpose save the temporary relief of one victim of our industrial system.

But it is not by help to individual instances of suffering, nor by temporary aid, that such evils as these stories indicate can be met, for they are merely infrequent samples taken from a prevailing set of evil conditions. The object of the Exhibition, of which these pages preface the Handbook, is to marshal a considerable number of instances of the rates of pay, and, so far as possible, of the conditions or labour in the lowest ranks of various trades, and to confront the public with them, so that an effect may be produced which will not be transitory, and will lead to the serious consideration of remedies which shall be permanent, and which shall embrace not only individuals, but the whole of sweated labour. This class of labour is that which offers no resistance, and, by the pressure or competition, is forced to a level at which bare subsistence alone can be maintained. Every now and then it descends below that level and news of "another death from starvation" may find its way to the public ear. The resistance which labour offers to the capitalist is created either by trade protection – that or the Trade Union – or by the State protection, entailing regulated conditions of employment imposed by the law. Therefore the larger class of sweated industry is found among the home workers – too scattered to act together for their corporate interest, and for whom legislative protection exists least, and where it exists is worst administered.

Wages having been forced down to the lowest point, it follows that, to eke out the family budget, every available human being in the home becomes a wage-earner. The aged and infirm, the crippled and the half-witted are pressed into the service, while children toil early and late, often during as well as after and before school hours, to complete their tale of work; and while we feel the pathos that those who have earned rest, or are physically unfilled for labour, should be forced into the ghastly struggle, the suffering of the children carries with it the stronger appeal for help; after all it is with them that the future lies.

"Indoor work . . . in insanitary homes is generally bad, and accounts for many of the pale faces and stunted frames to be found in the schools," says the Inter-Departmental Committee's Report on the Employment of School Children; and one of the cases officially cited, in which four children, aged from eight to ten years, were employed at home from 44 to 50 hours a week in wood chopping after and before school hours, gives point to the remark. How shall we put heart and energy into citizens reared under such conditions as these?

In home work, less perhaps than in any other class of work, does the stated wage represent the amount received. "In the making of women's clothes by starving women in this town," writes one of the Factory Inspectors deductions reduce to insignificance any wage that starts by being fair." Cotton and needles and materials, as well as the payment for carrying work to and from the shop, mount to a goodly sum. An unavoidable accident which has slightly damaged the value of the work done may entail its forced purchase by the worker and the purchase of her work, at 1s., 11d. a mat, may be the fate, for example, of the Matmaker, who has drawn the strands a trifle too tight. Because of the depression and ignorance of these lowest strata of labour, a trade may be found lingering which, under ordinary and healthy circumstances, would have long since died out as a home industry. Side by side with the elaborate blouses or underclothing made for a few pence and sold by shop or factory for as many shillings, are trades like matchbox or tie making or straw plaiting, where prices are depressed, not by the cupidity of the employer, but by a competition with machinery, and a hopeless sacrifice of unproductive labour ensues.

I spoke of the squalid room of the woman whose story forms my text. Rent is a terrible item to the dwellers in big cities, and labour such as that of which I speak gets crushed into any cranny or hole. It may be carried on in basement kitchens, in wretched attics, among conditions of dirt and disease. In such homes the hours given to cleaning and tidying are grudged, since they lessen the week's earnings, while a demand on the landlord for repairs or improvement must be avoided as that means a raised rent and the consequent search for another home. "In some instances," says Miss Vine, H.M. Inspector of Factories. in a Report she made on out-work in 1904–, "one room has to serve the manifold use of bath room, laundry, drying ground kitchen, scullery, bed room, living room, sick room, workshop, and, it may be, mortuary as well. One can only wonder at the patient courageous life, at the ceaseless, tireless energy displayed in the midst of such misery and dirt in the face of such tremendous odds." She sums up well – but with our admiration for the victim goes also our contempt for the ignorance, the inertia, which permits their sacrifice. That our legislature must have made some attempt to check so great an evil is obvious; that the efforts made have been tentative and fumbling goes without saying. It is well to consider them now.

The evil has been long with us. About eighteen years ago, the Government, confronted with the problem and bewildered by it, took that favourite step of Governments in a difficulty, and appointed a Committee of the House of Lords to enquire into the Sweating System. The Committee sat two years, took much invaluable evidence, and issued a definition of the Sweating System. The Blue Books which contain the evidence have long grown dusty on bookshelves, but the definition arrived at by the Committee that "Sweating meant unduly low rates wages, excessive hours of labour, and insanitary state of work places," pointed the direction in which legislation was needed, and the fumbling and tentative attempts at remedy so far enacted have been directed at these conditions. The attempts at regulating wages have been small indeed: they comprise the recently acquired power of the Secretary of State to extend to these home workers, trade by trade, the protection of the Particulars section, so that they can compute when work is given out to them the payment they will receive for any given job. The Truck law has so entirely broken down that a Departmental Committee has just been appointed to consider what is to be done with it, while, so far as the Particulars section is concerned, those trades recommended for its protection in 1902 have not yet received that protection. Hours of Labour are touched only in Domestic factories or workshops where, if children and young persons are regularly employed, certain periods of hours are specified, but owing to the complication of the law and the difficulties of inspection, it is almost impossible to enforce them. There is also the much evaded regulation by which those who have done a full day's work in factory or workshop are forbidden to take work home to do there. More attempts have been made to fight insanitary conditions, and in this direction the local authority has much power to deal with dilapidation and dirt.

In certain trades the employer must keep and furnish lists of out workers for the convenience of local authority and factory inspector and to the former have also been given powers as to the prohibition of the giving out of work. This sounds well, but the powers are vague, and, leaving many loopholes of escape from action for a dilatory or apathetic local authority, result, save in the instance of one or two active authorities, such as Glasgow, in the accomplishment of little.

Those into whose hands this catalogue will fall, will sec the Sweated Industries' Exhibition, and realise that these forty workers, at one penny or twopence an hour, are typical of hundreds of thousands of their fellow-citizens, and that, under circumstances of squalor and privation impossible to depict in such an exhibition, they are creating things necessary for our convenience or amusement. Visitors will have realised also that the sin of such employment lies at our door. The time was when people hugged themselves in the delusion that this condition of things was caused by the introduction of middlemen who doled out the work and consumed the profits. This idea has been discredited by the Committee itself, by every tract and pamphlet since issued, and by the investigations of such bodies as our Christian Social Union or the Women's Industrial Council. We find that, except in certain instances, such as those for example of the agents who transmit the work in parts of Ireland or in the South of England, no one interposes tween the employer and the worker, and that the sweater is in fact ourselves. "The sweater," says Mrs. Sidney Webb, "is the whole nation," for employer, shopkeeper, and purchaser all contribute to create and keep alive the system I have described, and our guilt is not only that which attaches to the passive tolerance by us as citizens of any wrong or suffering in the state, but amounts to active, if ignorant, participation in oppression.

Sometimes this participation is of a very definite character and is carried on under the guise of Charity. The homeworkers' struggle is rendered more acute by the competition with goods produced under favoured conditions and subsidised in institutions. The underselling thus arrived at is peculiarly mischievous, and this amateur method of partially supporting Homes, Institutions, or Societies by underselling ordinary labour cannot be too strongly condemned.

We turn then to the suggested remedies. There are many who urge that a system of preferential dealing and of boycotting ill-paid goods commends itself to them as a piece of personal service, as something that they individually can do. It is truly well where one becomes aware that goods have been made under bad conditions and for insufficient pay, to avoid their purchase. but no voluntary system such as this can really meet the sweating evil. Lists of fair shops arc a thoroughly illusory recipe. With all the ramifications of modem industry, it is impossible to cope, at the end of the scale represented by the retail salesman, with a deep-seated trouble: we must get at the other end and protect the workers themselves. And as they suffer through the action of the whole nation, so they must be protected by its action. The laws protecting the home worker must be so developed and administered that this protection shall be as efficient for the tie maker who works in one room as for the textile operative among the clanging machinery of a northern mill northern mill.

We claim for honourable labour, wherever carried on, proper conditions of employment and an adequate reward. This reward, in the case of the textile worker of whom I have spoken, is secured by magnificent organisation. The home worker, scattered and oppressed, is incapable of organisation, and a living wage must be secured for her by other means. One of the points which strikes us most in investigating the conditions of the home worker, is the varying rate of pay given by different firms for the same work. Just as the pay of one employer may be a ½ d. an hour more than that of another, so prices may be varied arbitrarily in the same firm with no relation to the market rate or to anything except increased profits. I will quote as an example the gradual lowering from 9d. to 5d. of the pay for making elaborately strapped and stitched skirts by a firm, which is obviously becoming increasingly prosperous. These discrepancies in pay, governed here mainly by the greed or the kindness of individual employers, are in some Colonies dealt with by law, and the instance which always appears to me to be most applicable to our own condition is that which obtains in Victoria. By this plan, a Committee of Employers and Employed in a given trade is officially called into existence; its members meet and thresh out their trade difficulties and decide on a given rate of pay, subject to a revision according to the changes of the market. The last report of the Victorian Chief Inspector is well worth attention. From it we find that there are thirty-eight Boards at present in operation, and that these determine rates of pay in such industries, among others as those which represent our sweated trades, i.e., clothing, underclothing, dressmaking, shirtmaking, fruit preserving.

The Clothing Board has raised the rate of wages 1/2 a week for each employee; the Shirt Board has, since its inception, gained an average increase of 1/3 a week for each worker in the trade; the Board regulating wages in the jam trade, a rise of 1/5 a week. The effect of the recent adoption of a Wages Board for the dressmaking trade is still more interesting. It was found on investigation that girls working eight or nine years in the trade were earning, in many instances, a weekly wage of only as many shillings. The rate, are now fixed, so that after five years' service a dressmaker must receive a minimum wage of 16/- a week, and though in many cases this raised the pay received by as much as five or six shillings, the reports of the inspectors point to the fact that the trade has settled down without difficulty to the change, customer and employer alike benefiting by the increased efficiency of the workers which shows itself when the receipt of a living wage enables them to command additional food and comfort.

It is good to note that, according to the last report, the initial difficulties in working the scheme seem to have disappeared; "the Determinations appear to be well observed, and the Department has now comparatively little difficulty in enforcing the rates fixed by the Boards."

The Women's Trade Union League has long advocated the adoption of some such plan in our own country. What is needed is the joint consideration of the best workers and the best employers in the sweated women's industries, to study the market rates and decide on the highest rate of pay admissible. Why should not such a board be started in some selected trade? If the result of experiment in, say, the sack making industry, was to raise wages one shilling or even sixpence a week, this would mean a substantial improvement for workers who earn fivepence to sevenpence a day, and it is unnecessary to lay stress on the incidental value which would attach to the organisation and knowledge of the trade thus gained. A Wages Board Bill, intended for these feeble trades, has been for some years introduced by Sir Charles Dilke at our request. It is modelled on the Victorian scheme, and has a memorandum stating that the widest discretionary power would be left to the Board as to fixing time or piece-work rate, and as to varying that rate according to the class of persons employed.

Next to the "unduly low rates of wages" which characterise sweating, came, in the House or Lords' definition, "excessive hours of labour;" and here the imagination of Reformers has failed to see a way. How, in the thousands of poor homes to which work is given out, is the regulation of hours to be devised or enforced? Already in the domestic workshops – the place where children or young persons, members of the family dwelling there, have a legal limit placed upon their hours – it is found impossible in practice to enforce it; and to legislate further for the regulation of hours in the home would be to pass a stillborn law. This is one of the facts that induce many of us to welcome the modern tendency to concentrate work in factories and workshops. Here the responsibility of the employer for the conditions under which work is carried on is beyond challenge, laid down by excellent laws, and enforced by comparative ease of inspection, with the strong pressure of public opinion which publicity brings.

Hidden away in the holes and corners of our cities, homework is susceptible or no such influences, and the giver-out of work escapes his obligation to those he employs, for it is a survival of different labour conditions, and has really no place in healthy, modern industrial life.

For the last point of the Lords' definition, the "insanitary state of the workplaces," far more is proposed and far more can be done. One of the suggestions made before the Committee and urged by Mr. Oram, ex-Chief Inspector of Factories, was for the compulsory registration of all places where work is carried on, and this in an extended form, modelled on precedent found to work successfully in some of the States of the American Union, forms the chief point urged by the Women's Industrial Council. By this means it is proposed to penalise the employer who gives out work to any save those who can show a certificate from the Factory Inspector that their home is one suitable for the purpose, the certificate to be revoked if there is a lapse from a proper standard of sanitation and ventilation. Other proposals, the logical development of our present factory and workshop law, are embodied in the Model Bill introduced by Mr. H. J. Tennant. The principle on which the law which safeguards our code is based is that the occupier or employer is responsible for the conditions under which the work is carried out, and it rests on him to see that these are healthy – that rooms are not overcrowded, that the air is pure, that all that makes for decency and health is present. The proposals of Mr. Tennant's Bill are to extend this protection to the home into which work enters, so that if for his convenience the employer gives work to be done outside his workshop, he shall see that proper conditions for carrying on the work obtain there also. In the home, as in the workshop, the Inspector of the Local Authority is to enforce the amended law, and if the local authority fails in its duty another authority comes into play. If the sanitation of the workshop be neglected, the Factory Inspector, by virtue of his supervisory control, interferes, and so it is proposed that in the home, if the local authority be found defaulting, the Factory Inspector shall have power to act. Here we shift from the shoulders of the already over-burdened out-worker to those of the giver-out the responsibility for the condition of the place in which the work is done and provide that wherever work goes, there goes with it efficient inspection and control. I say efficient; but in this matter of administration, just as in the initial agitation to obtain complete regulation, the onus must rest upon ourselves. As the initiation of new laws is the result of an awakened public opinion, so their enforcement is in proportion to our watchfulness and keenness. The absence of effective bye-laws and the sluggishness of many local authorities reflect the absence of municipal life in a town, just as the unequal incidence of our laws protecting the worker have reflected the sluggish state of English public opinion on questions affecting the nation's life.

We look to this new Parliament to give the strong remedial measures which the country needs, for there men have found a place where they can speak at hand of the wrongs and suffering borne by those who form the lowest strata of our people. But those measures will depend for their enforcement on ourselves. The nation which has the best laws is by no means necessarily that in which the best conditions prevail, since for adequate administration are needed citizenship and public spirit. We have much to retrieve, and it remains with us to work individually and collectively – first to agitate for adequate laws, and then to watch over their administration. It is only by so doing that we can wipe out the reproach or the words I have quoted – "the Sweater is the whole Nation."

60

PARTICULARS OF WORKERS AT STALLS, DAILY NEWS SWEATED INDUSTRIES EXHIBITION, 1907

Source: Richard Mudie Smith, Compiler, 'Particulars of Worker at Stalls', *Sweated Industries Being a Handbook of The "Daily News" Exhibition.* Part PP, Worker's Section. May 1906 (Bradbury, Agnew & Co., Ltd.), 89–117.

EDITORIAL HEADNOTE

This selection is self-evident, giving detailed information on sweated workers represented in the exhibition, with occasional comments and editorialising.

PARTICULARS OF WORKERS AT STALLS

The attention of Visitors is directed to the fact that the Workers are forbidden to accept any gratuities.

DE PROFUNDIS

The following letter, addressed to the organizing Secretary is printed because it represents the experience of a host of similar sufferers. The name and address of the writer are, for reasons needless to name, withheld, but for every statement made she is prepared to produce chapter and verse.

April 17th, 1906.

'Sir, – The following is an account of my past experience as a City machinist. I sought work from firms now in existence, and obtained work at these prices: –

Flannel and cotton chemise plain bands with trimming on them and on sleeves . . . 1/- doz

Flannel and cotton small children's chemises and knickers, no trimming . . . 8d. "

Flannel and cotton nightdresses, with insertion and frills on neck and sleeves . . . 2/9 "

DOI: 10.4324/9781003676669-66

Flannelette bathing gowns, trimmed with braid . . . 3/- "
Ladies' flannel and cotton shirts. Plain . . . 1/9 "
The velvet ones 2/3 & 2/9 "
Ladies white muslin shirts trimming down fronts, 1 row each side, tucks in between, making about 20 tucks . . . 3/- "
Pinafores with tucked yoke lace insertion let in, tucked frills round yoke and sleeves, skirt with broad hem insertion and lace let in . . . 3,-"
Dressing gowns, flannelette and cotton with Watteau pleat pointed collar with lace and stitched band . . . 5/6 "
Or yoke top with frill of same down front as far as band . . . 3/6 "
Buttons on both buttonholes made at warehouse, sateen slips, plain . . . 10d "

After paying for cotton and railway journey, I had 7/- per week on an average, sometimes less, and paid 5/- for rent: I worked from six a.m. in morning till ten at night, only taking about one hour for my meals. While at warehouses I saw some had notices up that work kept longer than four days would not be paid full price. Work must be counted before taken away, or any deficiency must be paid for. A difficult matter to measure trimmings and count parts in a hurry, especially when you sometimes only had the floor to pack up on. Some could not understand why the Inspector never called on them, but some thought they never had their full number of outdoor workers until the Inspector had been. I myself never had a visit unless I put a bill in a window to try and get a girl. The home workers who get on the best are those who have number of machines and take learners, whom they send off when their time is up and have fresh ones.

I had some flannelette shirts, lined sent me at 1/9. I could stand it no longer; took them to St. Pancras Vestry; showed them to the lady inspector, who sent me to the Working Women's League, who could do nothing then unless the workers would strike.

"Yours truly,
"An Ex-Machinist."

Stall I. Worker No. 1

Description of Work	......	Trouser Making
Rates Paid		Men's, 1/9 to 2/6 per dozen
		Boy's, 1/6 per dozen
Worker's outlay for thread, &c.		About 4 ½d. per dozen
Time lost in fetching and returning work		About half-hour daily
Average working day		10 or 12 hours
Average earnings		Best week, 10/6 (very exceptional); sometimes between 3/- and 4/-

Regular or intermittent work		Fairly regular, but subject to slack seasons
Retail price of article		Unknown
Worker's rent		5/- weekly
No. of rooms		Two

Process. – The process includes all the machining on the trousers, including the pockets, and takes nearly an hour per pair.

Remarks.—Worker is a widow with four children, the eldest of whom is 9 years and the youngest 3 years. She is in receipt of parochial relief. "The children all look healthy, and are kept very nicely."

Stall I. Worker No. 2

Description of Work		Cabinet Making
Rates Paid		see "Earnings"
Worker's outlay for sundries.		Considerable
Time lost in fetching and returning work		....
Average working day		....
Average earnings		almost 15/-
Regular or intermittent work		Intermittent
Retail price of article		Varies
Worker's rent		7/6
No. of rooms		Two

. . .

Stall II. Worker No. 3

Description of Work		Matchbox Making
Rates Paid		2d. gross
Worker's outlay for sundries.		Has to find paste, hemp (for tying up), and firing to dry wet boxes
Time lost in fetching and returning work		About 2 hours a day
Average working day		12 hours a day

Average earnings		Not 5/- a week. Highest is 8/2 for full week, including Sundays
Regular or intermittent work		Occasionally works Sunday and Monday. Otherwise the average is five days a week
Retail price of article		The matches retail at from 2d. per dozen boxes
Worker's rent		2/6 per week
No. of rooms		One small room (7 persons)

Remarks. – This worker has five children – the eldest of whom is 11. She also has to support her husband, who is consumptive, and who has been unable to work for 6 years. They have been compelled to take parish relief intermittently since 1901, in time of sickness, &c. The eldest girl (11), after morning school, makes a gross of outside cases before going back to afternoon lessons at 2 p.m., and again works from 4.30 to 5.30 p.m., fitting up the boxes.

Stall II Worker No. 4

Description of Work		Making Matchboxes
Rates Paid		2¼ per gross
Worker's outlay for sundries.		Finds own paste and bass for tying, 2¼ d. for 14 gross
Time lost in fetching and returning work		Several hours each week
Average working day		16 hours
Average earnings		5/- weekly
Regular or intermittent work		No work to be got during 5 months of year
Retail price of article		....
Worker's rent		5/-
No. of rooms		Three

Remarks. – Husband out of work. Three children – eldest daughter helps to earn the 5/weekly. IN fetching work, has 1 ½ hours walk – sometimes has to wait 2 hours for work.

Stall III. Worker No. 5

Description of Work		Carding Hooks and Eyes
Rates Paid		8d. and 9d. per 24 gross. Bar hooks, 11d.; midgets, 1/3
Worker's outlay for thread, &c.		4d in every 3/-
Time lost in fetching and returning work		Worker pays another woman 3d weekly for the fetching and returning of the work
Average working day		From about 5 p.m. when the work arrives, till 11 a.m. next day when it has to go back. 'A few hours' bed.' Say at least 14-hours day.
Average earnings		¾ weekly between two – mother and daughter. When work is plentiful, and the children are made to help, the *whole family* can earn 6/- a week, 'sticking as close as glue' to the work.
Regular or intermittent work		Work had through a middle-woman is always rather intermittent, and quality also varies.
Retail price of article		1d. per card of 2 dozen
Worker's rent		3/6
No. of rooms		Three. No water in house.

Process. – Hooks and Eyes are given out loose, by weight; cards are given, and the work is paid for by the 24 gross. The eyes have to be sorted out and stitched on to the card; then the hooks are disentangled and linked into the eyes, usually by the children when they come home from school; then the eyes are stitched down. The bars, though better paid, are dreaded, being so tiresome to get hold of. Midgets are also disliked, for, though paid for at 1/3 per 24 gross, they are so minute to pick up and so trying to the eyes to sew, that less can be earned at them. Ordinary black hooks are the best. The worker does 384 *for a penny*, and one person, working eighteen hours a day, can earn about 5/- a week.

Remarks. – This worker's husband was with the Midland railway for 33 years. When 54 years of age he fell from a boiler, but, not realising he was seriously hurt, made no report. The next day he found he had lost the use of his right arm. He was dismissed and told he had no claim on the Company, 'because he had not reported the accident the same day.' Hence he has received neither compensation nor pension. . . .

Stall III. Worker No. 6

Description of Work		Carding Buttons
Rates Paid		3/-. per 100 gross.
Worker's outlay for thread, &c.		2d in every 3/-
Time lost in fetching and returning work		At least one hour daily. Lives near the factory, but often kept waiting.
Average working day		15 hours. From 8 a.m. to 11 p.m. this old woman and her brother sit and sew steadily.
Average earnings		3/6 weekly (*between the two*).
Regular or intermittent work		Four holiday weeks lost. Otherwise the work is fairly regular.
Retail price of article		1d. per card of a dozen buttons. With the boot buttons a buttonhook is also attached.
Worker's rent		3/9
No. of rooms		Kitchen and two bedrooms.

Process. – Buttons are given out daily, by weight, and cards are provided by the firm, but *not needles or thread.* Each button has to be firmly stitched on to its little square, drawn on the card. The cards are then neatly tied up in packs and taken back to the factory each day. The buttons are weighed out, not counted. Workers have been heard to complain that weight does not always tally with the number (they are paid for by the gross). But any shortage has to be paid for by the worker.

Remarks. – For nearly 11 years this worker kept clean two large Church Schools for 12/6 weekly, out of which she had to find soap, &c. The moving of heavy desks, &c., left her with a strained heart and consequent weakness. Worker and her brother have an aged sister – once a servant, but too old for service – who does their housework and helps to card. This sister is allowed a small pension by her former mistress which she adds to the family funds; and the old brother gets about 2/–every Sunday for selling cakes.

Stall IV. Worker No. 7

Description of Work		Tennis Ball Sewing
Rates Paid		4½d. to 6d a dozen
Worker's outlay for thread, &c.		1½d. gross for thread; ¾d. to 1d. for needles. Wears thimbles fast, also
Time lost in fetching and returning work		30 minutes daily.

Average working day		10 hours. A quick worker takes 2½ hours to do a dozen.
Average earnings		This worker only made about 6/- a week
Regular or intermittent work		Busy from February to August, rest of the year slack or no work.
Retail price of article		10/6 to 12/- dozen
Worker's rent		2/-
No. of rooms		One.

Process. – See Stall.

Remarks. – Worker now does shirtmaking which provides more constant work.

Stall IV. Worker No. 8

Description of Work		Racquet Ball Covering
Rates Paid		2/- to 4/- gross. Depending on size.
Worker's outlay for thread, &c.		Nil.
Time lost in fetching and returning work		Half an hour daily, or less
Average working day		11 or 12 hours
Average earnings		5/- weekly
Regular or intermittent work		regular, but occasional slack times.
Retail price of article		....
Worker's rent		....
No. of rooms		....

Process: – See Stall

Remarks. – Worker now married, but was engaged in this industry till her marriage.

Stall V. Worker No. 9

Description of Work		Slipper Making
Rates Paid		2/6 per dozen, women's 3/- "men's
Worker's outlay for thread, &c.		65 per dozen
Time lost in fetching and returning work		2 hours per day

Average working day		13 to 15 hours a day.
Average earnings		12/- weekly
Regular or intermittent work		Loses about 8 weeks per year
Retail price of article		¼, 1/6, 1/11, according to sizes.
Worker's rent		4/6.
No. of rooms		Two

Process. – See Stall

Remarks. – A widower, with four children, whom he is struggling to bring up well. When fetching work he sometimes has to wait all the morning – 'Employer out', &c. . . .

Stall V. Worker No. 10

Description of Work		Making Children's Boot Uppers
Rates Paid		1/2 to 1/9 per dozen
Worker's outlay for thread, &c.		Finds ink, thread, oil, needles wax, thread, paste (excluding machine rent).
Time lost in fetching and returning work		1½ hours daily
Average working day		10 hours 'working hard'.
Average earnings		5/- to 9/- weekly.
Regular or intermittent work		Worker only made 2 full weeks' work since last August Bank Holiday'.
Retail price of article		1/11 to 2/3 per pair
Worker's rent		4/6 per week
No. of rooms		Six

Process. – See Stall XXIV.

Remarks. – Widow with four children. Ekes out her earnings with parish relief.

Stall VI. Worker No. 11

Description of Work		Me's Umbrella Maker
Rates Paid		1/6 per dozen
Worker's outlay for thread, &c.		1d reel does 3 dozen
Time lost in fetching and returning work		Some hours each week

Average working day		Very irregular
Average earnings		'Last week, working each day, earned 6/4'.
Regular or intermittent work		Intermittent
Retail price of article		2/11 each
Worker's rent		8/-
No. of rooms		Two and a kitchen

Process. –

Remarks. – This worker is valued by her employers, and has preference when work is given out.

Stall VI. Worker No. 12

Description of Work		Covering Sunshades
Rates Paid		6d. per dozen
Worker's outlay for thread, &c.		2d. each 6 dozen
Time lost in fetching and returning work		12 hours a week
Average working day		'Often 6 a.m. to midnight'.
Average earnings		8/9 (96 hour week!) if in full work.
Regular or intermittent work		Regular
Retail price of article		Unknown
Worker's rent		2/6
No. of rooms		One small top.

Process. – See Stall. Each Sunshade has to be matched in cotton, which costs 2d. per reel. There are often 13 shades of colour in one parcel of Sunshades. Worker's sight is failing through working constantly in bright colours.

Remarks. – Worker is a widow with 10 children, 2 of whom are dependent.

Stall VII. Worker No. 13

Description of Work		Making Grummets
Rates Paid		5d., 7d., and 8d. per 100
Worker's outlay for thread, &c.		Nil.
Time lost in fetching and returning work		4 hours per week
Average working day		11 hours

Average earnings		6s. weekly.
Regular or intermittent work		Intermittent
Retail price of article		Unknown
Worker's rent		6s.
No. of rooms		Three

Process. – See stall. 'Grummets' are washers used by boiler-makers, for bolts. They are made from jute and manilla rope in three sizes.

Remarks. – The worker is a married woman, with five children under nine years of age. Her husband is in work, earning about 25s, per week. Often on three-quarter-time. He has had much illness and several accidents.

Stall VII. Worker No. 14

Description of Work		Sack Making
Rates Paid		see 'Earnings'
Worker's outlay for thread, &c.		Nil.
Time lost in fetching and returning work		some hours weekly
Average working day		10 hours.
Average earnings		6/3 weekly.
Regular or intermittent work		Only to be had for part of last year
Retail price of article		....
Worker's rent		2/6
No. of rooms		One (small).

Process. – See Stall

Remarks. – This worker belongs to a family of sack makers. Her mother has had 21 children (8 of whom are now dependent), and has worked at sack making since the age of 9. Her husband (worker's father) is a labourer, out of work. The worker's husband is also a labourer, out of work. Worker, calling for material at 9.30 a.m., often has to wait till 12.30. If the sack be spoiled in making, 9d. is deducted – if the sack be of better quality, this may reach 2/6.

Stall VIII. Worker No. 15

Description of Work		Making babies Bonnets
Rates Paid		2/- per dozen; making complete bonnet

Worker's outlay for thread, &c.		3 ½ d. per week.
Time lost in fetching and returning work		5 hours per week
Average working day		13 hours – 'when work is plentiful'.
Average earnings		....
Regular or intermittent work		Intermittent
Retail price of article		Unknown
Worker's rent		About 7/- weekly
No. of rooms		Three

Process: – 'Babies' millinery requites not only long training, but special aptitude. The materials are supplied from the factory, the cashmere being cut to shape. The lace to make the frilling is supplied in bulk. Her prices touch the high-water mark of payment for home industries. Her work is all done by hand; and she knows with automatic certainty where to put every stitch.'

Remarks. – Worker lost her husband, in a very tragical manner, some years ago; he maintained her and the two weakly children in cleanliness and respectability, without assistance. She wishes to acknowledge the kindness of her employer in furnishing her with the materials for the bonnets to be made at the Exhibition.'

Stall VIII. Worker No. 16

Description of Work		Tie making
Rates Paid		4½d. to 5d. dozen
Worker's outlay for thread, &c.		1d. on each 1/- earned, for thread; a girl kept to travel to City with the work, and fetch it, at 2/6 weekly (tea given); 2/- weekly travelling expended. Total cost 5/6 weekly.
Time lost in fetching and returning work		....
Average working day		8 hours.
Average earnings		12/-.
Regular or intermittent work		Intermittent. Four months per annum lost (at least), even when working for 3 firms and getting work from one when the others are slack.
Retail price of article		....
Worker's rent		7/6
No. of rooms		3.

Process. – The Derby ties are sent out with the silk already cut; the linings have to be cut to shape and fitted and the machined together. The tie is next folded in half and 'slipped' along the turned-in edges. 'Six or eight can be done in an hour by a quick worker.' The ties are then carefully ironed and pressed, folded in half and half again, and tied up in parcels of 1/2 dozen of 1 dozen each, as the firm requires. A coal fire or gas ring has to be used continually, and the work has to be sent to the City two or three times a day. This worker also has an 'out-worker,' who works at a lower rate, but has no travelling expenses. The work is trying to the sight.

Remarks. – Worker's husband is a railway employé – average earnings, 29/- weekly. The tie making is done to support the worker's widowed mother, whose mainstay she is. Worker has for some years suffered from anæmia.

Stall IX. Worker No. 17

Description of Work		Brush Drawing
Rates Paid		6½d. per 1000 holes ('A little over 4 hours to do a thousand.')
Worker's outlay for thread, &c.		Nil.
Time lost in fetching and returning work		7½ hours weekly
Average working day		....
Average earnings		6/- a week at most.
Regular or intermittent work		Fairly regular.
Retail price of article		....
Worker's rent		2/- weekly
No. of rooms		One.

Process. – See Stall.

Remarks. – A widow – has worked at brushes for 57 years. Began when 6 years old

---

Stall IX. Worker No. 18

Description of Work		Fur Sewing
Rates Paid		See 'Earnings.'
Worker's outlay for thread, &c.		....
Time lost in fetching and returning work		....
Average working day		11½ hours.

Average earnings		14/- weekly (3 months), 9/- weekly (5 months).
Regular or intermittent work		Intermittent – 8 months in year only
Retail price of article		....
Worker's rent		3/- weekly.
No. of rooms		One.

Process. – See Stall

Remarks. – Lives alone; maintains herself on her earnings.

Stall X. Worker No. 19

Description of Work		Vamp Beading (Ladies' Shoes).
Rates Paid		1/7 to 2/6 per dozen pairs
Worker's outlay for thread, &c.		2d. weekly 'and find own needles.'
Time lost in fetching and returning work		....
Average working day		14 hours.
Average earnings		6/- weekly.
Regular or intermittent work		Slack from December to June.
Retail price of article		....
Worker's rent		3/.
No. of rooms		Onne

Process. – Each bead has to be put separately by hand. See Stall.

Remarks. – This is an experienced worker who can do high-class work.

Stall X. Worker No. 20

Description of Work		Beading Ornaments
Rates Paid		2½d. to 6½d. dozen, according to size.
Worker's outlay for thread, &c.		1½d. weekly.
Time lost in fetching and returning work		About 3 hours weekly.
Average working day		12 hours.
Regular or intermittent work		6 months in year only.
Average earnings		5/- weekly, 'at most'.

Retail price of article		....
Worker's rent		....
No. of rooms		....

Process. – The worker has, first, to cut out the buckram, bind it, and then to put on the sequins and beads, *each one separately*. The work is bad for the eyes.

Remarks. – This worker has two small children dependent on her. Three others are in work, but can allow her very little – has had to 'pawn things, to make ends meet.' Husband (an old man, out of work) helps his wife and between them they can make 7/- a week at most.

Stall XI. Worker No. 21

Description of Work		Blouse Making
Rates Paid		2/4 per dozen, fancy blouses
Worker's outlay for thread, &c.		2¼d. every dozen blouses.
Time lost in fetching and returning work		6 or 7 hours a week (in addition to 'bus fares – say 6d. weekly)'
Average working day		....
Average earnings		5/- weekly.
Regular or intermittent work		Regular for 5 months of the year only.
Retail price of article		....
Worker's rent		....
No. of rooms		....

Process. – See Stall.

Remarks. –

Stall XI. Worker No. 22

Description of Work		Blouse Making. (Better quality blouses than made by worker No. 21.)
Rates Paid		5/3 per dozen
Worker's outlay for thread, &c.		About 3d. dozen
Time lost in fetching and returning work		Considerable
Average working day		12 hours.
Average earnings		About 12/- weekly.

Regular or intermittent work		Regular
Retail price of article		6/11
Worker's rent		7/6
No. of rooms		Six

Process. – The work is cut out at the factory and worker has to make and finish it.

Remarks. – Worker is married, and does this work to add to her income, which is not otherwise sufficient to keep them comfortably. Her mother helps with finishing, or the worker would not earn as much.

Stall XII. Worker No. 23

Description of Work		Shawl Fringeing.
Rates Paid		See 'Earnings' and 'Remarks'.
Worker's outlay for thread, &c.		....
Time lost in fetching and returning work		an hour daily.
Average working day		17 hours.
Average earnings		Average earnings over the year 5/-. May rise occasionally to 8/-, or even 9/-.
Regular or intermittent work		Often idle for a month at a time.
Retail price of article		....
Worker's rent		11/- monthly
No. of rooms		Two

Process. – Worker plaits the fringe and knots it. She was engaged on a large black shawl, which she had to go round twice, being 16 yards of fringeing, for 10d.

Remarks. – Widow of Baker. Has lost her voice through an attack of diphtheria. Has four children. Complains of falling rates of pay: used to get 5/- for work, which now only produces 2/-.

Stall XII. Worker No. 24

Description of Work		Making Children's Knickerbockers
Rates Paid		1/10 per dozen, all sizes
Worker's outlay for thread, &c.		8d. weekly

Time lost in fetching and returning work		3 or 4 hours weekly.
Average working day		10 hours.
Average earnings		6/- weekly.
Regular or intermittent work		Very irregular.
Retail price of article		1/- to 1/9 per pair
Worker's rent		3/-
No. of rooms		Two

Process. – Material straight from cutters at factory. The cloth, and also the linings, have to be seamed by machine; also all bits for the flies, fly linings and pockets made, all seams pressed, linings and knickers joined and turned, buttons and button-holes worked. After being finished off by hand, inside and outside are pressed and tickets sewed on ready to take back to the factory.

Remarks. – Husband out of work. Three small children.

Stall XIII. Worker No. 25-

Description of Work		Belt Making.
Rates Paid		Varies – 1/- dozen for some qualities
Worker's outlay for thread, &c.		10d. weekly, sometimes more.
Time lost in fetching and returning work		Average about 5 hours weekly.
Average working day		10 hours 'working hard'.
Average earnings		5/-
Regular or intermittent work		From September to January almost no work.
Retail price of article		....
Worker's rent		....
No. of rooms		....

Process. – See Stall.

Remarks. – Worker aged 23. Eldest of a family of 16.

Stall XIII. Worker No. 26

Description of Work		Military Embroidery
Rates Paid		....
Worker's outlay for thread, &c.		....
Time lost in fetching and returning work		Considerable
Average working day		8 or 9 hours.
Average earnings		12/- weekly in a good week.
Regular or intermittent work		Intermittent – 'has a good deal of slack time.'
Retail price of article		....
Worker's rent		2/6 – her share of 3 rooms
No. of rooms		

Process. – See Stall.

Remarks. – Worker is somewhat crippled. Besides the military embroidery does other kinds of embroidery when she can get them, viz., for railway-men's uniforms, school badges, &c.

N.B. – Although this work is done for the Government, the present War Minister is so anxious to put an end to sweating that he has assisted the Committee of the Exhibition by supplying the material on which this worker is engaged.

Stall XIV. Worker No. 27

Description of Work		Hosiery Making
Rates Paid		1/2 per dozen pairs
Worker's outlay for thread, &c.		....
Time lost in fetching and returning work		Considerable
Average working day		9 or 10 hours.
Average earnings		8/- or 9/- weekly.
Regular or intermittent work		....
Retail price of article		From 1/3 to 1/6 per pair
Worker's rent		5/6 per week
No. of rooms		Five

Process. – See Stall.

Remarks. – Worker is married; has four small children; owns her own machine.

Stall XIV. Worker No. 28

Description of Work		Glove Stitching
Rates Paid		1½d. per dozen
Worker's outlay for thread, &c.		Nil.
Time lost in fetching and returning work		....
Average working day		....
Average earnings		2/- weekly.
Regular or intermittent work		....
Retail price of article		....
Worker's rent		4/-.
No. of rooms		Four

Process. – 'Picking up stitches at finger-ends – 120 fingers for 1½d. If working hard with no hindrance, can earn the noble sum of 1d. per hour, but average is only ¾d. per hour.'

Remarks. – Worker's husband is ill at home. There are six small children.

Stall XV. Worker No. 29

Description of Work		**Making Confirmation Wreaths**
Rates Paid		Wreaths containing 1 gross of white flowers, 1/9 *per dozen wreaths*.
Worker's outlay for thread, &c.		6d. weekly, for paste and gum.
Time lost in fetching and returning work		Half an hour a day.
Average working day		12 hours.
Average earnings		7/- weekly.
Regular or intermittent work		Fairly regular
Retail price of article		Unknown
Worker's rent		4/- weekly
No. of rooms		One

Process. – See Article on 'Artificial Flower- Making.'

Remarks. – Worker has been a Widow Thirty years. Has had no parochial relief, in spite of the irregularity of the work. Was working in the factory at the age of seven – now 72. Is a most accomplished and skilful worker.

Stall XV. Worker No. 30

Description of Work		Making Pinafores
Rates Paid		2/- per dozen
Worker's outlay for thread, &c.		'Purchased own machine (£9 12s.) finds cotton.'
Time lost in fetching and returning work		'One to three hours, according to time kept waiting at shop.'
Average working day		12 hours.
Average earnings		10/- weekly.
Regular or intermittent work		Fairly regular.
Retail price of article		....
Worker's rent		3/6
No. of rooms		One

Remarks. – Worker lives alone. She has a small allowance from a relative, but is obliged to work hard at her sewing to make ends meet. Used to be able to earn 30/- weekly when prices were better and herself stronger. Constant machining has much impaired her health. 'Is frequently obliged to stay in bed for a day.'

Stall XVI. Worker No. 31

Description of Work		Cigarette Case Making
Rates Paid		4½d. per thousand.
Worker's outlay for thread, &c.		Nil.
Time lost in fetching and returning work		....
Average working day		Varies
Average earnings		8/- to 10/- weekly.
Regular or intermittent work		Intermittent – 'work terribly uneven' – at present slack.
Retail price of article		....
Worker's rent		....
No. of rooms		....

Remarks. – See Article, page 57 [Notes on the Manufacture of Cigarette Cases].

Stall XVI. Worker No. 32

Description of Work		Pipe and Cigarette-Holder Making
Rates Paid		'Small cigarette-holders sold to wholesalers at 8d. to 1/- pre gross.'
Worker's outlay for thread, &c.		About 1/- per 6 gross for clay.
Time lost in fetching and returning work		Much time lost in hawking the wares. (See 'Remarks.')
Average working day		Varies – 10 to 12 hours, or more.
Average earnings		8/- to 1/- weekly ('bad week may be 5/-, good one, 15/-).
Regular or intermittent work		See Remarks.
Retail price of article		¼d. to 1d. each.
Worker's rent		5/-
No. of rooms		Three rooms and a yard.

Process. – The clay is pressed into a mould by hand-press. After drying, the pipes and holders are fired in a small kiln in the yard. Each pattern, of course requires a separate mould, and the worker has but one or two sort. The holders are sometimes coloured to look like briars, when they fetch rather more.

Remarks. – 'This worker is in business on her own account. A hard-working woman of excellent character; she has one child ill in the infirmary, and has had, occasionally, to claim outdoor relief.'

Stall XVII. Worker No. 33

Description of Work		Chemise Making
Rates Paid		2d. each
Worker's outlay for thread, &c.		6d. weekly (and sewing machine to be kept in repair).
Time lost in fetching and returning work		Journeys, 1 hour weekly, *but 5 hours weekly lost in waiting.*
Average working day		14 hours
Average earnings		2/- per day
Regular or intermittent work		Fairly regular, but in slack season can earn only 4d. a day.

Retail price of article		Unknown.
Worker's rent		5/3.
No. of rooms		Two.

Process. – Has to cut out and make entirely.
Remarks. – Worker is married; 2 children. Her husband is out of work.

Stall XVII. Worker No. 34

Description of Work		Making Ladies' Fancy Aprons
Rates Paid		1/8 and 1/10 per dozen
Worker's outlay for thread, &c.		2d. per dozen
Time lost in fetching and returning work		Half a day twice *weekly* (also fare).
Average working day		14 hours.
Average earnings		'Worker must earn 18/- per week, and so works long hours; does not stop for meals and gets help at home.'.
Regular or intermittent work		Intermittent
Retail price of article		1/6 to 1/11.
Worker's rent		4/-
No. of rooms		One

Process. – See Stall

Remarks. – A particularly quick worker, who has done all kinds of machining, both well paid and badly paid.

Stall XVIII. Worker No. 35

Description of Work		Shirt Making
Rates Paid		Some 9 ½ *per dozen*, others 1/- and up to 1/9 ½ per dozen, *for making shirt throughout*.
Worker's outlay for thread, &c.		....
Time lost in fetching and returning work		About 2 hours daily.
Average working day		See 'Process.'

Average earnings		9/- weekly.
Regular or intermittent work		
Retail price of article		1/11 to 2/3 per pair
Worker's rent		4/6 per week
No. of rooms		Six

Process. – For the shirts paid at 1/9½ *per dozen*, the following work is required: – make and line yoke and bottom bands, put in 4 gussets, hem skirts, run and fell side seams, make sleeves and put them in. Being a very expert worker, she can do this – which is skilled work – at the rate of a dozen shirts in 10 hours or so. The shirts paid at 9d. *per dozen* require her to hem necks, button-stitch 2 stud-holes, sew on 6 buttons and clip threads from all seams. These take 4½ hours per dozen. The shirts at 1/- per dozen have 2 rows feather-stitching, 6 buttonhole, 8 buttons, 4 seams bridged, and 8 fastenings made. It is very hard work to do a dozen of these in 6 hours.

Remarks. – Wife of a tradesman irregularly employed.

Stall XVIII. Worker No. 36

Description of Work		Shirt Finishing
Rates Paid		1½d. dozen, taking 1½ hours per dozen; 3d. dozen, taking 4 hours per dozen.
Worker's outlay for thread, &c.		1d or 1½d. off 1/6 earned.
Time lost in fetching and returning work		From 1½ to 2 hours.
Average working day		17 hours.
Average earnings		12/- to 14/- per month.
Regular or intermittent work		
Retail price of article		
Worker's rent		14 per month.
No. of rooms		Two.

Process. – The finishing of shirts at 1½d. a dozen includes the bridging of 4 seams, sewing on of 4 buttons and turning down of a collar *(being the sewing on of 48 buttons, 48 bridgings, and 12 collar turnings for 1 ½ d.)* Those at 3d. dozen require 8 buttons on each shirt, bridging of 4 seams, clipping of threads from 4 seams and putting in a stud *(being the sewing on of 96 buttons, 48 bridgings, 48 thread clippings, or more, and 12 stud fixings, for 3d.)*

Remarks. –

Stall XIX. Workers Nos. 37 and 38

Description of Work		Artificial Flower-making
Rates Paid		Violets, 7d. gross; geraniums, 7d. gross; buttercups, 3d. gross; roses, 1/3 to 3/6 gross.
Worker's outlay for thread, &c.		6d. weekly for paste.
Time lost in fetching and returning work		2 hours a day
Average working day		14 hours.
Average earnings		10/- weekly.
Regular or intermittent work		Irregular
Retail price of article		Various.
Worker's rent		4/6 weekly.
No. of rooms		One.

Remarks. – A clever woman and magnificent worker. Cannot read or write; 'For fifty years she has made artificial flowers and for skill and indomitable perseverance she has no superior. The basket of flowers seen in the picture (see illustration 'Flower-makers') is her creation. (Her husband is also a flower-maker, but is nearly blind and quite an invalid. Until recently they occupied an underground room, for which 4s 6d. weekly was paid. To support herself and her husband without parish relief or philanthropic aid, she has often worked fourteen, and even sixteen, hours a day; her only respite has been to carry her finished flowers to the factory and bring back other materials. On her way home, sometimes she will purchase a little black silk, and some black bristles, and when other work fails, these she will make into black tulips, or 'ragged roses,' and other symbols of bereavement and sorrow, and the half-blind husband will rise from his bed, wander into the streets, and dispose of them at a mourning warehouse for 3½d. per complete spray. (These mourning flowers soon increase in value, for the tradesman marks them 6¾d. or 8¾ d per spray.)'

Stall XX. Worker No. 39

Description of Work		Steel Bodice Work
Rates Paid		2¾ d gross, "hard work to do a gross and a half per day
Worker's outlay for thread, &c.		Nil.
Time lost in fetching and returning work		Nil.

Average working day		14 hours. "Has got up at 6 a.m. and worked till 12 p.m. and only done 2 gross."
Average earnings		2/- a week.
Regular or intermittent work		Intermittent. "Not getting any at present".
Retail price of article		1/11 to 2/3 per pair
Worker's rent		6d week, "because living with her married daughter, who helps her."
No. of rooms		

Process. – see: stall

Remarks. – A widow 69 years of age.

Stall XX. Worker No. 40

Description of Work		Book Folding – mostly Bibles and Prayer Books
Rates Paid		1d. per 100 sheets – on some Bibles 1¼d. for 100 sheets.
Worker's outlay for thread, &c.		....
Time lost in fetching and returning work		1 to 1½ hour.
Average working day		12 hours
Average earnings		9/- to 10/- weekly.
Regular or intermittent work		6 months in the year only.
Retail price of article		....
Worker's rent		8/6 weekly
No. of rooms		Three.

Process. – The sheets have to be first cut, then folded, and put into the right order.

Remarks. – The worker's husband is out of employment. There are six children, three of whom are earning. Worker has broken down in health, and "the doctor says she must not do any more of the work." Her breakdown is due to the severity of the work – cutting some of the heavier books (poems) strained her heart.
N.B. This worker attends the Exhibition to show the process, but will not be continuously busy.

Stall XXI Worker No. 41

Description of Work		Cardbox Making
Rates Paid		1/2 gross for small boxes about 5 inches by 3 inches.
Worker's outlay for thread, &c.		Finds glue and string – quite 6d. weekly
Time lost in fetching and returning work		About 2 hours per day
Average working day		10 hours to make 1 gross.
Average earnings		5/- weekly, full week 8/-
Regular or intermittent work		4 of 5 days a week
Retail price of article		These boxes are not retailed
Worker's rent		4/6
No. of rooms		One.

Remarks. – This worker was married in 1890, and has had 7 children. Three of these: are now living and "cared for" by mother. Her husband died in the Infirmary of Pulmonary Tuberculosis, September 1905. During his illness and the worker's confinement, trifling amount of parochial relief accepted. None applied for since husband's death. Five shillings represents the most ever spent on food – the average being 6d. to 1/- per day, according to earnings; this buys 2 ounces tea, a loaf, and some margarine. Worker very occasionally has 2/- from a cousin. She has been compelled to pawn for food and rent.

Stall XXI. Worker No. 42

Description of Work	**......**	**Paper-bag Making**
Rates Paid	......	Two sizes 6d. per 1,000.
Worker's outlay for thread, &c.	......	Finds own paste.
Time lost in fetching and returning work	......	5 hours a week
Average working day	......	12 hours.
Average earnings	......	4/6 a week.
Regular or intermittent work	......	Very irregular.
Retail price of article	......	....
Worker's rent	......	5/-
No. of rooms	......	Three, and scullery.

Process. – Worker's paper is square, and has to be cut to shape, each separately; then fold; then paste; then pack in ½-gross bundles.

Remarks. –

Stall XXII. Worker No. 43

Description of Work	......	Drawing, Clipping and Scolloping of Lace (Machined Made).
Rates Paid	......	See "Earnings".
Worker's outlay for thread, &c.	......	Nil.
Time lost in fetching and returning work	......	Varies from 5 to 30 minutes
Average working day	......	12 hours or more in the season.
Average earnings	......	2/- per day for quick hands, working 12 hours or more a day.
Regular or intermittent work	......	Intermittent. "Some weeks a single day, and some weeks they will work the clock round".
Retail price of article	......	Varied according to character, quality, width and demand.
Worker's rent	......	....
No. of rooms	......	....

Process. – See Stall.

Remarks. – This worker attends the Exhibition to show work done by home workers at above rates. She herself works in a factory for fairly good wages.

Stall XXII. Worker No. 44

Description of Work	......	**Accoutrement Sewing. (Government Contract Work)**
Rates Paid	......	Belts, 1½ d., 1¾d. each; bandoliers, 1/7 each; frogs, 1½d. each; bottle covers, 1d. each; mess tin covers, 3d. dozen; haversacks, 4½d. dozen.
Worker's outlay for thread, &c.	......	....
Time lost in fetching and returning work	......	....
Average working day	......	....

Average earnings	......	10/- weekly.
Regular or intermittent work	......	....
Retail price of article	......	....
Worker's rent	......	....
No. of rooms	......	....

Remarks. – This worker is now doing shirt work, and thinks it pays about as well.

N.B. – Although this work is done for the Government, the present War Minister is so anxious to put an end to sweating that he has assisted the Committee of the Exhibition by supplying the material on which this worker is engaged.

Stall XXIII. Worker No. 45

Description of Work	......	**Fruit-Basket Making**
Rates Paid	......	3/- per gross 1 lb. size.
Worker's outlay for thread, &c.	......	Wood per gross, 1/6
Time lost in fetching and returning work	......	Considerable – 'bus fare 2d.
Average working day	......	12 hours
Average earnings	......	1 1/3 per day
Regular or intermittent work	......	Regular about 4 months in summer; little or none in winter.
Retail price of article	......	Sold to customers direct; maker hawks them in the market
Worker's rent	......	7/- per week
No. of rooms	......	Two

Process. – See Stall.

Remarks. – The competition of machinery has cut prices by about 50 per cent during past few years.

61

HOW TO DO AWAY WITH THE SWEATING SYSTEM, 1892

Beatrice Webb

Source: Beatrice Webb, 'How to Do Away with the Sweating System', A paper read at the twenty-fourth annual congress of Co-operative Societies, held at Rochdale, June 1892, in *Problems in Modern Industry*, Sidney and Beatrice Webb (Longmans, Green and Co., 1898), 139–48.

EDITORIAL HEADNOTE

Beatrice Webb (1858–1943, born Martha Beatrice Potter) was a social reformer and politician, and among the most prominent and productive pioneers of social science in Britain together with her husband, Sidney James Webb, Baron Passfield (1859–1947), with whom she maintained a close working relationship. It is notable that they were, and are, often referred to as 'the Webbs', and the ODNB produced a joint biography of the couple. Born into wealth and comfort, she had an intellectual education, later bemoaning her lack of domestic skills. In her early years she searched for religious meaning, the ways and means of service to humanity and gradually rejected capitalism (see entry in ODNB). She, like her sisters, in fact, became anti-feminist and she signed a petition opposing female suffrage in 1899. Having seen the conditions of sweated female workers in the London tailoring trades in the 1880s, she became hostile to the form of feminism that placed civic equality before economic emancipation. As female suffrage rose up the political agenda, she recanted in 1906. Even so, her feminism was not of the narrow suffrage kind, as her activities and writings show. From the 1880s, she evinced respect for independent women like Octavia Hill and other philanthropists, but recognizing that it was seen as 'ladies' work, and she shifted toward social analysis, to develop a more scientific understanding of poverty. Taking a number of forays into social observation, she became committed to the principles of co-operation. Working in the East End of London, she developed her observational skills and gained an understanding of the structural nature of poverty. She

DOI: 10.4324/9781003676669-67

became one of the original team deployed by Charles Booth, a cousin, in his pioneering study of East End poverty, and worked as a jobbing tailor to gain insight to the sweating industry. Rejecting individualism, she became a socialist during this period. Reading an essay by Sidney Webb in the collection *Fabian Essays in Socialism*, she liked his historic sense and was introduced to him shortly after by another cousin, Margaret Harkness. She initially only sought an intellectual friendship and in this they had much in common. She joined the Fabian Society at his prompting and together they dominated the organisation until shortly before the First World War.

Fittingly, this extract on sweating comes from a paper read at a Co-operative Society congress and was published in the Webb's joint volume *Problems in Modern Industry*. She starts by defining sweating and then examining the causes as preliminary to indicating how to eliminate it. It is informed by her intellectual journey and her practical work, including her time working in the industry. She wrote on dock work and tailoring for Booth, whose *Life and Labour* she references frequently, and these industries reappeared in the speech.

Before we can hope to solve the problem which forms the subject matter of this paper, we must answer two preliminary questions. First, we must decide what we mean by sweating and the sweating system; and secondly, we must determine what are the causes of these evils. For it is obvious that without an exact conception of the nature of the suffering which we desire to remedy, without some idea of the sources of the evils which we are determined to cure, we shall fail to grapple with the practical question of 'How to do away with the Sweating System.'

Fortunately for us the first question has already been adequately answered by an august authority. Almost the only result of the elaborate inquiry into the sweating system,[1] conducted by a Committee of the House of Lords in 1888–90, was an accurate definition of sweating at once comprehensive and concise. Lord Derby and his colleagues finally decided that sweating was no particular method of remuneration, no peculiar form of industrial organisation, but certain conditions of employment – viz. unusually low rates of wages, excessive hours of labour, and insanitary workplaces. When we get any one of these conditions in an extreme and exaggerated form – for instance, when we find a woman sewing neckties in her own home, straining every nerve to earn only a halfpenny an hour – still more, when we see all these conditions combined, as in the cellar dwellings in which the Jewish boot-finishers work sixteen or seventeen hours a day for a wage of 12s. per week – then we say that the labour is sweated, and that the unfortunates are working under the sweating system.

Let us, therefore, pass on to the second point. What are the causes that produce these evils? Some persons maintain that sweating is restricted to industries in which sub-contract prevails; that, in fact, it is the middleman who is the sweater; that this man grinds the face of the poor, and takes from them the fruits of their labour. You will remember a cartoon that appeared in Punch about the time of the House of Lords' inquiry, in which the middleman was represented as a bloated man-spider sucking the life-blood out of men and women who were working around him. Now, before I studied the facts of East London industries for myself I really believed that this horrible creature existed. But I soon found out that either he was purely a myth, or that the times had been too hard for him, and that he had been squeezed out of existence by some bigger monster. For I discovered that in the coat trade, and in the low-class boot trade – which are exclusively in the hands of the Jews – where the work is still taken out by small contractors, these middlemen, far from being bloated idlers, work as hard, if not harder, than their sweated hands, and frequently earn less than the machinist or presser to whom they pay wages. On the other hand, in those trades in which English women are employed – such as the manufacture of shirts, ties, umbrellas, juvenile suits, etc. – the middleman is fast disappearing. It is true that formerly the much-abused sub-contract system prevailed in these trades – that is to say, some man or woman would contract with the wholesale manufacturer to make and deliver so many dozen garments for a certain sum. He would then distribute these garments one by one in the homes of the women, or perhaps he would engage women to make them in his own house. He might receive a shilling for the making of each garment, but he would give only tenpence to the actual workers, pocketing twopence in return for his trouble and risk. But of late years the more enterprising wholesale manufacturers have thought it most unjust that the middleman should pocket the twopence. To remedy this injustice they have opened shops all over the East End of London, where they give out work just as the middleman used to do, first to be machined and then to be finished. But, strangely enough, they still pay tenpence to their workers, the only difference being that instead of the middleman getting the balance they pocket the twopence themselves. Nor do they trouble themselves in the very least where these garments are made. The women who support themselves and perhaps their families by this class of work live in cellars or in garrets, sometimes two or three families in one room. This does not concern the wholesale manufacturer. No doubt he would tell you that the middleman was the sweater and that he had destroyed him. But, unfortunately, he did not destroy, or even diminish, what the practical observer means by sweating. The actual worker gains absolutely nothing by the disappearance of the subcontractor, middleman, or so called sweater. In East London the change has been, so far as the workers are concerned, from out of the frying-pan into the fire.

And if we leave the clothing trade, and pass to the lower grades of the furniture trades, in which all the evils of sweating exist, we may watch the poverty-stricken maker of tables and chairs hawking his wares along the Curtain Road, selling direct to the export merchant, or to the retail tradesman – or perchance, to the private customer. In the manufacture of cheap boots in London, of common cutlery at Sheffield, of indifferent nails at Halesowen, we meet with this same sorrowful figure – the small master or out-worker buying his material on credit, and selling his product to meet the necessities of the hour; in all instances underselling his competitors, great and small. Respectable employers, interested in a high standard of production, trade unionists, keen for a high standard of wage, agree in attributing to this pitiful personage the worst evils of the sweating system. Here, not only do we fail to discover the existence of sub-contract, but even the element of contract itself disappears, and the elaborate organisation of modern industry is replaced by a near approach to that primitive higgling of the market between the actual producer of an article and the actual consumer – to that primaeval struggle and trial of endurance in which the weakest and most necessitous invariably suffers.

I do not wish you to imagine that I deny the existence of the sweater in the sweated industries. But I deny that the sweater is necessarily or even usually the sub-contractor or employing middleman. The sweater is, in fact, the whole nation. The mass of struggling men and women whose sufferings have lately been laid bare are oppressed and defrauded in every relation of life: by the man who sells or gives out the material on which they labour; by the shopkeeper who sells them provisions on credit, or forces them under the truck system; by the landlord who exacts, in return for the four walls of a bedroom, or for the unpaved and undrained back-yard, the double rent of workshop and dwelling; and, lastly, by every man, woman, and child who consumes the product of their labour. In the front rank of this, the most numerous class of sweaters, we find the oppressed workers themselves. The middleman where he exists is not the oppressor, but merely one of the instruments of oppression. And we cannot agree with Punch's representation of him as a spider devouring healthy flies. If we must describe him as a noxious insect we should picture him much more truly as the maggot that appears in meat after decay has set in. He is not the cause, but one of the occasional results of the evil. He takes advantage of the disorganised state of the substance which surrounds him, and lives on it; if he does not do so, some other creature will devour both him and his food. What we have to discover, therefore, is the origin of the disorganisation itself.[2]

Now, in all the manufacturing industries in which 'sweating' extensively prevails we discover one common feature. The great mass of the production is carried on, not in large factories, but either by small masters in hidden workshops, or by workers in their own dwellings. And, as a natural consequence of this significant fact, the employer – whether he be the profit-making middleman, wholesale trader, or even the consumer himself – is relieved from all responsibility for the conditions under which the work is done. The workers, on the other hand, incapacitated for combination by the isolation of their lives, excluded by special clauses for the protection of the Factory Acts, are delivered over body and soul to the spirit of unrestrained competition, arising from the ever-increasing demand for cheap articles in the great markets of the world. If we compare this state of things with the industries in which sweating does not exist, we see at once that in the case of the engineer, the cotton-spinner, or the miner, the men work together in large establishments, and the employer becomes responsible for the conditions of their employment. The mill-owner, coal-owner, or large iron-master, is forced to assume, to some slight extent, the guardianship of his workers. He is compelled by the State to provide healthy accommodation, to regulate the hours of labour of women and young persons, to see to the education of children, to guard against and insure all workers against accident. Trade unions, arising from the massing of men under the factory system, insist on a recognised rate of wages. Public opinion, whether social or political, observes the actions of a responsible employer in the open light of day. Willingly or unwillingly, he must interpose his brains and his capital between groups of workers on the one hand, and the great mass of conscienceless consumers on the other. These are the services exacted from him by the community in return for the profits he makes. He is, in fact, the first link between the private individual intent on his own gain, and the ideal official of the Socialistic State administering the instruments of production in trust for the people. It is the absence of this typical figure of nineteenth century industry which is the distinguishing feature of the sweating system.

On the other hand, we have seen, in the sweated industries, how, by the system of home-work, the virtual employer altogether escapes the responsibilities of his position. He gives out his work from an office to a miscellaneous and scattered set of workpeople, whose places of abode he scarcely even knows; his work is done in uninspected domestic workshops, it may be under the most insanitary conditions; his employees must, as he knows, often toil far into the night to comply with his demands, but he incurs no penalty. Alike from the obligations and the expenses of the factory owner, the sweater is free. Meanwhile, the slum landlord is receiving, for his cellars and attics, the double rent of workshop and dwelling without incurring the expensive sanitary obligations of the mill-owner. In short, it is home work which creates all the difficulties of our problem. For it is home work which, with its isolation, renders trade combination[3] impracticable; which enables the manufacturer to use as a potent instrument, for the degradation of all, the necessity of the widow or the creed of the Jew. And more important still, it is home work which, by withdrawing the workers from the beneficent protection of the Factory Acts, destroys all legal responsibility on the part of the employer and the landlord for the conditions of employment.

Clearly we must first see to it that our own house is in order. I am glad to think that co-operators as employers already recognise their duty as regards the payment of fair wages, the exaction of reasonable hours of labour, and the provision of sanitary workplaces for all their employees. This special responsibility of co-operators as employers has often been dwelt upon. The shirt-making shops of the Scottish Co-operative Wholesale Society at Shieldhall offer a brilliant example of what may be done by co-operative enterprise in an industry usually abandoned to the sweater.[4] But it is useless to shut our eyes to the fact that cooperators can never hope to become the employers of the great mass of the workers who suffer under the sweating system. Taken as a whole the sweated industries may be said to work mainly for export. The low-class clothing made in East London is largely worn, not by our own people, but by the inhabitants of Australia and the Cape. The common boots and shoes turned out wholesale by the Jewish families of Whitechapel, or the Leicestershire villagers, equally supply the Colonial market. The sweated knives of Sheffield disgrace her name and injure her commercial prestige throughout the whole world. Even the most patient Conservative would not ask us patiently to watch the degradation of large sections of our countrymen whilst the Co-operative Wholesale Society is enroling, as members, the dusky Indian or the almond-eyed Mongolian, who are to so large an extent the virtual employers of the sweated workers. And even in those cases where the cheap and nasty products of the sweating system are used at home, they supply the needs neither of co-operators nor of those among whom co-operation is ever likely to flourish. The evil influence of the export sweating trade extends to that which supplies a nearer market. It is the woman earning a halfpenny an hour at clothes for the Cape who buys the cheap furniture hawked about the Curtain Road. It is the Jewish boot-finisher working for abroad who, in his turn, buys the slop clothing displayed in the sweater's front shop. We are thus in a vicious circle, where sweating itself creates the conditions for the sweating system.[5] For can we expect the nail-maker, toiling sixteen or seventeen hours a day for bare subsistence, or the children brought up in the one-roomed homes of East or South London, to develop that high level of moral and intellectual character which experience has proved to be absolutely essential to any considerable growth of co-operative association? As a matter of fact, the officials of the co-operative movement have met with as great obstacles to the spread of co-operation among the victims of the sweating system as an ardent co-operator would experience if he insisted on going as a co-operative missionary to the South Sea Islanders.

And if it be impracticable to transform the sweater's victim into a co-operative consumer, still more impossible will it be to change him into a co-operative producer. We may differ as to the desirability of Associations of Producers in other departments of industry. But it will be needless to remind the experienced co-operator that the idea of the East End female necktie-makers, the Staffordshire nail-makers, or the Jewish boot-finishers ever being able to set up in business for themselves as associations of producers is simply chimerical. Whether or not the self-governing workshop be the goal of industrial organisation, it is certainly not the starting-point. Indeed, those who believe most firmly in associations of producers insist most keenly that it requires for its success an exceptional amount of character and intelligence on the part of the workers. Moreover, the self-governing workshop, pledged to a high standard of wage, would be subject, in the sweated industries, to the competition of the home-work system, with its degraded labour and cheap products. Should we desire, therefore, the rapid spread of co-operative production, carried on by associations of producers, our first step must be to root up and destroy the evils of sweating.

Are co-operators, then, powerless to do away with the sweating system? We must, I fear, admit that neither as employers nor as associated workers can they deal directly with the evil outside their ranks. Yet co-operators, of both schools, are most vitally interested in maintaining throughout the whole community a high standard of industrial morality. For not only does the sweating system practically exclude from their membership whole sections of their fellow-workers, but even in their own market they are unfortunately only too liable to be attacked by unscrupulous private competitors. The failures of promising experiments in co-operative production have too often been attributed to the difficulty of obtaining a market for well-made goods. Nearly every quarterly meeting bears unconscious witness to the insidious influence of the low-priced manufacturer of low-class goods, in the complaint that the Co-operative Wholesale Society or the retail store is charging, for some articles, more than the private trader. And in all the labour troubles which perplex the co-operative committee-man, it is the ever present fear of the competing sweater which at times prevents our ready acquiescence in that generous treatment of co-operative employees advocated by our most enlightened administrators.

See also in this collection, Vol 4.

Source Endnotes

1 The voluminous Report and Evidence of this committee is published as a parliamentary paper, H.L. 62 of 1890. An article by the present writer in the *Nineteenth Century* for May 1890, entitled 'The Lords and the Sweating System,' gives a critical analysis of the recommendations. A useful summary of the evidence is published by the Women's Liberal Federation, price id. A systematic analysis of the whole problem is concisely given in Fabian Tract, No. 50, Sweating, its Causes and Remedy.

2 The common assumption that sweating arises principally from the struggle for existence among destitute aliens appears to me to be inaccurate. No one would deny that the evils of sweating are aggravated by the presence of workers – such as the Jews, with an indefinitely low standard of life and an absence of skill. (See the preceding chapter, 'The Jews of East London.') But all the evils of sweating exist where neither Jews nor foreigners have yet penetrated (as, for instance, in the chain and nail industry); or where their competition is but little felt (as in the low-grade furniture trade). Even in the clothing trades the competition of Jewish immigrants is practically limited to some branches of the tailoring and boot and shoe trades. On the other hand, we are everywhere confronted with a large supply of cheap female labour, far exceeding in numbers even the most exaggerated estimate of alien immigration. The evil effect of Jewish immigrants on the labour market is, indeed, not a question of fact, but a question of proportion. The Jews are counted by their thousands; the women, dragging in their real semi-dependent husbands and a huge force of unprotected children, may be numbered by hundreds of thousands. This aspect of the subject is discussed in various chapters in Mr. Charles Booth's *Life and Labour of the People*; and in *Industrial Democracy*, part ii. chap. x. sec. 4, 'The Exclusion of Women.'

3 I have not attempted in this paper to deal with home work from the standpoint of trade unionism; but if systematic home work be unfavourable to the growth of co-operation, it is absolutely fatal to the stability, or perhaps even to the existence, of trade combination. Trade unionists are, of all reformers, the most vitally interested in the abolition of workplaces withdraw it from the jurisdiction of law, trade-union regulation, and public opinion. On this point see Industrial Democracy, vol. ii. part ii. chap. xii.

4 The movement against sweating would be assisted if co-operators invariably insisted that no order should be given to any but 'fair' houses innocent of sweating. Every town

council or other public authority should be urged to follow the example of the London County Council, in insisting on the payment by all contractors of the standard rate of wages in each occupation, and in rigidly refusing all tenders from 'unfair' firms. The cheapness of the sweater (often, by the way, delusive) is the price of blood.

5 The industrial demoralisation of East London is, I believe, caused mainly by the two factors of home work and intermittent dock labour, and even the existence of so large a class of irregularly-employed dock labourers is, to a large extent, rendered possible only by the home work done by their wives. I doubt if co-operation can ever flourish in East London until these continuing sources of degradation are removed. See *Industrial Democracy*, part iii. chap. iii. sec. 4, 'Parasitic Trades.'

62

HOMEWORK AND SWEATING, THE CAUSES AND REMEDIES, 1907

B. L. Hutchins

Source: B.L. Hutchins, *Homework and Sweating, the causes and the remedies*, Fabian Tract No. 130 (The Fabian Society, 1907), 3–7, 9–10, 17–18.

EDITORIAL HEADNOTE

Having opened this volume with B.L. Hutchins, her essay in the *Fabian Tracts* is a fitting partner to Beatrice Webb's paper. Like Webb, she starts by trying to define sweating and tends to agree that there were many sweating systems, a point this volume also makes. Her essay also makes the link between handicraft work and its deterioration into sweating and sweating as an extension or offshoot of the factory. She deals with factors that have become familiar: why sweating worked to the advantage of the employer, the issue of wages, raised earlier, the case for regulation, but interestingly introduces the issue of 'alien' immigrants which is largely a shadow issue in most accounts, and far more common in American texts, many of which appear in later volumes in this collection.

WHAT IS MEANT BY THE SWEATING SYSTEM

The phrase, the Sweating *System* is misleading. All experts agree that there is no one industrial system co-extensive with, or invariably present in, the Sweated Trades. Mr. Booth expresses this by saying that it is not with one but many sweating systems we have to deal: Mr. Schloss says that no sweating *system* whatever is discoverable; and the House of Lords Committee, whilst reporting that the evils complained of could "scarcely be exaggerated," said that they had been unable to find any precise meaning attached to the phrase. An enquiry into sweating resolves itself, therefore, into an enquiry into the conditions under which the "sweated industries" are worked. Here at least a painful and striking

DOI: 10.4324/9781003676669-68

uniformity is met with, and accepting it as a starting point, the Lords Committee defined Sweating as: –

1. Unduly low rates of wages.
2. Excessive hours of labor.
3. Insanitary state of the workplaces

Mr Schloss has added the important point, taxing of working-power to an unreasonable extent, or getting sixpenny-worth of work out of fourpenny-worth of pay ("driving").[a] The broadest definition we can find for the term sweating, is "grinding the faces of the poor." Professor Ashley has given us a new and vivid phrase "cheap and docile labor," which helps to explain the special characteristic of sweated industry.[1] Sweated workers are sweated because either by reason of sex, age, infirmity or want of organization and support, they have to let their work go cheap. They are compelled by need to sell their labor to the first purchaser who will take it, and cannot make conditions. They must work at the rates of pay the employer thinks good enough for them, and the smallness of the pay automatically extends the hours of work.

Sweating is no new thing. It occurs usually as a symptom of one of two kinds of industrial change: either as the decay of a handicraft or as an extension or offshoot of the factory system. Handloom weaving is an instance of the former kind that will occur to us at once. Long before machinery was introduced we find the scattered weavers suffering from their lack of organization, subject to continual oppression by the factors who disposed of the stuff Elizabeth's ministers were so impressed with the gravity of the evil that they drafted a bill to "avoid deceits done by Spinners of Woollen yarn and weavers of woollen cloth, and *to increase their wages.*" (S. P. Dom. Eliz. Vol. 244.) In more recent times the handloom weavers vainly petitioned Parliament to revive the assessment of wages in their trade. In 1815 it was argued before Peel's Committee on the Employment of Children in Cotton Mills that it was unjust to limit the hours of children working in the mills while the handloom weavers, being grievously underpaid, often had to keep their children working far into the night to make up a living. In Germany and Austria and elsewhere the decaying handicraft, or *Hausindustrie*, is well known and widely spread. It is not only the competition of handworking with machinery that cuts down the rates of pay. The chain making at Cradley Heath shews that a handicraft can be grossly underpaid and sweated, although as yet no machine has been invented to do the work. But in England the sweated industry now more often takes the form of an auxiliary to the factory. Tailoring, clothing, shirts, blouses, ties, shoes, slippers and various trifles such as toys, crackers, match-boxes, instead of being made in the factory, are given out to be made or partly made in the workers' homes. This at first sight seems mysterious, for the economy and efficiency of factory industry (production on a large scale) has been demonstrated over and over again, in theory and in practice. How is it that blouses or match-boxes continue to be made in homes if they could be better and more cheaply made in a factory?

The Reason why Sweating Pays the Sweater

Although, broadly speaking, the factory is the more economical method, yet the employment of home-workers offers an advantage in that very little capital is needed for starting or extending a business, and also because the sweating employer or contractor is able to shift some of the cost on to other people's shoulders. The manufacturer has to pay rent and rates for his factory; the sweater leaves the workers to pay rent for themselves. The manufacturer has to observe Factory Act requirements as to the cleaning, ventilation and sanitation of his factory; the sweater does not trouble about the condition of the workrooms to which he gives out work, as long as he gets the work done. The manufacturer may only employ women, children and young persons, for a certain period and within certain hours; the sweater's hands may work all night if they and he see fit. But there is another circumstance which gives the sweater an advantage, or apparent advantage, and that is in the complete lack of organization among these out-workers. It is true, no doubt, that factory women also are generally unorganized, but the mere fact of working and being paid together helps to maintain some sort of a standard, though often low enough. Out-workers are mostly very poor people, scattered about in their little homes, knowing nothing of one another, sometimes very shy and shrinking; they are often women who sorely need a few shillings to supplement the less irregular earnings of the head of the house, but are not entirely dependent on their own industry. If they ask for better pay or attempt to protest against a reduction of rates, there is one answer for them; others will be thankful to get the work. Some of these women get a little charity; many have poor relief; some have husbands who earn 16s or 17s. a week when they are lucky enough to be in work at all. Some depend entirely on their wretched trade, and their case must be little better than prolonged starvation. All of them constitute however a force of "cheap and docile labor" which can be made profitable after a fashion, though it can obviously be applied to some industries only. Work that depends on delicate or costly machinery, or on skilled supervision and organization, is safe from any competition from the home. But the needlework trades and certain small objects that can be made with little skill, boxes, toys, crackers, etc., offer a field to the enterprise of the sweating employer, because the work can so easily be transferred from the factory or shop to the home. And the peculiarly unfortunate feature of this competition between the two industrial modes is that every improvement in the Factory Law or in its administration tends to drive work out of the factory into the home. If a local authority resolves to adopt a higher standard of requirements in regard to "suitable and sufficient" sanitary accommodation, the occupier of a workshop may decide to send away women and give them work to do at home; on the other hand, stricter inspection of out-workers will help to disgust their employer, who will think he would rather take on more indoor hands than be worried over the infectious diseases of people he knows very little about. The exact effect of the law in force in deciding the choice between outdoor and indoor employment is a point on which fuller information is much needed. But one thing is plain; the legal regulation of home work must be amended and extended in order to do away with the unfair advantage obtained by the employer; otherwise the benefit of the Factory Act to the worker will in certain industries involve the giving more work out to homes.

Wages

The unfair advantage enjoyed by the sweater is of two kinds: first, the evasion of factory legislation, already mentioned; second, the extreme lowness of the wages paid. Of the low wages so much has been heard lately that it is hardly necessary to labor the point further. We may take a few instances at random from The *Daily News* Exhibition Handbook.

A. Trouser maker, widow with 4 children, works 10 or 12 hours a day, her best earnings (exceptional) are 10s. 6d.a week; more often 3s. or 4s.; receives parochial relief.
B. Match-box maker, works 12 hours a day, earns on an average les than 5s. a week. Highest earnings 8s. 2d. for a full week including Sunday.
C. Button carder. Two old people work together, earn 3s. 6d. per week.

Such instances could be multiplied *ad nauseam.* The Cradley Heath chain makers, after deducting cost of fuel, earn only 5s. to 6s. weekly for hard work, of a kind really skilled in its way, and not yet replaceable by machinery. The present writer has personally visited home workers in London, Birmingham and Cradley Heath, and has met with one, a skilled waistcoat maker, who was paid a living wage. The next most favourable instance was that of a remarkably quick, capable girl, making girls' frocks, lined throughout and trimmed, at 8d. each, deducting cost of cotton. She said she could make five or even six a day on occasion; but "you have to move yourself to do it"; and one could well believe it. This was an exceptionally quick worker; what would have been the earnings of an average or slow worker? In match-box making and similar wretched trades, about 1d. per hour seems to be what the piece rates yield. The lowest depths of all perhaps are reached by workers who sew hooks and eyes, buttons, etc., on cards. Carding hooks and eyes I have found paid at 14d. per gross cards in Birmingham. The employer was threatening to reduce the price to 10½d. for there were middlewomen who could farm the work out to "very poor people," and thus cut the recognized price of 14d. per gross. The average earnings of women in this work are only about 3s. 3d. weekly, even when they work long hours.[2] In all these small home industries the wages appear to tend steadily downwards, although in factory work women's

Image 8 Jacob A. Riis. Sewing Pants for the Sweater's in Gotham Court, New York, 1890s. Public Domain

wages have been rising for a considerable period.[3] The explanation is not far to seek; whereas the factory industry, aided not only by machinery which can be seen, but by improvements in organization and supervision which are not seen (or not so easily), becomes more efficient and produces at a less cost, in home work there is no scope for these improvements, and employment is given to "cheap and docile labor" only. In so far as these women consent to take lower and lower rates, they can get work. . . .

Protection of Home Industries

Protection of home industries is sometimes urged as a possible remedy for sweating. The evidence collected for the Berlin exhibition of sweated industries shewed however that sweating is quite as rampant in protected Germany as in free-trade England; and there are colonies of home-workers in Chicago and New York where even the very high tariff maintained in America does not make wages or conditions any better than in the worst parts of London. Regulation of sweating would do far more for trade than any import duty on manufactured goods, as it would deprive the sweater of the unfair advantage he now gets by employing "cheap and docile labor" unregulated workrooms, and more custom and a larger share of the export trade would then go to the traders who are carrying on business honestly under fair conditions.

Alien Immigration

Restraint of immigration is often urged as a remedy for sweating but the Aliens Act of 1905 achieved little or nothing, and it is unlikely that even a much more drastic Act would really check the evil. It must be remembered that the alien population is comparatively small, though, no doubt, in one or two districts it forms a high percentage. Sweating is quite equally rampart where the alien is a negligible quantity. There are practically no foreigners in the cutlery or nail and chain-making industries, yet there the sweater flourishes. Even in the tailoring trades, the competition of destitute foreigners is as nothing compared with the great mass of unskilled and unorganized female labor which crowds the market. The removal of all Jews from the sweated trades would be but a partial and temporary relief. The evil effect of the Jew's competition lies in the characteristics which render him a fit subject for the pestilential conditions of home work: he overcrowds whole districts; his standard of comfort is low; and his ingenuity has created or organized new industries to suit the circumstances. In the factory, English skilled labor has the preference: abolish the conditions that now specially favor the demoralizing competition of the Jew, and the difficulty will be got over without an impracticable policy of exclusion. The latest factory inspector's report from New Zealand (June, 1906) says that though there has been a considerable influx of labor into the colony of late years, no displacement or unemployment of their own people has ensued. Why? Because *the system of employment in the colony permits no undercutting in wages,* and "thus gives to those possessing knowledge of local conditions and requirements advantage over the visitor, unless the latter shows decidedly superior attainments." . . .

Conclusion

There are those who will say that the measures of reform here sketched out will have the effect of throwing out of work those poor people who are not worth employing at the wages and under the conditions that would be required under an amended Factory Act, with a minimum wage and strictly sanitary conditions required for out-workers as well as indoor hands. M. Aftalion, in a recent interesting study,[4] declares that to regulate home work is to destroy it, and cites the example of Victoria, where the establishment of a minimum wage has driven almost all the work into factories. We believe, judging from the analagous [sic] case of factory regulation, that the unemployment which would result from a well thought out scheme of home work regulation would be much less than these critics expect. Some workers would go to the factory; some, as already pointed out, would no longer need to take work out, if the head of the family were assured a living wage. Some workers, now underpaid, underfed, underwarmed, and badly clothed, would quickly respond to improved conditions and pay, and would in a short time become really more efficient. Moreover, we must remember that the payment of larger wages to a class of workers previously underpaid would in itself be a beneficial stimulus to trade, and lead to an increased demand for employment in the production of the food and clothing required. But let us admit that most probably there would be some workers unable to earn the minimum wage, and consequently thrown out of employment. These, we must remember, would be the workers either so unhealthy, so old, or so exhausted with a life of underpaid toil, that they would not be worth employing under the changed conditions and improved standard set. Here, surely, if ever, is the case for liberal poor relief. It would be far cheaper to the community in the end to pension off these victims of unregulated competition than to allow them to compete in the labor market, lower the rate of wages, and through their cheapness thrust the more capable out of work. For it must be remembered we are not here discussing those who are "unemployable" because of drink, extravagance or excess. The pathetic part of the sweated industries is that it is often the very virtues of these people that are their ruin. Miss Clementina Black, in her introduction to the cases investigated and tabulated by the Women's Industrial Council,[5] says "many of them are of the highest respectability and maintain a standard of conduct and cleanliness quite heroic. . . . The majority of these 44 women are industrious, even painfully industrious; most are thoroughly respectable; scarcely one is paid a living wage." They will sit up all night, and work for what is given them, and submit. Theirs is indeed "cheap and docile labor." They represent an out-of-date tradition and a superseded method, and only the wise and careful intervention of the State can save them and their children from a slow process of deterioration through want. "There is no person in this kingdom – or in any of the states that are called civilized – who does not partake of the proceeds of underpaid labor; and the conditions of such labor are not growing better; they are, if anything, growing worse, and underpayment is rather spreading than decreasing."[6]

Source Endnotes

1 *The Tariff Problem*, 1903. p. 110.
2 Daily News Handbook, p. 39
3 See G.H. Wood, F.F.S, I the Journal of the Statistical Society, June 1902.
4 *Le Développement de la Fabrique, et le Travail à Domicile*. Paris: Larose, 1906.
5 *Interim Report on Home Industries of Women*, p. 44.
6 *Interim Report on Home Industries of Women*, p. 45

Editorial Endnotes

a D.F, Schloss, Methods of Industrial Remuneration, 1898.

63

THE 'PIECE-WORK' SYSTEM AND TUBERCULOSIS

Jane Addams and Alice Hamilton

Source: Jane Addams and Alice Hamilton, MD, Hull House, 'The "Piece-Work" System as a Factor in the Tuberculosis Of Wage-Workers', *Transactions of the Sixth International Congress on Tuberculosis*, vol. 3. (William Fell, 1908), 139–40.

EDITORIAL HEADNOTE

Jane Addams and Alice Hamilton speak about an important health issue which was endemic in sweated trades, tuberculosis or 'consumption', and especially, as they argue, in piece-work. Alice Hamilton (1869–1970) identified many workplace hazards and worked to improve the health of the inner-city poor. She promoted 'industrial medicine' and laws to protect employees from dangerous substances in the workplace. From one of the founding families of Fort Wayne, Indiana, she planned to become a doctor, but as her boarding school largely ignored sciences she spent a summer getting tuition in chemistry and physics before attending the University of Michigan Medical School, where her interest in pathology led her to become a researcher rather than a physician. She later went with her sister, a classicist, to study in Germany where many universities closed their doors to her before Frankfurt accepted her. Returning to the States, she became a research assistant at Johns Hopkins Medical School. In 1897, Hamilton accepted an appointment as professor of pathology at the Women's Medical School of Northwestern University, which was dissolved soon after. She later worked as a bacteriologist at Chicago's Memorial Institute for Infectious Diseases.

In Chicago, she lived for many years at Jane Addams's Hull House, the most famous of the settlement houses founded by churches and universities at the dawn of the 20th century. Settlement houses, often staffed by idealistic college graduates, offered help to immigrants and other poor people who lived and worked in congested and rundown inner cities.

DOI: 10.4324/9781003676669-69

While at Hull House, Hamilton applied her medical expertise to finding the causes for the high incidence of typhoid fever and tuberculosis in the surrounding community. She identified bad working conditions as one of the factors that weakened the resistance of poor immigrants to the disease. Because of Hamilton's public-health experience, in 1908 the governor of Illinois appointed her to the Illinois Commission on Occupational Diseases. The commission decided to conduct a broad survey of industrially related diseases in Illinois – a groundbreaking study, which Hamilton agreed to oversee. From 1911 to 1920 she served as a special investigator for the U.S. Bureau of Labor Statistics, where she performed a landmark study on the manufacture of white lead and lead oxide. As the leading expert in industrial medicine, she was appointed assistant professor at Harvard Medical School, the first woman professor ever appointed at Harvard University.

Jane Addams (1860–1935) is more widely known as a pioneer social worker, feminist and internationalist, as well as a Nobel Prize winner. From Cedarville, Illinois, she suffered from a congenital spine injury which was much later surgically corrected. She graduated from Rockford Female Seminary in 1881 but received her bachelor's degree after it was accredited as the Rockford College of Women the next year. Intending to become a doctor she had to give up her studies because of poor health and spent time reading, travelling in Europe and contemplating her options. In 1887, with her friend Ellen G. Starr, she visited London's Toynbee Hall, the settlement house in the east end, which focused her ideas of opening a settlement house in the poorer areas of Chicago. This they did in 1889, to foster education and philanthropy and to investigate and improve conditions in industrial areas of Chicago. In its second year, its success meant some 2000 people attended every week: they held kindergarten classes, clubs for older children in afternoons and clubs and classes for adults in the evening, virtually becoming a night school. They added an art gallery, a public kitchen, a coffee house, gymnasium, swimming pool, a cooperative boarding club for girls, a book bindery, an art studio, a music school, a drama group, a circulating library, an employment bureau and a labour museum. Addams was busy promoting philanthropy and led investigations into midwifery, narcotics, milk supplies, sanitation and even accepted the post of garbage inspector on the nineteenth ward, earning $1000 a year. An ardent feminist and pacifist, she spoke against the First World War and became Chairman of the Women's Peace Party and then President of the International Congress of Women at the Hague in 1915; this later became the Women's International League for Peace and Freedom, with her as honorary president until her death. Too ill to attend the Nobel Prize ceremony in 1931, the Committee later published an edited version of her autobiography, *Twenty Years at Hull House*, in the *Nobel Lectures.*

It has been shown that excessive bodily effort lowers the resistance to infection, and that, in consequence, great fatigue must be regarded as one of the predisposing causes of tuberculous disease.

There are at the present time many kinds of factory and household work carried on by women which require great muscular effort and are injuriously fatiguing, but the women who are employed under the so-called "piece-work" system probably suffer, on the whole, the greatest degree of fatigue, because the pressure under which they work is so great. It occurred to us, during the last summer, that it would be worth while to study the effects of this system on factory girls, by inducing them to submit to certain physiological tests which are used to determine the rate of fatigue and then to compare the results with those obtained from girls who were working at a normal rate of speed.

"Piece-workers" are paid according to the amount of work accomplished, and not by the day. As a rule, in factories where this system is in force, a day's rapid work earns an ordinary day's wage, but a very active or skillful worker can do more than the standard amount, whereas a slow, awkward girl must exert herself to the utmost not to fall below it. There is thus an enormous incentive to rapid work under this system, and the effect is especially clear in the case of girls and women, for, as is well known, they are more reckless of their health than men are.

The speed attained by girls doing "piece-work" is often amazing, and is usually at the expense of the girl's health. In some factories the nervous strain of such rapid work is increased by the use of dangerous machinery, for the girl's attention must then be given not only to maintaining her speed, but to protection of her hands or eyes as well. In this way it comes about that factories which have ample light, space, and air, and which are free from dust and poisonous substances, may, nevertheless, have a high tuberculosis rate, simply because of the "speeding up" – the excessive fatigue – of the workers. Girls who work each day to the very limit of their strength cannot fully recuperate during the night, and are therefore constantly in a condition of lowered resistance to tuberculous infection.

We choose as subjects for our study four trades, two of them light and not exhausting except for the speed required, – the paper-box makers and the glove-makers, – and two heavier, – the overall-makers and core-makers. This summer was not altogether favorable for such an investigation, because most factories were working short-time – four and a half days or less. Still the girls in some places were showing the effects of exhaustion as much as, or even more than, when working full time, for they were speeding madly in the effort to approximate their usual wages. Some girls told us that they worked with a clock beside them, and tried each day to break their record of the day before at a given hour.

It was easy to convince ourselves of the fact that the "piece-work" system as it is usually carried on is the cause of very great fatigue in girls, but we failed to secure scientific proof, as we had hoped to do. The machine which we were advised to use, the ergograph, which is in use in physiologic laboratories, failed to give logical and consistent results.

Evidently the scientific testing of chronic fatigue is a complicated matter. The weariness of one day extends over to the following day, so that the worker does not begin the morning in a normal condition, but with a sluggish circulation and a great disinclination to effort. After an hour or so she "gets into the swing," her circulation is more active, she begins to work more easily. Then comes usually a second period of depression, which may last until the end of the day, but is often followed by second burst of activity – when the girl sees that the day is almost over and "spurts" for the last hour or two. Some girls declare that the morning is the hardest time; others, the hours from two to four in the afternoon.

A well-planned series of tests applied to a group of "piece-workers" and to an equal number of women employed in work of the same character, but without the excessive speed, would, we feel convinced, show that "piece-work" is far more exhausting than work done at a natural rate of speed. And, since excessive fatigue lowers the resistance to infection, the "piece-work" system as it is now carried on undeniably plays a part in the tuberculosis of factory workers.

Part 7

THE LAST WORD

64

THE SEWING MACHINE AND WORKING AT HOME

Ottilie Baader

Source: Ottilie Baader, 'The Sewing Machine and Working at Home', *Ein steiniger Weg. Lebenserinnerungen einer Sozialistin* [*A Rocky Path: Life Reminiscences of a Female Socialist*] (JW Dietz Nache, GMBH, 1921), 17–21.

EDITORIAL HEADNOTE

Ottilie Baader (1847–1925) typified the industrial homeworker, and this passage from her autobiography expresses the tedium and oppressions that many such women suffered. She had a relatively good education in Frankfurt am Oder, and when the family moved to Berlin at age thirteen, she went to work in a factory, first as a manual labourer, then sewing. By 1879, she had become an activist for working women and gave a speech to a group of shift workers. She joined a middle-class worker's association which offered free classes and went on to become one of the founders of the Association of Berlin Mantle Sewers, the first trade union organisation for women in Germany; she received her first sentence in prison, but an amnesty on the accession of Friedrich III (1888, husband of Princess Victoria, oldest daughter of Queen Victoria) saved her from serving the sentence. In early 1890s, Baader left work at the Sternberg cuff and collar factory in Berlin and started to work from home to care for her disabled father. Baader established her own independence and identity through participation in socialism, where she found the means of self-assertion against gender and class inequalities, and spent the rest of her life as an activist in social democratic organisations and the women's movement.

DOI: 10.4324/9781003676669-71

Image 9 Vrouw achter naaimachine, (Woman behind a sewing machine) Herman Heijenbrock, 1881–1925. Rijksmuseum. Public Domain.

It wasn't until the 1860s that the sewing machine industry in Germany was far enough advanced for machines to be in general use. This produced a great revolution in the work that women did, especially the manufacturing of white goods and shirts. The making of collars and cuffs (heretofore they had been a fixed part of men's shirts) now developed into a separate industry. At this time there were four or five companies in Berlin that produced large quantities of these articles.

As I said, I had tried all kinds of work. But now I learned to sew on a machine and worked in one of these factories on Spandauerstrasse [Spandau Street). There were about fifty women working at sewing machines and about an equal number engaged in preparing the pieces for the sewers. Every sewer was teamed with a preparer and the pay was split between them.

The workday lasted from eight in the morning until seven at night without any significant breaks. At noon you ate the bread you'd brought with you, or else you ran to the canteen next door to get something hot for a few groschen. Together, the preparers and the sewers got seven, at most ten, talers a week. Since the machine sewing was more strenuous than the preparing, it was customary for the sewer to get $17\frac{1}{2}$ and the preparer *$12\frac{1}{2}$* groschen of every taler. But before the division was made, they deducted the cost of the wasted thread and broken needles, which usually came to about $2\frac{1}{2}$ groschen per taler.

The first stimulus for us to change these conditions came with the Franco-Prussian War. Immediately after its outbreak, business in the clothing industry came to a standstill. Women were let go and stood around penniless because they hadn't been able to save anything on their low wages. Our company wanted to take the "risk" of keeping up full employment during the slack time if we wanted to work for half pay. We had no conception of any organization and were in a crisis situation since most of the women depended on themselves for support; they lived, so to speak, from hand to mouth. So we agreed to try it for a week.

So we started the drudgery. But the result was pitiful. The full cost of thread and needles was still deducted from our half wages. The owner's brutal actions made us start thinking. We decided unanimously that it was better to quit than to work for such wretched pay, which you couldn't even exist on. We selected three women, among them me, to tell this to the boss. When our delegation announced our common decision, he tried to calm us by telling us that as soon as there was news of victory in the war, business would go back up and wages would climb. He carefully avoided saying that they would "reach their former levels." Luckily we had the presence of mind to say that the wages would never rise as fast as they had been cut and, moreover, that there was a full warehouse of articles produced at the lower wages. When the boss realized that he couldn't fool us so easily, he got so angry his face turned red and he screamed at us, "OK, then I'll pay you the full wages again! Are you going to work now?" We told him curtly, "Yes, we'll work again."

We ourselves were surprised by our success. And it was just as much a novelty to the owner that working women would get together and make common demands. He had been taken by surprise, but it was also true that collar makers were very much in demand at that time. Shortly thereafter the boss called me into his office and told me that I didn't have to fear that my participation in this matter would hurt me at work. As long as he had work, there would be a place for me. That sounded very good, but it really wasn't true. He began to find fault with my work, and it wasn't long before I got tired of this and left voluntarily. The unity of the women, which had brought us the success, did not last long. Business did not pick up very quickly after the news of the victory. But the owners had learned. They didn't act as brutally as before but rather proceeded more carefully. They negotiated individual wage cuts with women who were in particularly dire straits. Of course this generated mistrust instead of unity among the women, and it took many years before they understood what was happening and confronted management with closed ranks. For many women it was a long and hard path.

I now bought my own machine and worked at home. I got to know all too well the fate of women working at home. I pedalled at a stretch from six o'clock in the morning until midnight, with a one-hour lunch break. At four o'clock I got up and did the housework and prepared meals. There was a little clock in front of me as I worked, and I watched carefully that each dozen collars took no longer than the previous dozen. Nothing made me happier than being able to save a few minutes.

This went on for five years, years that went by without my noticing that I was young, years in which life gave me nothing. Many things had changed around me. My sister and then my brother had gotten married, and my youngest sister had drowned during a boating party. My father had not been able to work for a long time, and so my fate was the same as many single daughters who don't make their own happy life at the right time: they have to hold everything together, to be both mother and father at the same time, and support those family members who can't support themselves. I supported my father for over twenty years, and I was always able to work hard enough to have an apartment with a living room and a kitchen.

My brother's wife died when their first child, a girl, was still very small. I took the child in, and during the year I had her, she brought me much joy. She learned to walk with me. When my brother remarried, I had to give her back. My brother himself died a few years later, and I often had the two boys from his second marriage with me because their mother had to work.

I can't say that I was always very happy. I'd hoped for something else out of life. Sometimes I was just sick of life: Sitting year after year at the sewing machine, always the collars and cuffs before me, one dozen after another; there was no value to life, I was just a work machine with no hope for the future. I saw and heard nothing of all the beautiful things in the world; I was simply excluded from all that.

For a while things were even worse. The endless work made me ill and the doctor said I'd have to give up the continuous sewing-machine work. I started to work on aprons which also took some handwork. I also got a half-day position doing alterations on finished goods. That was some variety, but basically work went on as before.

65

THE SONG OF THE SHIRT, 1843

Thomas Hood

Source: Thomas Hood, 'The Song of the Shirt', *Punch, or the London Charivari*, 5 (1843), 261.

EDITORIAL HEADNOTE

A Londoner, Thomas Hood (1799–1845) learned engraving, joined a literary society, and began writing prose and poetry. He became sub-editor of the *London Magazine* and continued to contribute to and edit many of the contemporary magazines. Mostly published in magazines and journals, he suffered financial and health difficulties, lived in Europe for some years and died in London. As he was popular, his fellow writers secured a pension on the civil list for his wife. His writing was both flippant and serious, and he spoke out for the poor and oppressed who suffered in the midst of Victorian prosperity. *The Song of the Shirt* highlighted the plight of the underpaid seamstresses of the day and was written in honour of a Mrs. Biddell, a widowed seamstress living in wretched conditions. She sewed trousers and shirts at home using materials supplied by her employer for which she was required to give a £2 deposit. In a desperate attempt to feed her starving infants, she pawned the clothing she had made, accruing a debt she could not pay and was sent to the workhouse. What happened to her is unknown.

With fingers weary and worn,
  With eyelids heavy and red,
A Woman sat, in unwomanly rags,
  Plying her needle and thread –
  Stitch! stitch! stitch!
In poverty, hunger, and dirt,
And still with the voice of dolorous pitch
She sang the "Song of the Shirt!"

DOI: 10.4324/9781003676669-72

"Work! Work! Work!
While the cock is crowing aloof!
And work – work – work,
Till the stars shine through the roof!
It's O! to be a slave
Along with the barbarous Turk,
Where woman has never a soul to save
If this is Christian work!

"Work – work – work
Till the brain begins to swim,
Work – work – work
Till the eyes are heavy and dim!
Seam, and gusset, and band,
Band, and gusset, and seam,
Till over the buttons I fall asleep,
And sew them on in a dream!

"O, Men with Sisters dear!
O, Men! with Mothers and Wives!
It is not linen you're wearing out,
But human creatures' lives!
Stitch – stitch – stitch,
In poverty, hunger, and dirt,
Sewing at once, with a double thread,
A Shroud as well as a Shirt.

"But why do I talk of Death!
That Phantom of grisly bone,
I hardly fear his terrible shape,
It seems so like my own –
It seems so like my own,
Because of the fasts I keep;
O God! that bread should be so dear,
And flesh and blood so cheap!

"Work – work – work!
My labour never flags;
And what are its wages? A bed of straw,
A crust of bread – and rags.
That shatter'd roof, – and this naked floor –
A table – a broken chair –
And a wall so blank, my shadow I thank
For sometimes falling there!

"Work – work – work!
From weary chime to chime,
Work – work – work –
As prisoners work for crime!
Band, and gusset, and seam,
Seam, and gusset, and band,
Till the heart is sick, and the brain benumb'd,
As well as the weary hand.

"Work – work – work,
In the dull December light,
And work – work – work,
When the weather is warm and bright –
While underneath the eaves
The brooding swallows cling,
As if to show me their sunny backs
And twit me with the spring.

"O, but to breathe the breath
Of the cowslip and primrose sweet! –
With the sky above my head,
And the grass beneath my feet;
For only one short hour
To feel as I used to feel,
Before I knew the woes of want
And the walk that costs a meal!

"O, but for one short hour!
A respite however brief!
No blessed leisure for Love or Hope,
But only time for Grief!
A little weeping would ease my heart,
But in their briny bed
My tears must stop, for every drop
Hinders needle and thread!

"Seam, and gusset, and band,
Band, and gusset, and seam,
Work, work, work,
Like the Engine that works by Steam!
A mere machine of iron and wood
That toils for Mammon's sake –
Without a brain to ponder and craze
Or a heart to feel – and break!"

– With fingers weary and worn,
With eyelids heavy and red,
A Woman sat, in unwomanly rags,
Plying her needle and thread –
Stitch! stitch! stitch!
In poverty, hunger, and dirt,
And still with a voice of dolorous pitch, –
Would that its tone could reach the Rich! –
She sang this "Song of the Shirt!"

66

KLÖPPLERINNEN (THE LACE-MAKERS), 1840

Louise Otto-Peters

Source: Louise Otto-Peters, *Klöpplerinnen (The Lace-Makers) Oederaner Stadtanzeiger*, 1840.

EDITORIAL HEADNOTE

Born in Meissen, Louise Otto-Peters (1819–1895) was a German woman's rights activist, who was founder of then 1865 of the General German Women's Association (Allgemeiner Deutscher Frauenverieín). She wrote novels, poetry and political articles and published journalism in democratic newspapers. Germany was an autocratic state and after the failure of the 1848 revolution she began the Women's Newspaper (*Frauen Zeitung*), which prompted a Saxony law prohibiting women from becoming newspaper editors. Moving the paper to Gera, outside Saxony, she continued publishing until 1853. She also founded the women's journal *Neue Bahnen* in 1865, continuing to edit it until her death. One of her main themes was better working conditions for women, and *Klöpplerinnen*, like the *Song of the Shirt*, is a plea for recognition of the evils of homework

Do you see them sitting at the bobbin cushion?
Their cheeks pale and their eyes red!
They toil for a bite,
For a bite of black bread!
Grandmother has blinded her eyes,
She waits until death frees her –
She twists her hands in silent prayer:
God protect us in these difficult times.

The children move their little hands,
The bobbins fly up and down,

DOI: 10.4324/9781003676669-73

Toil and worry, no end, no end.
That is their future course.

All the maidens, may God have mercy,
They know nothing of the joy of youth,
Misery embraces them in his arms,
Want nestles against their breasts.

Do you see them sitting at the bobbin cushion?
You see the lace they have woven:
You rich, great people – has your conscience never trembled in the innermost parts of your soul?
You revel and feast where they perish,
Enjoy life in luxury,
While they die of hunger,
Thanking God that the torment is now over!

Do you see them sitting on their bobbin pillows
And still talk beautifully about trusting in God?
You have ripped it from our souls:
Because we see you yourselves godless!

Do you see them sitting on their bobbin pillows
And feel no mercy in such a time:
Then your death pillow will be
The curse of poverty and all its suffering!

SELECTED BIBLIOGRAPHY

Abbott, Edith, *Women in Industry, A Study in American Economic History*. D. Appleton and Company, 1909.

Albert, Alice J. 'Fit Work for Women: Sweated Home-workers in Glasgow, c. 1875–1914,' in *The World is Ill Divided: Women's Work in Scotland in the Nineteenth and Early Twentieth Centuries*. Eleanor Gordon and Esther Breitenbach, eds, pp. 158–177. Edinburgh University Press, 1990.

Albrecht, Sandra L., 'Industrial Homework in the United States: Historical Dimensions and Contemporary perspective', *Economic and Industrial Democracy*, vol. 3 (1982): 413–430.

Aston, Jennifer, 'Female Business Ownership in Birmingham 1849–1901', *Midland History*, Vol. 37 No. 2 (Autumn 2012), 187–206.

Barker, Hannah (1997), 'Women, work and the Industrial Revolution: Female involvement in the English Printing Trades', in Hannah Barker and Elaine Chalus (eds.), *Gender in Eighteenth-century England*. Longman, 88–100.

Barker, Hannah, *The Business of Women, Female Enterprise and Urban Development in Northern England, 1760–1830*. Oxford University Press, 2006.

Baxandall, Rosalyn, Linda Gordon and Susan Reverby, eds. America's Working Women. Vintage, 1976.

Berg, Maxine, 'What Difference did Women's Work Make to the Industrial Revolution?', *History Workshop*, 35 Spring 1993.

Berg, Maxine, 'Women's Work and the Industrial Revolution', *ReFresh*, 12, Spring 1991

Berg, Maxine. *The Age of Manufactures, Industry, Innovation and Work in Britain, 1700–1820*. Fontana Press, 1994.

Bouvier, Jeanne, *My Memoirs*. In *The French Worker* edited by Mark Traugott. The University of California Press, 1993.

Boxer, M.J. 'Protective Legislation and Home Industry. the Marginalization of Women Workers in late nineteenth century and early twentieth century France.' *Journal of Social History*, (1986): 45–65.

Boxer, Marilyn J. 'Women in Industrial Work: The Flowermakers of the Parisian Belle Epoque,' *French Historical Studies*, 12 (1981).

Campbell, Robert. *The London Tradesman, being a compendious view of all Trades, Professions and Arts . . . calculated for the information of Parents, and Instruction of Youth in their Choice of Business*. T. Gardner, 1747.

Clarkson, L.A. *Proto-Industrialization: the First Phase of Industrialization?* Macmillan,1985.

Collins, Brenda. 'Sewing Outwork in Ulster'. In *Markets and Manufacturers in Early Industrial Europe*, edited by Maxine Berg. Routledge, 1991.

Commons, John R. 'The Sweating System'. In *Out of the Sweatshop* edited by Leon Stein. Quadrangle, 1977.

Craig, Beatrice, *Female Enterprise: Behind the Discursive Veil in Nineteenth-Century Northern France*. Palgrave Macmillan, 2017.

Craig, Beatrice. *Women and Business since 1500. Invisible Presences in Europe and North America?* Palgrave, 2016.

Cunningham, Hugh. *Children and Childhood in Western Society since 1500*. Longman, 1995.

de Vries, Jan, 'Between Purchasing Power and the World of Goods: Understanding the Household Economy in Early Modern Europe,' in John Brewer and Roy Porter, eds. *Consumption and World of Goods*, 85–132. Routledge, 1993.

de Vries, Jan, *The Industrious Revolution*. Cambridge University Press, 2006.

Dunlop, O. J. and R. D. Denman. *English Apprenticeship and Child Labour – A History*. Fisher Unwin, 1912.

Engels, Friedrich, *The Condition of the Working-Class in England in 1844*. Translated: Florence Kelley. George Allen and Unwin, 1892.

Erickson Amy, 'Clockmakers, Milliners and Mistresses: Women trading in the City of London companies, 1700–1750'. Working Paper, Cambridge Group for the study of Population, https://doi.org/10.17863/CAM.109861.

Sjögren, Fredrik Guy Neville, 'Entrepreneurship and Technological Change: The Birmingham and District Cut-Nail Trade, c. 1811–1913, PhD University of Birmingham, June 2019.

Hobsbawm, Eric J. *The Age of Revolution, 1789–1848*. Weidenfeld and Nicolson, 1962.

Holley, John, 'The two family economies of Industrialism: Factory Workers in Victorian Scotland', *Journal of Family History*, 6, 1 (1981): 57–69.

Hope, Emily, Mary Kennedy, Anne de Winter. 'Homeworkers in North London'. *Dependence and Exploitation in Work and Marriage.* eds Diana Leonard Barker, Sheila Allen, eds., 88–108. Longman Group Limited, 1976.

Hudson, Pat, 'Protoindustrialisation', *ReFresh*, 10, Spring 1990.

Lanza, Janine, Amanda Lewis Nang'ea and Deborah Simonton, *Global History of Women's Work*. Routledge, forthcoming.

Le Play, Fréderic, *Les Ouvriers Européens: Travaux, Vie Domestique Et Condition Morale Des Populations,* 2nd ed. Tours: A. Mame et fils, 1877.

Lown, Judy, *Women and Industrialization: Gender at Work in Nineteenth-century England*. Polity Press, 1990.

Mann, Alistair J. 'Embroidery to Enterprise: the Role of Women in the Book Trade of Early Modern Scotland', 137–51 in Elizabeth Ewan and Maureen Meikle, eds. *Women in Scotland, c.1100–c.1750*. Tuckwell, 1999.

Mayhew, Henry. *London Labour and the London Poor; a cyclopaedia of the condition and earnings of those that will work, those that cannot work, and those that will not work.* 3 vols. G. Newbold, 1861.

McKendrick, Neil. 'Home Demand and Economic Growth, A New View of the Role of Women and Children in the Industrial Revolution.' In *Historical Perspectives, Studies in English Thought and Society*, edited by Neil McKendrick. Europa Publications.

McKendrick, Neil, John Brewer and J. H. Plumb. *The Birth of a Consumer Society; the Commercialization of Eighteenth-century England.* Hutchinson, 1983.

McMillan, James. *Housewife or Harlot: The place of women in French Society, 1870–1940.* Saint Martin's Press, 1981.

Meade, Teresa A. and Merry E, Wiesner-Hanks, *A Companion to Global Gender History.* Wiley-Blackwell, 2020.

Medick, Hans. 'The Proto-industrial Family Economy: the structural function of household and family during the transition from peasant society to industrial capitalism.' *Social History,* 3, (1976): 291–315.

Medick, Hans. 'Plebian Culture in the transition to capitalism.' *Culture, Ideology and Politics, essays for Eric Hobsbawm.* Raphael Samuel and Gareth Stedman Jones, eds. 84–113. Routledge, 1983.

Mendels, Franklin F. 'Proto-industrialization: the first phase of the industrialization process'. *Journal of Economic History.* 32 1 (1972): 241–261.

Milhaud Caroline, L'Ouvriere en France: sa condition presente, les reformes necessaires. Félix Alcan, Éditeur, Librairies Félix Alcan et Guillaumin Réunies, 1907.

Mitchell, B.R. *International Historical Statistics: Europe*, 4th ed. London: Macmillan, 1998.

Nenadic, Stana. 'Businessmen, the urban middle classes, and the 'dominance' of manufacturers in nineteenth-century Britain'. *Economic History Review* 44, 1 (1991): 66–85.

Nenadic, Stana, 'The Social Shaping of Business Behaviour in the Nineteenth-Century Women's Garment Trades'. *Journal of Social History*, 31, 3, 1998.

Norwood, Arlisha R. 'Florence Kelley', National Women's History Museum, 2017. https://www.womenshistory.org/education-resources/biographies/florence-kelley, accessed 25 September 2024.

Ogilvie, Sheilagh C. and Markus Cerman, 'The Theories of Protoindustrialisation', 1–11 in *European Proto-Industrialization: An Introductory Handbook.* Cambridge University Press, 1996.

Pinchbeck, Ivy. *Women Workers and the Industrial Revolution 1750–1850.* Routledge and Sons, 1930; Virago 1981.

Prior, Mary. 'Women in the Urban Economy: Oxford, 1500–1800'. In *Women in English Society, 1500–1800*, edited by Mary Prior. Methuen and Co. Ltd, 1985.

Richards, Eric. 'Women in the British Economy Since about 1700, an Interpretation,' *History*, 59, 197 (June 1974): 337–57.

Riis, Jacob. *How the Other Half Lives: Studies among the Tenements of New York.* Charles Scribner's and sons, 1890.

Rose, Sonya O. *Limited Livelihood: Gender and Class in Nineteenth Century England.* Taylor & Francis Group, 1992.

Sheridan, Geraldine. 'Views of Women at Work by the Royal Academicians: The Collection, Descriptions des arts et metiers (1761–1789)', in *Studies in Eighteenth-century culture*, 32, (2003): 155–91.

Simonton, Deborah. 'Milliners and *Marchandes de Modes*: Gender, Skill and Creativity in the Workplace', 19–38. In Anne Montenach, Marjo Kaartinen and Deborah Simonton, eds. *Luxury and Gender in European Towns, c.1700–1914.* Routledge, 2014.

Simonton, Deborah. '"Sister to the tailor": Guilds, gender and the needle trades in eighteenth-century Europe', 135–58. In Johanna Ilmakunnas, Marjatta Rahikainen, Kirsi Vainio-Korhonen, eds. *Early Professional Women in Northern Europe, c. 1650 to the 1850s.* Routledge, 2017.

Simonton, Deborah. *The Education and Training of Eighteenth-Century English Girls, with special reference to the working classes*. PhD Thesis, University of Essex, 1988.

Simonton, Deborah. *A History of European Women's Work.* Routledge, 1998.

Simonton, Deborah. *Gender in the European Town.* Routledge, 2023.

Sloman, Susan Legouix. 'Artists' Picture Rooms in Eighteenth-century Bath'. *Bath History*, 6 (1996): 132–54.

Smout, T. C. *A Century of the Scottish People, 1830–1950.* Fontana Press 1987.

Thompson, E. P. 'Patrician Society, Plebeian Culture,' *Journal of Social History,* 7, 4. (Summer 1974): 382–405.

Thompson, E. P. 'Time, Work Discipline, and Industrial Capitalism.' In *Essays in Social History*, edited by M. W. Flinn and T. C. Smout. Clarendon Press, 1974.

Thompson, Paul and Eileen Yeo. *Unknown Mayhew.* Penguin, 1984.

Treble, James H. 'The Characteristics of the Female Unskilled Labour Market and the Formation of the Female Casual Labour Market in Glasgow, 1891–1914.' *Scottish Economic and Social History,* 6, (1986): 33–46.

Tweedale, Geoffrey. 'Backstreet capitalism: An analysis of the family firm in the nineteenth-century Sheffield cutlery industry', *Business History*, 55, 6 (2013): 875–891.

Williams, Rosalind. *Dream Worlds: Mass Consumption in Late Nineteenth-century France*. University of California Press, 1982.

Wrigley, E. Anthony. *Continuity, Chance, and Change. The Character of the Industrial Revolution in England.* Cambridge, 1988.

You, Xuesheng. 'The Missing Half: Female employment in Victorian England and Wales', Cambridge Group for the History of Population, [c. 2019] https://www.campop.geog.cam.ac.uk/research/occupations/outputs/onlineatlas/femaleemployment.pdf. Accessed 24 September 2024.

INDEX

For Product Safety Concerns and Information please contact our
EU representative GPSR@taylorandfrancis.com Taylor & Francis
Verlag GmbH, Kaufingerstraße 24, 80331 München, Germany